The Jossey-Bass
Higher and Adult Education Series

Academic Advising

A Comprehensive Handbook

Virginia N. Gordon, Wesley R. Habley, and Associates

NACADA
National **ACADEMIC ADVISING** Association

JOSSEY-BASS
A Wiley Company
San Francisco

Published by Jossey-Bass
A Wiley Imprint
989 Market Street, San Francisco, CA 94103-1741   www.josseybass.com

Jossey-Bass books and products are available through most bookstores. To contact Jossey-Bass directly call our Customer Care Department within the U.S. at (800) 956-7739, outside the U.S. at (317) 572-3986 or fax (317) 572-4002.

Jossey-Bass also publishes its books in a variety of electronic formats. Some content that appears in print may not be available in electronic books.

Library of Congress Cataloging-in-Publication Data

Academic advising handbook / Virginia Gordon and Wesley R. Habley,
editors. — 1st ed.
    p.   cm. — (The Jossey-Bass higher and adult education series)
Includes bibliographical references and indexes.
    ISBN 0-7879-5025-4 (alk. paper)
    1. Counseling in higher education—United States—Handbooks, manuals,
etc. 2. Faculty advisors—United States—Handbooks, manuals, etc. I. Gordon,
Virginia N. II. Habley, Wesley R. III. Series.
    LB2342 .A29 2000
    378.1'94—dc21   00-008177

Printed in the United States of America
FIRST EDITION
HC Printing   10 9 8 7 6 5 4

Contents

Part One
Foundations of Academic Advising

Part Four

Training, Evaluation, and Recognition

Part Five

Dealing with Change in the Future of Academic Advising

The National Academic Advising Association

The National Academic Advising Association (NACADA) is the leader within the global higher education community for the theory, delivery, application, and advancement of academic advising to enhance student development. Its mission includes

- Affirming the role of academic advising in student success and persistence, thereby supporting institutional mission and vitality.
- Championing the educational role of academic advisors to enhance student learning and development in a diverse world.
- Anticipating and fulfilling the academic advising needs of twenty-first century students, advisors, and institutions.
- Advancing the body of knowledge on academic advising.
- Fostering the talents and contributions of all members and promoting the involvement of diverse populations.

NACADA strives to fulfill this mission through its members by providing a network of professional colleagues and resources for the professional development of all advisors. These resources include a semiannual professional journal, a quarterly newsletter, regional and national conferences, teleconferences direct to campuses, special publications addressing advising issues, an advisor training video, member commissions to address specific to special populations or situations, an Academic Advising Summer Institute, career services, and many other helpful services.

NACADA membership information is available at www.ksu.edu/nacada

We dedicate this book to all the academic advisors
in the trenches who have committed their professional lives
to students and who have contributed more than they know
to the realization of innumerable goals and dreams.

Preface

The college students who are matriculating in this new millennium are, according to Howe and Strauss (1993), the thirteenth generation of Americans to attend college since the first students entered the colonial colleges when the nation was born. Yale, Brown, and other early colleges were cognizant of their students' academic and personal concerns, and academic advising became the natural process for attending to those individual students' needs. Since then, academic advising has played an important role in the lives of students. True, it has experienced many cycles of reemphasis and renewal, and the advising process itself has been defined and redefined in many forms, but its acceptance as an integral part of higher education has never been stronger than it is today.

As the size of institutions increased over the years to accommodate growing numbers of students and as curricula expanded and became more complex, advising took on new and sometimes expanded responsibilities. Community colleges have played a predominant role in advising's latest rebirth, because they are the portal of entry for many new students such as older adults and minority students. In the 1960s and 1970s, students were demanding more personalized attention in their academic planning. It is no accident that this was when Crookston's (1972) and O'Banion's (1972) models for a more humane and developmental approach to advising students appeared. Later, many institutions began to realize the importance of advising in the retention of students, especially during their initial enrollment. This brought about a major examination of how advising was delivered on some campuses, and as a result, reorganization took place at many institutions. The advising center was introduced on some campuses as a vehicle for offering a more visible and centralized location that students could use in place of or in addition to their regular faculty advising system.

The advent of technology has already had a profound effect on how advisors interact with students and on how administrative advising tasks function. Many advisors believe that technology will completely revolutionize advising, teaching, and learning. Rather than depersonalize contact between advisor and student, technology is expected to encourage more meaningful and frequent contact.

In this new, exciting milieu, it seems appropriate to update and document the current status of academic advising in a detailed way. The need to learn from its past and project its role into the future has never been stronger. *Academic Advising: A Comprehensive Handbook* has been written to accomplish just that. This volume is intended to be a handy reference for professional advisors—those who spend their day working with students who have a variety of academic, vocational, and personal needs. Faculty advisors will find much helpful information about students, resources, and advising techniques in these pages. Administrators can review the many approaches to advising that are possible and perhaps find new ways of thinking about how their delivery systems might become more student responsive. The many complex elements of the advising process described in this book can open new vistas for everyone involved in the advising enterprise.

It is obvious that academic advising is not an isolated function but an integral part of the mission of higher education. This book will help those involved in advising either directly or indirectly and at every level not only to appreciate the importance of good advising in students' lives but also to understand how it can contribute to the purpose of higher education itself.

This handbook contains five parts representing every important facet of academic advising. The chapters in each part are authored by experts who are well equipped to share their expertise in these areas.

Part One provides the historical, philosophical, and theoretical foundations for academic advising. It reviews the current state of advising practices nationally and outlines ethical and legal considerations that influence the practice of advising.

In Chapter One, Susan H. Frost traces the history of academic advising from colonial times to the present. She divides this historical perspective into three periods: higher education before academic advising was defined, advising as a defined and unexamined activity, and academic advising as a defined and examined activity. Don G. Creamer, in Chapter Two, examines the theoretical frameworks that have influenced the advising process. He addresses those aspects of theory use about which there is agreement within the profession by outlining the scope of academic advising, delineating some central concepts of developmental theories used, and discussing practice-oriented generalizations about the use of theories in advising.

Using data from five national surveys of academic advising conducted by ACT, Inc. (formerly known as American College Testing), in Chapter Three Wesley R.

Habley reviews current practices in faculty advising, advising centers, and the goal achievement and overall effectiveness of advising programs. In Chapter Four, Katherine Simon Frank discusses ethical considerations and obligations involved in advising. She examines professional codes of ethics and forms of ethical principles as guides for delivering service professionally. Because of the increasing litigiousness of American society, in Chapter Five Barbara A. Becker emphasizes the importance of advisors' understanding of current legal trends and the application of those trends to their daily work. The understanding of students' legal rights will contribute to better advising and improved working relationships with students.

Part Two concentrates on the diverse types of students we are called upon to advise and describes some of the needs and characteristics of these varying populations. In Chapter Six, M. Lee Upcraft and Pamela S. Stephens set the stage for this examination by providing an overview of today's students and how they have changed over the years. This profile includes both demographic and ideographic information and focuses on the advising needs of these changing students.

Chapter Seven defines the unique academic and career advising needs of students at different educational levels. Gary L. Kramer outlines how developmental theory can help advisors understand how undergraduate, graduate, and professional students' personal and academic adjustment concerns differ as they progress through their college experience. He offers suggestions for creating a growth-producing environment that responds to the needs of students at these many levels of academic performance. In Chapter Eight, Ronnie Priest and Sidney A. McPhee discuss the importance of understanding differences among multicultural students and offer suggestions for advising students from diverse ethnic backgrounds.

Chapter Nine focuses on students with special needs. Steven C. Ender and Carolyn J. Wilkie describe those students whose concerns are of a more specific academic or physical nature, including students with high ability, those who enter college underprepared, or those who are having academic difficulty. Some special students, such as disabled students or student athletes, are often advised in more than one campus office, so greater coordination among units is required. Gay and lesbian students are also discussed and special advising considerations are offered for assisting them. Chapter Ten addresses groups of students who have in common the characteristic of undergoing a transition. George E. Steele and Melinda L. McDonald describe undecided students, those who change their majors, adult students, and transfer students. Advising approaches or models to help these students move successfully through their transitions are provided.

Many students equate the choice of academic major with a career choice, so in Chapter Eleven Betsy McCalla-Wriggins describes the critical elements in career planning and outlines the basic knowledge and skills that all advisors need to help students understand how these two decision areas may or may not be related. She also emphasizes the need to integrate advising and career sources on campus.

Part Three of the handbook focuses on the organization and delivery of academic advising services. In Chapter Twelve, Eric R. White underscores the important relationship between the institutional mission and the goals and objectives of the academic advising program. White stresses the need for all units on campus that provide advising to develop goals and objectives, and he provides advice on the development of goal statements. The institutional mission statement is also a critical consideration in the implementation of an organizational model for the delivery of advising services. Celeste Pardee, in Chapter Thirteen, discusses that relationship and provides an overview of seven organizational models categorized into central models, shared models, and decentralized models. Pardee also provides insights on the coordination, effectiveness, and strengths and weaknesses of each of the seven models.

Although faculty members continue to be the primary providers of advising services on college campuses, additional personnel play a pivotal role in the delivery of advising. Alice G. Reinarz provides in Chapter Fourteen an overview of the strengths and areas of concern associated with several advisor types. Reinarz reviews faculty, professional advisors and counselors, and peer and paraprofessional advisors, concluding that the best delivery derives from a shared delivery system that focuses on the complementary strengths of various advisor types.

Chapters Fifteen and Sixteen focus on the actual delivery of academic advising services. Charlie L. Nutt, in Chapter Fifteen, outlines the skills and competencies necessary to build an effective one-to-one advising relationship. In Chapter Sixteen, Nancy S. King provides examples of the ways in which group strategies can augment the delivery of high-quality advising.

The influence of technology has shaped, and will continue to shape, the academic advising process. In Chapter Seventeen, Michael E. McCauley reviews the uses of technology that support the macrolevel environment of academic advising. Included in McCauley's chapter are descriptions of student information systems, degree audits, and transfer articulation systems. The use of technology at the microlevel is the focus of Chapter Eighteen by Remy R. Sotto. She provides descriptions of the various synchronous and asynchronous technologies that may be used in the delivery of advising services.

Because the quality of a student's educational and career decisions is directly related to the amount of information that is brought to bear on those decisions, Chapter Nineteen by Thomas J. Grites focuses on the role of cognitive and noncognitive assessment in support of the academic advising process. In addition, Grites provides suggestions on best practices in the use of assessment instruments.

Because all five ACT national surveys on advising practices continue to point to shortcomings in cornerstone functions that support academic advising, Part Four of this book focuses on the three most critical aspects of a quality academic advising program: training, evaluation, and recognition and reward.

Three chapters are devoted to design, content, and exemplary practices in training programs for academic advisors. In Chapter Twenty, Margaret C. King provides an overview of the essential elements of advisor training and describes a variety of available external resources that support it. Linda C. Higginson, in Chapter Twenty-One, focuses on the content of advisor training programs, organizing her chapter around what advisors need to understand, know, and demonstrate. Phillip J. Farren and Faye Vowell describe exemplary training practices in Chapter Twenty-Two. They make the case that successful training efforts result from understanding institutional mission, establishing a clear definition of advising, and identifying the training needs of individuals who serve as academic advisors.

Two chapters in Part Four focus on the second cornerstone: the evaluation of academic advising. Michael L. Lynch, in Chapter Twenty-Three, describes the major components of a qualitative and quantitative assessment of the campus's advising program. Lynch makes the case for, and provides illustrations of the uses of, process evaluation along with the valuation of outcomes as effective mechanisms for assessing the overall impact of an advising program. Elizabeth G. Creamer and Delores W. Scott review the essential elements of individual advisor evaluation in Chapter Twenty-Four. They suggest that individual advisor data, whether utilized for formative or summative assessment, must come from multiple sources and must be tied to a clear statement of advisor expectations.

The final cornerstone of quality academic advising is the focus of Chapter Twenty-Five by Thomas J. Kerr on recognition and reward for excellence in advising. The ACT national surveys suggest that recognition and reward is the area of greatest dissatisfaction and it had the lowest effectiveness ratings, so there are few exemplary programs from which to generalize. Nevertheless, Kerr builds a strong case for development of recognition and reward programs for advisors and provides suggestions for including a reward structure as an important stimulus to improved advising.

Part Five concentrates on the future and on how higher education and thus advising might meet the needs of students as well as the institution's own needs. In Chapter Twenty-Six, Victoria A. McGillin addresses the need to identify the future directions that the field of advising should be considering. A brief overview of existing research is provided with an emphasis on delineating the critical advising issues that will be confronted in the future. Virginia N. Gordon focuses in Chapter Twenty-Seven on how higher education might prepare future learners for the workplace of tomorrow, and on the role that advising can play in that future. Finally, Herta Teitelbaum describes in Chapter Twenty-Eight some possible areas of future change in higher education and how advising can implement specific actions now to ensure that it will still be viable and relevant in a new age.

This book has been written under the auspices of the National Academic Advising Association (NACADA), an internationally recognized professional organization dedicated to the advancement and improvement of academic advising. The authors hope that the thoughts and ideas they have put on these pages will greatly enhance the practice of advising and will consequently have an even more positive impact on the lives of students.

The authors would also like to acknowledge the assistance provided by individuals who contributed to this book from its inception to completion. We thank Nancy King for her leadership and vision for this project and her commitment to its successful conclusion. Gale Erlandson, editor of the Jossey-Bass Higher Education Series, contributed to the original conception of this manuscript and was helpful in every phase of its development. We also thank Jamie Dolan of the ACT Center for her clerical assistance.

August 2000

Virginia N. Gordon
The Ohio State University
Wesley R. Habley
American College Testing

References

Crookston, B. B. "A Developmental View of Academic Advising as Teaching." *Journal of College Student Personnel,* 1972,13, 12–17.

Howe, N. and Strauss, W. *13th Gen: Abort, Retry, Ignore, Fail?* New York: Vintage, Books, 1993.

O'Banion, T. "An Academic Advising Model." *Junior College Journal,* 1972, 42, 89–125.

The Authors

BARBARA A. BECKER is an attorney with the Student Legal Service at the University of Minnesota, Twin Cities (UM-TC). She has twenty years of experience directing nonprofit and educational organizations, including nine years as director of student services for the College of Liberal Arts at UM-TC. She holds an M.S. degree (1977) in Higher Education from Iowa State University and a J.D. degree (1985) from William Mitchell College of Law. As a consultant, Becker presents workshops and lectures on legal issues in higher education.

DON G. CREAMER is professor and program leader of higher education and student affairs at Virginia Polytechnic Institute and State University (Virginia Tech) and director of the Educational Policy Institute of Virginia Tech. He earned a B.A. degree (1960) in history and an M.Ed. (1961) in counseling and guidance from Texas A&M–Commerce. Prior to joining Virginia Tech, Creamer served the Dallas Community College District as dean of students at El Centro College. His primary research interest is in student development practices, particularly in two-year colleges. He has published several articles and four books, the most recent of which is *Improving Staffing Practices in Student Affairs* (1997). Creamer has served the American College Personnel Association (ACPA) as president (1979) and senior scholar (1989–1995) and is the recipient of the ACPA Contribution to Knowledge Award (1999).

ELIZABETH G. CREAMER is associate professor at Virginia Polytechnic Institute and State University (Virginia Tech). She spent the early part of her career in financial aid and academic advising administration. Although she continues to be responsible for an advising center and directs the interdisciplinary major for the College of Arts and Sciences, her primary role on the faculty is teaching undergraduate courses in women's studies and graduate classes in higher education and student affairs, focusing on such topics as gender and diversity. Creamer has served in a number of important roles with the National Academic Advising Association, including regional representative and vice president for development. She is the author of more than thirty journal articles and book chapters, as well as the book *Assessing Faculty Publishing Productivity: Issues of Equity* (1998). She is currently working on a second book, to be published in 2000, *Working Equal: Academic Couples as Collaborators.*

STEVEN C. ENDER is a professor in the Learning Center at Indiana University of Pennsylvania (IUP). He earned his M.Ed. degree (1986) in student personnel services and his Ed.D. degree (1981) in counseling and human development from the University of Georgia. As a faculty member at the University of Georgia, Kansas State University, and IUP, Ender has taught both graduate and undergraduate courses focusing on learning enhancement programs. In addition to serving on the editorial boards of the *NACADA Journal* and the *Journal of College Student Development,* Ender has edited or coauthored six books, fourteen book chapters, and sixteen articles in professional journals on academic advising, the contribution of student affairs to the learning process, and training undergraduates to serve as peer educators. His most recent book is *Students Helping Students* (with Fred B. Newton, Jossey-Bass, 2000).

PHILLIP J. FARREN is director of the Student Personnel Program at Emporia State University, Kansas. He has served Emporia State as both vice president for student affairs and vice president for finance and administration. He earned his Ph.D. (1969) in higher education from the University of Northern Colorado. Farren has presented and published numerous book chapters and journal articles in the areas of the future of advising, the fiscal impact of advising, marketing advising, and the centrality of academic advising to all aspects of the campus community.

KATHERINE SIMON FRANK holds a B.A. degree (1964) in sociology from the New School for Social Research and an M.L.S. degree (1999) in social movements and change from the University of Minnesota. She serves as advisor, curriculum administrator, and coordinator of undergraduate advising in the sociology department at the University of Minnesota. Simon Frank has won both campus and national awards for her outstanding academic advising. A social activist, she studies, writes, teaches, and utilizes decision-making tools for resolving ethical dilemmas. She was instrumental in the development of the National Academic Advising Association's statement of core values.

SUSAN H. FROST, vice provost and adjunct associate professor at Emory University, earned her Ph.D. degree (1989) in higher education at the University of Georgia. Her current research interests include the strategic development of universities and the nature of intellectual community. Her books are *Using Teams in Higher Education: Cultural Foundations for Productive Change* (1998), *Inside College: Undergraduate Education for the Future* (with Ronald Simpson, 1993), and *Academic Advising for Student Success: A System of Shared Responsibility* (1991). Her articles have appeared in the *Journal of Higher Education, Research in Higher Education,* and the *Journal of College Student Development.* Frost consults frequently with colleges and universities on issues related to academic advising.

VIRGINIA N. GORDON is assistant dean emeritus and adjunct associate professor at The Ohio State University. She has extensive experience in teaching, administration, advising, and counseling in higher education settings. Her bibliography includes more that forty books, monographs, book chapters, and articles on the administration of advising, career advising, working with undecided students, and advisor training. She is a past president of NACADA and the founder and first director of the National Clearinghouse on Academic Advising. Dr. Gordon has received national acclaim and numerous awards for her contributions to the field, the most fitting of which is NACADA's naming of its award for outstanding contributions to the field of academic advising the Virginia N. Gordon Award.

THOMAS J. GRITES is assistant to the vice president for academic affairs at the Richard Stockton College, New Jersey. He earned his B.S. (1966) in mathematics and M.S. (1967) degrees in guidance and counseling education from Illinois State University and his Ph.D. degree (1974) from the University of Maryland in student personnel and higher education. He worked in college residence halls before beginning his thirty-year career in academic advising. Grites regularly teaches education courses on his campus and has also taught graduate classes in academic advising at Teachers College, Columbia University. He served on the steering committee that later evolved into the National Academic Advising Association (NACADA). In addition to other major contributions to the association, Grites served two terms as NACADA's president. He is the recipient of the NACADA Award for Excellence in the Field of Advising and the Alumni Achievement Award from Illinois State University. He has authored or coauthored more than fifty publications, including *Developmental Academic Advising* (1984); has given more than seventy conference presentations; and has served as a consultant, evaluator, and workshop leader on more than one hundred campuses.

WESLEY R. HABLEY directs the American College Testing (ACT) Center for the Enhancement of Educational Practices. Prior to joining ACT in 1985, he served first as an academic advisor and later as director of the Academic Advisement Center at Illinois State University and director of academic and career advising at the University of Wisconsin–Eau Claire. He holds a B.S. degree (1968) in music education and an M.Ed. degree (1970) in student personnel from the University of Illinois–Urbana/Champaign, and a Ed.D. degree (1978) in higher education from Illinois State University. Habley has served the National Academic Advising

Association (NACADA) in a variety of roles, including treasurer and president. He is the recipient of NACADA awards for outstanding contributions to the field of advising and for service to NACADA. He is lead researcher and author of monographs on three ACT national surveys on campus practices in academic advising, the most recent of which was published in 1998 in the NACADA monograph series. Additional material has appeared in the *NACADA Journal,* the *NASPA Journal,* the *Journal of College Student Personnel,* several volumes of the Jossey-Bass New Directions in Higher Education series, and in various monographs published by NACADA and the First Year Experience Program at the University of South Carolina. Habley has served as consultant to or workshop leader at more than 125 colleges and has made more that two hundred presentations at professional meetings.

LINDA C. HIGGINSON is associate dean for student and academic support in the Commonwealth College of Pennsylvania State University (Penn State). She earned her B.A. degree (1970) in mathematics at the University of Delaware and both her M.Ed. (1971) and D.Ed. (1981) degrees in counselor education at Penn State. Before assuming her current role, she held several positions in student affairs, advising and counseling, and academic advising administration at Penn State. She has served in several roles on the National Academic Advising Association's (NACADA) board of directors, for which she has received five Certificates of Recognition. She has represented NACADA on the Council for the Advancement of Standards in Higher Education (CAS) for almost a decade. Since 1990, she and colleague Eric White have provided annual NACADA workshops on the use of CAS standards and guidelines and the CAS self-assessment guides. Higginson's teaching has focused on helping skills for human service practitioners. She is also the recipient of Penn State's Diversity Recognition Award.

THOMAS J. KERR is dean of the College of Evening and Professional Studies at Drexel University. In the past he has served as associate provost for academic services at Rowan University and as associate dean of academic and student affairs in the College of Engineering at Boston University. President of the National Academic Advising Association (NACADA) from 1993 to 1995, Kerr has also served NACADA in a variety of other positions, including leadership of task forces on several strategic initiatives. He has been a faculty member at the Summer Institute on Academic Advising, and his publications on advising issues include *Redefining Faculty Roles for Academic Advising* (1994), *Retention Is Not an Isolated Event* (1990), and *Advisors Beat the Budget Cut Blues* (1992).

MARGARET C. KING is assistant dean for student development at Schenectady County Community College, with direct responsibilities for academic advising, counseling, and job placement services. She holds a B.A. degree (1965) in history from Ursinus College, an M.S. (1970) in student personnel, and an Ed.D. (1984) in educational administration and policy studies from the State University of New York (SUNY) at Albany. A founding member of the National Academic Advising Association (NACADA), King served as president from 1991 to 1993 and currently chairs the NACADA Consultants Bureau. She has been a member of the faculty of the Summer Institute on Academic Advising since its inception in 1987 and serves as a consultant and speaker on academic advising. In addition to publishing several works on advising in two-year colleges and on organizational models and delivery systems, King was editor of the New Directions for Community Colleges monograph *Academic Advising: Organizing and Delivering Services for Student Success* (1993). She is a recipient of the SUNY Chancellor's Award for Excellence in Professional Service, and of the NACADA awards for service and for excellence in the field of advising.

NANCY S. KING is vice president for student success and enrollment services and professor of English at Kennesaw State University, Georgia. She holds a B.A. degree (1964) in English and psychology from Mercer University and M.A. (1970) and Ph.D. (1984) degrees in English from Georgia State University. She has served the National Academic Advising Association in several positions, including president (1997–99) and vice president for member services (1993–95). King has also been actively involved in the Golden Key National Honorary Society, serving as a member of the National Advisory Board and chartering advisor of the Kennesaw State University chapter. She has been the recipient of campus awards for advising, leadership, service, and scholarship as well as national awards from the National Resource Center for the First-Year Experience and Golden Key. King also serves as a consultant and speaker on the topics of academic advising, freshman seminar programs, and student success.

GARY L. KRAMER is associate dean of admissions and records and professor of counseling and special education at Brigham Young University. He received his Ph.D. degree (1977) in education and administration from Oregon State University. He has published nearly fifty scholarly papers in nine refereed journals, edited five monographs, authored seven monograph and book chapters, and delivered more than 150 presentations to a wide variety of professional organizations. In addition to serving the National Academic Advising Association (NACADA) as president and monograph editor, Kramer has received the association's awards for researcher of the year, service to NACADA, and excellence in the field of advising.

MICHAEL L. LYNCH is assistant vice president for educational and personal development and associate professor of counseling and educational psychology at Kansas State University. He earned his B.S. degree (1967) in education and his M.S. (1970) and Ed.D. (1972) degrees in counseling and guidance from Indiana University. Lynch is past editor of the *NACADA Journal* and currently serves as editor of the NACADA Monograph Series. He teaches in the areas of research methods and design and statistics. His research interests include student retention and performance and academic advising. He has made numerous presentations on conducting advising research and qualitative methodologies for the study of advising effectiveness.

BETSY MCCALLA-WRIGGINS is director of career and academic planning at Rowan University. She earned her B.S. degree (1969) in home economics education and M.S. degree (1974) in educational psychology from the University of Tennessee–Knoxville. At Rowan, McCalla-Wriggins oversees the career development, counseling, student work, cooperative education, and academic advising units and was responsible for the creation of a fully integrated career development and academic advising unit. She serves on the faculty of the Summer Institute for Academic Advising and is president-elect of the National Academic Advising Association.

MICHAEL E. MCCAULEY, director of academic systems at Ball State University, earned his B.S. (1963) and M.A. (1967) degrees in history from that institution. He served as academic advisor and advising administrator from 1967 to 1987, when he became involved in the development, implementation, and maintenance of academic affairs information systems. A founding member of the National Academic Advising Association, McCauley has served the association as treasurer, vice president for development, and president and is the 1987 recipient of NACADA's service award. He has coauthored chapters on the use of technology in advising in two NACADA monographs and serves as a faculty member for the Summer Institute on Academic Advising. He has presented numerous workshops and concurrent sessions at local, regional, and national conferences.

MELINDA L. MCDONALD served as program coordinator for the Alternatives Advising Program in the University at The Ohio State University prior to her appointment as program administrator specialist (K–16) for the Ohio Board of Regents. She earned her B.A. degree (1977) in Spanish education and her M.A. degree (1982) in counselor education at Rollins College, and her Ph.D. degree (1991) in counselor education from The Ohio State University. She is the recipient of the National Academic Advising Association's Outstanding Advisor Award. Her research interests include career development and decision making with undecided and major-changing students.

VICTORIA A. MCGILLIN is dean of academic advising and adjunct professor of psychology at Wheaton College, Massachussetts. She holds a B.S. degree (1971) in psychology and an M.S. degree (1973) in clinical psychology from the Pennsylvania State University and a Ph.D. degree (1979) in clinical psychology from Michigan State University. McGillin has held faculty appointments at Clark University, the University of Connecticut, and Michigan State University. Her current research includes the study of risk and resilience in higher education. She has served the National Academic Advising Association as chair of the research committee and as vice president for development. She is a member of the American Association for Higher Education, the New England Psychological Association, and the think tank for the New England Resource Center for Higher Education, and a fellow of the American Orthospychiatric Association.

SIDNEY A. MCPHEE, who has held administrative positions at the University of Louisville and the University of Memphis, currently serves as vice chancellor for academic affairs and strategic planning for the Tennessee Board of Regents. McPhee holds a B.A. degree (1976) in sociology from Prairie View A&M University, an M.A. degree (1979) in education administration from the University of Miami, and a Ph.D. degree (1982) in applied behavioral studies from Oklahoma State University. He has published extensively on a wide variety of topics in local, national, and international publications.

CHARLIE L. NUTT has served since 1993 as vice president for student development services at Coastal Georgia Community College after serving as professor of English and director of advisement and orientation. He holds a B.S. degree (1977) in English education from the University of Georgia, an M.Ed. degree (1981) from Georgia Southern University, and an Ed.D. degree (1999) from Georgia State University. Prior to his work at Coastal Georgia, Nutt served as an English teacher, department head, and school administrator in the Georgia public schools. He has been actively involved in the National Academic Advising Association, the National Council for Student Development, the American College Personnel Association, and Phi Delta Kappa. He has served as a community college consultant in the areas of retention, advising, student success, institutional effectiveness, and learner-centered campuses.

CELESTE F. PARDEE is the director of the Office of Academic Services in University College at The University of Arizona. She earned her B.S. degree (1971) in secondary education and her M.Ed. (1982) in guidance and counseling from Texas Tech University. She also earned an M.S. degree (1976) in geography from Texas A&M University. Pardee's research has focused on how academic advising programs evolve. She has published articles on the practice of developmental academic advising and advising program development. Pardee has served the National Academic Advising Association as a regional representative and association secretary. In addition, she was one of the founders of the professional advising council at the University of Arizona and of the State Conference of College and University Advisors.

RONNIE PRIEST is chairperson of the Department of Counseling, Educational Psychology, and Research at the University of Memphis. He earned his Ph.D. degree (1990) in counselor education from the University of Alabama. His research interests include counseling multiracial individuals, diversity, and counseling sexually victimized children, adults, and their families. He is the recipient of the Martin Luther King Jr. Humanitarian Award.

ALICE G. REINARZ began her advising career as a faculty advisor, which led to positions in the administration of advising programs. Her current role in the College of Literature, Science, and the Arts at the University of Michigan is director of the Academic Advising Center. She holds both B.A. (1967) and Ph.D. (1972) degrees in microbiology from the University of Texas and has integrated her disciplinary training with the design and revitalization of effective academic advising units. Her work with undergraduate students has included teaching, mentoring, and advising. A recipient of the Carski Foundation Outstanding Teaching Award (1990) from the American Society of Microbiology, she teaches a class on infectious diseases as part of her college's first-year seminar program. Reinarz has published in the areas of undergraduate curriculum reform and careers for science majors and is coeditor of the Jossey-Bass monograph *Teaching Through Academic Advising* (1995).

DELORES SCOTT is associate provost for retention and academic support at Virginia Polytechnic Institute and State University (Virginia Tech). She earned her B.A. degree (1970) from Virginia Union University, her M.Ed. degree (1982) from Virginia State University, and her Ph.D. degree (1995) in higher education from Virginia Tech. She recently chaired the university task force on academic advising and is charged with providing leadership of initiatives to improve advising and retention of undergraduate students. Scott is responsible for oversight of the Center for Academic Enrichment and Excellence, the academic support center for undergraduate students at Virginia Tech.

REMY R. SOTTO is a counselor at Pima Community College in Tucson, Arizona. She earned her M.S. degree (1985) in physical education from San Diego State University. Sotto's expertise, publications, and national conference presentations focus on the use of technology in advising and in advising distance learners. She has coordinated a Title III project, has served on a variety of National Academic Advising Association committees and task forces, is currently consulting with Western Governor's University, and is serving on an advisory board for the Western Interstate Commission for Higher Education.

GEORGE E. STEELE is currently director of the Ohio Learning Network. He was coordinator of Advising in University College at The Ohio State University. In that position, he was responsible for the coordination of advising services for undecided and major-changing students. Steele earned his B.A. (1976), M.A. (1978), and Ph.D. (1986) degrees in education from The Ohio State University. He is coauthor of several journal articles about undecided and major-changing students. With Virginia N. Gordon and Melinda L. McDonald he has shared national recognition for programs implemented in the University College over the years. Steele is active in the National Academic Advising Association and has served as director of the Clearinghouse on Academic Advising. In addition to his work with undecided students, Steele is interested in the use of technology in advising.

PAMELA S. STEPHENS is career coordinator in the Office of Career Development at Temple University and a doctoral candidate in the graduate program in higher education at Pennsylvania State University (Penn State). She received her B.A. degree in English from Penn State and her M.A. degree in educational leadership from Troy State University. Her research and professional interests include student affairs administration, academic and career counseling, student development, and student demographics.

HERTA TEITELBAUM is assistant dean in the Advising Center of Cornell University's College of Arts and Sciences. She served previously as associate dean of University College at the University of Utah, providing campuswide coordination of academic advising for undergraduates and advisor training and development programs. She holds a Ph.D. degree (1976) in linguistics and has taught courses in statistics, research methods, and student development. Her publication topics include linguistics, higher education, and academic advising.

M. LEE UPCRAFT is research associate in the Center for the Study of Higher Education, assistant vice president emeritus for student affairs, and affiliate professor emeritus of higher education at Pennsylvania State University. He received his B.A. degree (1960) in social studies and his M.A. degree (1961) in guidance and counseling from the State University of New York–Albany, and his Ph.D. degree (1968) in student personnel administration from Michigan State University. His research and professional interests include student retention, assessment in student affairs, the first-year experience, the impact of technology on student learning, and student demographics.

FAYE VOWELL is vice president for academic affairs at Western New Mexico University (WNMU), following multiple administrative assignments at Emporia State University. WNMU is noted for its application of quality principles to higher education. Vowell has been active in advising and with the National Academic Advising Association (NACADA) since 1984. She has authored a number of articles and edited a variety of monographs on advising as well as leading a team of advisors in the creation of a video training program for advisors. She is currently leading a NACADA initiative to create an on-line advisor training course.

ERIC R. WHITE is executive director of the Division of Undergraduate Studies and affiliate assistant professor of education at Pennsylvania State University (Penn State). He has previously served Penn State as a psychological counselor; coordinator of testing, counseling, and advising; and director of undergraduate studies. He earned his B.A. degree (1966) in history from Rutgers University and his M.S. (1967) and Ed.D. (1975) degrees in counseling psychology from the University of Pennsylvania. White has served in a number of positions in the National Academic Advising Association and is currently the association's treasurer. He is the author of several monograph chapter and journal articles and coeditor of the Jossey-Bass monograph *Teaching Through Academic Advising*.

CAROLYN J. WILKIE is a professor with the Learning Center at Indiana University of Pennsylvania (IUP). She earned her B.S. degree (1971) in English and her M.Ed. degree (1973) in language education at IUP, and her Ph.D. (1996) in curriculum and instruction from Pennsylvania State University. Wilkie's published works include articles on classroom environment research, the effect of work-study employment on academic progress, the effectiveness of freshman seminar programs, predicting academic probation, and reentry women. She has earned numerous awards for teaching, publications, and research, including recognition by the National Association for Developmental Education, the College Reading and Learning Association, and organizations within the state of Pennsylvania.

Academic Advising

Part One

Foundations of
Academic Advising

Academic advising has a long and fascinating history. Its foundations lie in the history of American higher education, from the colonial colleges to today's diverse array of colleges and universities. To comprehend advising's evolution and its place on today's campuses, one must understand how social, economic, and political forces have affected change in higher education since the seventeenth century.

In Chapter One, Susan H. Frost not only traces this history but also extrapolates from it the successful practices that need to be continued and the pitfalls that need to be avoided. On the basis of this broad history, she concludes by offering challenges to advising researchers, practitioners, and administrators to advance to the next stage of development, in which both thought and action will be critical.

In the past several decades, theoretical frameworks have been ascribed to the process of academic advising. Perhaps the most influential theoretical foundations have been developmental theories—of student, cognitive, adult, and career development, to name a few. In Chapter Two, Don G. Creamer describes the theories that relate most directly to the process of academic advising, and discusses practical applications of theoretical concepts.

Although advising's historical context provides a framework from which to observe change, Wesley R. Habley, in Chapter Three, reviews the current status of advising by examining data from a recent national survey. He describes the significant changes that advising has experienced in the past two decades and compares past data with the current information.

Two foundation areas, ethical and legal issues, have become increasingly important in the past two decades. Advisors are sometimes confronted with moral and ethical dilemmas, presented to them by their advisees and in their dual roles as student advocates and employees of the institution. In Chapter Four, Katherine Simon Frank describes ethical standards and principles that are relevant to advising practices. Attorney Barbara A. Becker, in Chapter Five, outlines important legal issues that may arise in certain advising situations. She discusses contract and statutory law in this context and offers practical suggestions for avoiding litigation.

These chapters introduce the reader to the past and current status of academic advising and impart valuable insights into how theory can be used as a foundation for advising practices. They also provide advisors with important information about their ethical and legal obligations. Overall, at the end of Part One readers should have gained a comprehensive understanding of the foundations that undergird advising and a complete knowledge of its roots and general practices.

Chapter One

Historical and Philosophical Foundations for Academic Advising

Susan H. Frost

Beginning with the earliest colleges and universities in the United States, faculty members have advised students about their courses of study. The topics of this advice have ranged from requirements imposed by institutions, departments, and outside agencies to students' notions about their intellectual interests and vocational goals. For the most part, students have valued this advice. This chapter investigates some of the ideas and events that have shaped advising as it is constructed today. It presents lessons that can help improve both current methods and interaction between students and advisors. Are there successes we would do well to emulate? Are there pitfalls we would do well to avoid?

Before examining these questions, it is useful to note two historical aims of undergraduate education: to involve students with the content of their learning and to involve them with the teacher. In the 1930s and 1940s, American philosopher and University of Chicago professor John Dewey thought deeply about these goals. Over the course of his career, Dewey searched for ideas that mediated between the conflicting notions of fact and value, thought and nature, and the individual and society. Encouraging educators to go beyond merely viewing students as empty vessels and arranging interactions to fill them, Dewey advocated involving students in action with the world and the forces that shape it. What a student learns in one situation, he claimed, enables that student to meet the next situation effectively (Borgard, 1981). Dewey seems to have captured a value that has developed over the long course of higher education. Teaching is more than the transmission of facts. Even from the earliest days of higher education, interaction between students and the content of learning has been key.

Some years before Dewey, another educator, John Henry Newman, wrote two volumes of essays about such matters: *Historical Sketches* (1872) and *The Idea of a University* (1873). *Historical Sketches* is a series of essays in which Newman considered the rise and progress of the university. In several of the essays, Newman described the essence of another aim: to involve students with the teacher in meaningful ways. He described, for example, the Sophist Hippocrates, whose students were likely to find him pacing among them, bewitching them with his voice, and fielding their questions on topics from physics to astronomy. The gathering seemed as much social as serious, for until that time teaching adults had not been acknowledged as an intellectual activity or granted standing of its own. The Sophists, who seem to have been the first paid teachers, offered knowledge and not political connections or other fashions of the day (Dewey, 1993).

Thus, we can link the Sophists and their students to some defining ideas of formal higher education. Among the Sophists' first students was Socrates, who later taught using a debating technique we know as *Socratic dialogue.* Socrates' style was the basis of the Academy of Athens, which Socrates' student Plato founded in 387 B.C. Some identify this academy as the first university in Europe. Plato's student Aristotle is thought to have devised notions of causality, logic, and scientific thought, which form the foundations of modern western thinking.

Modern Western thinking is the foundation of U.S. higher education. The history and foundation of higher education frame the review of advising presented in this chapter. This review spans the years from the founding of Harvard in 1636 to the 1990s. To add clarity, these years are divided into three periods that mark the development of academic advising: higher education before academic advising was defined as an activity, higher education when academic advising was defined but for the most part unexamined, and academic advising as a defined and examined activity. The first period spans the years from the founding of Harvard to the emergence of research universities in the late nineteenth century. The second period dates from the late nineteenth century to the 1970s, when theory-based research on advising began to shape practice. The third period began in the 1970s and continues today. Early in the first period, clear purpose guided the development of colonial colleges, and this purpose influenced the nature of higher education for many years.

Higher Education Before Academic Advising Was Defined

The English colonists who settled America believed deeply that an educated citizenry and a learned clergy were essential aspects of the society they wanted to establish. Therefore, a brief sixteen years after landing at Plymouth Rock in 1620, the Puritans founded Harvard College. Fifty-seven years later, in 1693, the state of Virginia opened the College of William and Mary, which was followed by Yale in 1701 and others. By 1776, thirteen colleges existed, representing the colonists' intent to establish social order in communities, instill civic responsibility in inhabitants, and educate privileged young men without having to rely on the universities the settlers had left behind in England.

In time, borrowing from both the English residential college scheme and the governing patterns of German universities, the colonial colleges taught a classical curriculum that emphasized ideas, or the life of the mind. In these early American schools, both the curriculum and the teaching method were standard. Students had little or no choice of courses, and recitation by students was the only teaching method faculty used (Herbst, 1982; Rudolph, 1962).

In the residential communities these colleges formed, students and faculty lived in the college, and strict rules governed all aspects of students' lives. For example, the faculty supervised not only the students' studies and living environment, but their worship as well (Bush, 1969). In one case, two Yale students attended Separatist church services with their parents while vacationing at home. Objecting to this lapse, Rector Thomas Clap and his faculty moved to govern the students' worship, even when the students were at home (Hofstadter and Smith, 1961). In other settings, tutors offered less rigid direction. Generally, colonial college tutors worked with one or more classes in all subjects, providing most of the guidance that colonial college students received (Roche, 1986).

As the attitudes and ideology developed that led to the colonies' political revolution, students seemed less willing to follow the rules. By 1770, some students expressed revolutionary attitudes openly, debating on campus the natural rights of individuals and the contractual basis of government, for example. During this time, the mission of American colleges evolved from educating for service to church and state to educating for citizenship in a new republic. Individualistic ideas were forming, and following the Revolution these notions brought great change to colleges in America.

After the Revolution, the colonial colleges continued to advance republican ideals among privileged young men, and on the western frontier new colleges opened to educate a broader component of the population. Designed for the most part to promote religious freedom, these colleges expanded the curriculum to include the information and skills that settlers needed to survive (Potts, 1971). In time, reflecting Jacksonian views of individualism, optimism, and materialism, colleges prepared students to serve not the state but rather the students' individual aims. Religious influence diminished as students demanded a curriculum that would advance their more personal goals.

The distance between faculty and students continued to widen, however. At times faculty made rules and regulations and used force to impose them. The distance did not go unmarked. For example, in 1832 a Harvard student named Samuel Osgood observed, "I do not think that professors and tutors generally show enough personal interest and regard for their pupils. . . . The two parties are too often found set against each other in mutual suspicion, each mistrusting and mistrusted" (Bush, 1969, p. 599). Some students reacted to this distance by changing the focus of their attention. By 1840, extracurricular activities and pastimes were more important to many students than formal programs of study.

The era of the Civil War modernized all aspects of American life, including higher education. During this period, new colleges were founded and others changed to offer real choice in the curriculum. In 1862, Congress passed the Morrill Act, authorizing land grant colleges in each state to teach practical subjects to the citizens. The Second Morrill Act of 1890 provided funds to states that extended higher education to all races (Veysey, 1965).

Another important development occurred between 1790 and 1850 when some institutions began to educate women. Women first received liberal education at academies and seminaries, then in 1847 Lucy Stone became the first woman in Massachusetts to receive the bachelor of arts (A.B.) degree. Soon higher education for women was in widespread demand. In 1889 Columbia president Frederick Barnard wrote of Columbia's need to address the issue of admitting women: "In more than half the colleges of the United States, young women are admitted on the same terms as young men, and attend the same instructors in the same lecture halls at the same hours. . . .The presence of young women . . . has the effect to raise rather than to depress the average scholarship of the classes to which they belong" (Russell, 1937, pp. 251–253). By 1930, 44 percent of all U.S. college students were women (Solomon, 1985, p. 63).

During this time three distinct educational philosophies emerged: utility, liberal culture, and research. *Utility* called for a practical, real-life approach to all courses, even the most traditional. Cornell's emphasis on public service was an early example of utility, as was Harvard's extensive elective system. Acting on the ideas of President Lincoln Steffens, the University of Wisconsin advanced utilitarianism to a greater degree. Steffens envisioned the university as a "kind of living reference library for the state as a whole" (Veysey, 1965, p. 107). This example was known as the Wisconsin Idea.

Promoting the pursuit of art and beauty for their own sake, *liberal culture* had its roots in the classical curriculum of the colonial colleges. With passionate supporters at Princeton and Yale, for example, liberal culture in the late 1880s opposed both utility and research. Although few scholars supported liberal culture, those who did were both militant and prolific, writing more about the problems of higher education than the advocates of research (Veysey, 1965). In universities, departments of philosophy, fine arts, and languages evolved from liberal culture; some aspects of current undergraduate education are rooted in its ideas.

Those who emphasized *research* looked to Europe for new developments, especially to Germany, where investigation and writing defined a university education. In America, faculty interested in research benefited from the gradual loss of religious control over colleges, which helped make it possible for scholars who studied abroad to influence the development of institutions at home. Professors who advocated a research philosophy devoted their energy to research and scholarship and tended to ignore their students (Bush, 1969). They were intellectuals who placed less value on America's traditional devotion to the education of select young men than on their own work to advance knowledge. As Cowley (1938) noted, American professors who studied in Germany brought home "the degree of Doctor of Philosophy and substantially succeeded in establishing it as the *sine qua non* of the professorship. They taught their subjects as ends in themselves rather than as means for the educating of college students. And, most important of all, they abandoned the holistic conception of the historic American college and announced themselves frankly and completely intellectualistic" (pp. 472–473).

Many undergraduates, however, wanted no part of the new tendency to specialize. Most attended college for general instruction and for the activities they considered more important: athletics, student publications, dramatics, or talking with their friends. They went to class because it was required and never aimed for more than a C grade (Cowley, 1938). Before long, faculty came to consider it inappropriate to speak to students on a personal basis, and students considered it improper to approach faculty. Although a few great teachers broke the silence, most students and faculty had the most impersonal of relationships (Bush, 1969). At best, historical ideals about the teacher guiding the learner had become obscured; at worst, they had been lost.

Academic Advising as a Defined and Unexamined Activity

By the early twentieth century, three types of American higher education institutions existed: the Eastern colleges, with their mostly homogeneous student bodies; Eastern universities, with more heterogeneous profiles; and the generally heterogeneous Western universities. Although the missions of these types were distinct, they shared an unfortunate trait. For the most part, chasms existed between students and faculty, who each defined the academic experience differently enough to suggest that their minds almost never met. Growing administrative structures contributed to this distance, as did formally organized structures for departments and deans, and hiring practices were based more on research capacity than on teaching ability. As presidents came to associate themselves with the identity and ambition of their schools, the public perceived them as the "personality" of the institution (Veysey, 1965).

Also during the first years of the century the elective principle became a defining characteristic of American higher education. In addition to providing students with choices about their courses of study, the elective principle "moved the individual to the center of the educational universe and boldly asserted that all educated men need not know the same things" (Veysey, 1965, p. 305). Knowledge had expanded beyond the mastery of one person, providing a foundation on which academic departments were built.

By 1910 six institutions had enrollments of five thousand or more. As some formerly distinctive colleges competed for both students and financial support, they blended into the same kind of institution. Their future was bright, however. The industrial revolution had created a significant number of millionaires in America, and many of these millionaires supported universities and colleges. At first they funded general education, but by 1920 they directed their wealth more to research. Partly in reaction to this new connection, scientists moved to emphasize objectivity and the scientific method. By considering their findings morally neutral, faculty avoided circumstances in which lines of inquiry might offend powerful donors. According to some observers, faculty also declined to take responsibility for the consequences of their work (Bender, 1997).

Due in part to this factor, new knowledge increased exponentially in the 1920s and early 1930s. By 1933 the Depression had reduced private wealth and the federal government stepped in. According to historians, the technology that made victory possible in World War II came from university research conducted during these years (Geiger, 1986). Also in this period, most institutions continued to grow and become more complex. Although the administrations of both public and private universities were more and more insulated from the work of scholars and academic departments, both sectors of higher education remained distinctive.

As noted, one characteristic of this time was the growing distance between faculty and undergraduate students. In 1909, A. Lawrence Lowell, the new president of Harvard, took measures to close the gap. He announced a return to the "ideals of the collegiate way of living; in brief, to the ideals of holism . . . the restoration of personal relations between faculty and students by means of the tutorial system. . . . [C]ollege students are whole people. . . . [I]t is bad psychology and bad education to assume that they are disembodied intellects and that education is intellectual training alone." (Cowley, 1938, p. 474). Lowell seemed to build on the philosophy of former president Charles Eliot Norton, who in the late nineteenth century wrote that faculty should give advice and assistance to students outside the classroom as well as inside. "Every student on his entrance to college is referred to a member of the Faculty, who will act as his advisor in regard to all matters in which he may stand in need of counsel" (Bush, 1969, p. 607).

One early attempt to connect students and faculty more closely took the form of a system of academic advising, introduced at Johns Hopkins in 1889. Other institutions soon emulated the practice of having faculty members advise students about their courses of study (Grites, 1979). In fact, Veysey (1965, p. 297) reports that the advisor system for selecting courses was the "fad of the moment at Columbia in 1906" but soon degenerated into brief, impersonal interviews. By the late 1930s almost all institutions had formalized advising programs (Raskin, 1979). The following examples provide a sense of some other attempts to connect students and faculty.

Acknowledging the charge of a liberal arts college to give educational and vocational guidance to students, in 1938 Wesleyan University determined to offer such guidance. President Albert Hill wrote about Wesleyan's program, observing that Wesleyan offered it without interfering with the "high cultural aims" of the college (Hill, 1938, p. 124). To implement the goal, Hill established a committee of faculty and others to encourage students to explore their interests. Although the program seemed directed more at information about careers than at college course selection, it had developmental goals. For example, the committee advised students that their preferences might change during their time in college. Faculty encouraged students to explore new interests and questions as they developed.

A decade later, Alfred University took a similar approach. In 1947 the president of Alfred charged a committee of faculty and others to formulate a plan to give "visible form and progressive depth" ("With the Technicians," 1952, p. 40) to the advising of freshmen and sophomores at the university. The committee recommended that Alfred establish a "personnel" office to orient freshmen to the history and tradition of the university, to study methods, and to general conduct, and that it subscribe to the "faith and philosophy underlying general faculty advising" (p. 41). Defining this faith as more humanist than related to specialty in psychological counseling, Alfred established a system that supplemented rather than replaced faculty in the advising process.

Perhaps Wesleyan president Hill borrowed from published reports when he used the word *personnel* to describe the office he envisioned. By 1934 reports of "student-personnel work" had begun to appear in published reports of higher education practice (Lloyd-Jones, 1934). Described as work having to do with individual students outside the classroom, this function attempted to interest the student in developing his or her own body, mind, and character. This work, which included educational guidance and vocational counseling, was largely undefined in the minds of those who carried it out. However, even at this early stage, proponents of the function recognized the value of "spontaneous participation on the part of each member" (Lloyd-Jones, 1934, p. 143). Leaders cautioned those who worked in student personnel to offer integrated services to students and require them to take part in the conversation.

Syracuse University also used an integrated approach. To improve students' adjustment to college, Syracuse reported on a study of 173 freshmen women to learn the nature of the problems they encountered when adjusting to academic demands, and techniques for alleviating these problems. The investigators, student deans who were also graduate students with training in psychology and related areas, devoted half their time to studying the women in residential cottage settings. Superior students seemed to have fewer problems adjusting to academic life, especially if their problems were scattered across the types the study identified. Another finding was that some students' lives had been so controlled and directed at home that they had little capacity to direct themselves in college. Investigators recognized that all students warranted help with academic adjustment and recommended that Syracuse provide this help in both group and individual settings (Smith, 1939).

Various other reports associated academic advising with student personnel programs. However, most scholars who have investigated the evolution of advising agree that during this period advising was primarily a function of academic affairs. Regardless of functional location, ideas about help with academic adjustment and academic advising seem to have developed during this time from an undefined concept to defined components of some formal programs. Although advising programs at institutions like Wesleyan, Syracuse, and Alfred developed during the same period that educators like Eliot and Lowell discussed goals of faculty-student interaction, actual programs did not always reflect the views of such men. Both Eliot and Lowell called for faculty and students to interact, not only in the classroom but outside as well. Some accounts describe programs that either do not involve faculty or assign to them much smaller roles. However, these programs did offer students a venue to investigate their interests. They also provided a basis for a more intensive period of development for the concept of academic advising as we define it today.

Academic Advising as a Defined and Examined Activity

In 1950, the federal government established the National Science Foundation to fund scientific and technological research in the United States. Both this massive funding and the GI Bill to enable veterans of World War II to attend college tuition free produced record enrollment and unmatched research activity in the years following the war.

The end of World War II, the founding of the National Science Foundation, and increasing enrollments due to the GI Bill helped change many universities from smaller, more insulated and homogeneous teaching institutions into the research institutions they are today. These forces influenced all sectors of higher education. Between 1949 and 1999, the number of colleges and universities in the United States increased from 1,800 to more than 3,600, enrollments grew from 2.2 million to more than 14.3 million, and federal support for research increased from about $100 million to more than $12 billion (National Center for Education Statistics, 1998; "1998–1999 Almanac," 1998). In the 1960s, American higher education grew more than it had in the three preceding decades. Indeed remarkable, this growth brought higher learning to broad segments of the population and prosperity to many institutions. It brought growing pains as well.

Although most institutions set their own course during the first half of the twentieth century, by the 1960s society was beginning to shape the tasks that universities and colleges were compelled to perform. For example, the public became more interested in access to higher learning and in solutions to immediate problems than in new knowledge and the traditional methods of the disciplines. Additionally, student protest welled up in the late 1960s. Although most radical activity had dissipated by 1971, students continued to work through organizations and more informal groups to change both the rules and the practices of the academy (Geiger, 1993).

Also during these years, student populations changed from being largely homogeneous to being increasingly diverse on many fronts. For example, during the 1980s the U.S. population growth rate was at a historic low, yet minority populations grew at two to fourteen times the rate of the nonminority group. From 1972 to 1995 the percentage of college students who were members of minority populations increased from about 15 percent to 25 percent of all students (National Center for Education Statistics, 1998). The increase was due primarily to growth in the enrollment of Hispanic and Asian students. For each of these groups, enrollment as a percentage of all college students increased about 4 percent each year. During the same period, enrollment rates for eighteen- to twenty-four-year-old African American students who had completed high school increased from 27 percent to 36 percent; corresponding rates for students who were Hispanic increased from 26 percent to 34 percent. In 1996, students who were African American accounted for 10 percent of the total college and university enrollment; students who were Hispanic accounted for 8 percent; Asian–Pacific Islanders accounted for 6 percent; and American Indian–Alaskan Natives constituted 1 percent. As these numbers suggest, in 1995 about one in four students was a member of a minority population.

Accompanying these changes on university and college campuses was the advancement of the community college. Between 1966 and 1976, the number of community colleges increased from 565 to 1,030, and enrollment increased by almost 200 percent. Community colleges came to represent the central point of entry into higher education for both lower-income and working adult students. Perhaps more than any other segment of higher education, community colleges developed strong links to their local communities (Koltai, 1985).

Continued formalization of academic advising on most campuses was one response to two forces: student populations that were increasingly numerous and diverse, and faculties that were devoted to research. By the late 1970s, academic advising had begun to resemble an organized profession. In 1979 the National Academic Advising Association (NACADA) was formed and attained five hundred members by the end of its first year. To increase interest in informed and improved practice, the association supported an annual national conference, advising-related research, a refereed journal, and other outlets for publication and professional development. NACADA appears to have improved advising programs and enhanced the professional status of advisors. Today NACADA flourishes and works to improve both knowledge and practice related to advising.

National interest in improving the experience of first-year students also developed during this time. Under the leadership of John N. Gardner, all types of institutions demonstrated their interest in the first year of college. Before long, many colleges and universities organized formal programs not only to orient and advise students, but also to strengthen the students' experiences during the entire first year.

Despite these efforts, national reports and other data suggested that improvements in advising practice were less numerous and less powerful than some accounts indicated. In its 1984 report, *Involvement in Learning,* the National Institute of Education identified advising as one of the weakest components of the undergraduate academic experience. Other observers agreed. After both two and four years of college, only about half of students responding to a survey designed to measure the quality of services expressed satisfaction with advising (Astin, Korn, and Green, 1987). The influence of NACADA and national attention to the problem notwithstanding, published reports of advising's effectiveness did little to dispute the claims.

In an effort to encourage both reflection and improved practice, in 1979 the American College Testing Service (ACT) began a series of comprehensive surveys of advising practice. The ACT surveys conducted in 1979, 1983, and 1987 provide the most comprehensive research on advising during the period. According to findings, in 1979 the delivery of information to students was the primary goal of most programs. By 1987, the only goal approaching satisfactory achievement was to provide information (Carstensen and Silberhorn, 1979; Crockett and Levitz, 1983; Habley and Crockett, 1988). Because advising remained largely unevaluated at that time, scholars knew little about the effects of services on students (Frost, 1991).

By the early 1990s, conflicting attitudes toward advising at the national level and reports of actual campus practice indicated that change was needed not only at the program level but among higher education leaders as well. Additionally, new ideas about some theoretical foundations of advising and about the specific ways students benefit from college also came forward. Some offered promising routes to improved practice.

One line of research revealed new information about why students persist in college and succeed. Beginning in 1975, investigators suggested that for the most part students who are involved in college are more successful than students who are uninvolved. Alexander Astin (1984, 1985), Ernest Boyer (1987), and Vincent Tinto (1975, 1987) were three of the prominent scholars who advanced this view. For example, Astin (1984) described involvement as an investment of energy measured along a continuum of qualitative characteristics such as commitment and quantitative characteristics such as time. Learning, he suggested, is directly proportional to both the quality and the quantity of involvement, which successful policies and practices seem to advance.

Also in the early 1970s, a new concept of academic advising was promoted. Working independently, Burns Crookston (1972) and Terry O'Banion (1972) linked advising to theories of student development and used this link to explain advising as a form of teaching. Crookston organized his concept around two principles: higher education provides opportunity for persons who are developing to plan to achieve self-fulfilling lives, and teaching includes any experience that contributes to individual growth and that can be evaluated. Crookston framed a new definition of academic advising. First, he defined traditional or prescriptive advising as a relationship built on the authority of the advisor and the limitation of the student. In a prescriptive advising setting, for example, the student brings problems to the advisor for solutions. Advisors tend to answer specific questions but rarely address more comprehensive academic concerns (Crookston, 1972; Fielstein, 1994).

Second, Crookston linked his new concept to the belief that students and advisors should share responsibility for both the nature of the advising relationship and the quality of the experience. Developmental advising, as Crookston called his idea, is a rational process. As such, it employs environmental and interpersonal interactions, behavioral awareness, and problem-solving, decision-making, and evaluation skills. In Crookston's estimate, the advising *relationship* is vital; determining and achieving both long-term and immediate goals are in its domain. Crookston believed that this relationship could be accomplished better through application of his concepts than through traditional advising practices.

Crookston, O'Banion, and others who offered similar ideas looked to Chickering's (1969) psychosocial theory for conceptual support. Chickering's theory is organized around seven concepts that Chickering called *vectors*. Developmental advising is directly related to three of these vectors: developing competence, developing autonomy, and developing purpose (Gordon, 1988). These vectors support characteristics of developmental advising that make the concept unique. For example, developmental advising is a process, not a routine endorsement of course taking; it is concerned with growth, especially personal goals and objectives; and it depends on ongoing interaction (Ender, Winston, and Miller, 1982; Frost, 1991). Such specific clues about characteristics of the concept offered practitioners the promise of substantive change.

Along with these developments, a more comprehensive line of inquiry offered some clarity about ways in which effective undergraduate learning takes place. In 1991, Ernest Pascarella and Patrick Terenzini summarized the findings of this inquiry in their comprehensive volume, *How College Affects Students*. They explained their strongest conclusion about the academic experience: "The greater the student's involvement or engagement in academic work or in the academic experience of college, the greater his or her level of knowledge acquisition and general cognitive development. . . ."(p. 616). As evidence indicates, some instructional and programmatic interventions not only increase the student's active engagement in learning and academic work, but also enhance knowledge acquisition and some dimensions of both cognitive development and psychosocial change. Astin, Tinto, Pascarella, and Terenzini seem to agree that student involvement is critical. Although this knowledge has enriched theoretical work on the positive effects of college, it does not appear to have brought widespread change to practice.

In 1994 the *NACADA Journal* led a reflection on both the theory and practice of developmental advising. In the fall issue, twenty-seven theorists and practitioners wrote critically about Crookston's and O'Banion's ideas, addressing the authors' influence on thought and action. In that volume, O'Banion (1994) updated his views. In practice not enough has changed, he observed. Those who would implement developmental advising seem to know more about the aims of the concept than about how to accomplish those aims.

It was suggested earlier in this chapter that Newman's and Dewey's aims are at the core of undergraduate education. Reflecting on these aims and on the development of academic advising, I agree with O'Banion. Although theory and research offer improvements to advising and to similar components of the academic experience of undergraduates, too little has been done to incorporate these theories and research into actual gain. In other words, action lags behind thought, leaving a gap to be filled.

Perhaps trends in the demand for undergraduate education hold clues about this gap. Before 1993, the population of high school graduates in the United States had decreased almost every year for fifteen years. Consequently, leaders worried about issues relating to declining enrollments, student retention, and tuition-based revenue, for example. As they moved to devise ways to attract and retain students, research about improving college gained importance.

Then, in 1994 the population of high school graduates began to increase, and fears of declining enrollments gradually faded. Other pressures came forward, especially those concerning program quality and faculty work. Thus, perhaps before new knowledge could lead to wide improvements in advising and other student-centered programs, leaders turned their attention elsewhere.

Today we remain in the cycle of increasing demand for higher education. In this climate, this volume seems particularly well-timed. By its nature, it provides for broad reflection on both theory and practice. Perhaps it will advance the next stage of advising development, in which both thought and action ought to advance.

In anticipation of this work, this chapter ends with questions for three groups of readers: theorists and researchers, advising practitioners, and higher education leaders.

For Theorists and Researchers

- What do we know about the effects of college that might improve academic advising and related components of undergraduate learning?
- Considering our knowledge of faculty-student interaction and student learning styles, for example, how can faculty best be involved? How can students best be engaged?

For Advising Practitioners

- What are the effects of advising on your campus?
- How do these effects differ among all types of student populations? By type of advising interaction?
- Considering your students and your advisors, what should your program aspire to achieve? How will you measure progress toward your goals?

For Higher Education Leaders

- Considering the distance between thought and action, how can we best close the gap? For example, how can we use what we know about effective advising relationships to improve the experiences of both students and advisors?
- What are the ideal educational goals of advising? How can we best use our resources to achieve these goals?

Meeting the challenges that these questions imply could not only shape the future of academic advising; it could also advance the broader aims of education. Although academic advising is just one component of undergraduate education, it is at the core of learning. Thus, by its nature it is a likely place for change to begin.

References

"1998–1999 Almanac." *Chronicle of Higher Education,* 1998, *1,* 005.

Astin, A. W. "Student Involvement: A Developmental Theory for Higher Education." *Journal of College Student Personnel,* 1984, *25*(4), 297–308.

Astin, A. W. *Achieving Educational Excellence.* San Francisco: Jossey-Bass, 1985.

Astin, A. W., Korn, W., and Green, K. "Retaining and Satisfying Students." *Educational Record,* 1987, *68*(1), 36–42.

Bender, T., and Schorske, C. E. *American Academic Culture in Transformation.* Princeton, N.J.: Princeton University Press, 1997.

Borgard, J. H. "Toward a Pragmatic Philosophy of Academic Advising." *NACADA Journal,* 1981, *1*(1), 1–6.

Boyer, E. L. *College: The Undergraduate Experience in America.* New York: HarperCollins, 1987.

Bush, N. B. "The Student and His Professor: Colonial Times to Twentieth Century." *Journal of Higher Education,* 1969, *40*(8), 593–609.

Carstensen, D., and Silberhorn, C. *A National Survey of Academic Advising: Final Report.* Iowa City, Iowa: American College Testing Program, 1979. (ED 232 525)

Chickering, A. W. *Education and Identity.* San Francisco: Jossey-Bass, 1969.

Cowley, W. H. "Intelligence Is Not Enough." *Journal of Higher Education,* 1938, *9*(9), 469–477.

Crockett, D. S., and Levitz, R. S. *A National Survey of Academic Advising.* Iowa City, Iowa: American College Testing Program, 1983.

Crookston, B. B. "A Developmental View of Academic Advising as Teaching." *Journal of College Student Personnel,* 1972, *13,* 12–17.

Dewey, J. *Philosophy and Education in Their Historic Relations* (E. R. Clapp, trans.; J. J. Chambliss, ed.). Boulder, Colo.: Westview Press, 1993.

Ender, S. C., Winston, R. B., and Miller, T. K. "Academic Advising as Student Development." In R. B. Winston Jr., S. C. Ender, and T. K. Miller (eds.), *Developmental Approaches to Academic Advising.* New Directions for Student Services, no. 17. San Francisco: Jossey-Bass, 1982.

Fielstein, L. L. "Developmental Versus Prescriptive Advising: Must It Be One or the Other?" *NACADA Journal,* 1994, *14*(2), 71–75.

Frost, S. H. *Academic Advising for Student Success: A System of Shared Responsibility.* ASHE-ERIC Higher Education Report, no. 3. Washington, D.C.: George Washington University, School of Education and Human Development, 1991.

Geiger, R. L. *To Advance Knowledge: The Growth of American Research Universities, 1900–1940.* New York: Oxford University Press, 1986.

Geiger, R. L. *Research and Relevant Knowledge: American Research Universities Since World War II.* New York: Oxford University Press, 1993.

Gordon, V. N. "Developmental Advising." In W. R. Habley (ed.), *The Status and Future of Academic Advising: Problems and Promise.* Iowa City, Iowa: American College Testing Program, 1988.

Grites, T. J. *Academic Advising: Getting Us Through the Eighties.* AAHE-ERIC Higher Education Research Report, no. 7. Washington, D.C.: American Association for Higher Education, 1979. (ED 178 023)

Habley, W. R., and Crockett, D. S. "The Third ACT National Survey of Academic Advising." In W. R. Habley (ed.), *The Status and Future of Academic Advising: Problems and Promise.* Iowa City, Iowa: American College Testing Program, 1988.

Herbst, J. *From Crisis to Crisis: American College Government, 1636–1819.* Cambridge, Mass.: Harvard University Press, 1982.

Hill, A. G. "A Guidance Program." *Journal of Higher Education,* 1938, *9*(3), 124–126.

Hofstadter, R., and Smith, W. (eds.). *American Higher Education: A Documentary History,* Vol. 1. Chicago: University of Chicago Press, 1961.

Koltai, L. "Community Colleges: Making Winners out of Ordinary People." In A. Levine (ed.), *Higher Learning in America, 1980–2000.* Baltimore: Johns Hopkins University Press, 1985.

Lloyd-Jones, E. "Personnel Administration." *Journal of Higher Education,* 1934, *5*(3), 141–147.

National Center for Education Statistics, U. S. Department of Education. *The Condition of Education: 1998.* Washington D.C.: Government Printing Office, 1998.

National Institute of Education. *Involvement in Learning: Realizing the Potential of American Higher Education.* Washington D.C.: National Institute of Education, 1984. (ED 246 833)

Newman, J. H. *Historical Sketches.* London: Basil Montagu Pickering, 1872.

Newman, J. H. *The Idea of a University.* London: Basil Montagu Pickering, 1873.

O'Banion, T. "An Academic Advising Model." *Junior College Journal,* 1972, *42*(6), 62–69.

O'Banion, T. "Retrospect and Prospect." *NACADA Journal,* 1994, *14*(2), 117–119.

Pascarella, E. T., and Terenzini, P. T. *How College Affects Students: Findings and Insights from Twenty Years of Research.* San Francisco: Jossey-Bass, 1991.

Potts, D. B. "American Colleges in the Nineteenth Century: From Localism to Denominationalism." *History of Education Quarterly,* 1971, *11,* 363–380.

Raskin, M. "Critical Issue: Faculty Advising." *Peabody Journal of Education,* 1979, *56,* 99–108.

Roche, J. F. *The Colonial Colleges in the War for American Independence.* Millwood, N.Y.: Associated Faculty Press, 1986.

Rudolph, F. *The American College and University: A History.* New York: Vintage Books, 1962.

Russell, W. F. (ed.). *The Rise of a University, Vol. 1: The Later Days of Old Columbia College.* New York: Columbia University Press, 1937.

Smith, C. M. "Academic Adjustment Problems." *Journal of Higher Education,* 1939, *10*(7), 369–374.

Solomon, B. M. *In The Company of Educated Women.* New Haven, Conn.: Yale University Press, 1985.

Tinto, V. "Dropout from Higher Education: A Theoretical Synthesis of Recent Research." *Review of Educational Research,* 1975, *45,* 89–125.

Tinto, V. *Leaving College: Rethinking the Causes and Cures of Student Attrition.* Chicago: University of Chicago Press, 1987.

Veysey, L. R. *The Emergence of the American University.* Chicago: University of Chicago Press, 1965.

"With the Technicians." *Journal of Higher Education,* 1952, *23*(1), 40–49, 58.

Chapter Two

Use of Theory in Academic Advising

Don G. Creamer

Academic advising is an educational activity that depends on valid explanations of complex student behaviors and institutional conditions to assist college students in making and executing educational and life plans. These explanations are commonly found in sound theories. Given the scope of the academic advising phenomenon, advisors may be required to understand many theories—not only one or two—in order to grasp sufficient knowledge to be useful in advising students. Sound theory provides plausible explanations of a complex phenomenon. It distills the phenomenon to its essence and makes systematic observations about apparent relationships or underlying principles. Good theory is also useful in practice; it illuminates complex circumstances and makes puzzling things understandable.

Recently, Gordon and Steele (1995) dramatized the need for using theory in advising by describing an apparent relationship between effective academic advising practices and many related theories. They asserted that the effective academic advisor needs knowledge of student development theory, career development theory, learning theory, decision-making theory, multicultural theory (such as racial identity theory), retention theory, personality theory, moral development theory, adult development theory, sociological theory, and organizational theory. Understanding such a broad spectrum of theories is a daunting task.

Academic advising is a form of teaching that is both complex and puzzling, and its effectiveness depends on the sound use of multiple theories about students and the educational institutions in which they study. Because advising focuses on helping individuals achieve their own goals and interests, it is also a moral endeavor (Goodlad, (1997). As a special form of teaching, advising generally occurs outside the classroom, but it uses instructional methodologies in a disciplined fashion, as is done in classroom settings, to help students make and execute plans to achieve their educational and life goals. Ironically, although most educators agree that effective teaching relies on knowledge of relevant theories pertaining to the facts or circumstances being taught, there is at the same time little consensus about whether there is a need for theories about the process of advising (or teaching) itself.

This chapter addresses those aspects of theory use about which there is agreement within the profession by outlining the scope of academic advising, delineating some central concepts of developmental theories used in advising, and discussing practice-oriented generalizations about the use of theories in advising.

Scope of Academic Advising

Five widely held beliefs establish the practical boundaries of academic advising. These beliefs are grounded in the Statement of Core Values of the National Academic Advising Association (1994). Taken together, they express why, how, and under what circumstances academic advising is undertaken in higher education.

First, the *purpose* of academic advising is student learning and personal development. This purpose is precisely the same purpose that shapes all other forms of teaching, both inside and outside the classroom. Whether one is a teacher of literature, of out-of-classroom leadership programs, or of athletic skill, the purpose of teaching is to promote student learning and personal development. Promoting student learning and development is clearly not the sole purview of academic advisors. All educators share this purpose for education. Likewise, all advising responsibilities cannot be performed by academic advisors alone (Habley, 1984). Advising is a responsibility shared by all educators in a differentiated fashion.

Second, the art or science of teaching is the *pedagogy* of academic advising. Teaching methods that employ active or collaborative learning tactics and that recognize the social nature of learning are more effective than tactics that depend solely on didactic methods. Thus, advising programs that employ group activities, activities based in an academic advising center, or both are often able to acknowledge these standards practically. This is one of the major reasons that developmental advising is more effective than prescriptive advising with a broad range of students.

Third, the *context* of academic advising is educationally compelling circumstances calling for the formation and implementation of educational and life plans. Academic advising derives its meaning from the setting and achieving of student goals. Advising practices are conducted within educational environments and are conditioned by policies and practices that shape the limits and potentialities for achieving student goals.

Fourth, the *focus* of academic advising is the whole person. Developing realistic plans for students' lives and careers requires a holistic perspective, on both the person making the plans and the environment in which the plans will be carried out. All aspects of a student's background and current circumstances and the totality of the educational environment must be taken into account for effective advising to occur.

Fifth, the *content* of academic advising is constructed knowledge about students' educational and life plans. Together, students and advisors construct knowledge about the students' opportunities and how they can be realized. Although many students may follow similar educational paths, each student devises a plan containing some unique features, including dreams and perceptions of reality. Advisors must recognize this aspect of educational planning and incorporate such features into each student plan.

Thus it can be seen that advising is a developmental function; it is teaching in out-of-class settings to promote student learning and personal development.

A Framework for Effectiveness in Academic Advising

Based on generalizations from literature and practice, certain tentative hypotheses about the conditions that influence effectiveness in academic advising may be asserted:

- Students succeed at setting goals and making and executing plans to achieve them depending on their knowledge and understanding of themselves, their knowledge of the institutional resources available to them, and their motivation and will to make and accept the consequences of their choices about educational and life opportunities.

- Advisors succeed at influencing student choices and actions depending on their knowledge of institutional resources and of students' developmental and maturational levels, their sensitivity to students' needs and plans, and their skills in intervention and communication.

- The richness of institutional resources, including especially the comprehensiveness of curricular offerings and their accessibility for the making and executing of student plans for life and work, influences both student and advisor success.

Central to these hypotheses of effective academic advising is that students' understanding of themselves, from both their internal perspective and the advisor's external perspective in a real-world context, is associated with effectiveness. For the advisor to achieve this understanding of students, theories of development and learning are especially useful. Toward this end, this chapter outlines useable developmental, typological, and career theories, then discusses certain applications of these theories in advising practice.

Use of Student Development Theories in Advising

Relevant theories of student development are generally classified into clusters, such as psychosocial theories, cognitive-developmental theories, and typological theories. Psychosocial theories always include and sometimes focus exclusively on identity development; cognitive-developmental theories always focus on how we think and make meaning from our experiences; and typological theories always focus on distinguishing personality features and the patterns among them.

Clearly, knowledge of student identity, of the ways in which students make meaning, and of distinguishable and sometimes predictable patterns of student behavior is extremely useful to academic advisors. Such knowledge enables insights that allow advisors to explain conditions in students' lives that are often confusing and that sometimes block effective planning and learning.

Several thorough reviews of developmental theory can be found in recent literature. Evans, Forney, and Guido-DiBrito (1998) provide a comprehensive overview of these theories. Evans and her colleagues give a historical perspective and offer practical uses for the theories they review. Their review categorizes these theories in a psychosocial, cognitive-developmental, and typological format. Another useful review of developmental theories can be seen in Komives, Woodard, and Associates (1996). This work demonstrates the usefulness of developmental theories in broad arenas of student affairs. Both of these excellent sources also give appropriate attention to available theories to explain developmental phenomena in minority students, women, and students with alternative lifestyles. Especially useful to advisors may be a chapter by King (1996) that addresses student cognition and learning.

Older but still useful reviews may be found in Creamer and Associates (1990) and Chickering and Havighurst (1981). Creamer and his associates' reviews stress cognitive-developmental theories, psychosocial theories, and the assessment of both types of theory. Chickering and Havighurst provide one of the early but most thorough reviews of adult development, especially in their consideration of the developmental tasks associated with stages or periods of development.

To illustrate the useful nature of developmental theories, let's return to the larger themes within them—identity, ways of making meaning, and personality patterns of behavior. These themes are constant or recurring issues in academic advising and therefore offer a practical set of guides for considering developmental theories.

Identity Theories

Erikson (1968) provides the foundation theory for most psychosocial theories that focus on identity. He postulates eight stages of development: basic trust versus mistrust, autonomy versus shame and doubt, initiative versus guilt, industry versus inferiority, identity versus identity confusion, intimacy versus isolation, generativity versus stagnation, and integrity versus despair. The focus in understanding college students is generally on the stages pertaining to identity and intimacy. Both stages represent major concerns for traditional-age college students.

Chickering's (1969) theory is perhaps the best known and most widely used theory in explaining college students' identity development. In its latest version (Chickering and Reisser, 1993), identity is the central feature among seven vectors of development: developing competence, managing emotions, moving through autonomy toward interdependence, developing mature interpersonal relationships, establishing identity, developing purpose, and developing integrity. These elements of Chickering's theory and the concept of vectors have proven to be popular and of considerable utility in programming for student learning and development, and they seem to describe well many of the personal conflicts and dilemmas faced by traditional college students.

Building on Marcia's (1980) four identity states—diffusion, foreclosure, moratorium, and achievement—which are marked by the presence or absence of crisis and commitment, Josselson (1987) sought to explain distinctive aspects of identity development in women. She postulated variations on Marcia's states that show unique features of women's identity development and called them *purveyors of the heritage* (foreclosures), *pavers of the way* (identity achievements), *daughters of the crisis* (moratoriums), and *lost and sometimes found* (identity diffusions). Josselson's work shows the complexity of identity development and how it may vary by gender.

Racial and ethnic identity development models are emerging and may be helpful when used with selected populations of students. These models include Cross's (1971, 1995) Model of Psychological Nigrescence, Helms's (1995) Model of White Identity, and Phinney's (1990) Model of Ethnic Identity. Cross's model, developed originally in the 1970s and later revised, describes the identity development process for blacks in stages: preencounter, encounter, immersion-emersion, internalization, and internalization-commitment. Helms's model attempts to explain movement from racism to nonracism and includes two stages: abandonment of racism, which includes contact, disintegration, and reintegration; and defining nonracist white identity, which includes pseudo-independence, immersion-emersion, and autonomy. Phinney's model acknowledges the influence of culture, loyalty, and kinship in shaping identity, and the need to resolve certain conflicts involving stereotyping and prejudice. This model is composed of three stages (similar to Marcia's [1980] theory): diffusion-foreclosure, moratorium, and achievement.

Theories pertaining to gay, lesbian, and bisexual identity development are also emerging in the literature. Cass (1983–1984) and D'Augelli (1994) offer two relevant theories from these perspectives. Cass's theory is based on stages beginning with identity confusion and moving through identity comparison, identity tolerance, identity acceptance, identity pride, and identity synthesis. D'Augelli's model views gay, lesbian, and bisexual development as social construction, depending more on circumstances and environment than on movement through sequential stages. D'Augelli's life-span model sees identity development occurring from personal activities and actions, interactive intimacies, and sociohistorical connections.

Theories About Making Meaning

Piaget's (1952) work is the foundation for cognitive-developmental (or structural) theories and relies heavily on the function of assimilation and accommodation in the process of integrating new information into current ways of thinking. Development occurs when the cognitive structure is changed, thus enabling new ways of incorporating experience.

One of the best known and most widely used theories pertaining to changing how we make meaning is Perry's (1968) theory of intellectual and ethical development. Perry saw cognitive development occurring through a series of positions, beginning with basic duality and moving through multiplicity, relativism, and commitment. Consistent with how most theorists see development actually occurring, the uneven patterns of development that Perry noted among college students included temporizing, escape, and retreat. He also observed that growth is uneven, although certain overall patterns can be seen.

Belenky, Clinchy, Goldberger, and Tarule (1986) described women's ways of knowing or their unique epistemological perspectives on viewing the world. Like many other theories, their theory is constructed around patterns or perspectives, including silence, received knowledge, subjective knowledge, procedural knowledge, and constructed knowledge. Baxter Magolda (1992) adds to these perspectives in her model of epistemological reflection, which contains four stages, with gender-related patterns in three of them: absolute knowing, which includes receiving knowledge and mastering knowledge; transitional knowing, which includes interpersonal knowing and impersonal knowing; independent knowing, which includes interindividual and individual patterns; and contextual knowing.

King and Kitchener's (1994) Reflective Judgment Model (RJM), developed to describe how people decide what they believe about vexing problems, builds on Piaget's work and Perry's model. The RJM includes seven stages that can be clustered into three categories: prereflective thinking, quasi-reflective thinking, and reflective thinking. Reflective thinkers, for example, are contextual reasoners; to reach conclusions, they base their judgments on data and principles.

Kohlberg's theory of moral reasoning (1976) is structured around preconventional, conventional, and postconventional or principled levels of reasoning. Each level is composed of two stages of development and addresses different relationships between the self and society's rules or expectations. At the center of Kohlberg's theory is the application of justice in making moral judgments.

Gilligan (1981, 1993), conversely, based her theory on an ethic of care in making moral judgments. She challenged Kohlberg's principle of universality regarding the sequential and universal development of cognitive structure by demonstrating an alternative to justice reasoning—an ethic of caring, which she claimed is more common to women than to men.

Thus all of these theories deal with structural or cognitive growth and explain how people think. Some cognitive-developmental theorists, such as Kohlberg (1976), claim that these structural changes are universal, that is, that they apply to such growth in all persons regardless of gender, race, or cultural attributes. As has been outlined here, however, some of the more recent theorists point out certain variations in these structural changes, especially in gender-related issues. There appears to be enough evidence from these new theories to suggest real caution in the application of the principle of universality in cognitive-developmental growth.

Typology (or Personality) Theories

These theories are not developmental—that is, they do not explain growth and change—but they do add considerable insight about the ways in which personality attributes influence learning. Kolb's (1981, 1984) theory of learning, for example, explores the process by which knowledge is created by experience. He sees learning as a four-stage cycle consisting of concrete experience, reflective observation, abstract conceptualization, and active experimentation. These cornerstone elements of the cycle are then translated into four styles of learning: the *accommodator* (action oriented, good at carrying out plans), the *converger* (prefers technical tasks, excels at problem solving), the *assimilator* (emphasizes ideas, good at inductive reasoning), and the *diverger* (people oriented, imaginative, and good at generating alternatives). In this conceptualization, persons may prefer or possess a dominant style of learning, but may still use other styles.

The Myers-Briggs Type Indicator (Myers and McCaulley, 1985) and the Keirsey Temperament Theory (Keirsey, 1987) are very popular typology theories for explaining patterned variations in behavior, but they do little to explain development. They may, however, help to explain students' comfort level with certain styles of teaching they encounter in classrooms.

Criticism of Current Developmental Theories

One of the difficulties in taking full advantage of developmental theories arises from certain well-known weaknesses in the theories and in the research about them. Evans, Forney, and Guido-DiBrito (1998) in their concluding commentary offer some suggestions for improving theories. They call for more comprehensive and less linear theories, for theories that are less dependent on Eurocentric models of development, and for theories that give voice to student populations not currently considered in theories. They call for theories that consider the entire life span and knowledge of how the environment affects development. These sweeping recommendations expose serious weaknesses in current theoretical knowledge about student development. Thus, although use of developmental theories can be helpful to advisor and student alike, such theories should be used prudently and, perhaps, conditionally. Generalizations about the behavior of minority students; of gay, lesbian, and homosexual students; or of women students that are based on theories developed exclusively about white, middle- to upper-class (and sometime exclusively male) eighteen- to twenty-two-year-old college students should be made with caution.

Academic advisors are faced with two serious problems in using developmental theories. First, there are many such theories and they typically are intended to explain some relatively narrow developmental phenomena when considered alone. Second, there are at least as many developmental phenomena that are not explained by current theories as there are those that offer reasonable explanations. Particularly troubling in this latter problem is the rudimentary nature of emerging theories that purport to explain even generally common phenomena such as identity development in persons of color; in persons of diverse cultural, ethnic, and religious backgrounds; and in women.

Use of Career Development Theories

There are many types and classifications of career development theories. Among the more prevalent classifications are trait and factor or type theories, developmental theories, decision-making theories, and social learning theories. These theories and many others are presented in detail, including their applications for various counseling purposes, in recent works by Sharf (1997); Osipow and Fitzgerald (1996); Zunker (1994); Peterson, Sampson, and Reardon (1991); and Seligman (1994). These authors, especially Osipow and Fitzgerald (1996) and Zunker (1994), also describe current knowledge of theory development and its use with women and minorities.

Trait and Factor Theories

Trait and factor theories combine traits of individuals and work requirements to describe the benefits or salience of working under the combined conditions. These theories, beginning with Parsons (1909), have been very durable in the field and are commonly known and used by counselors and advisors, but they are subject to persistent criticism, especially for being one-size-fits-all and for their almost exclusive use of measurement instruments to derive individual and work traits or factors.

Holland's (1973) typological theory allows individuals to project their preferences on occupational titles and roles and assigns individuals to modal personality styles, including realistic, investigative, artistic, social, enterprising, and conventional. From these styles, Holland derives theoretical implications for vocational choice. One important aspect of Holland's theory is the concept of *congruence,* that is, the theoretical implications for satisfaction and growth of the individual given the closeness of fit between the individual's personality type and the occupational type.

Developmental Career Theories

Representatives of developmental theories of career development include Ginzberg, Ginsburg, Axelrad, and Herma (1951) and Super (1990). Ginzberg and his associates theorized that career development occurs generally from about age eleven to age seventeen or in young adulthood and moves through three stages: fantasy (childhood), tentative (early adolescence), and realistic (middle adolescence to young adult). Movement occurs from play orientations through recognition of work requirements to integration of capacities and interests. According to Super, one of the best-known career theorists, career development occurs throughout the life span and includes stages of crystallization (14–18), specification (18–21), implementation (21–24), stabilization (24–35), and consolidation (35 and older). Super was especially interested in developmental tasks associated with various stages of career maturity, and he formulated helpful concepts of cycling and recycling through these tasks. The concepts of career patterns that emerged were most descriptive of his thinking about career development.

Decision-Making Theories

Decision-making theories may be represented by Miller-Tiedeman and Tiedeman's (1990) "lifecareer" theory. This theory argues for the efficacy of inner wisdom and self-views. It is an ego development theory and suggests that one looks within to find career direction. It focuses on increased self-awareness, life learning, and decision making.

Social Learning Theories

Social learning theories are well represented by the work of Krumboltz, Mitchell, and Gelatt (1975) and by Mitchell and Krumboltz (1990). According to these theories, career development involves the interaction of four factors: genetic endowments and special abilities, environmental conditions and events, learning experiences, and task approach skills. Thus, unique learning experiences over the life span lead to career choices.

Theories of Minority Career Development

Theories of minority career development, mostly derived from racial and ethnic identity models, are emerging, such as Cross (1971). Atkinson, Morten, and Sue (1993), for example, offer a theoretical perspective on career development that focuses on identity development among oppressed groups. Christensen (1989) elaborates a five-stage model of career development: unawareness, beginning awareness, conscious awareness, consolidated awareness, and transcendent awareness. Thus, minority career development patterns may differ from that of the majority because of important variations in identity development in minorities.

Other Views of Career Development Theories

Another perspective on the classification of career development theories is offered by Peterson, Sampson, and Reardon (1991). They classify major career development theories as those that emphasize self-knowledge (such as trait and factor theory), those that integrate occupational knowledge and self-knowledge (such as Holland's [1973] theory of career choice), those that emphasize decision-making skills (such as Miller-Tiedeman and Tiedeman, 1990), those that emphasize executive processing (such as Super, 1990), those that emphasize contextual influences on career choice (such as Krumboltz, Mitchell, and Gelatt, 1975), those of ethnic awareness (such as Atkinson, Morten, and Sue, 1993, and Christensen, 1989).

Seligman (1994) offers helpful observations about certain commonalities among career development theories, including the following:

- Career development is a process that follows relatively predictable yet variable stages throughout the life span.
- Career information is useful at several transitional periods in the life span.
- Personal factors such as gender, family background, biology, personality, thinking and learning styles, values, interests, and abilities serve as influencers in career development.
- Career choices are greatly influenced by self-image, and accuracy of self-image is related to rewarding careers.
- Time, society, environment, geography, economics, and chance serve as external influencers of career development.
- Satisfying careers are related to congruence between career choices and well-defined and prominent personality patterns.
- Approaches to assisting with career choices should consider social and family goals, leisure interests, and geographic choices as well as occupational preferences.
- Approaches to assisting with career choices should emphasize personal responsibility and empowerment to enable independent, purposeful, deliberate, rewarding, and attainable goals.

The sources of these theories are displayed in Exhibit 2.1 according to the type of development the theories explain. The exhibit provides an easy reference for advisors who may wish to read more thoroughly about some or all of the theories.

All of these theories explain some aspect of students' learning and development. They are best used, however, when they can be synthesized into strategic advising approaches.

Generalizations About the Use of Theory in Academic Advising

Several generalizations can be made about advising to illustrate the value of synthesizing such theoretical knowledge for use in a particular educational manner.

Development represents internal change from simple to complex forms and from differentiation to integration (Thomas and Chickering, 1984). As development occurs, students experience their world differently than before and

Student Development Theories				Typological Theories
Identity Theories	Theories About Making Meaning	Theories About Gender, Race, and Gay, Lesbian, and Bisexual Identity	Summaries of Developmental Theories	Learning and Personality Pattern Theories
Erikson (1968)	Piaget (1952)	Cross (1971, 1995)	Evans, Forney, and Guido-DiBrito (1998)	Kolb (1981, 1984)
Chickering (1969)	Perry (1968, 1981)	Helms (1995)	Komives, Woodard, and Associates (1996)	Myers and McCaulley (1985)
Chickering and Reisser (1993)	Belenky, Clinchy, Goldberger, and Tarule (1986)	Phinney (1990)	Creamer and Associates (1990)	Keirsey (1987)
Marcia (1980)		Cass (1983–1984)		
	Baxter Magolda (1992)	D'Augelli (1994)	Chickering and Havighurst (1981)	
	King (1996)			
	King and Kitchener (1994)			
	Kohlberg (1976)			
	Gilligan (1981, 1993)			

Career Development Theories					
Trait and Factor Theories	Developmental Career Theories	Decision-Making Theories	Social Learning Theories	Theories of Minority Career Development	Other Views of Career Development Theories
Parsons (1909)	Ginzberg, Ginsburg, Axelrad, and Herma (1951)	Miller-Tiedeman and Tiedeman (1990)	Krumboltz, Mitchell, and Gelatt (1975)	Cross (1971)	Sharf (1997)
Holland (1973)	Super (1990)		Mitchell and Krumboltz (1990)	Atkinson, Morton, and Sue (1993)	Osipow and Fitzgerald (1996)
				Christensen (1989)	Zunker (1994)
					Peterson, Sampson, and Reardon (1991)
					Seligman (1994)

Exhibit 2.1. Representative Student and Career Development Theorists by Selective Phenomena of Interest to Academic Advisors.

assimilate learning into their lives in a more holistic fashion. In short, *students' needs for advising change with each new plateau of development.* Whether development occurs psychosocially or cognitively, students' perspectives on their educational experiences are altered. Thus, successfully promoting development in students changes the role of the advisor for each student over time and as experiences mount.

Let's consider this point further. *The role of academic advising changes as students learn and develop.* Use of theory in academic advising occurs in real-life developmental circumstances. As has been shown, developmental theory has direct value to advisors in helping to explain many of the complicated issues facing students; however, issues and circumstances change over time because students are in the process of learning and developing. First-year students, for example, present academic advisors with very different developmental circumstances than fourth-year students. Students' perspectives are modified as they experience change, and their capabilities grow as they amass experiences that shape their views.

This ever-changing situation is depicted in Figure 2.1, which shows the changing needs for and contexts of advising. Students' needs change significantly over time from information-dominant forms to consultation-dominant forms. Contexts of advising also change as students progress in the undergraduate experience and as conditions within the environment are modified. These situations may change regularly, even, in some circumstances, from one advising contact to another. Certainly we should expect the individual to change as learning and development shapes him or her over time. Additionally, we should expect that students' needs for formal advising will change over time as learning occurs about how to be self-sufficient within the college environment. Further, perspectives on life may also take on different forms as students progress through their undergraduate experience.

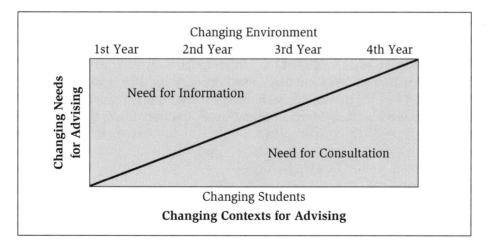

Figure 2.1. Changing Needs and Contexts for Advising.

The environment in which advising occurs, such as the academic depart-ments or the institution itself, may also change as institutions face new reali-ties and assume new educational properties. Curricular changes such as adding or deleting academic programs create new alternatives for students. Thus, aca-demic advisors must be adaptable in their use of theory as students grow and develop in constantly changing educational environments.

Knowledge and use of developmental theory helps to define advising tasks, identify outcomes of advising, and promote development directly (Creamer and Creamer, 1994). Creamer and Creamer propose a developmental model for advising that embodies setting career and life goals, strengthening self-insight and self-esteem, broadening interests, improving interpersonal relations, clari-fying personal values and styles of life, and enhancing thinking and reasoning. Their model may suggest which dimensions of students are essential and most likely to change. Creamer and Creamer assert that developmental advising calls for an understanding of the relationships between the types of presenting ques-tions students bring to advising and the outcomes of effective advising that both students and advisors expect. Knowledge of the types of developmental theory presented earlier are essential to this model, because it calls for sensitivity to the real developmental meaning behind the questions asked by students of their advisors, and to the strategies available to advisors for fostering self-sufficiency in students and for addressing their current needs.

Academic advising represents only a part of the overall developmental effort of an institution. To be most effective, academic advising should be seen as an effort that is thoroughly coordinated with other units of the college or univer-sity to help students gain self-sufficiency and develop fully. As Habley (1984) points out, academic advisors are not the only professionals in higher educa-tion who rely on developmental theory to assist students, and they should not attempt to achieve the full measure of development by themselves. Certainly most student services are actively engaged in the developmental education of students. They often adhere to precisely the same educational goals as acade-mic advisors. Many teachers of academic disciplines also rely on developmental theory to guide their pedagogical approaches. Even academic departments, and increasingly institutions themselves, describe their work in developmental terms. Academic advisors do not have to act unilaterally to achieve the devel-opmental goals of students and they should not organize their work as if it were necessary. Thus, *the developmental academic advisor must know theory, know others who use it in their educational endeavors, and coordinate these multiple efforts.*

Conclusion

This chapter reviewed some fundamental boundaries or parameters of acade-mic advising, summarized selective theories of student development, and offered some applications of the theories by way of generalizations about their use. Scope of advising was described as including purpose, pedagogy, context, focus, and content. A set of hypotheses about effective advising was sketched to illustrate broadly the complexities of the process.

Student development theories and certain corresponding career development theories were presented as among the most essential for effective academic advising practice. These theories were summarized according to the primary phenomena they explain, such as identity theories, theories of making meaning, typological theories, trait and factor theories, career development theories, decision theories, social learning theories, and theories of minority career development. Some of the shortcomings of developmental and career theories were also highlighted. Many of the available theories are especially wanting in regard to their appropriateness for explaining development in minorities, gay and lesbian persons, and women.

Although no theories of academic advising are currently available, the need for such theories is increasingly evident. Professionals currently engaged in the process of using related theories in practice are in the best position to observe and conduct systematic research on the advising process in higher education. They should become builders of theories that can explain the complex phenomena associated with effective practice. Assertions such as those made in this chapter about the relationship between effective advising and student knowledge of self and institutional resources deserve to be tested empirically. Likewise, claims that effectiveness is related to students' motivation and their will to make and accept the consequences of their choices should be examined. Similar assertions about the relationship between effective advising and advisor understanding of student developmental needs should be studied.

References

Atkinson, D. R., Morten, G., and Sue, D. W. *Counseling American Minorities: A Cross-Cultural Perspective.* (4th ed.) Madison, Wisc.: Brown and Benchmark, 1993.

Baxter Magolda, M. B. *Knowing and Reasoning in College: Gender-Related Patterns in Students' Intellectual Development.* San Francisco: Jossey-Bass, 1992.

Belenky, M. F., Clinchy, B. M., Goldberger, N. R., and Tarule, J. M. *Women's Ways of Knowing: The Development of Self, Voice, and Mind.* New York: Basic Books, 1986.

Cass, V. C. "Homosexual Identity: A Concept in Need of Definition." *Journal of Homosexuality,* 1983–1984, *9*(2–3), 105–126.

Chickering, A. W. *Education and Identity.* San Francisco: Jossey-Bass, 1969.

Chickering, A. W., and Havighurst, R. J. "The Life Cycle." In A. W. Chickering and Associates, *The Modern American College: Responding to the New Realities of Diverse Students and a Changing Society.* San Francisco: Jossey-Bass, 1981.

Chickering, A. W., and Reisser, L. *Education and Identity.* (2nd ed.) San Francisco: Jossey-Bass, 1993.

Christensen, C. P. "Cross-Cultural Awareness Development: A Conceptual Model." *Counselor Education and Supervision,* 1989, *28,* 270–287.

Creamer, D. G., and Associates. *College Student Development: Theory and Practice for the 1990s.* Washington, D.C.: American College Personnel Association, 1990.

Creamer, D. G., and Creamer, E. G. "Practicing Developmental Advising: Theoretical Contexts and Functional Applications." *NACADA Journal,* 1994, *14*(2), 17–24.

Cross, W. E. Jr. "The Negro to Black Conversion Experience: Toward a Psychology of Black Liberation." *Black World,* 1971, *20,* 13–27.

Cross, W. E. Jr. "The Psychology of Nigrescence: Revising the Cross Model." In J. G. Ponterotto, J. M. Casas, L. A. Suzuki, and C. M. Alexander (eds.), *Handbook of Multicultural Counseling.* Thousand Oaks, Calif.: Sage, 1995.

D'Augelli, A. R. "Identity Development and Sexual Orientation: Toward a Model of Lesbian, Gay, and Bisexual Development." In E. J. Trickett, R. J. Watts, and D. Birman (eds.), *Human Diversity: Perspectives on People in Context.* San Francisco: Jossey-Bass, 1994.

Erikson, E. H. *Identity, Youth, and Crisis.* New York: Norton, 1968.

Evans, N. J., Forney, D. S., and Guido-DiBrito, F. *Student Development in College: Theory, Research, and Practice.* San Francisco: Jossey-Bass, 1998.

Gilligan, C. "Moral Development." In A. W. Chickering and Associates, *The Modern American College: Responding to the New Realities of Diverse Students and a Changing Society.* San Francisco: Jossey-Bass, 1981.

Gilligan, C. *In a Different Voice: Psychological Theory and Women's Development.* Cambridge, Mass.: Harvard University Press, 1993.

Ginzberg, E., Ginsburg, S. W., Axelrad, S., and Herma, J. L. *Occupational Choice: An Approach to General Theory.* New York: Columbia University Press, 1951.

Goodlad, J. I. *In Praise of Education.* New York: Teachers College Press, 1997.

Gordon, V. N., and Steele, G. E. "Toward a Theory of Academic Advising." Paper presented at the National Academic Advising Association's Nineteenth National Conference, Nashville, Tenn., 1995.

Habley, W. R. "Integrating Academic Advising and Career Planning." In R. B. Winston Jr., T. K. Miller, S. C. Ender, T. J. Grites, and Associates, *Developmental Academic Advising.* San Francisco: Jossey-Bass, 1984.

Helms, J. E. "An Update of Helms's White and People of Color Racial Identity Models." In J. G. Ponterotto, J. M. Casas, L. A. Suzuki, and C. M. Alexander (eds.), *Handbook of Multicultural Counseling.* Thousand Oaks, Calif.: Sage, 1995.

Holland, J. L. *Making Vocational Choices: A Theory of Careers.* Englewood Cliffs, N.J.: Prentice Hall, 1973.

Josselson, R. *Finding Herself: Pathways to Identity Development in Women.* San Francisco: Jossey-Bass, 1987.

Keirsey, D. *Portraits in Temperament.* Del Mar, Calif.: Prometheus Nemesis, 1987.

King, P. M. "Student Cognition and Learning." In S. R. Komives, D. B. Woodard Jr., and Associates, *Student Services: A Handbook for the Profession.* (3rd ed.) San Francisco: Jossey-Bass, 1996.

King, P. M., and Kitchener, K. S. *Developing Reflective Judgment: Understanding and Promoting Intellectual Growth and Critical Thinking in Adolescents and Adults.* San Francisco: Jossey-Bass, 1994.

Kohlberg, L. "Moral Stages and Moralization: The Cognitive-Developmental Approach." In T. Lickona (ed.), *Moral Development and Behavior: Theory, Research, and Social Issues*. Austin, Tex.: Holt, Rinehart and Winston, 1976.

Kolb, D. A. "Learning Styles and Disciplinary Differences." In A. W. Chickering and Associates, *The Modern American College: Responding to the New Realities of Diverse Students and a Changing Society*. San Francisco: Jossey-Bass, 1981.

Kolb, D. A. *Experiential Learning: Experience as the Source of Learning and Development*. Englewood Cliffs, N.J.: Prentice Hall, 1984.

Komives, S. R., Woodard, D. B., and Associates. *Student Services: A Handbook for the Profession*. (3rd ed.) San Francisco: Jossey-Bass, 1996.

Krumboltz, J. D., Mitchell, A., and Gelatt, H. G. "Applications of Social Learning Theory to Career Selection." *Focus on Guidance*, 1975, *8*, 1–16.

Marcia, J. E. "Identity in Adolescence." In J. Adelson (ed.), *Handbook of Adolescent Psychology*. New York: Wiley, 1980.

Miller-Tiedeman, A. L., and Tiedeman, D. V. "Career Decision Making: An Individualistic Perspective." In D. Brown, L. Brooks, and Associates, *Career Choice and Development: Applying Contemporary Theories to Practice*. San Francisco: Jossey-Bass, 1990.

Mitchell, L. K., and Krumboltz, J. D. "Social Learning Approach to Career Decision Making: Krumboltz's Theory." In D. Brown and L. Brooks (eds.), *Career Choice and Development: Applying Contemporary Theories to Practice*. (2nd ed.) San Francisco: Jossey-Bass, 1990.

Myers, I. B., and McCaulley, M. H. *Manual: A Guide to the Development and Use of the Myers-Briggs Type Indicator*. Palo Alto, Calif.: Consulting Psychologists Press, 1985.

National Academic Advising Association. *Statement of Core Values*. [http://www.ksu.edu/nacada/choice2/corevalu.htm]. 1994.

Osipow, S. H., and Fitzgerald, L. F. *Theories of Career Development*. (4th ed.) Needham, Heights, Mass.: Allyn & Bacon, 1996.

Parsons, F. *Choosing a Vocation*. Boston: Houghton Mifflin, 1909.

Perry W. G. Jr. *Forms of Intellectual and Ethical Development in the College Years: A Scheme*. Austin, Tex.: Holt, Rinehart and Winston, 1968.

Peterson, G. W., Sampson, J. P., and Reardon, R. C. *Career Development and Services: A Cognitive Approach*. Pacific Grove, Calif.: Brooks/Cole, 1991.

Phinney, J. S. "Ethnic Identity in Adolescents and Adults: Review of Research." *Psychological Bulletin*, 1990, *108*, 499–514.

Piaget, J. *The Origins of Intelligence in Children*. New York: International Universities Press, 1952.

Seligman, L. *Developmental Career Counseling and Assessment*. (2nd ed.) Thousand Oaks, Calif.: Sage, 1994.

Sharf, R. S. *Applying Career Development Theory to Counseling*. (2nd ed.) Pacific Grove, Calif.: Brooks/Cole, 1997.

Super, D. E. "A Life-Span, Life-Space Approach to Career Development." In D. Brown and L. Brooks, and Associates, *Career Choice and Development: Applying Contemporary Theories to Practice*. (2nd ed.) San Francisco: Jossey-Bass, 1990.

Thomas, R. E., and Chickering, A. W. "Foundations for Academic Advising." In R. B. Winston Jr., T. K. Miller, S. C. Ender, T. J. Grites, and Associates, *Developmental Academic Advising.* San Francisco: Jossey-Bass, 1984.

Zunker, V. G. *Career Counseling: Applied Concepts of Life Planning.* (4th ed.) Pacific Grove, Calif.: Brooks/Cole, 1994.

Chapter Three

Current Practices in Academic Advising

Wesley R. Habley

Academic advising has been a fixture on the higher education scene since colleges were first established in colonial America. Advising in those colleges was a function fulfilled by faculty who assumed responsibility for the intellectual, ethical, and moral development of students in a mentoring capacity. Although this mentoring role remained essentially intact for nearly two centuries, several significant events and movements have gradually reshaped the nature and purpose of American higher education. Among these have been the enactment of the Morrill Act, which established land grant colleges; the broadening of the curriculum; the appointment of individuals from among the faculty to serve as chief advisors; the rapid influx of students following World War II; and the burgeoning growth of community colleges (Habley, 1995). These changes have in turn led not only to an evolving definition of the nature and purpose of a college education, but also to an examination of the role and function of academic advising on the college campus.

Although several alternative and successful approaches to academic advising existed prior to 1970, three critical events took place during the 1970s that increased the focus on the role and function of academic advising. First, the publication of two articles created the framework for an expanded definition of academic advising. Crookston (1972) and O'Banion (1972) suggested that advising was far too critical to be defined as a perfunctory, clerical function that involved only the prescriptive selection and scheduling of courses. In addition, significant declines in the enormous increase in the number of college students that had been fed by the baby boomer generation loomed on the horizon. This decline began in the late 1970s, and colleges faced with the prospect of a dwindling number of matriculating students were forced to look seriously at ways in which they could better serve, satisfy, and retain the students who enrolled.

Finally, by the second half of the decade, what had been a loosely coupled network of individuals with an interest in academic advising became a national organization known as the National Academic Advising Association (NACADA). Following two national meetings on academic advising, NACADA was chartered in the spring of 1979 and the first NACADA national conference was convened in Omaha in the fall of 1979.

Although ACT (formerly known as American College Testing) had delivered a series of advising workshops and was informally involved with academic advising as early as 1970, growing interest in the field of advising led to ACT's first national survey of campus practices in academic advising (Carstensen and Silberhorn, 1979). Since that time, ACT has conducted additional surveys (Crockett and Levitz, 1983; Habley, 1988; Habley, 1993; and Habley and Morales, 1998). This chapter provides an overview of these five ACT surveys by reviewing change (or the lack thereof) in campus practices over the span of nearly two decades.

Clearly the surveys have undergone modifications over time. Many items have been deleted, new items have been added, and new concepts have been explored. Regardless of these modifications, there are two major reasons that it is possible to comment on changes in academic advising during the last two decades. First, all of the surveys studied a set of core topics including coordination, policy, training, evaluation, recognition, and reward. Second, all of the surveys are consistent in methodology in terms of sample size, sampling techniques, and survey administration and follow up. In the case of the most recent survey, a stratified random sample of two-year, four-year, public, and private institutions was drawn from a population of 2,710 accredited institutions offering an associate's or bachelor's degree. Based on the response rates from the previous four surveys, as well as the fact that national response rates have generally diminished over time, the largest sample ever drawn for the advising survey (1,395 colleges) constituted the group to which the fifth national survey was mailed. Responses were received from 754 colleges, a 54.1 percent response rate. The return rate and the distribution of the actual set of responding institutions very closely corresponded with that of the sampling frame. As a result the findings of the survey could be generalized to the national population of colleges.

This chapter provides an overview of national trends for all institutional types, although because of the length restrictions of the chapter, these trends are discussed without including a myriad of descriptive tables from the surveys. Readers interested in a breakdown of tabular data by public and private and two-year and four-year institutions are encouraged to refer to the final reports of each of these five surveys. Following are some observations on the surveys.

Campus Advising Policy

One of the essential elements of a quality academic advising program is the articulation of the program's basic purpose, function, and components in a campus advising policy.

When campuses were queried on this topic in the 1979 survey, only about one-quarter of the institutions indicated that they had a published statement on advising (Carstensen and Silberhorn, 1979). By 1983, this figure had increased to 63 percent (Crockett and Levitz, 1983). Since then, however, there have been no appreciable changes in this percentage, with the most recent survey indicating that 61 percent of campuses had a published statement of advising policy (Habley and Morales, 1998).

Beginning with the 1983 survey, the contents of the advising policy statements were also studied. Across the last four surveys, several topics were included in the majority of campus policy statements: philosophy of advising, goals for advising, responsibilities of advisors, responsibilities of advisees, and delivery strategies. There are also several topics that were not generally included (defined as less that 30 percent of institutions reporting) in advising policies: selection of advisors, training of advisors, evaluation of advising, and recognition and reward for advisors.

Coordination of Advising Services

A second critical element in the development of a quality academic advising program is the need for coordination of effort among many service delivery units. Although the collection of survey data has not been consistent across the five surveys, three trends stand out. First, the assignment of coordination of services to a director or coordinator of academic advising has nearly doubled since the first survey. Currently, 31 percent of college campuses report having a director or coordinator of advising. In addition, the coordination of advising services remains (with the exception of two-year colleges) primarily an academic affairs function. In the 1997 survey, 69 percent of the campuses reported that a vice president or assistant vice president for academic affairs either served as or had administrative responsibility for the coordinator of advising (Habley and Morales, 1998). Finally, it is clear that the coordination of advising is not the main task of the individual to whom it is assigned. Although the percentage of time devoted to the coordination of advising has gradually increased across all of the surveys, the 1997 survey indicated that on 71 percent of college campuses, the individual responsible for the coordination of advising devoted 50 percent or less of his or her time to that function.

Organization of Advising Services

The first two ACT surveys focused in only a limited fashion on the ways in which campuses organized for the delivery of academic advising. In 1987, however, the survey collected information on the prevalence of seven organizational models first proposed by Habley (1993). Although these models are described in detail in Chapter Thirteen of this book, it is important to note that there have been some obvious shifts in the utilization of the models since data were first collected in 1987. Most noteworthy among these shifts is that the tendency to rely solely on faculty to deliver advising has declined to fewer than half of the campuses included in the 1997 survey. Data from the most recent survey also indicate that campuses are more likely to provide specialized advising services for a variety of student subpopulations, such as exploratory, at-risk, or nontraditional students. Finally, it is becoming apparent that more campuses are viewing academic advising as a system of shared responsibility involving faculty, academic administrators, and advising offices or centers, as well as a variety of related support services.

Advising Offices and Centers

Of all the trends that characterized advising practices between 1979 and 1997, increases in the development of advising offices are most obvious. In 1979, 205 of the 820 institutions surveyed (25 percent) indicated that an advising office was in place on their campus. By 1997, that percentage had nearly tripled to 73 percent.

Further understanding of the scope of advising center practices and responsibilities was facilitated through a major change in survey design in 1987. In that survey, and in those that followed, practices in advising offices were separated from practices in faculty advising. Section 2 of the survey focused on practices in faculty advising delivered in academic subunits while section 3 studied practices in advising centers and offices.

As a result of this change in survey design, and as a result of the data derived from the surveys, Habley (1993, 1998) has suggested that advising centers are in a state of crisis created by increasing expectations and responsibilities without allocating necessary human and fiscal resources. In comparison to previous surveys, the 1997 survey indicated that advising offices and centers

- Were less likely to provide staff training
- Were less likely to provide group interventions
- Had fewer student contacts per term than faculty advisors
- Had inordinately high student-advisor ratios
- Were much less intrusive
- Did not always evaluate staff
- Provided fewer information sources to advisors.

Additional evidence of this crisis is that the 1997 survey shows that advising centers are far less likely to intervene when students make important educational decisions. Of the six occasions when students were required to contact the advising center, all six showed a steady decline between the 1987 and the 1997 surveys. Additional declines were noted in the number of support materials (handbooks, articulation worksheets, campus referral directories, and so on) and student information sources (high school transcripts, assessment results, grade reports, and so on) provided to advising center staff.

As a result of these findings, Habley concluded, "If steps are not taken to deal with these critical issues, it is virtually certain that the advantages once attributed to advising centers will all but disappear" (Habley and Morales, 1998, p. 64).

Faculty Advising

Data that provide a better understanding of faculty advising are taken from two sources. The first source includes an overview of practices that support faculty advising and is taken from the five ACT surveys of national practices that provide the foundation for this chapter. The second data source includes information on student opinions about faculty advising and is taken from a 1999 normative report on ACT's (1999) Survey of Academic Advising. This survey collected information from students on their satisfaction with academic advising.

Practices in Faculty Advising

With the development of separate sections on faculty advising and advising centers that have characterized the ACT national surveys since 1987, it became possible to identify trends and articulate critical issues confronting faculty advising.

Among these trends, as Habley and Morales (1998) have observed, virtually all faculty are expected to advise as a result of their faculty status. In addition, typical faculty advisors have four advising contacts per term, have a typical load of twenty-six advisees, and spend approximately 11 percent of their time advising students. Finally, on a positive note, 1997 survey data indicated that faculty advisors are more likely than they had been in previous surveys to intervene on occasions when students make important educational decisions.

Observing some of the critical issues in faculty advising, Habley and Morales (1998) report that across the last three surveys there have been only incremental and situational gains in the practices that support faculty advising. They further suggest that many important aspects of support for quality faculty advising are nonexistent on some campuses and unsystematic on many others. In support of these contentions, Habley and Morales offer the following evidence:

- Only about one-third of campuses provide training for faculty advisors while less than one-quarter of the campuses require faculty training in advising.

- The vast majority of training programs focus solely on the communication of factual information, with little time devoted to concepts and relationship skills.

- Less than one-third of campuses include advising in the evaluation of faculty performance.

- Less than one-third of campuses include academic advising in the reward structure for faculty members.

- The most common form of advisor recognition is minor consideration in promotion and tenure; yet that form of recognition is utilized in all departments at only 8 percent of the campuses surveyed.

It is clear from these data that many of the essential practices (training, evaluation, and recognition and reward) that support faculty advising are far from exemplary.

Student Opinions of Faculty Advising

Although the national surveys on advising provide quantitative data on practices in faculty advising, ACT's (1999) Survey of Academic Advising, a student evaluation of advising, provides qualitative insights into faculty advising. In a ten-year period ending December 31, 1998, more than 100,000 students at 250 colleges from thirty-eight states completed this survey of opinions and attitudes. The survey collected data on both students' needs and their impressions of their faculty advisors. In reporting on these data, Habley (2000) concluded that although there were areas of concern, faculty advisors were satisfactorily meeting students' needs, and students in general had favorable impressions of the traits and characteristics of their faculty advisors.

Goals for Academic Advising

Four national surveys of advising practices have collected data on the achievement of eight goals for academic advising. The goals were developed by a NACADA task force that was charged with providing input to the Council for the Advancement of Standards (CAS) in 1980. These goals formed the basis for the development of the CAS Standards for Academic Advising and the CAS Self-Assessment Guide for Academic Advising:

1. Assisting students in self-understanding and self-acceptance (values clarification; understanding abilities, interests, and limitations)
2. Assisting students in considering their life goals by relating their interests, skills, abilities, and values to careers, the world of work, and the nature and purpose of higher education
3. Assisting students in developing an educational plan consistent with their life goals and objectives
4. Assisting students in developing decision-making skills
5. Providing accurate information about institutional policies, procedures, resources, and programs
6. Referring students to other institutional or community support services
7. Assisting students in evaluating or reevaluating progress toward established goals and educational plans

8. Providing information about students to the institution, college, academic departments, or some combination thereof.

Respondents were asked to use a five-point scale (5 = very satisfactory, 1 = very unsatisfactory) to rate their level of satisfaction with the achievement of each goal. In 1983, the mean responses ranged from 2.55 (decision-making skills) to 4.01 (providing accurate information), and the overall mean for all goals was 3.19. In addition to the goal on decision-making skills (goal 4), the goals of consideration of life goals (goal 2) and self-understanding (goal 1) fell at or below the midpoint of the five-point scale. Overall goal achievement means improved only slightly on the 1987 and 1992 surveys to 3.22 and 3.31, respectively, while the lowest ratings remained the same as they were in the 1983 survey. The 1997 survey suggested that strides have been made as the overall mean reached 3.64. In spite of the gains in goal achievement, it is important to note that the only goal for which an overall rating of satisfactory (4.0) was obtained was goal 5, providing accurate information. The means for the remaining goals all fell between neutral (3.0) and satisfactory (4.0), with the most developmental goals (1, 2, and 4) recording the lowest mean ratings.

Program Effectiveness

Effectiveness criteria were introduced in the 1987 survey. Although minor revisions were made in some of the effectiveness variables, it is possible to make comparisons across the surveys. The effectiveness variables that respondents rated on a scale from 1 (very ineffective) to 5 (very effective) are as follows:

1. Providing for the overall academic advising needs of your students
2. Identifying and selecting high-quality advisors
3. Implementing training programs for advisors
4. Providing advisors with timely and accurate information about their advisees
5. Providing appropriate levels of coordination, direction, and supervision
6. Systematically evaluating the advising program
7. Systematically evaluating the effectiveness of academic advisors
8. Rewarding good advising performance
9. Providing communication among advisor, deans, department heads, and the coordinator of advising, if such a position exists
10. Meeting students' advising needs within the limits of human and fiscal resources
11. Providing advisor accountability, both to a higher level of authority and to advisees

Among the more revealing findings of the study of effectiveness variables is that there has been little change in the overall mean from 1987 to 1997 (from 2.9 to 3.1). Equally compelling, however, is that the ratings of four variables—accountability, training, evaluation, and recognition and reward—fell below the midpoint of the effectiveness scale on the 1987 survey and remained below the midpoint in the 1997 survey. These areas are fundamental components of quality, yet they continue to be stumbling blocks in the development of quality academic advising programs.

Conclusion

In many respects, summarizing the results of five ACT surveys on academic advising provides the reader with a twenty-year retrospective on the field of advising. As this chapter has noted, there has been tremendous growth in the field of advising. Stimulated by a dramatic decline in the number of traditional-age students, the development of theoretical frameworks, and the establishment of a national organization, the field of academic advising has moved from a peripheral support function into a position of increasing prominence in higher education. There have been increases in the percentage of campuses with advising centers, in the appointment of individuals to coordinate advising on campus, and in the establishment of advising policy statements, as well as in the membership of and services provided by the NACADA.

There have also been increases in diversity in the organization, focus, and delivery of advising services on college and university campuses, not only in the diversity of institutional missions in American higher education but also in the diversity of students being served by that system. This diversity is a healthy sign that campus advising programs are also characterized by diversity. New organizational patterns have emerged, personnel engaged in advising or advising-related functions are more variable, and indeed, definitions of advising are more likely to be tailored to reflect diversity.

Finally, and perhaps most telling, it is abundantly clear that the cornerstones in the delivery of quality services are developing the skill levels of individuals who deliver the services (training), measuring the effectiveness of services (evaluation), and providing recognition and reward to individuals whose performance is exemplary. A recurrent theme, however, found in all five ACT surveys, is that training, evaluation, and recognition and reward have been, and continue to be, the weakest links in academic advising throughout the nation. These important institutional practices in support of quality advising are at best unsystematic and at worst nonexistent. They are unsystematic because on many campuses even the exemplary practices in these areas exist in only a few of the departments or offices delivering academic advising. On other campuses, training, evaluation, and recognition and reward efforts are minimal, perfunctory, and unsatisfactory. When respondents were asked to rate the effectiveness of training, evaluation, and recognition and reward on the fifth survey, the overall means for all three functions fell below the midpoint (3.0) of the scale: training fell to 2.9, evaluation to 2.7, and recognition and reward to 2.2.

For the most part, however, these practices do not exist at all. Only 18 percent of campuses have a policy statement that includes training, 11 percent have a policy statement that includes evaluation, and only 4 percent include recognition and reward. In addition, respondents to the fifth survey indicated that only 23 percent of campuses require training for faculty advisors, 29 percent evaluate faculty advising, and 31 percent recognize and reward faculty advising, usually as a minor consideration in promotion, tenure, and salary decisions.

In conclusion, one must marvel at the dynamic growth and diversity of advising programs that have taken place over the last two decades of the twentieth century. Yet academic advising will not arrive as a fully functional contributor to institutional well-being or reach its full potential until decision makers and resource allocators recognize the importance of training, evaluation, and recognition and reward. The future status of academic advising rests in these functions.

References

ACT, Inc. *Normative Data Report on the Survey of Academic Advising.* Iowa City, Iowa: ACT, Inc, 1999.

Carstensen, D. C., and Silberhorn, C. *Final Report: A National Survey of Academic Advising.* Iowa City, Iowa: ACT, Inc., 1979.

Crockett, D. S., and Levitz, R. S. *A National Survey of Academic Advising: Final Report.* Iowa City, Iowa: ACT, Inc., 1983.

Crookston, B. B "A Developmental View of Academic Advising as Teaching." *Journal of College Student Personnel,* 1972, *13,* 12–17.

Habley, W. R. *Fulfilling the Promise: Final Report of the ACT Fourth National Survey of Academic Advising.* Iowa City, Iowa: ACT, Inc., 1993.

Habley, W. R. "Faculty Advising: Practice, Performance, and Promise." In G. L. Kramer (ed.), *Reaffirming the Role of Faculty in Academic Advising.* National Academic Advising Association Monograph Series, no. 1. Manhattan, Kans.: National Academic Advising Association, 1995.

Habley, W. R. "What Do Students Think of Faculty Advisors?" Presentation at American Association of Higher Education Conference on Faculty Roles and Rewards, New Orleans, 2000.

Habley, W. R. (ed.). *The Status and Future of Academic Advising: Problems and Promise.* Iowa City, Iowa: ACT, Inc., 1988.

Habley, W. R., and Morales, R. H. *Current Practices in Academic Advising: Final Report on ACT's Fifth National Survey of Academic Advising.* National Academic Advising Association Monograph Series, no. 6. Manhattan, Kans.: National Academic Advising Association, 1998.

O'Banion, T. "An Academic Advising Model." *Junior College Journal,* 1972, *42*(6), 62–69.

Chapter Four

Ethical Considerations and Obligations

Katherine Simon Frank

People do business daily with many different service and product providers—from obtaining food, clothing, and transportation to getting grooming, health, recreational, educational, and legal needs met. Likewise, faculty, academic advisors, and academic advising administrators provide direct service daily to students and student-oriented offices at educational institutions. These systems operate smoothly, and professionals and their staff feel good interacting with one another within these systems when established expectations and standards set the tone for how to treat other people, how to represent what everyone is responsible for, how to carry out the service that is offered, and so on. An important element that helps determine the collective quality of life for students on college campuses is the caliber with which faculty and professional advisors render their service.

This chapter considers ethics—the "principles of conduct governing an individual or group" or "the science of ideal human character" (Gove, 1965, p. 285)—and how the principles that define good and bad behavior shape the practice of advising. After defining ethics in the abstract, the chapter looks at some guides—in the form of professional codes of ethics—that will help the reader understand how practitioners can deliver their service to students professionally. Faculty and advisors can utilize ethical principles as tools and techniques to resolve dilemmas they face. They can learn to put these operating principles to work to help reach solutions when they are presented with dilemmas, and to achieve program quality in their practice of academic advising.

Ethics Defined

It is possible to define *ethics* simply, as in the previous paragraph, but that definition alone does not convey the process by which people in a given setting interpret the governing principles of conduct to determine whether behavior is good (appropriate) or bad (inappropriate), nor how to implement what this "science" means in practical terms.

Philosophy of Ethics

Philosophically, ethics is the study of moral (or exemplary) human behavior. It is not a description of customs and behavior. Rather, ethics is the process of determining what one considers right and wrong. Instead of establishing a set of rules that constrain behavior, ethics guides one in establishing—for given behaviors or situations—what is right, what is wrong, what is good, what is bad, what the social rules are, and what the standards are for proper conduct in groups, large or small. The ethics of a situation does not control one's behavior; rather, it helps one determine what is the right action to take (Nowell-Smith, 1954). Acting (doing) does not always require thinking about the act, but ethics always involves thinking about and evaluating how to act to achieve the best possible outcome.

Ethics is concerned with "construct[ing] a rational system of moral principles, and direct[ly] and systematic[ally] examin[ing] the underlying assumptions of morality," including working toward, among other aims, "establish[ing] the validity of a set of norms or standards for governing behavior, an ideal of human character to be achieved, or ultimate goals to be striven for" (Denise and Peterfreund, 1992, pp. 5–6). When people refer to the rules that they and others follow in their daily lives, they are actually considering the standards that guide them. Many rules or standards of a society were established as a response to the environment, to early religion, or to customs. They had the purpose of ensuring that everyone got a fair chance, considered as many angles of the circumstances causing a situation as possible, made a reasonable decision in determining the outcome of a situation, and most important, minimized harm to self, to immediate others, and to the larger group (society) as a whole when making a decision (Durkheim, 1993).

Though one important goal of ethical thinking and the application of ethical problem solving is to do no harm, this is not always possible. Sometimes one can find options in which no one is harmed or troubled by the final decision. Other times, the goal should be to minimize the injury to one party while setting right the situation for another. In other words, the goal in resolving an ethical dilemma is to find a balance where the least harm is done to everyone involved.

This is not an easy task; many factors may complicate the discovery of an equitable solution. First, institutions of higher education, where faculty and professional advisors practice their academic advising, are intricate and complicated social structures. Next, each institution has its own rules based on its values. Also, advisors and faculty bring to work their own personal assortment of morals and opinions based on what they think is most important. They interact each day with many individuals, each of whom also has a personal array of needs, opinions, beliefs, and values. It is this mixture of individual and group values, goals, and social rules; institutional goals and rules; and other cultural factors that makes ethical problem solving a challenge.

Situations can get even more complex when an employee is asked to make decisions in a multivalue setting such as the workplace, which may have its own rules and priorities, different from those that are important in other settings. Employees should first define their own work ethic and then consider what it means to respect another's work ethic or be troubled by another's poor work ethic. A work ethic defines how people conduct themselves in carrying out their job responsibilities and how they follow the rules of their workplace and of the culture out of which they come—such as how they treat their fellow employees and their clients, and what they expect in terms of quality, quantity, and promptness of work.

In addition to needing to operate within the workplace culture, some service and helping professionals are also charged with making decisions as representatives of their institutions, or at least with interpreting their institution's rules to outsiders and newcomers. If employees have been given the responsibility to make decisions on behalf of the organization, the employer needs to provide these employees with guidelines for making those decisions. With the privilege or charge to make decisions comes the employees' responsibility to abide thoroughly by and understand the mission of the workplace and the rules in force there. In the role of decision maker, one has the complicated task of operating as an employee of the institution with its particular culture, while at the same time bringing to that work environment one's individual knowledge of the rules of the broader culture (heritage, family, peer group, community, and the like). Each of these cultures has rules of its own, some of them unique.

Sometimes one's personal values, or the qualities that are of greatest worth in one's life, may come into conflict with those of the institution or workplace, or one may be asked to perform an activity or make a decision that is contrary to the values of the workplace but compatible with one's own values. Situations such as these are the root of ethical dilemmas. People can use ethical principles to help resolve these quandaries.

Cultural Influences of Ethical Dilemmas

When moving into a culture that is different from one's own, one needs to learn where one's native values overlap with and where they differ from the values of the new circumstances. This need applies even to the differences between personal and family values and the values of the workplace and other institutions where one spends significant amounts of time. An ethical dilemma arises when there is a conflict between the values of one or more of these interacting sites.

An example of the conflict of values may be seen in the following scenario. Not uncommonly, and very unfortunately, at colleges and universities students copy exam answers from neighboring students, plagiarize term papers, hire a proxy to sit for an exam, or collaborate on assignments meant to be done alone. In North American culture, the academic community agrees that all of these activities are cheating, which is considered bad and inappropriate behavior. But ethics are embedded in social contexts; rules determining appropriate behavior differ across cultures and may depend on the culture's conception of the ways people are obligated to one another. A person from a different culture may have learned that it is essential to help a fellow member of the group achieve success. Helping someone to get the right answers on a test, or writing a passing paper for another person—behavior that is judged to be cheating in this culture—may be considered loyal helping behavior by people in a different culture who may be studying in North America.

One might understand more about this conflicting behavior if one learns that the person cheating comes from a culture where loyalty to one's fellow is valued more than individual accomplishment, even if an institutional rule in American culture dictates against providing such help to another person. Therefore, sharing answers to a test, for example, or collaborating on an assignment may reflect behavior valued by one's culture's. However, this value may conflict with the valued behavior of the educational institution or dominant culture. The scholastic standards committee at a college might decide to handle a case of cheating differently if they understand the cultural context that influenced the behavior. For example, for a first offense they might give a warning to the student from the other culture as a way of educating her about the institutional culture, thus giving a more lenient punishment than they would to a student who had been raised in the culture where copying is unambiguously considered cheating; a more severe consequence should be levied against the student from the local culture.

Less frequently one hears about incidents in which a potential student is admitted to a college despite the lack of acceptable academic credentials to support the admissions decision. Examples of such admissions decisions include the young woman who was considered suitable for the entering class because she has a special talent in a sport, or the young man whose father, influential in raising money for the school's large endowment, is currently serving as president of the college's alumni association. In these cases, different kinds of moral issues are raised. Do these admissions considerations warrant ethical consideration? What is right and what is wrong with admitting these students? Even though one may value (and even need) some characteristics (beyond academic qualifications) of each applicant, the risk of compromising other institutional values, including the institution's basic academic standards, must be considered carefully.

Ethical decision making requires objective questioning. Through such questioning, one is guided in making choices that are appropriate for a given situation. Ethics helps one decide what is right after looking at many possibilities. In resolving an ethical question, one must understand that there might not be a single best answer or outcome. Even after successfully generating several scenarios as a result of ethical questioning, it may be difficult to determine which outcome is the best. The differences between the outcomes may be subtle. Usually one or a small number of the solutions will appear to be more workable, or will, in the long run, result in better consequences (or least harm) for most parties involved, even though the outcome may not be ideal for everyone.

Think, for example, about an extreme case: cannibalism. In this society, eating human beings is not sanctioned. When the Donner Party set out from the Great Basin in 1846 to make their way through the mountains toward California, they were trapped by a great blizzard that halted their progress. The group had to make a profound decision—would they eat those who died from expo-sure to the cold and snow, thus promising the survival of some of them? Or would they continue to insist that in this society no one ever eats fellow humans and, as a result, ensure that everyone would most certainly die? They debated this question, eventually deciding to save as many lives as possible by eating those who died because of the cold. As a result, forty-seven of the eighty in the party survived. The choices were either everyone dies or only some die because the survivors have made an ethical decision to set aside a moral conviction (that eating human beings is bad) so they may remain alive.

Another group from the same society may have decided differently, saying that no matter what, it is wrong to eat fellow humans, even if everyone starves to death as a result. Because ethical behavior is "culture bound"—that is, what is right and what is wrong varies from society to society—individuals from a completely different society might have had no trouble at all making the deci-sion with which the Donner party struggled.

Fortunately, in academic advising the issues with which advisors grapple every day are rarely, if ever, matters of life and death. More often, they include issues of convenience, preference, success, and achievement. They involve issues that affect people who have needs and opinions. Even so, the debate over a given issue requires ethical consideration, with no obvious best-choice out-come. Although it is not the object of this chapter to analyze specific ethical dilemmas in detail, the preceding examples indicate the complications present in seemingly straightforward situations.

Ethics in Advising

Advisors may periodically be confronted with ethical dilemmas in their prac-tice. The dilemmas may involve scholastic achievement or admissions decisions, as mentioned earlier, or quite different issues. They may be issues with which the advisor can wrestle alone, or they may require consultation with other indi-viduals and other services. At the very least, the advisor must rely on widely based knowledge of her own values and of her institution's values. She must understand how to apply these values to a problem with no clear right answer and plunge in to look at many options.

Advisors as Advocates

Advisors, whether faculty or professional, work on behalf of students, help them execute their academic programs, and support them to complete their education. Advisors also represent their universities and their institution's policies. The insti-tution hires student support staff and faculty with the expectation that these peo-ple will be consistent, fair, and equitable in their dealings with students, other faculty and staff, and administrative people; and that they will follow the institu-tional rules and be good citizens of the institution. In addition, advisors have per-sonal beliefs regarding right and wrong, good and bad, that they have learned in a variety of settings (community, home, school, and workplace, to name a few).

Sometimes people discover that the values of others or of one's institution or employer do not seem right to them. They must then evaluate to what extent they feel compromised by continuing to interact with the individual or institution that has different values. They may need to decide whether to continue to participate in that setting or seek another setting more compatible with their own values. They may begin to ask questions about the ethics involved, and search for options that may lead to a resolution of their discomfort. If they cannot set aside their own values to look objectively at the options, they may find a colleague to serve as advocate for the student with whom they are working.

Advisors as Interpreters

Academic advisors are entrusted with working with students who need guidance in a multitude of areas: understanding the institution's requirements and rules; navigating through various academic programs (for example, the major, the minor, and general education requirements); choosing courses; exploring careers; learning about opportunities for individual studies with faculty, both on and off campus, study abroad, and cocurricular activities; learning how to make good decisions and evaluate personal and academic goals; working toward resolving personal issues; finding a personal, engaged, congenial, and nurturing connection within an otherwise seemingly impersonal institution; and a variety of other services that help students achieve success in their college years. Advisors need to relate well to undergraduates, have a strong academic record, be well trained for their work, and be informed of the limitations of their authority (Miller, 1999).

Advisors as Models for Ethical Behavior

Students and the institutions for which advisors work expect advisors to be honest, fair, loyal, and committed to excellence and decency; to respect and care for others; to keep promises; to be principled and faithful; to be responsible citizens; and to be accountable to everyone they serve (Josephson, 1988). There is no better model than for students to see their advisors acting in principled ways, solving problems and basing decisions on values. In this way, students can learn how to think and solve problems ethically as well.

Advisors have numerous responsibilities and, consequently, expectations from many different constituencies about how to carry out their duties. The rest of this chapter addresses these expectations and how advisors make ethical decisions, with the guidance of a core of institutionally endorsed values added to or reinforcing their own.

Codes of Ethics

Many professional associations have a set of guidelines or rules called a code of ethics that sets the standard for the profession and defines its ideals about appropriate treatment of clients and colleagues, behavior within the institution and the larger community, and participation within the profession. The code also helps protect professionals in their practice by defining the limits of the practice, thus clarifying what is realistic for the practitioner to expect and for the client to experience. In many cases, codes specify sanctions for noncompliance with the rules and explicitly state that a condition of membership in the association is acceptance of the terms of the code.

Not all codes of ethics are a listing of rules, of dos and don'ts for the profession. Some serve as a moral authority—a document against which professionals can check their behavior in the abstract, and a resource and reference when the professional needs guidance and direction.

Codes do not happen by accident. For a code to be embraced by an association's members, adopted, and effective, the drafting group should publicize its efforts, make its drafts available for members' comments, and seriously consider their feedback in making revisions. Professionals want a sense of ownership of the standards that the code defines. Without input from those who are expected to abide by it, the code would carry less meaning and have less impact.

Critics of associations that have a code of ethics express concern that some members might interpret the code too strictly, using it as a "mechanical formula for doing right" (Lowenstein and Grites, 1993, p. 60) rather than understanding the process of ethical problem solving and decision making. Some critics are concerned that professionals who are not members of the association might believe that the code and its recommended process do not apply to them in their practice, so they can ignore the standards promoted in it (Lowenstein and Grites, 1993).

The Statement of Core Values of the National Academic Advising Association (NACADA, 1994) addresses these concerns. It states that it exists "to provide the guidance which many academic advisors have sought" (p. 4), and that "anyone carrying out advising functions should be expected to perform in a professional manner. The Core Values . . . provide a framework against which those who advise can measure their own performance" (p. 1). It cautions the association to keep the core values "in line with current professional practices and thinking" (p. 4), which also makes the core values more likely to be accepted by advising professionals generally.

Academic advisors may be held accountable to several codes. Some advisors are located within academic programs or departments. Many discipline-orientated professional associations have codes of ethics (for example, the American Sociological Association, the American Association of University Professors, the American College Personnel Association, and the National Association of Student Personnel Administrators), as do many large institutions. Because most codes of ethics address issues such as honesty, fairness, respect, care for others, decency, loyalty, responsibility, accountability (Josephson, 1988), and safety, there is apt to be more overlap than conflict between codes. There may be conflicts, however, so in cases where an advisor's practice is guided by several codes from different associations, the advisor should seek clarification about which code should take precedence.

NACADA's Statement of Core Values

Academic advising is relatively new as a formal field of practice. In the association's beginning, there was no formal ethical guidance, so NACADA, advising offices, and other student services providers looked to the Standards and Guidelines for Student Services/Development Programs produced by the Council for the Advancement of Standards (CAS) for guidance relating to standards of practice (Miller, 1999). In 1991 a small group of NACADA members began to lobby for the development of a code of ethics. They wrote drafts, conducted workshops for and gathered feedback from members at regional and annual association meetings, and ultimately drafted a final version that was submitted to the association and adopted in 1994. (The entire document appears as Appendix A in this handbook.) The Statement of Core Values approved by NACADA was seen as a stepping stone to a possible future code of ethics.

The Statement of Core Values affirms the benefit of advisors using an advising philosophy or model that best meets their needs and the specific needs of their students. "It is through our Core Values that students' expectations of academic advising are honored" (NACADA, 1994, pp. 1–2). In addition, the statement acknowledges advisors' diversity. It suggests that advisors draw on their strengths and on their own interpretation of advising, as well as expand on the unique attributes of their institutions. The statement indicates values as "reference points" rather than as equally weighted items, recognizing that "some Core Values [are] more important than others" (p. 1).

The Statement of Core Values recognizes that academic advising is a complex responsibility. No matter how advisors are trained, it says, and no matter what their experience is, all are ultimately guided by their own personal values when they work with students and others in the context of the university (NACADA, 1994, p. 2). Furthermore, the statement reinforces that many advisors share similar values with others. With the support of the Statement of Core Values, advisors may feel confident about "communicat[ing] to others what [students] can expect from [advisors, that] may be used to validate [advisors'] conduct in [their] diverse roles and [their] relationships within the academic community" (p. 2).

According to the statement, students who seek advising have a right to expect "dependable, accurate, respectful, honest, friendly, and professional service" (p. 2), values specified earlier in this chapter as characteristics that advisors can use when modeling ethical behavior. It goes on to define advisors' responsibilities: to work with students, to engage others who work in a wide range of support services in the advising process, to honor the institution where the advisor works, to uphold higher education principles generally, to advocate on behalf of one's college or university within the community, and to attend to their professional role and themselves personally. In each of these areas, the statement lays out the parameters for appropriate behavior. The Statement of Core Values never explicitly declares how an advisor should advise, but it provides general principles that all advisors should adopt.

The Council for the Advancement of Standards Guidelines

The CAS standards are more directive than NACADA's Statement of Core Values. For example, part 12 of the CAS General Standards reads, in part, as follows:

> All staff members must ensure that confidentiality is maintained. . . . [Advisors must comply with] all requirements of the Family Educational Rights and Privacy Act (Buckley Amendment). . . .
>
> All staff members must ensure that students are provided access to services on a fair and equitable basis.
>
> All staff members must avoid any personal conflict of interest so they can deal objectively and impartially with persons within and outside the institution. . . .
>
> Whenever handling funds, all staff members must ensure that such funds are handled in accordance with established and responsible accounting procedures.
>
> Staff members must not participate in any form of sexual harassment. . . .
>
> All staff members must recognize the limits of their training, expertise, and competence and must refer students in need of further expertise to persons possessing appropriate qualifications" [Miller, 1999, p. 7].

In addition, the CAS Standards and Guidelines for Academic Advising (Miller, 1999) include an item regarding advisors' responsibility to impart accurate information to those outside the university community, and an item regarding advisors' obligation to comply with institutional policies and regulations.

Both the Statement of Core Values and the CAS Standards and Guidelines serve to guide advisors in their practice. The Core Values leave room for interpretation of a situation while the CAS Standards may be more useful in helping advisors respond to specific clearly defined situations.

Modeling Ethical Decision Making

Advisors model for their students the process of learning to make decisions based on moral and ethical principles. Students see advisors actively attending to ethical issues as they arise. By talking about the elements present in a question, advisors can verbally evaluate the content of the issues. The next step is to apply values or ethical principles to the question by evaluating various strategies for reaching a solution. Rather than being directive (and encouraging the student to be passive), advisors need to engage their students in the process of questioning, listen to them carefully as they express their own values, even if the advisor does not share those values entirely, and guide students to look at many alternatives before making a decision.

Ethical Dilemmas and Ethical Problem Solving

At one time or another everyone will face an ethical dilemma and need to reach a solution to it. The key is how to begin to think about complicated situations that have no clear solutions.

Advisors begin with a set of standards, such as a code of ethics or a statement of core values learned through membership in their professional association, an academic discipline, or their employment. A common set of standards based on NACADA's Statement of Core Values might be as follows (NACADA, 1994):

1. Treat students with respect. Let them or help them learn to make their own decisions, set their own goals, and make progress toward those goals. Keep their matters private and their information confidential. Give them accurate information, and facilitate referrals to others when the students' needs would be better met elsewhere.

2. Treat colleagues with respect. Remain neutral and nonjudgmental even in the face of criticism of a colleague by a student or other colleague. Communicate with administrators the importance of academic advising and the need for ongoing support for it. Advocate for changes in our institutions when policies, practices, or both interfere with students' learning.

3. Honor the concept of academic freedom. Utilize appropriate theories of student development in delivering services to students. Guide students, with their participation, through their academic programs so they may maximize their education and their opportunities to learn from faculty. Teach students to understand and make connections between their university or college learning and their everyday lives. Encourage students to perform their best, and advocate for the improvement and creation of programs and services to meet students' needs.

4. Learn about and understand the institutional culture, its mission, its goals, its expectations. Compare the compatibility of the institution's values and professional and job values and then work toward change within the institution and the professional practice, to bring about a balance between the two. Inform yourself about local, state, and federal laws and policies that govern the practice of the advising profession. Understand the legal ramifications to the institution from advisors' decisions and from actions taken on the basis of those decisions.

5. Interpret the institution's mission, goals, and values to the community so that the community will respond appropriately to the institution's programs and services.

6. Obtain the education and training required to do what the advisor is hired to do. Seek professional development to keep your skills honed. Pay special attention to your own personal, physical, emotional, and

spiritual needs. Seek nurturing from and provide nurturing to colleagues, maintain personal boundaries, and seek support inside and outside the institution.

Following is another way of presenting ethical principles (Kitchener, 1985, pp. 19–25):

Respecting autonomy: allowing others and oneself freedom of action and freedom of choice

Doing no harm, either directly to others or by putting others at risk

Benefiting others: contributing to another's welfare, development, and growth

Being just: giving equal treatment to all and considering only relevant factors

Being faithful: keeping promises, being loyal and considerate

The Standards in Practice

These standards do not provide answers. They set a tone, remind advisors of their responsibilities (broadly construed), and offer advisors alternatives to consider as they engage in the problem-solving process. Advisors are encouraged to engage ideas from the Statement of Core Values as well as to bring their own values into play. Probably the most important reminder is that effective problem solving happens in a neutral climate.

Advisors need to develop tools for resolving ethical dilemmas if they do not already have them. When looking at an ethical dilemma, one must stay objective while exploring many options and alternative solutions. People want answers and they want them *now!* A sure prescription for difficulty and frustration is to try to find a right answer to an ethical dilemma. It is necessary to remember that there is no single, simple right answer, nor is there an absolutely wrong one. However, there may be one answer that is better than others.

Most important, seek support while grappling with ethical dilemmas. As advisors practice this new kind of decision making, they must maintain open and frequent communication with others who understand the issues with which they are grappling.

Problem solving within an ethical context is a process. Take an active role; practice is essential. There are no mistakes to be made. There is no right or wrong answer; there may be many answers.

People are used to questions having right and wrong answers that are relatively readily available, but with ethical dilemmas it takes time to find a solution. Ethical issues cannot be resolved in black and white; rather, answers will be found in a wide range of grays. One must be patient with the process of exploring and generating options.

Gather facts about the people and situation involved. Ascertain relevant policy. Look at a set of guiding principles (like the Statement of Core Values) where one can expect to see what behavior is minimally acceptable. Begin to question or examine personal values, the values of the advising profession, the values of one's institution, and often others' values as well (for instance, compare notes with colleagues). Weigh the conflicting principles and elements. Ask, What in this situation is ethical and what is unethical? Between what values does one need to decide (for example, truth and loyalty, or truth and fairness)? Examine what is best for the student and what is allowable within institutional rules.

The goal of ethical problem solving is to reduce complexity by introducing general principles that apply across the board. One can apply relevant values from one's personal toolbox of values and the Statement of Core Values. People want to make decisions based on what is defined as good, what is defined as right, and what is proper within allowable guidelines. They want to learn to develop criteria to evaluate rules and make judgments of good and right. They want to be able to apply those criteria to issues, then to analyze the issues using the criteria, and finally to evaluate them afterwards.

Advisors should come to know their own minds. They should decide what solutions fit best within their own set of values, because they need to feel comfortable with the final decision. Embedded in ethical decision making is an element of judgment, a critical eye. The ultimate goal is to discover to the best of one's ability what is worth doing, whether others approve or not. Those are key words. Some may not agree with the conclusion one reaches. As long as the solution is morally defensible, as long as no harm is done, or the harm done to those involved is minimal and the good done for another is maximized, one is on safe ground.

Conclusion

All individuals have systems of rules that guide their behavior and help them make choices. From their families, communities, and the institutions in which they work, study, and worship, people learn, both explicitly and implicitly, basic rules of right and wrong that govern how to relate individually to family members and (as one grows and the number and kind of relationships expand) to those in wider circles of friends, acquaintances, colleagues, and even strangers. These rules (values or morals) that people develop are essential and precious in their lives and they guide their behavior.

Individuals' morals dictate or forbid certain behaviors. The rules may be accompanied by consequences to ensure that they are enforced. These rules of morality give everyone in a given society a common, stable grounding with everyone else; they enable members of that society to feel safe, to predict others' behavior, and to operate comfortably and productively in their day-to-day lives (Phillips, 1986).

Taking the time and effort to ponder thoroughly and thoughtfully the ethical questions that arise out of a conflict of values ultimately cuts down on conflicts. It helps create a social environment that is consistent, fair, respectful, responsible, and accountable. It helps people develop tools for determining what is right and what is wrong.

Academic advising deals in the language of ethical philosophy: advisors help students with their choices (for example, what courses to take, how much time to devote to a job versus studies, and what major to pursue), with their beliefs and values (honesty in completing one's own work, and setting priorities), with shoulds and oughts (degree requirements and minimum grade point achievement), with accepting responsibility for their actions, with being accountable for those actions, and with respecting another's autonomy (leaving the ultimate decision for course selection and major, for example, up to the student). So, in a sense advisors deal with students every day utilizing the ethical principles discussed in this chapter. Understanding some of the philosophical underpinnings of ethics and ethical problem solving helps advisors confront otherwise troublesome situations more competently.

Resources

The author looked at numerous codes of ethics. The best representative sampling of codes are contained in the following works:

Canon, H. J., and Brown, R. D. (eds.). *Applied Ethics in Student Services.* New Directions for Student Services, no. 30. San Francisco: Jossey-Bass, 1985.

Rich, J. M. *Professional Ethics in Education.* Springfield, Ill.: Thomas, 1984.

Van Hoose, W., and Kottler, J. A. (eds.). *Ethical and Legal Issues in Counseling and Psychotherapy.* (2nd ed.) San Francisco: Jossey-Bass, 1985.

References

Denise, T. C., and Peterfreund, S. P. *Great Traditions in Ethics.* (7th ed.) Belmont, Calif.: Wadsworth, 1992.

Durkheim, E. *Ethics and the Sociology of Morals* (R. T. Hall, trans.). Amherst, N.Y.: Prometheus, 1993.

Gove, P. B. (ed.). *Webster's Seventh Collegiate Dictionary.* Springfield, Mass.: Merriam-Webster, 1965.

Josephson, M. "Teaching Ethical Decision Making and Principled Reasoning." *Ethics: Easier Said Than Done,* 1988, *1*(1), 27–33.

Kitchener, K. S. "Ethical Principles and Ethical Decisions in Student Affairs." In H. J. Canon and R. D. Brown (eds.), *Applied Ethics in Student Services.* New Directions for Student Services, no. 30. San Francisco: Jossey-Bass, 1985.

Lowenstein, M., and Grites, T. J. "Ethics in Academic Advising." *NACADA Journal,* 1993, *13*(1), 53–61.

Miller, T. K. (ed.). "Standards and Guidelines for Academic Advising." *CAS Blue Book.* College Park, Md.: Council for the Advancement of Standards for Student Services/Development Programs, 1999.

National Academic Advising Association. *Statement of Core Values.* Manhattan, Kans.: National Academic Advising Association, 1994.

Nowell-Smith, P. H. *Ethics.* Baltimore, Md.: Penguin Books, 1954.

Phillips, D. *Toward a Just Social Order.* Princeton, N.J.: Princeton University Press, 1986.

Chapter Five

Legal Issues in Academic Advising

Barbara A. Becker

Experience is a good teacher, but she sends in terrific bills.
—Minna Thomas Antrim, *Naked Truths and Veiled Illusions,* (1901)

S tudent lawsuits against colleges and universities have resulted in court review of academic decisions. With the increasing litigiousness of our society, respecting students' legal rights is important for both ethical and practical reasons. While experience is usually a desirable goal, experience as a defendant or as a witness for the defense is best avoided. An understanding of current legal trends will help faculty and advising professionals to respond effectively to the legal implications of their daily work and to avoid legal entanglements that are costly in terms of time, money, and emotions. Equally important, advisors' understanding of students' legal rights will contribute to better advising and improved working relationships with students.

Sources of Law: The Academic Contract and Statutory Law

What is the source of a school's legal duty to its students? Courts today base decisions on the contractual relationship between a college and its students, defining the contract in terms of the actual promises made in college catalogues, bulletins, and handbooks as well as the verbal promises of administrators, instructors, and advisors. In addition to considering these explicit contract terms, the court will add implied terms by looking at past practices and customs of the institution. Finally, many courts will imply terms necessary to a school's fair treatment of students.

This chapter provides an overview of legal issues and does not purport to give specific legal advice. If you have a specific concern, consult legal counsel.

As a brief historical note, contract theories were first used *against* students in the 1920s. In 1924, the New York Supreme Court allowed Syracuse University to require "the withdrawal of any student at any time for any reason" and without explanation. In this case, a female student was dismissed from Syracuse University because of rumors that she was not "a typical Syracuse girl" (*Anthony* v. *Syracuse University,* 1928). Such unreined authority continued until the mid-sixties, when institutions functioned under the "reasonable parent" standard, exercising over a student whatever authority a parent could. This still gave colleges leeway to operate virtually unchecked. However, with the activism of the mid-sixties, contract theories were reborn as students went to court. The contract between the student and the university became a tool for dissatisfied student consumers seeking redress.

In addition to honoring the academic contract, educational institutions are also obligated to follow federal and state laws, whether enacted by legislatures, judges (case law), or administrative agencies. Some federal laws apply to nearly all educational institutions while others apply only to public and not to private schools. For example, federal laws on privacy of student information (discussed later in this chapter) apply to all institutions that receive federal funding, even if the funding is only indirect, such as student financial aid. Federal prohibitions against discrimination (based on race, national origin, sex, age, or disability) apply to private and public schools due to Congress's regulation of either recipients of federal funds or employers. In contrast, federal constitutional protections of free speech and religion, for example, apply only to governmental action and usually not to acts of officials at private schools, unless some connection to government can be established.

Academic staff must also be aware of laws within their own state that govern their activities, such as state data privacy laws, state human rights laws, local ordinances, and case law establishing precedent for common law claims, such as negligence or intentional torts.

Changing Curriculum and Academic Programs

Despite the extensive roll call of lawsuits brought against academic institutions, most courts are reluctant to overturn decisions and actions that are truly academic—in other words, those decisions that require the expertise of academic professionals. Courts review academic decisions not to substitute their own views as to the academic merits but to determine whether a school's action has broken the academic contract with a student. This is in contrast to court review of decisions made by the university acting in other capacities—as an employer, for example. Likewise, this concept of *academic abstention* does not protect schools from judicial scrutiny of procedural matters.

A Minnesota case involving the academic dismissal of a student illustrates this idea. In *Abbariao* v. *Hamline University School of Law* (1977), a student was dismissed because of his low grades. He sued for breach of contract, contending that tutoring—which was promised in the school bulletin but later discontinued—would have made a difference in his academic performance. There had also been a grading system change during the student's enrollment. Relying in part on a bulletin statement that changes could be made without notice, the court said the contract was not breached. This case, and many similar cases, stand for the following propositions: (1) colleges have a duty to follow their own established policies and procedures, (2) schools have a right and responsibility to establish and maintain appropriate academic standards, and (3) course requirements and programs may be changed if the changes themselves are reasonable and if students are given reasonable warning. Thus, schools may make reasonable changes in curriculum and degree content almost at will in exercising their educational responsibility if students are given reasonable warning of the changes.

Given courts' emphasis on providing students with "reasonable" notice of changes, how much notice is required? There is no absolute answer, but as a guideline some courts have held that the academic contract is renewed each time tuition is paid, usually each term. Therefore, minimal notice would be given at least one term before a change is contemplated, and considerably earlier than that for a change that could hinder a student's degree progress or program choice. In practice, it is wise to give a year's notice or more for significant changes such as alteration or elimination of academic majors or degrees.

The outcome of these alleged academic breach-of-contract cases depends on the specific facts of each case, but courts will examine the following factors: the express and implied promises made to the student, the reasonableness of the student's reliance on the promises made by the school, the hardship to the student, and the student's opportunity to avoid the harm. For example, a New York state court in *Healy* v. *Larsson* (1974) ordered a community college to grant a degree to a student who took courses his advisor had recommended. After he had taken the courses, the student found that the coursework did not match the stated requirements for the degree. The court ruled that the advisor's statements were part of the contract and that the student had justifiably relied on them, and on that basis the court ordered the community college to grant the degree.

Similarly, a New York state court ruled that a student's reliance on the advice of his advisor and other faculty was reasonable and ordered Brooklyn College to award a degree. The student received permission to complete and receive credit in two psychology courses without attending class. The college posted the credit to his transcript, but later refused to award his degree, based on a policy that courses completed without class attendance would not count toward a degree. The New York Supreme Court held that the college was estopped from asserting this policy on the basis of the permission and advice given by members of the faculty and the student's program advisor (*Blank* v. *Board of Higher Education of New York,* 1966).

Decisions in these types of *reliance* cases turn heavily on the particular facts, in view of the hardship to the student as a result of the misadvice. As a result, it is difficult to predict the outcomes of such cases. However, they remind advisors of the importance of accurate advice and should be incentive for institutions to be accountable when errors are made, while maintaining the integrity of the degree. As a policy matter, an institution might consider writing letters explaining delayed graduation to prospective employers, waiving tuition for courses that must be made up, or backdating degrees as appropriate. In egregious cases, granting a nonconforming degree might be necessary.

Academic and Disciplinary Hearings and Dismissals

Dismissal from a particular academic program or from an entire academic institution is almost always a contentious situation, and frequently litigated. This is especially true when the student is seeking an advanced or professional degree, such as in law, medicine, or a related profession. The time and cost of such an educational investment is considerable and the resulting expectations are high. Although the U.S. Supreme Court has not stated that students have a constitutionally protected right to continuing education, under certain circumstances a "property interest" has been implied. Both procedural and substantive due process is required by constitutional law in public schools and implied by contract in private schools.

Procedural Due Process

Courts require that proper procedures be followed in arriving at a decision to dismiss a student. That said, students do not have the rights that one might expect after watching a few hours of *The Practice* or *Ally McBeal*. Procedural due process within academe does not require the same rights as due process in a court of law (for example, the right to counsel or to cross-examine witnesses).

Students have no absolute right to notice and hearing prior to a dismissal, but they must be advised in advance of their academic deficiencies or specific misconduct and the possibility of suspension or discipline. Although it is not necessary to allow a student to have an attorney present at a dismissal or disciplinary hearing (unless the school has its attorney at hand), it is good practice to allow the student to bring a nonlawyer advocate, such as an advisor, teacher, or friend. In addition, the student must be offered the opportunity to clarify any errors and to appeal the decision. Equally important, a court will require that a school follow its own established policies and procedures. The typical remedy when a procedural error is made is for the school to go back and do it right and reach an independent, second decision.

Substantive Due Process: Is the Decision Fundamentally Fair?

When analyzing the merits of an academic decision, courts rarely substitute their judgment for the professional judgment of the faculty unless there has been a substantial departure from accepted academic norms. In fact, unless the decision appears motivated by bias, is capricious, or violates some law (such as a specific protection against discrimination), academic institutions usually win these cases on summary judgment motions (a ruling by the judge dismissing the case without a trial), because of the academic abstention philosophy mentioned earlier. A U.S. Supreme Court case, *Regents of the University of Michigan* v. *Ewing* (1985), not only illustrates this idea, but also provides some interesting comments on academia.

In *Ewing,* a student challenged his dismissal from medical school and was successful in the lower courts, but the university eventually appealed to the U.S. Supreme Court. The student had taken six years to complete coursework normally finished in four years and had failed his medical school boards with the worst score ever reported. The Court inferred that Ewing had a property interest in continued enrollment without a specific ruling on that matter. The key issue of the case was whether the University of Michigan had acted arbitrarily in dropping Ewing from medical school. The Court stated, "The record unmistakably demonstrates . . . that the faculty's decision was made conscientiously and with careful deliberation, based on an evaluation of the entirety of Ewing's academic career "(Kaplan and Lee, 1995, p.467).

The Court further explained its reluctance to override an academic decision, quoting from its decision in an earlier medical student dismissal case, *Curators of the University of Missouri* v. *Horowitz* (1978): "When judges are asked to review the substance of a genuinely academic decision, such as this one, they should show great respect for the faculty's professional judgment. Plainly, they may not override it unless it is such a substantial departure from accepted academic norms as to demonstrate that the person or committee responsible did not actually exercise professional judgment" (Kaplan and Lee, 1995, p. 468).

It is clear that the Supreme Court does not condone second-guessing expeditions by the lower courts, and that the justices know how academia works— by committee!

Privacy of Student Information

Lawsuits based on defamation and invasion of privacy are on the increase. Given the sensitivity of the information that advisors may access (such as grades, test scores, evaluations, references, and disciplinary records), careful management of this information is crucial. Privacy and confidentiality issues often arise from either inappropriate release of student record information or negative recommendations.

Student Records and the Buckley Amendment

Some readers may remember the day when students could not view the records that schools keep about them. This practice was displaced by federal and state "sunshine" laws of the mid-seventies aimed at opening records to those who had a legitimate reason to see them.

The Family Educational Rights and Privacy Act (FERPA) of 1974 (20 U.S.C. § 1232g), also known as the Buckley Amendment, governs how student education records should be handled and applies to any public or private institution that receives federal funds. All former and enrolled students are covered by this law. Applicants' records are exempt, although some schools voluntarily extend similar safeguards to applicants' records. Students may view their own records and may challenge any information they believe is inaccurate.

What Is an Education Record? Most student education records come within the purview of FERPA, unless specifically listed as exempt. FERPA defines educational records broadly as "any record maintained by the institution about a student." Exceptions include law enforcement records, records used exclusively for medical treatment, a parent's financial records, confidential letters of recommendation for which students have signed a specific waiver of access, and some notes of instructional personnel.

Public or Private Information? Information about students is classified as either directory (public) or nondirectory (private). Release of private information is restricted to anyone but the student, except under a few legally defined circumstances. In addition, notice must be given to the student whenever information is released, including directory information, if the student has requested that it be suppressed. FERPA allows institutions to designate as public selected student information, such as name, major, address, phone, class, dates of enrollment and termination, college, advisor name, degrees granted, and honors and awards received. Students must be allowed to state each year whether they want to have the directory information suppressed.

Private information may not be released to anyone but the student without the written consent of the student or a court order, or under the following FERPA-defined circumstances: a health or safety emergency, if the information is necessary to resolve the emergency; or to those within the university itself who have a "legitimate educational interest." Thus, release within a school is permissible for legitimate educational purposes—for example, to a faculty member who needs information about a student enrolled in her course, or even to a school's accounts receivable clerk who is attempting to collect a student's outstanding tuition debt.

In addition, in 1998 Congress amended the Higher Education Act of 1965 (U.S.C. § 951–95) and included several provisions permitting (but not requiring) colleges to disclose to a student's parents information about any violations of law or school policy related to the use or possession of alcohol or controlled substances, if the student is under twenty-one; and results of disciplinary proceedings for commission of violent crimes and sex offenses, including the student's name, the nature of the violation, and the sanctions imposed. Congress stated, however, that the provision related to drug and alcohol offenses would not supersede state laws that prohibit such disclosures. College administrators disagree about the appropriate response to these amendments and are struggling to balance student privacy concerns against the public interest in reducing illegal drug and alcohol use. For a discussion of these amendments and the various choices that colleges are making in response to them, see Carnevale (1999).

Advisor Notes. Some advisors keep personal notes about students separate from the official education record. An advisor may make such notes as a memory device or to keep sensitive information out of the official file. If the goal is to keep these notes from student view, this is a risky practice for several reasons. First, FERPA requires that notes of instructional, supervisory, administrative, or educational personnel must be kept in the sole possession of these personnel and not be revealed to anyone other than a substitute. If anyone else sees them, the notes become open to student view. Second, such records would likely be discoverable during a lawsuit and their contents could be damaging. Advisors who keep separate file notes should strive to keep comments about students as factual and objective as possible, in the event that the notes are one day viewed by students.

Remember, the individual states' laws governing release of education data may expand students' rights. In Minnesota, for example, an individual may sue a staff member directly for unauthorized release of private information and be awarded punitive damages. This should strike fear (or at least caution) in the hearts of advisors in states with similar laws.

On-Line Advising and Student Records

Most legal commentators agree that electronic records fall within the definitions of federal and state data privacy and freedom of information laws, with the accompanying legal implications. Students have a right to review student record information stored electronically (or the paper printouts). E-mail advising transmissions are education records and should be preserved, and their confidentiality should be maintained. This can present practical problems with insecure Internet transmissions, although encryption technologies are available. Student permission should be obtained and documented if private information is sent via e-mail. Electronic advising, while efficient and useful, requires thoughtful policies regarding record management, retention, and documentation—in effect, replicating the usual safeguards employed when handling hard-copy student information.

Advisor Recommendations

Advisors are sometimes asked by students to provide letters of recommendation for character or job references. When only positive things are said about a student, this is usually not a problem. If, however, an advisor feels that a qualified or negative recommendation is warranted, danger lurks ahead.

Recommendations should be given with care, due to the possibility of a lawsuit based on defamation or invasion of privacy. Defamation is a statement, either oral or written, that is damaging to the reputation of an individual and communicated to a third party. Advisors should avoid giving negative references, especially if a reference has not been solicited by the student or if there has been difficulty in the advising relationship. Such circumstances could negate the qualified immunity defense that normally exists when a reference is given in good faith and with no malicious intent, and when its contents meet a reasonable and prudent standard. Invasion of privacy claims require not proof of malicious intent but rather evidence of a "highly offensive" intentional intrusion upon the solitude or seclusion of another or her private affairs. If an advisor feels unable to give a positive recommendation, it is best to decline. For ethical reasons, an advisor may feel duty-bound to write an honest but negative reference. If this is the case, the advisor should proceed only after consideration of the legal risks and with certainty that any negative statements can be factually documented.

Protection Against Discrimination

Because of constitutional safeguards and federal laws protecting specified groups, public colleges cannot use information about students' race, color, creed, religion, national origin, sex, age, marital status, or disability as a basis for educational decisions, nor can this information be gathered, except to meet state and federal reporting requirements or perhaps to implement an affirmative action plan (see later discussion). Both public and private colleges receiving federal funds are subject to congressional enactments prohibiting discrimination in education and employment on the basis of race, sex, age, or disability. Colleges bear a heavy legal burden to establish that use of these classifications to distinguish between students or as a basis for educational decisions is proper. Although a thorough discussion of each type of discrimination would require a complete chapter, three areas that advisors might encounter either in their work with students or as employees are discussed here.

Race-Based Affirmative Action Plans

When may colleges implement voluntary affirmative action plans? In other words, if a court has not ordered affirmative action efforts, may a school institute plans to increase racial and cultural diversity on campus? In 1978, the U.S. Supreme Court made it clear in the well-publicized case *Bakke* v. *Regents of the University of California* (1978) that not all affirmative action attempts are legal. The *Bakke* court overruled a medical school admissions plan at the Davis campus, which reserved a fixed number (quota) of places for minority students. Although the Supreme Court did not rule out all attempts at affirmative action, it stated that they would be "strictly scrutinized."

Although the Supreme Court has not heard any higher education affirmative action cases since *Bakke,* judicial review of these plans by the U.S. Court of Appeals has become increasingly rigorous. The Fourth and Fifth Circuits of the Court of Appeals have overruled efforts to increase minority enrollments by, respectively, the University of Maryland and the University of Texas.

In *Podberesky* v. *Kirwan* (1994), the Fourth Circuit Court of Appeals overruled the University of Maryland's program that awarded merit-based scholarships to African American students. The court held that the university's program, which evaluated minority students separately from other students, was not "narrowly tailored" to remedy the effects of past discrimination because in addition to giving scholarships to Maryland residents, scholarships were also given to nonresident students who were not within the category of individuals subjected to past discrimination (Reklaitis and Tarasevich, 1996).

In the *Hopwood* v. *Texas* case (1996), the U.S. Fifth Circuit Court of Appeals held that the University of Texas's admissions policies violated the Equal Protection Clause of the Constitution. The university had targets for enrollment of minority Mexican American and African American students and set presumptively lower admissions scores for their admission in order to reach these targets. The law school justified the program based on two grounds: to promote a diverse student body and to remedy the present effects of past discrimination. The court rejected these arguments and overturned the program, stating that "any consideration of race or ethnicity by the law school for the purpose of achieving a diverse student body is not a compelling interest" (Reklaitis and Tarasevich, 1996).

Despite the courts' trend to restrict affirmative action, many schools and educational organizations pose strong policy arguments in favor of efforts targeted at broadening diversity within college campuses (American Civil Liberties Union, 1999). Schools that wish to implement voluntary affirmative action plans should consult legal counsel or guidelines published by education risk experts and insurers. (Reklaitis and Tarasevich, 1996). Educators in the states governed by the Fourth Circuit (Maryland, Virginia, West Virginia, and North and South Carolina) and Fifth Circuit Courts (Texas, Louisiana, and Mississippi) face almost insurmountable hurdles to developing a legal affirmative action plan.

Sexual Harassment

Under Title VII of the Civil Rights Act of 1964 (42 U.S.C. § 2000e et seq), as amended in 1972 and 1993, public and private universities face the same challenges and liabilities as other employers, to provide a workplace free of inappropriate, sexually harassing conduct. Sexual harassment is also a violation of Title IX of the Education Amendments of 1972 (20 U.S.C § 1681 et seq), which prohibits sexual discrimination in education programs at schools receiving federal funds. This is a highly litigated area of the law, as demonstrated by the fact that the Supreme Court accepted and reviewed four cases involving sexual harassment during its 1997–98 term (Engelmeier and Hegre, 1999). Advisors and supervisors must be aware of the legal obligation that a school has to intervene promptly and take reasonable action to stop reported sexually harassing behavior.

Sexual harassment is legally categorized as one of two types—either *quid pro quo,* in which sexual harassment by a supervisor or authority results in a tangible employment decision about an employee (such as a demotion or discharge), or *hostile environment,* in which an employer's sexually harassing actions create an abusive or "poisoned" environment. Examples of harassing conduct, as determined by the courts, include, among others, unwelcome sexual advances, sexual touching, requests for sexual favors, verbal jokes of a sexual nature, and name-calling. Both men and women can be targets of sexual harassment and the perpetrators can be of the same or opposite sex.

Sexual harassment (and other forms of employment discrimination under Title VII) is such a serious problem in the workplace that the Supreme Court has articulated unusual legal consequences, as compared to other civil lawsuits. For example, once a plaintiff has established that quid pro quo conduct has occurred, the employer can be liable for damages even if the employee has not actually reported the incident. Because of the acts of a responsible entity within the company, the employer is liable based on agency theories (Kaplan and Lee, 1995). In addition, in hostile environment cases, once the proof of illegal conduct is established, the plaintiff need not prove "serious harm" or resulting negative job consequences. The U.S. Supreme Court in a hostile environment sexual harassment case, *Harris* v. *Forklift Systems* (1993), stated, "Moreover, even without regard to these tangible effects, the very fact that the discriminatory conduct was so severe or pervasive that it created a work environment abusive to employees because of their race, gender, religion, or national origin offends Title VII's broad rule of workplace equality" (Kaplan and Lee, 1995, p. 245).

Employers should take proactive measures to set policies against sexual harassment and to publicize them to employees and supervisors.

Peer Sexual Harassment

The Supreme Court in May 1999 resolved a difference of opinion among the Federal Courts of Appeal on the issue of whether schools could be held liable for student-on-student sexual harassment. The Court ruled that a legal claim for damages may be brought by a private individual against a school board for student-on-student harassment, but only when the school is "deliberately indifferent to the sexual harassment, has actual knowledge of it, and that harassment is so severe, pervasive, and objectively offensive that it can be said to deprive the victims of access to the educational opportunities or benefits provided by the school" (*Davis* v. *Monroe County Board of Education*, 1999). These claims are brought against schools or other entities receiving federal funds under Title IX, which prohibits discrimination based on sex in educational opportunities.

In *Davis*, a female fifth grader was subjected to repeated incidents of verbal taunting and sexual touching by a male classmate ("G.F."). Despite the victim's numerous reports and the teachers' direct observation of several of the incidents, the school failed to take action to stop G.F.'s conduct, except to verbally warn him. No disciplinary action was ever taken against G.F., and the offensive conduct continued for almost five months. During that time the victim became increasingly upset, her previously high grades dropped, and she even contemplated suicide. The harassment finally stopped when G.F. was charged with and pleaded guilty to sexual battery.

In reaching its result the Court also noted that the board of education had not instructed its staff on how to respond to peer sexual harassment and had not established any policies on the issue—further proof of the school's failure to take reasonable action to stop the harassing conduct.

Disability Discrimination

Section 504 of the Rehabilitation Act of 1973 (29 U.S.C. § 794, as amended 1992) and the Americans with Disabilities Act (ADA)of 1990 (42 U.S.C. § 1201 et seq) are the primary sources of federal law that prohibit discrimination based on disability. The importance of these laws can be appreciated in view of the fact that according to a study by the American Council on Education, in 1992 nearly one in eleven first-year students reported that they had a disability (Kaplan and Lee, 1995). While Section 504 and the ADA vary slightly in their application, there are some key similarities.

First, plaintiffs must demonstrate that they have a disability, defined as either a mental or physical impairment that significantly limits one or more major life functions; must have a record of such an impairment; or must be regarded as having such an impairment. Examples of major life functions are walking, talking, hearing, performing manual tasks, caring for oneself, and working (Allred, 1991). Plaintiffs must also show that they are "otherwise qualified" to participate and meet the academic and technical requirements of the education program. Once a plaintiff meets these two threshold requirements, the school is then obligated to make reasonable accommodations. Courts have required schools to offer accommodations such as tutors, interpreters, lab assistants, special parking, access ramps, modified facilities, Braille or taped textbooks, extended time for tests, and quiet test rooms, to name some examples. It is important to note that schools are not expected to lower their academic standards or to make fundamental alterations in their academic programs. However, auxiliary aids must be provided, if they are reasonable. If an accommodation would result in undue hardship to a school, it is not reasonable. Some factors that courts consider in determining undue hardship include the nature and cost of an accommodation, the overall financial resources available, and the size of the school and its operations.

The disability itself is a factor that may be considered in determining whether a student is otherwise qualified, and in some circumstances may prevent the student from being able to meet the program requirements. For example, the U.S. Supreme Court upheld a community college's refusal to admit a deaf student to a nursing program on the basis that she was not otherwise qualified and could not meet the program's clinical requirements, which were based on safety considerations of patients. The Court theorized that although technology might eventually enable the student to meet these safety concerns, the school's present concerns were legitimate and prevented the student from qualifying for admission (*Southeastern Community College* v. *Davis,* 1979).

The Supreme Court surprised many commentators on June 22, 1999, with rulings in three related disability cases that restricted the reach of the ADA. The Court ruled that persons with "correctable" impairments do not come under the protection of the ADA. This decision means, for example, that a person with vision correctable to twenty/twenty may be refused a job as an airline pilot on the basis of her uncorrected vision (*Sutton* v. *United Air Lines, Inc.*, 1999), or that an individual whose high blood pressure can be controlled with medication may be refused a truck driver's license based on federal licensing regulations (*Murphy* v. *United Parcel Service, Inc.*, 1999).

This narrow definition of what constitutes a disability has been criticized by advocates for people with disabilities, including Professor Chai Feldblom of Georgetown Law School, who said, "[the rulings] create the absurd result of a person being disabled enough to be fired from a job but not disabled enough to challenge the firing" (Greenhouse, 1999, p. A16).

Conclusions

In today's litigious environment, careful reflection on students' legal rights yields benefits to both students and staff. Although faculty and advisors need not be experts in higher education law, they should be able to recognize situations that merit consultation with legal experts. Sources of useful legal information include university or consulting attorneys, professional organizations (see the list of additional resources at the end of this chapter), or even legal Web sites with education law links, such as findlaw.com.

Fortunately, understanding basic concepts of higher education law, following established policies, and applying principles of common sense and fairness will serve as a reliable compass, pointing advisors toward the legal expectations of the courts.

References

Allred, S. "The Americans with Disabilities Act: Some Questions and Answers." *School Law Bulletin*, 1991, *22*(1), 6–9.

American Civil Liberties Union (ACLU). "ACLU Briefing Paper: Affirmative Action." [http://www.aclu.org/library/pbp17.html]. 1999.

Antrim, M. T. *Naked Truths and Veiled Illusions*. Philadelphia: Henry Altemus, 1901.

Carnevale, D. "Education Department Proposes Guidelines for Changes in Law on Student Privacy." *Chronicle of Higher Education* [http://chronicle.com], June 3, 1999.

Engelmeier, S., and Hegre, J. "Lawyer Alert: What Your Law Firm, and Its Clients, Should Know About Workplace Sexual Harassment." *Hennepin Lawyer*, 1999, *2006*(1), 6–10.

Greenhouse, L. "High Court Limits Who Is Protected By Disability Law." *New York Times*, June 23, 1999, p. 1, A16.

Kaplan, W. A., and Lee, B. *The Law of Higher Education*. (3rd ed.) San Francisco: Jossey-Bass, 1995.

Reklaitis, R. F., and Tarasevich, D. A. *Promoting Equal Opportunity in Higher Education: Guidelines for Affirmative Action Programs*. Chevy Chase, Md.: United Educators Insurance Risk Retention Group, 1996.

Legal References

Abbariao v. Hamline University School of Law, 258 N.W.2d 108 (Minn. 1977).

Anthony v. Syracuse University, 224 App. Div. 487, 231 N.Y.S. 435 (1928).

Bakke v. Regents of the University of California, 438 U.S. 265 (1978).

Blank v. Board of Higher Education of New York, 273 N.Y.S.2d 796 (1966).

Curators of the University of Missouri v. Horowitz, 435 U.S. 78 (1978).

Davis v. Monroe County Board of Education, 119 S.Ct. 1661 (1999).

Harris v. Forklift Systems, 114 S.Ct. 367 (1993).

Healy v. Larsson, 323 N.Y.S. 625, affirmed, 318 N.E.2d 608 (N.Y. 1974).

Hopwood v. Texas, 78 F.3d 932 (5th Cir. 1996).

Murphy v. United Parcel Service, Inc., 119 S.Ct. 2133 (1999).

Podberesky v. Kirwan, 38 F.3d 147 (4th Cir. 1994).

Regents of the University of Michigan v. Ewing, 474 U.S. 214 (1985).

Southeastern Community College v. Davis, 442 U.S. 397 (1979).

Sutton v. United Air Lines, Inc., 119 S.Ct. 2139 (1999).

Additional Resources

Education Law Association, 300 College Park, Dayton, Ohio 45469–2280; phone: 937–229–3589; Web site: educationlaw.org.

National Association of College and University Attorneys, One Dupont Circle N.W., Suite 620, Washington, D.C. 20036; phone: 202–833–8390; Web site: www.nacua.org.

Part Two

Student Diversity
and Academic Advising

P art One of this volume outlined the historical changes that have affected academic advising over the centuries. The characteristics and number of students who have been advised over the years have changed just as dramatically. Part Two addresses the focus of advising—the individual student. To its credit, advising in American colleges has been student centered over most of its history. Although the characteristics of students have changed, the basic purpose of advising has been to assist students at the heart of the learning process. This focus recognizes the unique and diverse concerns that students present today.

M. Lee Upcraft and Pamela S. Stephens introduce in Chapter Six a general profile of today's college students, how their advising needs are influenced by who they are, and how they have changed ethnically and by gender, age, and enrollment status. Not only do we see a different demographic mix of students today than in previous years, but changes in their attitudes and values, family situations, and mental and physical health are apparent. Decline in students' preparedness to perform college-level work has perhaps been the most frustrating change to faculty and administrators. Chapter Six offers insights into how this and other factors have affected the advising function, and offers suggestions for a more personalized approach to such a diverse student population in general.

Chapter Seven takes into account the need to advise students who are at different levels of experience and maturity. Author Gary L. Kramer suggests that student development theory can help advisors understand students' differing personal and academic concerns from the first year to the graduate level. He outlines specific resources for advisors to consider as they advise students at such different levels.

The next three chapters examine specific groups of students, including those from different ethnic and cultural backgrounds. Ronnie Priest and Sidney A. McPhee in Chapter Eight emphasize the importance of cultural differences in advising. They offer insights into multicultural students' perceptions of their college experience and suggest thoughtful and caring advising interventions to ensure retention and graduation. In Chapter Nine, Steven C. Ender and Carolyn J. Wilkie describe and offer advising suggestions for high-ability as well as underprepared students. They outline the special advising needs of disabled students and student athletes, as well as gay and lesbian students, who may also need special advising considerations.

Academically and vocationally undecided students as well as major-changers and older adults are identified by George E. Steele and Melinda L. McDonald in Chapter Ten as students in transition. After describing the important characteristics of these students, the authors suggest advising approaches that can encourage and support them as they move through these sometimes difficult transitions.

The last chapter of Part Two discusses a universal concern of all college students: the inherent need to prepare for life after college. In Chapter Eleven, Betsy McCalla-Wriggins addresses the task of helping students integrate educational and career and life planning. She describes some basic elements in career exploration and planning of which advisors need to be cognizant, and outlines the basic career-advising knowledge and skills needed to help students make these important life decisions.

The chapters in Part Two offer a comprehensive portrait of today's college students and their astonishingly diverse backgrounds, needs, and concerns. The authors offer many helpful suggestions not only to help advisors acquire a deeper understanding of the students they advise, but also to help them sensitively tailor their approaches to take into account the unique needs of their individual advisees.

Chapter Six

Academic Advising and Today's Changing Students

M. Lee Upcraft, Pamela S. Stephens

College students have changed. Most of us associated with higher education recognize that fact, but the magnitude of the changes becomes apparent when we compare college students of today with those of forty years ago. A condensed description provided by Schoch (1980, p. 1) is as relevant today as when it was written twenty years ago: "Remember Joe College? The young man who, after working hard in high school, arrived at Berkeley, where he set out to sample the rich and varied intellectual feast at the University of California. Joe was independent, self-motivated, and academically well prepared. About his junior year, Joe settled on a major field of study, which he pursued with diligence and increasing confidence in order to graduate four years after his arrival."

Joe doesn't live here anymore, Schoch concludes, and a look at the 1998 entering class at Berkeley confirms his conclusion. That class was 40.9 percent Asian, 31.4 percent white, 13.2 percent Hispanic, 6.1 percent African American, 7.2 percent unknown, and 1.2 percent American Indian. In other words, at least 68.6 percent of students were nonwhite (Berkeley Office of Student Research, 1998).

But racial and ethnic diversity is only one indicator of how much students have changed, particularly in the last forty years. This chapter reviews the many ways in which students have changed, as well as the challenges academic advisors face because of today's students' physical and psychological health, their family dynamics, and other factors. The chapter concludes by exploring some of the implications of these changes for academic advising.

The Changing Demographics of Today's Students

There is ample evidence that students' demographics have changed drastically in the last thirty years, including race/ethnicity, gender, enrollment status, age, residence, disability, sexual orientation, and nationality.

Racial and Ethnic Diversity

The number of racial and ethnic groups accessing higher education has grown dramatically. In 1996, minorities constituted 25.2 percent of total enrollments, compared to 17.9 percent in 1986. Put another way, from 1986 to 1996, while overall enrollments increased 14.4 percent, American Indian enrollment increased 48.9 percent; Asian Americans, 83.8 percent; African Americans, 38.6 percent; Hispanics, 86.4 percent; and international students, 34.8 percent. Compare these figures with a 3.1 percent increase in white enrollment (Wilds and Wilson, 1998). If these trends continue, it will not be long before racial and ethnic minorities constitute more than one-third of the student population.

To be sure, racial and ethnic group participation is quite uneven by type of institution and geographic location. For example, nearly half (46.9 percent) of American Indians, Hispanic, Asians, and African Americans attend two-year institutions, compared to 30.3 percent for whites. In fact, more than half of American Indians (55.4 percent) and a majority of Hispanics (60.9 percent) attend two-year institutions (Chronicle of Higher Education Almanac, 1999). States with more than a quarter minority enrollment in higher education include, in rank order, Hawaii (71.0 percent); California (48.8 percent); Washington, D.C. (45.7 percent); New Mexico (44.9 percent); Texas (37.4 percent); Florida (32.9 percent); Louisiana (32.8 percent); Mississippi (32.7 percent); Maryland (32.2 percent); New York (31.6 percent); Georgia (30.8 percent); New Jersey (29.5 percent); Illinois (28.4 percent); and Alabama (27.0 percent) (Chronicle of Higher Education Almanac, 1998).

Interestingly, differences within minority groups may be as great as differences among them. For example, there are four major Hispanic-Latino groups in higher education—Mexican Americans, Puerto Ricans, Cubans, and Central and South Americans. Each group has a different history and different traditions and cultures (Justiz and Rendon, 1989). Within-group diversity is also evident with Asians, Native Americans, African Americans, and other groups, which means we must be very cautious in reaching conclusions about students based on gross categorizations of race and ethnicity.

Gender

The opportunity for higher education first belonged only to men. Not until the mid-nineteenth century were women allowed to go to college. But in the twentieth century, by around 1980, more women than men were enrolled in college.

Since 1978, women have outnumbered men among first-time enrollees (Wilds and Wilson, 1998). In 1997, 55.4 percent of undergraduate students were women (Chronicle of Higher Education Almanac, 1999).

Enrollment Status

Today more students enroll part-time. In 1997, 28.1 percent of all undergraduate students were enrolled part-time. Part-time students are most likely to be women over twenty-four years of age who are enrolled at two-year institutions. Nearly three out of five part-time students (59.1 percent) are twenty-five and older. Of male undergraduates enrolled part-time, 45.7 percent are twenty-five and older, while among females 65.2 percent are twenty-five or older (Chronicle of Higher Education Almanac, 1999).

As a consequence of their part-time enrollment, fewer students are completing bachelor's degrees in four years. According to a survey by the National Collegiate Athletic Association, only 56 percent of full-time first-year students graduate within six years. By racial and ethnic group, 64.0 percent of Asians graduated within six years, followed by 59 percent of Whites, 45 percent of Hispanics, 38 percent of African Americans, and 37 percent of American Indians (Wilds and Wilson, 1998).

"Stopping out" (the practice of dropping out and reenrolling at a later date) is also a more frequent occurrence than it used to be. According to the National Center for Education Statistics (1998), nearly one-third of all undergraduates depart institutions of higher education during their first year. In 1989–90, 15 percent of all students stopped out, with students enrolled at public two-year institutions stopping out at nearly twice the rate of those enrolled at four-year institutions.

Age

Since World War II and the GI Bill, older student enrollments have steadily increased, to the point where they represent 30.0 percent of undergraduate students enrolled in 1997. Students over twenty-five are more likely to be women, to enroll part-time, and to attend two-year institutions (Chronicle of Higher Education Almanac, 1999). The proportion of students over the age of forty has increased substantially in the last thirty years. In 1970, students forty years of age or older constituted 5.5 percent of total enrollments. Between 1970 and 1993 that number increased by 235 percent to 1.6 million, making such students the fastest-growing age group (*Chronicle of Higher Education*, 1996).

Residence

Given that more students are older, studying part-time, and enrolling in two-year institutions, it is not surprising that more of them are commuting and living off-campus. Hodgkinson (1985) reported that only about one in six students in postsecondary education is studying full time, is eighteen to twenty-two years old, and lives in a residence hall. Yet our popular stereotypes reflect the opposite. In fact, traditional-age students studying full-time and living on campus are a distinct minority among today's students.

Students with Disabilities

Students with disabilities had little access to higher education until the passage of the 1973 Rehabilitation Act. Section 504 of that act mandated equal opportunity for qualified handicapped people in the educational programs of institutions receiving federal assistance. Since then, enrollments of students with disabilities (impairments of mobility, vision, hearing, speech, learning, or others) have steadily risen, to the point where it is estimated that 9.0 percent of all students in 1994 had some disability (Henderson, 1995).

Sexual Orientation

Today's students are more open about their sexual orientations. According to some estimates, as many as 10 percent of today's students are gay, lesbian, bisexual, or transsexual, although most of them choose to remain "in the closet." Those who are open about their different sexual orientation frequently experience violence and discrimination, and those who are closeted live in fear of their sexual orientation being disclosed (Evans and Levine, 1990).

International Students

International student participation in U.S. higher education rose 48.6 percent from 1984 to 1995. The countries sending the most international students to the United States are, with one exception (Canada), exclusively Asian, including Japan, China, Korea, Taiwan, Malaysia, Thailand, Indonesia, and Hong Kong (Chronicle of Higher Education Almanac, 1998).

International students face various difficulties because of cultural differences. Among these differences are the emphasis on discussion in the classroom, the challenge of completing a heavy workload, departmental preferences for applied research, and the informality of the teacher-student relationship (Hu, 1997). In addition to these differences, international students also encounter difficulties resulting from prejudice, stereotyping, frustration, isolation, and low self-esteem. Furthermore, many international students are not accustomed to planning their own courses of study and are not familiar with the practice of academic advising (Do, 1996).

All this evidence suggests that Joe College has passed on or away and been replaced by a population of students that is so demographically diverse that a proper stereotype to replace dear old departed Joe is very difficult. But demographics tell only part of the changing student story. Students have also changed in other ways.

Changing Characteristics of Today's Students

Above and beyond these dramatic demographic shifts, other significant changes in college enrollments are occurring. They include changes in students' attitudes and values, their family dynamics, their physical and psychological health, their academic preparation, and their sources of financing their education.

Changing Attitudes and Values

Since 1966, the Cooperative Institutional Research Program at the University of California, Los Angeles, has tracked the attitudes, values, and aspirations of traditional-age high school students entering college. Compared to students of the mid-1960s, students of today are politically more conservative; less interested in developing a meaningful philosophy of life; more interested in making money; more concerned about getting a job after college; more interested in the fields of business, computer science, and engineering; and less interested in the humanities, fine arts, and the social sciences. Conversely, there has been little change in the percentage of entering students (about three in five) who list "obtain a general education" as a very important reason for deciding to go to college (Astin, Parrott, Korn, and Sax, 1997).

Depending on their age, today's students have been shaped by such events as the Great Depression, World War II, the Korean War, the civil rights movement, the Kennedy and King assassinations, the Vietnam War, the Reagan years, the collapse of the Soviet Union, the fall of the Berlin Wall, various economic booms and recessions (although traditional-age students may remember only the current run of expanding economic prosperity), the Challenger explosion, the Gulf War, the Clinton years, the Republican revolution, and many other important events.

Changing Family Dynamics

The American family is undergoing a transformation that is already having a significant impact on today's students. For example, the divorce rate increased rapidly through the 1960s and 1970s. The rate of divorce in 1985 was 5.0 per 1,000 people compared with 2.2 divorces per 1,000 people in 1960 (Friedberg, 1998). According to the Stepfamily Association of America (1998), 35 percent of all children born in the 1980s will experience life in a single-parent family for about five years before their eighteenth birthday. Additionally, students who themselves are divorced or single parents make up a significant part of our adult learner population.

But changing family stability is only part of the picture. Families characterized by physical violence, sexual abuse, alcohol and drug abuse, and other problems are on the rise (Gannon, 1989). Consequently, today we are seeing more students who are affected by family instability and dysfunction. Henton and others (1990) found that students who lack family support have a more difficult time adjusting to college. Likewise, many students from dysfunctional families have relationship problems and low self-esteem as well as higher suicide-attempt rates, sexual dysfunction, social alienation, physical ailments, and psychological trauma (Hoffman and Weiss, 1987).

Changes in Mental and Physical Health

Thirty years ago, students seeking help from college counseling centers presented problems clearly related to their college experiences, such as roommate problems, career indecision, academic difficulty, or relationship problems—in other words, "normal" students with "normal" problems. Today, students with problems present a very different picture. Witchel (1991) noted a substantial increase in psychological disturbance among today's college students. Counseling center directors report that waiting lists for treatment in college counseling centers are at an all-time high—very much a sign of the times. There is an increase in the number of students suffering from serious emotional distress, including self-destructive behavior, violence against others, anxiety, depression, and eating disorders, as well as victims of date and acquaintance rape, courtship violence, family or spousal abuse, and family drug and alcohol abuse (International Association of Counseling Services, 1998). Many of these conditions result not from students' collegiate experience but from their lives prior to or outside the collegiate environment.

Physical health problems are also on the increase and often closely linked to mental health problems. For example, eating disorders result from psychological problems, but they can very quickly become serious physical problems. Drug and alcohol abuse can also create significant physical as well as psychological problems, as can various kinds of violence, such as date rape. Further, the age diversity of today's students means that health issues reflect the spectrum of ailments rather than only those associated with late adolescence.

An even more alarming trend is the increase in sexually transmitted disease among students, the most serious of which is AIDS. The HIV-positive rate among today's college students is approximately 2.4 per thousand, compared to 1.0 per thousand in 1983 (E. Jurs, personal communication, Nov. 6, 1997). Much of this increase is attributable to the spread of the disease to heterosexuals, particularly women. Among younger age groups, the proportion of women infected with the HIV virus is approaching that of men (*Chronicle of Higher Education,* 1992).

Changing Academic Preparation

Perhaps no trend is more disturbing to faculty in higher education, and certainly to academic advisors, than the lack of academic preparation of today's students. A thirty-year decline in the Scholastic Aptitude Test scores between 1957 and 1987 has been well documented (Forrest, 1987), although in recent years this trend appears to have leveled off (Chronicle of Higher Education Almanac, 1999), and there are great discrepancies in scores by gender, race, and ethnicity, with men scoring higher than women, and majority students generally scoring higher than minorities, with the exception of Asians.

Perhaps even more important for academic advisors, more of today's students require remediation in basic reading, writing, and computational skills. According to a recent national report, approximately 29 percent of first-year college students enrolled in remedial reading, writing, or math in 1995, about the same percentage that enrolled in 1989. Of the students in remedial classes, 46 percent were twenty-two years of age or older, and 25 percent were over the age of thirty (Chronicle of Higher Education, 1998).

Changing Sources of Financing an Education

Before 1955, virtually all students paid for their education with their own or their parents' resources, or with limited academic scholarship aid. (A major exception was veterans who received GI Bill benefits after World War II and the Korean War.) In 1989, 56.4 percent of all undergraduates received some form of financial aid, including 70.4 percent of students enrolled in private institutions. Today, only about 20 percent of undergraduates between the ages of eighteen and twenty-two are pursuing a parent and student–financed education (National On-Campus Report, 1992).

Recent trends continue to put more financial pressure on students and their families. For example, according to the Citizens for Responsible Educational Reform (1998), since the 1980s college tuition has increased annually at the rate of two to three times the rate of inflation. Between 1981 and 1995, tuition at four-year public colleges and universities increased 234 percent, while during the same period median household income rose 82 percent and the consumer price index rose only 74 percent. Further, the typical bill for tuition, fees, room, board, books, and incidentals at public institutions is $10,069, a whopping 23 percent of the average American family's household income ("Can You Pay . . . ," 1998). At one Ivy League institution, tuition in 1976 was $3,790. Two decades later that same tuition bill was $21,130, nearly a sixfold increase (Larson, 1997). To be sure, by 1997 the average increase had dropped to a more manageable 5 percent, and a few brave institutions actually lowered tuition, but the damage has been done ("Can You Pay . . . ," 1998).

However, as costs have increased, so have the strategies that students and families use for dealing with them. These include government-sponsored incentives (such as education IRAs) to encourage families to start saving early for college, institution-based programs (such as prepaid tuition plans that lock in tuition rates at current levels), and federal and state loan programs and other financial aid (Upcraft, 1999). According to the College Board, in 1996–97 a total of 55.7 billion dollars were spent on student aid, of which approximately 54 percent came from federal loans, 19 percent from institutional grants, and 15 percent from federal or state grants (Cabrera, 1998). Today's students must cobble together a financial aid package that is complex, difficult to access, and more dependent on loans than ever before.

In addition to all these issues, more and more students must work to contribute to their college education. It is estimated that eight out of ten students work while studying for their undergraduate degrees. Two-thirds of working undergraduates must be employed in order to finance their education. Most of these students are attending classes full-time, and most are under twenty-four years of age and financially dependent on their families (Chronicle of Higher Education, 1998). The problem, of course, is that when students work too much, they are much more likely to drop out, and much less likely to earn good grades (Pascarella and Terenzini, 1991).

So today's students are quite different from Joe College. Meet "Josey College," a student far more typical of today's students than good old Joe. With a somewhat mediocre high school academic record, Josey College enrolled at the local state university because she had heard that college graduates get better-paying jobs. She lived at home, and financed her education with a part-time job, student loans, and a little help from her family. After she completed a developmental English course, she endured what she considered to be "boring" general education courses. At first she majored in computer science because she had heard there would be a good-paying job waiting for her when she graduated. During her second year, Josey stopped out for a semester because she ran out of money, was struggling academically, and was stressed out because of her parents' divorce. After getting herself together and saving money from a job, she returned a year later as an elementary education major (which she loved), and graduated five years after she had initially enrolled, approximately $15,000 in debt from student loans.

Implications for Academic Advising

Those of us who have been advising students for more than twenty-five years have seen a remarkable change in the role of the academic advisor. We more experienced advisors can remember when advising was a relatively simple process of helping students schedule classes, plan their courses, and choose their majors, and once in a while referring them to appropriate services on campus if they had personal or academic difficulties. But much has changed. Nowadays advisors face an almost impossible task. Clearly, in light of the changing student demographics and characteristics described earlier, academic advising is now a multirole job of part course scheduler, part remedial expert, part personal counselor, part career counselor, part financial aid resource, and part just about everything else students need when they cross our doorsteps. So our roles are changing as our students change.

Following are several implications for academic advising, given the enormously increased diversity of today's students:

1. *Know your students.* This seems like the proverbial no-brainer, but today's students are not like yesterday's students, nor will they be like tomorrow's students. Furthermore, even those advisors who keep up on the changing national picture may be limited if they do not know what students at their institution look like. National profiles may not resemble local profiles; institutions must keep advisors informed about enrollment trends, demographic shifts, and changing student characteristics. For example, we recommend that institutions publish annual profiles of their students, comparing currently enrolled students with previous generations of students. Profiles of entering classes are also very helpful. These should include as many of the demographics and characteristics discussed in this chapter as possible. It is especially important to profile students' academic skills and deficiencies, given the apparent decline in academic preparedness.

2. *Know your institution's resources and how to access them.* Even professional advisors cannot be all things to all students, and certainly faculty are limited in their ability to deal with many of the nonacademic problems faced by today's students. But both professional and faculty advisors must be skillful diagnosticians who can refer students to appropriate campus resources. This assumes, however, that academic advisors know about these services and can make successful referrals. Effective referrals are not merely handing the student the telephone number of a particular service and hoping for the best. Academic advisors today need to know these services well, including key personnel, and they need to be willing to persuade the student that a particular service will in fact help them.

3. *Advocate for campus resources that may be needed.* Knowing your institution's resources and how to access them assumes that your institution has appropriate resources to help students succeed. Unfortunately, sometimes institutional resources do not keep up with changing student profiles. For example, adult students may be turned off by orientation programs that assume that all new students are just out of high school and living on campus. They need orientation programs that cover issues such as transportation, child care, studying part-time, and managing job, family, and college responsibilities.

4. *Reconsider academic advising training programs in light of today's changing students.* How often do we hear an academic advisor lament that he or she just does not understand today's students. At worst, some believe that today's students are academic slackers who do not even believe that class attendance is important, let alone complete class assignments and pay attention in class. For some academic advisors who are white, advising Asians, African Americans, or any other racial or ethnic group is perceived as more complex and difficult than advising white students. As students diversify, their needs diversify, so training programs must help all academic advisors, regardless of their race or ethnicity, gender, or other characteristics, develop the attitudes and skills necessary to cope successfully with this diversity. As appropriate campus resources emerge in response to increased student diversity, training programs must help faculty keep up on the latest changes in services and programs.

5. *Develop collaborative relationships between teaching faculty and academic advisors.* In those instances where academic advising is done partly or entirely by professional academic advisors, establishing collaborative relationships between academic advisors and teaching faculty becomes critical. For example, advisors can provide teaching faculty with valuable information about today's students, while teaching faculty can help advisors better understand the unique classroom challenges they present. When teaching faculty and advisors share information and advice about students, everyone benefits, especially students.

6. *Reconsider academic advising policies and practices.* Some of our academic advising policies and practices are based on Joe College rather than Josey College assumptions about students. For example, adult students studying part-time may present challenges to some of our advising practices, such as offering services only between 8 A.M. and 5 P.M. Monday through Friday. Students who stop in and stop out with some frequency may make traditional graduation requirements dif-

ficult if not impossible to interpret. Answer the following basic questions: Do our advising policies and practices help our increasingly diverse student body, or do they get in the way? If so, how, and what must we do to correct this situation?

7. *Be alert for personal problems that may be inhibiting learning.* Students with personal problems are more likely to earn lower grades and drop out than more healthy students (Pascarella and Terenzini, 1991). There are times when students may turn to academic advisors for help with personal problems. Thirty years ago we were inclined to counsel students out of college until they resolved their personal problems. Today, most institutions assume some responsibility for helping troubled students while they are enrolled. We are not suggesting that academic advisors become psychotherapists and social workers, but we are suggesting that being alert to personal problems that may be getting in the way of students' academic success is an essential part of being an effective advisor for today's students. Referring them to appropriate on-campus or off-campus resources is also essential.

There are probably many more implications of increased student diversity for academic advising; we have presented what we believe to be a few of the most important ones. Again, local conditions will in large part dictate appropriate responses, but this assumes that institutions know their students and respond accordingly. We can only hope that this is the case, because failure to respond to the changing demographics and characteristics of our students will limit their ability to achieve their educational goals, and it will diminish the quality of education offered by our many and diverse institutions.

References

Astin, A. W., Parrott, S. A., Korn, W. S., and Sax, L. J. *The American Freshman: Thirty-Year Trends.* Los Angeles: Higher Education Research Institute, University of California, 1997.

Berkeley Office of Student Research.
[http://www.uga.berkeley.edu/ouars/level_2/camp_over.html]. 1998.

Cabrera, A. F. "Estimated Student Aid by Source, 1996–97." Unpublished paper, Pennsylvania State University, 1998.

"Can You Pay His Way Through College? *Time,* Aug. 17, 1998.

Chronicle of Higher Education, Dec. 12, 1992, p. A2.

Chronicle of Higher Education, Oct. 25, 1996, p. A44.

Chronicle of Higher Education, May 1, 1998, p. A72.

Chronicle of Higher Education Almanac. Aug. 28, 1998.

Chronicle of Higher Education Almanac, Aug. 17, 1999.

Citizens for Responsible Educational Reform. Washington, D.C.: National Commission on the Cost of Higher Education, 1998.

Do, V. T. "Counseling Culturally Different Students in the Community College." *Community College Journal of Research and Practice,* 1996, *20,* 9–21.

Evans, N., and Levine, H. "Perspectives on Sexual Orientation." In L. V. Moore (ed.),

Evolving Theoretical Perspectives on Students. New Directions for Student Services, no. 51. San Francisco: Jossey-Bass, 1990.

Forrest, A. "Managing the Flow of Students Through Higher Education." *National Forum: Phi Kappa Phi Journal,* 1987, *68,* 39–42.

Friedberg, L. *Did Unilateral Divorce Raise Divorce Rates? Evidence from Panel Study.* Cambridge, Mass.: National Bureau of Economic Research, 1998.

Gannon, J. R. *Soul Survivors: A New Beginning for Adults Abused as Children.* Englewood Cliffs, N.J.: Prentice Hall, 1989.

Henderson, C. *College Freshman with Disabilities: A Triennial Statistical Profile.* Research Report, Health Resource Center. Washington, D.C.: American Council on Education, 1995.

Henton, J., Hayes, L., Lamke, L., and Murphy, C. "Crisis Reaction of College Freshmen as a Function of Family Support Systems." *Personnel and Guidance Journal,* 1990, *58,* 508–510.

Hodgkinson, H. L. *All One System: Demographics of Education, Kindergarten Through Graduate School.* Washington, D.C.: Institute of Educational Leadership, 1985.

Hoffman, J., and Weiss, B. "Family Problems and Presenting Problems in College Students. *Journal of Counseling Psychology,* 1987, *2,* 157–163.

Hu, H. "Crossing the River by Touching the Stones: The Experiences of First-Year Asian Graduate Students at a Midwestern University." Paper presented at the American Educational Research Association Conference, Chicago, March 1997.

International Association of Counseling Services. *Annual Survey of Counseling Center Directors.* Pittsburgh, Pa.: International Association of Counseling Services, 1998.

Justiz, M., and Rendon, L. "Hispanic Students." In M. L. Upcraft and J. N. Gardner (eds.), *The Freshman Year Experience: Helping Students Survive and Succeed in Higher Education.* San Francisco: Jossey-Bass, 1989.

Larson, E. "Why Colleges Cost Too Much." *Time,* March 17, 1997.

National Center for Education Statistics. *Stopouts or Stayouts? Undergraduates Who Leave College in Their First Year.* Washington, D.C.: U.S. Department of Education, Office of Educational Research and Improvement, 1998.

National On-Campus Report, 1992, *20*(18), 5.

Pascarella, E. T., and Terenzini, P. T. *How College Affects Students: Findings and Insights from Twenty Years of Research.* San Francisco: Jossey-Bass, 1991.

Schoch, R. "As Cal Enters the 80s, There'll Be Some Changes Made." *California Monthly,* 1980, *90*(3), 1–3.

Stepfamily Association of America. [http://stepfam. org]. 1998.

Upcraft, M. L. "Affordability: Responding to the Rising Cost of Higher Education." In C. S. Johnson and H. E. Cheatham (eds.), *Higher Education Trends for the Next Century.* Washington, D.C.: American College Personnel Association, 1999.

Wilds, D. J., and Wilson, R. *Minorities in Higher Education 1997–98, Sixteenth Annual Status Report.* Washington, D.C.: American Council on Education, 1998.

Witchel, R. I. "The Impact of Dysfunctional Families on College Students' Development." In R. I. Witchel (ed.), *Dealing with Students from Dysfunction Families.* New Directions for Student Services, no. 54. San Francisco: Jossey-Bass, 1991.

Chapter Seven

Advising Students at Different Educational Levels

Gary L. Kramer

The past two decades have witnessed a dramatic shift toward student development in academic advising (Pascarella and Terrenzini, 1991; Astin, 1993; Tinto, 1993; Chickering and Reisser, 1993). In this context, advising is effective when based on the premise of student growth and success—a type of advising called *developmental academic advising.* Students are developmentally advised when advisors focus on growth that instills the following in students:

- Awareness of the relationship between education and life
- The ability to set realistic academic and career goals as well as a program to achieve them
- Awareness of life extending beyond the college years

A challenge that all academic institutions face is the diverse makeup of the student body. Students present a wide range of needs and skills, which calls for sensitive, knowledgeable people in the institution to help them understand institutional identity and fit, an awareness that is requisite to student academic success. Helping students take responsibility for their education depends partly on how well institutions adjust their goals to the goals that students set for themselves (Stark, 1989).

The questions we raise, the perceptions we share, the resources we suggest, the short-term decisions and long-range plans we help students think through—all should increase students' capacity to take charge (Chickering, 1994). Students who reported the greatest cognitive development were also most likely to perceive faculty (advisors) as being concerned with teaching and student devel-

Prescriptive Learning	*Developmental Teaching*
• Advisor has primary responsibility	• Advisor and student share responsibility
• Focus is on limitations	• Focus is on potentialities
• Effort is problem oriented	• Effort is growth oriented
• Relationship is based on status	• Relationship is based on trust and respect
• Relationship is based on authority and the giving of advice	• Relationship is based on equal and shared problem solving
• Evaluation is done by advisor	• Evaluation is a shared process

Exhibit 7.1. Advising as Teaching.

opment, and to report a close, influential relationship with at least one faculty member (Chickering and Reisser, 1993). Burns Crookston (1972) set the standard for developmental advising by advocating advising as a form of teaching. His description separated the tenets of *prescriptive learning* from *developmental teaching,* as shown in Exhibit 7.1.

As Frost (1995) points out, as developmentally advised students move through an academic institution, they increase their responsibility for educational planning and their reliance on the advisor decreases. For example, promoting concepts of shared responsibility, as Frost suggests, for the student, the advisor, and the institution can lead to students learning rather than merely supplying answers to specific questions; student involvement in their own academic and career futures; and collaborative planning that engages and motivates students to plan for success through strategic and quality efforts. A quality shared-advising effort leads to students' persistence to graduation, motivation to succeed in college, involvement in the institution, interaction with faculty, satisfaction with college, academic and career connection, personal and academic success, academic achievement, and cognitive development.

Evolving from *in loco parentis* to theoretical to practical student development and involvement in college, the approach to understanding today's college student must include a focus on students' diversity of background and situational circumstances, including gender, race and ethnicity, socioeconomic class, age, disabilities, degree status, part-time or full-time status, and transferring from other colleges (El-Khawas, 1996; Moore and Upcraft, 1990). For example, there has been a sharp increase in the number of students planning or seeking a master's or doctoral degree who thus require an increased focus on graduate student advising. Students' financial circumstances may play a significant role in their academic development. In particular, increasing economic pressures from a higher cost of living and increased tuition costs bear down on students; thus there is a swelling in the ranks of part-time study. Students who attend school part-time change the demographics of a college campus because a large part of the student body does not feel a part of the university.

Given the unique circumstances that students bring to the campus, academic advising today must be student centered and responsive to students' needs, support student growth and development, and involve continuous contact between the advisor and the student. For example, advisors, counselors, and faculty are acutely aware of older students returning to college to complete an undergraduate degree or seek a graduate degree. Fortunately, most older students have resolved to complete their education because they have experienced a need for a college degree, but they face a different set of challenges than younger students. Most older students are in school at great personal cost, and at great cost to their families (Krager, Wrenn, and Hirt, 1990). In the past decade, two main types of older students emerged: women reentering college after raising a family, and adults who realize the growing need for an education in all areas of life. Older students potentially face barriers often categorized as institutional (such as financial aid and admissions difficulties), situational (such as child-care problems and job pressures), or dispositional (such as lack of self-confidence and fear of change) (Harris and Brooks, 1998). As discussed in Chapter 10, older students have distinctive concerns that require a form of academic advising that is geared to their unique needs.

It is therefore important that advisors receive training not only in student race, gender, and age differences, but also in the developmental levels that students bring to the campus (Barr and Brown, 1990). Evidence suggests that campus advisement programs must make substantial improvement in training, delivery of services, and program evaluation (Habley and Morales, 1998). Compounding these matters is the behaviors and attitudes that students bring to the advising situation. For example, lack of student involvement in college can be problematic for advisors. Involvement in extracurricular clubs, organizations, athletics, intramurals, student government, and other campus activities is an important aspect of the student development process (Astin, 1985, 1993). It occurs only with student consent; that is, if students don't want to participate, they won't. Similarly, students often do not follow through with their intentions to attend developmental activities. Hess and Winston (1995) found that it is the students most in need of help who often do not use the resources or activities the college community provides. Conversely, students with strength in a particular area do attend activities in that area. Unfortunately, the Hess and Winston study concludes that college activities do not attract the students who need social interaction the most. However, students who have a high degree of self-regulation and are goal oriented generally succeed in college (VanZile-Tamsen and Livingston, 1999). Motivation and a self-regulated strategy, including self-efficacy and a learning-goal orientation, are important factors for both high and low achievers.

Long, Sowa, and Niles (1995) report similar findings in their study on career decisions among college seniors. They suggest that motivation is a key variable that distinguishes students who have a firm career choice from those who do not. Seniors who had made a career choice had a greater sense of purpose and an overall higher level of development than those who had not made such a choice, as measured by the Student Developmental Task and Life Style Inventory. Higher levels of development mean advanced social skills or the ability to deal with stress and academic difficulty. The authors conclude that students who are encouraged to make a career decision early in college find a greater sense of purpose in attending and succeeding in college. Advisors must not only address unique student backgrounds and developmental needs but they must do so equipped with unique preparation and training as collaborators, negotiators, and orchestrators of the student experience.

Another factor or student characteristic that advisors are very much aware of is the phenomenon of major change. Student major change is inevitable regardless of academic class or status. Although most students declare an academic emphasis before they enter college, the majority will change their course of study at least once (Kramer, Higley, and Olsen, 1994). One reason for the high rate of change is that most students lack information about and experiences in an academic discipline before they choose it. Even seniors lack confidence in their degree choice, particularly its career applications. It is important to consider why these changes are made and what their implications are for developmental advising.

When they enter college, most students lack planning and decision-making skills. Thus they often make wholesale major changes in the first year. Yet one-half of these students graduate with a major that matches their choice on the questionnaire given during the administration of the American College Test or their application major (Kramer, Higley, and Olsen, 1994; Kramer, Taylor, Chynoweth, and Jensen, 1987). Advisors' intervention techniques in these cases necessarily differ from those for juniors, seniors, and graduate students. (The Taxonomy of Student Services in Exhibit 7.2 suggests different approaches.) Stark (1989) points out the importance of institutions not only helping students identify their academic goals but also matching students' educational goals with those of the academic institution.

The open-major or undecided student presents another opportunity for advisor preparation and delivery of unique advising services. Lewallen's (1993) research, for example, suggests that undecided students do not necessarily fit advisors' preconceived notions about academic progress and retention in the institution. Lewallen sheds a different perspective on open-major students, who in the past have been labeled as attrition prone or at risk not to persist in their college education. His study suggests that not having decided on a major or career choice does not have an impact on academic persistence, just as the choice of a major is not synonymous with a commitment to educational goals.

General Academic and Career Advising Needs

I have discussed some issues in developmental advisement. Unfortunately, in the contemporary context of academic advising, there is little description of how to gauge student development, especially as students prepare for a successful

Themes by Academic Level	Needs or Educational Tasks	Advising and Career Services
Preentry		
Acquire accurate expectations	1. Prepare for entry into an academic discipline.	Provide new students with information on major courses of study and descriptions. Establish communications with new students and give assistance in decoding an academic discipline. Involve faculty from academic departments with new students. Assist in clarifying students' academic and career goals.
Prepare	2. Become familiar with college requirements, course contents, and course terminology (that is, credit hours, section, building abbreviations).	Ensure that new students receive the general catalog and relevant advisement information via Web (Internet, intranet) access. Provide walk-in, Web, or telephone assistance. Involve faculty in personalizing and clarifying academic program requirements and expectations.
	3. Complete initial registration.	Ensure that new students have received a class schedule and registration instruction, and supply a recommended first-year schedule. Conduct registration assistance via the Web or on campus.
	4. Learn to adjust class schedule before semester begins.	Provide add/drop instructions with course confirmation; where possible, develop specific instructions, especially for new students.
	5. Learn about financial aid and scholarship options and policies.	Provide walk-in, personalized faculty, or staff assistance, as well as Web or telephone access to key financial aid and scholarship planning information. Connect students with appropriate personnel for specialized information on grants, loans, and scholarships.

Exhibit 7.2. Student Services Taxonomy by Unique Academic Status.

Themes by Academic Level	Needs or Educational Tasks	Advising and Career Services
Freshman Year		
Become familiar with academic life	1. Become familiar with university resources.	Provide information on academic advisement programs and university resources. Conduct new-student orientation and introduce students to campus resources. Develop and produce a handbook (available through Internet) of related materials.
Set goals	2. Become acquainted with the college's mission, academic leaders (faculty, department chairs, deans) in major programs or interests.	Involve faculty in new-student orientation. Assign faculty advisors to meet with new students during orientation. Plan faculty-student orientation seminars.
		Help students understand their goals in relationship to the aims of the college.
		Explore opportunities for students to obtain personal meaning of the college's mission statement.
	3. Learn to adjust class schedule after semester has begun.	During orientation, acquaint freshmen with advisement and registration offices, general catalogue, and accessibility of campus intranet/Internet. Provide class-adjustment assistance.
Make commitments	4. Understand university and major requirements: • General education • Credit hours • Residence • Major courses • Prerequisites for admission to college or major	Automate academic requirements and provide student access via the Web. Provide walk-in academic advising services, seminars during new-student orientation, and faculty advisors.
		Maintain academic records for students, and provide individual access either through campus intranet or the Internet.

Exhibit 7.2. Continued.

Themes by Academic Level	*Needs or Educational Tasks*	*Advising and Career Services*
Use resources	5. Understand university policies and academic options, for example: • Academic warning and probation • Changing majors • Challenging classes • Advanced placement credit • Transfer credit • Independent study credit • Study abroad • Honors courses	Maintain and provide student access to up-to-date academic information. Disseminate it to students during orientation and through brochures, the Web, walk-in advising, and unique mailings. Initiate and promote faculty contact early in the first year.
Setting expectations and responsibilities	6. Develop accurate expectations of time and effort required to make successful academic progress, and timely graduation: • Time management • Study skills and habits • Graduation plan	Develop related seminars during the year. Regularly monitor student academic progress and make appropriate referrals. Faculty advisors help students develop and submit a graduation plan.

Exhibit 7.2. Continued.

Themes by Academic Level	Needs or Educational Tasks	Advising and Career Services
	7. Evaluate whether major and career choices match interests and abilities: • Identify interests • Assess abilities • Explore major/career options	Help students crystallize choice of major; work closely with career counselors to assess students' interests and abilities, that is, refer for appropriate career counseling. Develop related seminars and refer students appropriately. Connect career plans with academic plan (use Web links where possible).
	8. Assume responsibility for own educational progress.	Use college resources to provide accurate academic, financial, and career planning; that is, focus on enhancing student success in college.
	9. Learn how to associate with professors in and out of class.	Integrate faculty into advising program. Encourage and establish regular advising with faculty and departmental contacts.
Sophomore Year		
Crystallize academic plans	1. Determine academic path and expectations.	Establish contact with each sophomore student. Explore with students their academic direction. Electronically track and monitor student academic progress. Involve faculty advisor and department.
Development through student experience	2. Develop accurate expectations for selected major.	Develop, produce, and disseminate descriptive and interactive Web-based academic planning assistance. Provide students with a choice between technology and individualized service by promoting individual faculty assistance, college- and department-sponsored lectures and seminars, and so on.

Exhibit 7.2. Continued.

Themes by Academic Level	*Needs or Educational Tasks*	*Advising and Career Services*
Integrate with campus life	3. Explore career opportunities within major.	Refer students to career information counselors and relevant Web sites. Encourage contact with faculty advisors. Conduct college-sponsored lectures and seminars and create preprofessional clubs. Promote student-initiated discussions with university and community professionals. Refer students to related academic internships and other service-learning experiential opportunities. Involve students.
Reflection	4. Make well-defined education plans for up-to-date information on major and university requirements.	Provide academic information that sequentially details requirements and that allows students to interact with the data via a Web-based system, that is, individualized academic planning, as well as faculty advisors.
	5. Determine possible eligibility for financial assistance and/or scholarships.	Refer students to financial aid/scholarship office and promote financial-aid awareness and planning through a Web-based system or intranet, brochures, posters, and bulletin boards. Connect financial aid to an academic path to graduation, that is, a four-year plan.
Junior Year		
Integrate academic plans with career plans	1. Become acquainted with two or three faculty members in major field for academic or career planning and counseling and for future letters of recommendation.	Encourage faculty to post office hours and provide advisement. Monitor program progress. Faculty-student interaction must be fostered, particularly at this academic level.

Exhibit 7.2. Continued.

Themes by Academic Level	*Needs or Educational Tasks*	*Advising and Career Services*
Clarification	2. Clarify career goals and test career choice.	Connect students with career counselors to review career literature related to major, such as related Web links. Develop opportunity for internships, college-sponsored seminars with guest lectures, research projects, preprofessional clubs, co-op or academic internship experiences.
	3. Achieve intellectual competence in chosen field and confidence in professional ability.	Suggest group study, tutoring, lab experiences, major classes and seminars, internships, fieldwork, and research projects with faculty.
	4. If contemplating graduate school, consider institution-specific graduate program requirements and scholarships.	Explore with students or make available related institutional Web sites. Refer to graduate school catalogs. Provide information on graduate aid available and sources for scholarship applications.
	5. Determine academic standing.	Maintain and encourage students to monitor their academic progress. Suggest applying for graduation at the end of the student's junior year. Coordinate with graduation evaluation office to evaluate general education, major, and university requirements. Identify deficiencies. Clear academic status with faculty advisor.
Senior Year		
Preparing for transition to work or graduate school	1. Prepare for employment opportunities: • Prepare resume • Develop interviewing skills	Provide self-help guides on resume preparation and interviewing skills. Advisors should encourage students to obtain letters of recommendation from faculty, and provide other contacts. Promote career-planning seminars for advisees to attend.

Exhibit 7.2. Continued.

Themes by Academic Level	Needs or Educational Tasks	Advising and Career Services
Clarification	• Work with career placement center for interviews, contacts, etc. • Identify and pursue potential career opportunities.	
Transitional	2. Prepare for graduate/professional opportunities: • Prepare for and take entrance exams (GMAT, GRE, LSAT, MCAT) • Assess different schools and programs to match abilities, financial commitment, and geographical preference. • Understand and complete application procedures. • Select graduate school to attend from offers received.	Review programs and guidebooks on graduate programs. Refer to faculty advisors to suggest schools, write letters of recommendation, and provide counsel and contacts. Submit application(s) for entrance exams.
	3. Fulfill major, general, and university requirements for graduation.	Conduct a degree-audit interview with each student. Review status of academic plan.

Exhibit 7.2. Continued.

Themes by Academic Level	Needs or Educational Tasks	Advising and Career Services
	4. Meet graduation deadlines.	Advise students of graduation status. Notify by use of campus e-mail system, etc.
	5. Prepare for commencement.	Organize information for students to order cap and gown. Ensure that students are appropriately recognized during commencement with diploma or other honors.
Graduate Years		
Stage development*	1. Understand the structure of the field.	Establish a graduate advising program that coordinates central graduate school advisors with faculty advisors.
	2. Become acquainted with the language approach. Learn expectations and demands.	Develop a graduate advisor training program that focuses on the process of academic and social integration of new graduate students.
	3. Become acquainted with people, a group of peers, faculty sponsor.	Designate graduate faculty and graduate student peers to assist new students as socialization agents.
	4. Find a faculty sponsor	Assign faculty advisor; match students with compatible faculty members to help focus their interests.
	5. Obtain sufficient financial assistance	Identify faculty who can play a key role in helping students find institutional support and effective use of campus resources.
	6. Choose a committee.	Help students compose a committee of compatible individuals who have students' interests and success as a priority.

Exhibit 7.2. Continued.

* From Baird (1995).

Themes by Academic Level	Needs or Educational Tasks	Advising and Career Services
	7. Fulfill the dissertation or thesis requirement; that is, formulate the idea and method or approach.	Provide guidance through committees, peers, and faculty advisors. Mentor students by providing career advice as they embark on their professional careers, especially in the exploration of alternatives in the field. Review students' goals, interests, and priorities.

Exhibit 7.2. Continued.

transition from one academic year to the next. The literature does help identify key student academic needs, summarized in the Collaborative Undergraduate and Graduate Services Model (Figure 7.1). We do know, for example, that students who formulate plans of action and make commitments to educational goals move successfully through the stages of college life (Upcraft, and Kramer, 1995). As students set personal expectations according to the academic standards of the institution, they mature as they progress through the sophomore and junior years with increased aid from support services, including faculty-student interaction (see Figure 7.2). Students' integration into the academic institution is solidified as advisors become managers of the campus resources on behalf of students. Developmental advising in this context means that advisors enlist the aid of many campus services to satisfy and meet students' needs. Advising necessarily involves collaboration with all segments of the campus community. As the model in Figure 7.1 depicts, through choice and clarification seniors and graduate students are helped to crystallize academic and career plans.

Advising by Academic Class

One way to integrate advising and career services into the campus community is to consider students by academic class (Kramer, Taylor, Chynoweth, and Jensen, 1987). This approach focuses on the unique needs of freshmen, sophomores, juniors, seniors, and graduate students, each of whom faces different educational tasks. The following descriptions of each academic class and the taxonomic model are not inclusive; only the academic and career needs that distinctively represent each class are identified. The reader should already be aware of the diversity of students, the developmental differences between older and younger students, gender issues, race and ethnicity differences, and so on. Other chapters in this book address these concerns.

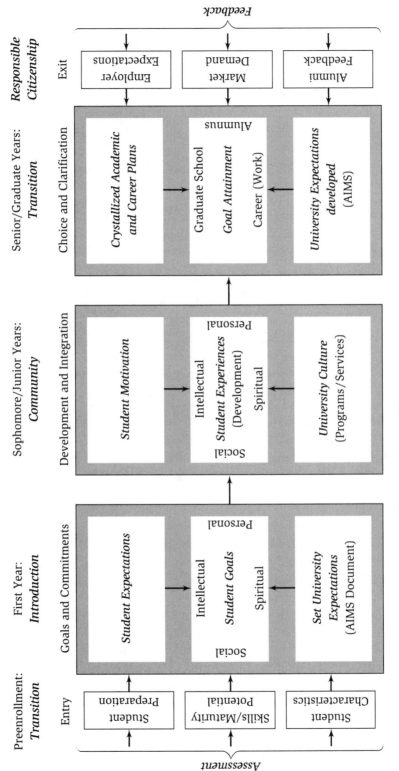

Figure 7.1. Collaborative Undergraduate and Graduate Services Model.

Source: Adapted from Kramer, 1996.

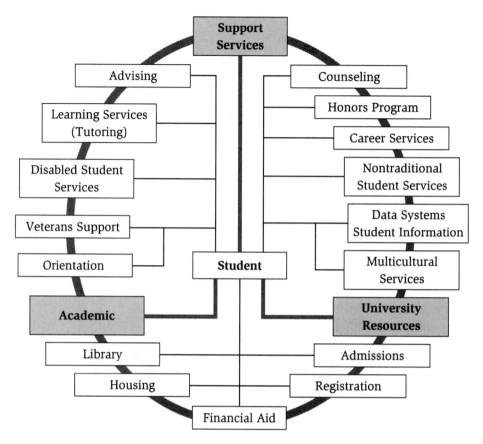

Figure 7.2. Campus Collaboration.

Source: Adapted from Kramer, 1996.

Freshman Year: Vulnerability

Freshmen students are vulnerable when it comes to good academic planning. In this regard, they are rather unsophisticated, unaware of the variety of resources available to them. Initially they must place a great deal of trust in their advisors, a trust that warrants quality programs and services. Freshmen expect the academic advising relationship to be characterized by both caring and competence: advisors are expected to be available, knowledgeable, and accurate (Gardner, 1995). The freshman year is especially important to the process of persistence: students are more prone to drop out of college during the first year and before the beginning of the second (Tinto, 1993). To prepare to advise freshmen, advisors must consider how and when the resources of the institution are marshaled to address the needs of the entering student and whether the advising goals are the same for both the student and the institution. Advisors must first know who is entering the system, then determine student expectations, aspirations, and needs before they even begin general advising, that is, registration. In other words, advisors need to see the educational system from the perspective of the student who moves through it.

The first year of college is at best transitional. Most freshmen enter college with pat, superficial, pseudo-plans. Freshmen are quite vulnerable to changes in their academic plans. Nearly half of all students who enter four-year colleges and universities never graduate from the institution they enter as freshmen, and close to 60 percent of students who drop out do so after their first year. Changes in academic major are also common among freshmen. Fifty-seven percent of freshmen change majors during their first semester (Kramer, Taylor, Chynoweth, and Jensen 1987; Kramer, Higley, and Olsen, 1994). Clearly the freshman year is a period of adjustment; it has been suggested that a half-year orientation course or seminar be established to focus on freshman needs and expectations and to facilitate career development and the use of campus resources.

Sophomore Year: Reflection

If there is a time when students need assistance but find little outreach, it is in their sophomore year. The second year of college presents some aspects of identity crisis better known as the *sophomore slump*. Compared to the freshman year, during the sophomore year students may feel less hopeful, less engaged, and less competent. It is a year of reflection on what they have achieved academically and on what they want to accomplish in the future (Kramer, Taylor, Chynoweth, and Jensen, 1987).

Easily detectable are several indicators of sophomore apathy: talk of changing majors or leaving school to work, questions regarding transfer to another school, and various problems in personal relationships. Some institutions have established sophomore programs that address these concerns.

Regardless of the causes of sophomore slump, personal attention from advisors may be an important factor in overcoming it. Advisors, aware of this critical period, should arrange appointments with sophomores to review their academic progress and integrate them into the academic community; to assess and, where appropriate, encourage and reinforce their abilities to succeed academically; and to assist them in crystallizing their academic paths. Effective discussions need to be advocated to ease the transition through the sophomore year.

Junior Year: Clarification

During the junior year, students are expected to stabilize their academic course of study, acquire the necessary background and study skills to perform maximally, pursue career information, and formalize relationships with faculty and significant others on campus. Clarifying and gaining confidence in both academic and career goals is an essential pursuit of the junior year. The third year of college has been aptly labeled a year of mastery and commitment (Kramer, Taylor, Chynoweth, and Jensen, 1987; Kramer, Higley, and Olsen, 1994).

Advisors should focus on providing a supportive environment in which students are stimulated to evaluate their own academic progress, recognize their academic accomplishments, and establish vital contacts with personnel in the institution. These contacts are important not only for clarifying goals but also for laying the groundwork essential to obtaining letters of reference.

Senior Year: Transition

Seniors have high expectations and are a captive audience (Gardner and Van der Veer, 1998). Because they are nearing the completion of their studies, they stand before transition into a graduate or work career. During the senior year, learning needs to be carried out both inside and outside the classroom. The future graduate must plan his or her career. Gardner and Van der Veer discuss several other senior-year issues, including capstone experience, leadership education, career planning, job search, and transition planning.

Schilling and Schilling (1998) add another dimension of the senior year assessment. Seniors are prone to ask, How do all these ideas fit together? What is important about what I've done? Where is this leading me? What are the implications of what I've studied for how I'll live my life? Thus the senior year is not only a transitional one but also a period of questioning and reflecting. Put another way, "The transitional status of the senior year supports reflection" (Schilling and Schilling, 1998, p. 262). Advisors would do well to engage seniors in the assessment process. Faculty, for example, during advising sessions, can greatly help seniors reflect on their views of their work at the institution. Moreover, engaging in assessment activities can provide seniors with materials not only for reflection but also for bridging the gap between the undergraduate years and the world that follows.

Students who are satisfied with their educational experience are those who succeed academically and are committed to a career choice as a result of proper direction, information, and understanding that began in their freshman year. Four years of undergraduate study should be capped by successful transition into the work world or graduate school. Advisors can help students in this important transition year by coordinating seminars on academic and career planning (such as resume writing, interviewing skills, and job search strategies) or by helping students apply to graduate or professional schools. It is also important that seniors know exactly how close they are to completing their academic requirements. Advisors should conduct an official audit of graduation-requirement deficiencies and prepare seniors for commencement.

Graduate Students: Professionalism

There is enormous diversity in graduate education today. Eighty percent of graduate students are enrolled in master's degree programs, and approximately two-thirds of master's students are enrolled part-time. About three-fifths of graduate students are women (O'Brien, 1992). Today's graduate students are likely to be older than their predecessors in previous years. Similarly, the number of minority students, international students, and students with disabilities in graduate schools is increasing (Issac, Pruitt-Logan, and Upcraft, 1995).

Research suggests three stages of a graduate career: the beginning, the middle, and the dissertation or thesis stage (Baird, 1995). Following are some of the issues that graduate students must work through:

- Understanding the structure of the field
- Becoming acquainted with the academic language and approaches
- Becoming acquainted with other graduate students, a group of peers in their discipline, and a faculty sponsor
- Obtaining financial assistance
- Identifying intellectual and professional interests
- Choosing a committee
- Fulfilling the dissertation or thesis requirement, that is, formulating the idea and method or approach

In short, graduate education is about the specialized knowledge, skills, attitudes, values, norms, and interests of the profession. These aspects suggest unique advising and guidance services, especially from faculty. This is particularly important, according to Baird (1995): "Because the different stages of the graduate career have different tasks and demands, the relations of students with faculty and other students also differ" (p. 26).

Exhibit 7.2, presented earlier, presupposes that the institution has clearly defined advising services, that these services are widely known throughout the campus community, and that a shared responsibility for advising exists. That is, university, advisor, and student responsibilities might be delineated as follows:

University Responsibilities

- Establish academic advisement and related policies, procedures, and resources.
- Publish timely and accurate information on program requirements.
- Connect academic and career counseling services.
- Emphasize and provide for timely student graduation.
- Assist advisors in professional development.
- Recognize and reward outstanding advisors.

Advisor Responsibilities

- Be familiar with program requirements.
- Make recommendations for registration and academic plan.
- Monitor student progress.
- Help students explore career options.

- Refer students to other campus resources.
- Look for potential in students.
- Motivate students to take responsibility for their own academic and career goals.
- Exhibit trust and confidence in students.

Advisee Responsibilities

- Prepare for and keep appointments.
- Establish and follow academic plans.
- Use university resources.
- Read the catalogue.
- Review academic progress.
- Attend and participate in class.
- Get involved in campus and community events.
- Take responsibility for and own decisions.

Conclusion

Advisors who recognize academic-class differences and successfully coordinate institutional resources to promote student development will be in a position to anticipate needs and discriminately offer students information and planning assistance. The taxonomy of advising and career services by academic class provided in Exhibit 7.2 has been devised to help advisors in this endeavor. The intent of the model is not to suggest a comprehensive offering of academic advising services, many of which may not be the function of the advising program. (Where student assistance is needed beyond the scope of academic advising, academic advising service personnel should refer students to an appropriate student service.) Rather, the purpose of the model is to suggest that students' academic needs differ and are generally associated with academic status. Most important, the taxonomy provides suggestions on what advisors can do to create a growth-producing environment for students.

References

Astin, A. W. *What Matters in College: Four Critical Years Revisited.* San Francisco: Jossey-Bass, 1993.

Astin, A. W. *Achieving Educational Excellence.* San Francisco: Jossey-Bass, 1985.

Baird, L. "Helping Graduate Students: A Graduate Advisor's View." In P. Isaac and A. Pruitt (eds.), *Student Services for the Changing Graduate Student.* New Directions for Student Services, no. 72. San Francisco: Jossey-Bass, 1995.

Barr, M., and Brown, R. D. "Student Development: Yesterday, Today, and Tomorrow." In L. V. Moore (ed.), *Evolving Theoretical Perspectives on Students.* New Directions for Student Services, no. 51. San Francisco: Jossey-Bass, 1990.

Chickering, A. W. "Empowering Lifelong Self-Development." *AAHE Bulletin,* 1994, *47*(4), 3–5.

Chickering, A. W., and Reisser, L. *Education and Identity.* (2nd ed.) San Francisco: Jossey-Bass, 1993.

Crookston, B. B. "A Developmental View of Academic Advising as Teaching." *Journal of College Student Personnel,* 1972, *13*, 12–17.

El-Khawas, E. "Student Diversity on Today's Campuses." In S. R. Komives and Associates, *Student Services: A Handbook for the Profession.* San Francisco: Jossey-Bass, 1996.

Frost, S. H. "Designing and Implementing a Faculty-Based Advising Program." *NACADA Journal,* 1995, *1*, 27–32.

Gardner, J. N. "Perspectives on Academic Advising for First-Year Students: Present and Future." In M. L. Upcraft and G. L. Kramer (eds.), *First-Year Academic Advising: Patterns in the Present, Pathways to the Future,* Monograph no. 18. Columbia: National Resource Center for the Freshman Year Experience and Students in Transition, University of South Carolina, 1995.

Gardner, J. N., and Van der Veer, G. *The Senior Year Experience.* San Francisco: Jossey-Bass, 1998.

Habley, W. R., and Morales, R. H. (eds.). *Current Practices in Academic Advising: Final Report on ACT's Fifth National Survey of Academic Advising.* Manhattan, Kans.: National Academic Advising Association, 1998.

Harris, M. B., and Brooks L. J. "Challenges for Older Students in Higher Education." *Journal of Research and Development in Education,* 1998, *31*, 226–234.

Hess, W. D., and Winston, R. B. Jr. "The Developmental Task Achievement and Students' Intentions to Participate in Developmental Activities." *Journal of College Student Development,* 1995, *36*, 314–326.

Isaac, P. D., Pruitt-Logan, A. S., and Upcraft, M. L. "The Landscape of Graduate Education." In P. Isaac and A. Pruitt (eds.), *Student Services for the Changing Graduate Student.* New Directions for Student Services, no. 72. San Francisco: Jossey-Bass, 1995.

Krager, L., Wrenn, R., and Hirt, J. "Perspectives on Age Differences." In L. V. Moore (ed.), *Evolving Theoretical Perspectives on Students.* New Directions for Student Services, no. 51. San Francisco: Jossey-Bass, 1990.

Kramer, G. L. "First-Year Academic Advising: Patterns in the Present." Presentation given at International Freshman Year Experience Conference, St. Andrews, Scotland, July 1996.

Kramer, G. L., Higley, B. H., and Olsen, D. "Changes in Academic Major Among Undergraduate Students." *College and University,* 1994, *69*, 88–98.

Kramer, G. L., Taylor, L., Chynoweth, B., and Jensen, J. "Developmental Academic Advising: A Taxonomy of Services." *NASPA Journal,* 1987, *24*(4), 23–31.

Lewallen, W. "The Impact of Being 'Undecided' on College-Student Persistence." *Journal of College Student Development,* 1993, *34*, 103–112.

Long, B. E., Sowa, C. J., and Niles, S. G. "The Differences in Student Development Reflected by the Career Decisions of College Seniors." *Journal of College Student Development*, 1995, *36*, 47–52.

Moore, L. V., and Upcraft, M. L. "Theory in Student Affairs: Evolving Perspective." In L. V. Moore (ed.), *Evolving Theoretical Perspectives on Students*. New Directions for Student Services, no. 51. San Francisco: Jossey-Bass, 1990.

O'Brien, E. M. *Master's Degree Students and Recipients: A Profile*. Research Briefs, vol. 3, no. 1. Washington, D.C.: Division of Policy Analysis and Research, American Council on Education, 1992.

Pascarella, E. T., and Terenzini, P. T. *How College Affects Students: Findings and Insights from Twenty Years of Research*. San Francisco: Jossey-Bass, 1991.

Schilling, K. L., and Schilling, K. M. "Looking Back, Moving Ahead: Assessment in the Senior Year." In J. Gardner and G. Van der Veer (eds.), *The Senior Year Experience*. San Francisco: Jossey-Bass, 1998.

Stark, J. S. *Student Goals for Colleges and Courses: A Missing Link in Assessing and Improving Academic Achievement*. ASHE-ERIC Report no. 6. Washington, D.C.: George Washington University, 1989.

Tinto, V. *Leaving College: Rethinking the Causes and Cures of Student Attrition.* (2nd ed.) Chicago: University of Chicago Press, 1993.

Upcraft, M. L., and Kramer, G. L. "First-Year Academic Advising: Patterns in the Present, Pathways to the Future." In M. L. Upcraft and G. L. Kramer (eds.), *First-Year Academic Advising Patterns in the Present, Pathways to the Future*, Monograph no. 18. Columbia: National Resource Center for the Freshman Year Experience and Students in Transition, University of South Carolina, 1995.

VanZile-Tamsen, C., and Livingston, J. A. "The Differential Impact of Motivation on the Self-Regulated Strategy Use of High- and Low-Achieving College Students." *Journal of College Student Development*, 1999, *40*, 54–58.

Chapter Eight

Advising Multicultural Students

The Reality of Diversity

Ronnie Priest, Sidney A. McPhee

The emerging multicultural literature on academic advising has benefited from research studies and findings dealing with multicultural and cross-cultural issues in psychology and counseling. The extant literature on culture and diversity and the resulting influence these factors have on understanding multicultural populations have helped with the knowledge and practice inherent in academic advising.

The study of multicultural advising and counseling has evolved into a major area of emphasis that focuses on all elements of the different cultural environments in a democratic society, including relevant theories, techniques, and practices (Axelson, 1993; Terenzini and others, 1994; Upcraft, 1996).

Since the early 1980s, American colleges and universities have expended considerable financial resources and human energies toward the recruitment of women and students of color. Educators and demographers have chronicled the growing number of students of color who are enrolling in institutions of higher education throughout the United States.

The United States is becoming increasingly diverse. Brown and Rivas (1993) alluded to a 1988 American Council of Education report that predicted that by the year 2000 one-third of the U.S. population would consist of ethnic minorities. It has been noted that African Americans, Latinos, Asians, and Native Americans represent approximately 23 percent of the American labor market (McPhee, 1990). This statistic points out a consistent growth in the ethnic minority population as a percentage of the general population. Wilson's (1993) research study determined that "the majority of the more than 1 million African American college students attend predominantly white institutions" (p. 4). Similarly, the increasing numbers of Native Americans, Asians, and

Latinos attending predominantly white institutions of higher learning is also impressive. Logically extended, this trend means that as colleges and universities pursue opportunities to increase their student enrollment, recruitment efforts will intensify to attract qualified ethnic minority students.

Although American institutions of higher education may have been relatively successful in recruiting ethnic minority students, they continue to struggle with retention of some of these students in academic programs. Retention studies have shown that effective academic advising is positively correlated to students' satisfaction with their college experiences, persistence in college, and graduation (Atkinson and Hord, 1983; Brown and Rivas, 1993; McPhee, 1990; Novels and Ender, 1988).

Any discussion of intervention considerations with ethnic minority students should first recognize that there is no such thing as a generic ethnic minority student. For example, Baldwin (1991) correctly discerned that African American students are not necessarily homogeneous and may demonstrate in-group cultural distinctiveness based on, among other things, gender, socioeconomic status, and level of acculturation to European American norms. Similarly, it should be recognized that Latinos, Native Americans, and Asian Americans represent a majestic array of diversity that cannot be described in generic terms. Lee (1991) offers that "educational counseling for ethnic minority individuals must be considered in a life-span developmental perspective"(p. 654).

With these considerations in mind, some identifiable themes and issues frequently occur when attempting to render cogent academic advising to ethnic minority students. Academic advisors are well advised to be prepared to address issues including but not limited to the following categories:

- Demographic overview
- Considerations related to class or being a first-generation college student
- Possible perceptions by ethnic minority students of the campus as a potentially hostile environment
- Exploration of students' proposed majors and long-term goals
- The need for advisors to engage in candid self-exploration of their personal perspectives
- The distinction (in terms of needs) between advising graduate and undergraduate students
- The need for follow-up advising during the semester and after graduation
- Recommended competencies for advisors who work with an array of ethnic minority students

It should be noted that these categories are by no means all-inclusive. The following paragraphs discuss some of the issues deemed most overarching in today's academic advising environment. (A final note of clarification involves the authors' use of the term *advisor*. There may be instances when advisors find themselves confronting emotional or psychological domains beyond their expertise. It is strongly suggested that when this occurs, the advisor should refer the student to a counselor or psychologist.)

Demographics

Recent U.S. Census Bureau data show that by the year 2000, ethnic minorities in the United States will comprise approximately 85 million people. Outtz (1995) notes that between 1980 and 1990, the population of the United States increased by 10 percent. This growth was primarily accounted for by the increase in the nonwhite population. This trend is projected to continue well into the twenty-first century.

Outtz suggests that higher education is connected to demographics in ways never before seen in the United States. For example, considering that the number of students who fit the traditional college student profile—white middle to upper middle class, ages eighteen to twenty-one—is decreasing, a demographic shift is apparent. Outtz writes, "The increase in the racial and ethnic diversity of college students is evident. College enrollment by non-whites has increased at a much greater rate than by whites. Between 1982 and 1992, the increase in the number of non-white ethnic groups enrolled in higher education was more than three times the increase among whites (26.6% and 8.7% respectively)" (p. 67).

First-Generation Students

A unique aspect of advising ethnically diverse students is that they may be the first in their family to attend college. Richardson and Skinner (1992) articulate that a primary reason that some first-generation students underachieve is directly attributable to lack of academic preparedness. This reality suggests an increased need for the student and his or her advisor to dialogue about the student's proposed program of study.

First-generation students also have the challenge of attending college without sufficient insight from their parents about what is entailed in successfully completing their studies. For example, a Latina student stated, "My mother told me college would be tough and I would have to study hard. She just never taught me how to study." It is important that advisors step into the "academic breech" and engage in comprehensive outreach when dealing with first-generation students (Rendon, 1992). One strategy that has proven effective for us is to have group advising sessions with first-generation students. Group advising affords an opportunity for similarly situated students to receive advising in a situation in which they are able to express their concerns and formulate solutions for challenges that confront them. From an administrative vantage point, group advising is also cost-effective.

Economic Considerations

It is not unusual for ethnic minority students attending college to experience an economic disadvantage when compared to many of their European American peers. This disadvantage can frequently be attributed to historical institutional socioeconomic inequities that rendered the ethnic minority individual in a "one down" position (Neighbors, Jackson, Broman, and Thompson, 1996). Consequently, it is not unusual for ethnic minority students to be compelled to work full-time as they acquire their college degrees or to seek financial assistance in the form of student loans or assistantships at rates higher than their European American counterparts (Wagner, 1993; Wilson, 1993).

Students in this situation frequently feel the dual press of needing to complete their academic endeavors while needing to be financially self-supporting. Consequently, some ethnic minority students may be at greater risk of making faulty courseload decisions (such as number of courses taken during a semester or combination of courses) due to their perceived need to complete a program of study as expeditiously as possible.

In discussing students' proposed majors, projected length of time for program completion, per semester courseload, and the rigor of the schedule should be directly addressed and, where appropriate, acknowledgment of the students' situation should be articulated. It is also crucial that advisors express the need for students to do their best even if it means students might need to stay in school an additional semester or year.

It is not unusual for some ethnic minority students to get so focused on the singular goal of completing their degree by any means necessary that they graduate while failing to attain a grade point average that accurately reflects their abilities. This shortsighted perspective born of urgency unfortunately overlooks the critical reality that these students may not be in a competitive position (with an overall 2.3 grade point average, for example) to gain entrance into graduate school. It is the academic advisor's responsibility to address these issues respectfully with students.

Advisors should also be knowledgeable about the availability of various forms of financial aid (such as loans, work-study, and or graduate assistant positions). We are not necessarily suggesting that advisors be aware of all the types of financial aid available. They should be able, however, to direct students to sources where the information can be located.

Exploration of Major and Long-Term Goals

It has long been understood that higher education presents challenges to most students. Neville, Heppner, and Wang (1997) suggest that college is a time when students negotiate an array of developmental tasks paired with academic concerns and newly formed interpersonal relationships. Consequently, academic advisors have a unique opportunity to explore with students their reasons for considering a particular major or series of courses. Due to lack of information, some ethnic minority students may consider a program of study that does not lead to a career that is commensurate with their college degree (Arbona and Novy, 1991). For example, a student might consider attaining a degree in an area of specialization that necessitates going to graduate school although the student has no intention of doing so. The obvious question is, What type of employment or career opportunities can the student reasonably expect to attain with an undergraduate degree? Ethnic minority students must be well informed about the relationship between academic and career decisions.

Perception of the Campus as a Hostile Environment

Whether their views are real or imagined, ethnic minority students may perceive European American campuses as hostile. Students furnish an array of reasons to buttress these perceptions. Strommer (1993) expresses the belief that "no campus is free of racial or ethnic prejudice" (p. 34). For example, instructors may be perceived as having different evaluative criteria for ethnic minority students than for other students (Green, 1989). Wilson and Linville (1982) conclude from their research that when students believed a hostile situation was temporary or transitory, they were able to enhance their academic performance. These findings offer a better understanding of how ethnic minority students can enhance their performance even though they envision the college campus as hostile. If in fact the campus atmosphere is hostile, advisors can assist students in formulating a plan to alter the college environment. They can encourage students to become involved in positively changing the academic environment.

Ethnic minority students may also conclude that their college campus is hostile when nonethnic minority students, faculty, and staff are overheard making what are deemed to be culturally insensitive remarks.

Where there are insufficient numbers of full-time minority faculty on campus, ethnic minority students may have a difficult time locating academic role models. Students may also have difficulty identifying faculty members they feel are sensitive to their situation. When advisors perceive that the campus is hostile, they should explore the reasons and take possible remediative actions.

Where there is a lack of ethnic minority representation within the faculty ranks, one feasible alternative is to invite ethnic minority professionals from a wide array of occupations to lead discussion groups with students. In addition, these professionals can often serve as mentors for students. Other remedial actions that academic advisors can take include identifying and applying solutions and coping strategies to specific situations. The mutually identified strategies should be realistic and attainable. Strommer (1993, p. 32) intones that "advisors in particular need to be sensitive to the climate for minority students on their campus and need to understand their special concerns."

Undergraduate and Graduate Advising

The distinction between advising undergraduate and graduate ethnic minority students may be one of degree as opposed to kind, yet salient issues are discernible. Some undergraduate students may be more invested in simply graduating than in seriously considering their choice of academic major. When students have parental financial assistance, they may have a greater opportunity than other students to enjoy college life.

In many instances it is assumed that graduate students have a greater level of maturity than undergraduate students. Consequently, the primary focus of academic advisors and counselors is on undergraduate students. The issue that is frequently overlooked, however, is that maturity does not necessarily equate with an innate ability to negotiate the rigors of a graduate program. Academic advisors have a responsibility to engage in outreach in their attempts to identify ethnic minority graduate students and provide supportive insights and mentoring.

Academic advisors should also recognize that in certain instances competent graduate students should be afforded opportunities to mentor undergraduate students. Graduate students invariably have insights into applying for, being accepted in, and successfully completing graduate study.

Ethnic Minority Male Students

Gibbs (1988) has suggested that ethnic minority males, especially African Americans and Latinos, may be an endangered species. From an academic vantage point, 26 percent of all eighteen- and nineteen-year-old ethnic minority males in these two groups either did not complete high school or were enrolled in high school during the 1980s (U.S. Bureau of the Census, 1981). Unfortunately, there are no indications that these statistics improved in the 1990s.

One of the authors spends what seems to be an inordinate amount of time diffusing the anger of a small but significant number of African American male students. Reggie (not his actual name) originally came to the office upset because "some students wanted to know what position I played. It is as if the only way I could get here is through athletics. I am here on an academic scholarship." The real issue is not so much that Reggie was angry, but rather the question, What suggested to the students Reggie had encountered that the only way he could be in college was through athletics? Carlos, a nineteen-year-old Puerto Rican sophomore student expressed his frustration at having students consistently consider him Chicano or illegally in the United States. "I am Puerto

Rican; there is no reasonable reason for people to assume otherwise. When I asked why they wanted to know my ethnicity in the first place, I was told, Don't be so sensitive." An attendant issue involved identifying for Reggie and Carlos alternative responses to these types of students that did not involve Reggie and Carlos getting distressed. The advisor also examined with them the issue of tolerance, "the ability to understand that all students on the college campus bring with them their own unique sets of personal experiences" (Roper, 1993, p. 58).

In hindsight, the advisor may have made a mistake by addressing the issue of intolerance with Reggie and Carlos. A more appropriate approach may have been to address the issue with the other students.

The existing literature relative to Native Americans, Latinos, and African American male students attending four-year colleges and universities suggests that they do not complete their degree program at a rate comparable to ethnic minority women or European Americans. Advisors would be well-served to increase their efforts in identifying the reasons for this phenomenon and to reduce its occurrence.

Kunjufu (1989) suggests, "We have to find more academic carrots that also stimulate students" (p. 73). Part of the academic carrot must be internal, in the form of personal motivation. Advisors must also recognize the importance of external motivation to male students, and afford them the opportunity to realize their potential and subsequently master their academic environment. Kunjufu astutely notes that "external motivation cannot be separated from role models" (p. 73).

Harris (1995) states that in counseling ethnic minority males, advisors and counselors should "increase their competency in interpreting social cues, differentiate among situations and individuals, develop a repertoire of alternative responses, evaluate and select situational and person-appropriate responses, and enact the chosen chain of behaviors with accuracy" (p. 282).

Candid Self-Exploration of Cultural Sensitivity

It is recommended that academic advisors acquire the requisite skills for effectively dealing with culturally diverse populations. Pederson (1994) suggests that counselors have the responsibility of examining their own knowledge, attitudes, perceptions, and feelings relative to interacting with ethnic minorities. Lee and Richardson (1991) have addressed salient dynamics, concerns, and pitfalls that are important for counselors interacting with culturally diverse groups. Johnson's (1990, p. 45) seminal work has conceptualized the role of multicultural counseling or advising as including an opportunity "to better comprehend the systems of relationships involved in multicultural counseling than they have in the past."

The question that must be addressed is, Where are academic advisors to go in order to acquire expertise relative to interacting successfully with ethnic minority students? Midgette and Meggert (1991) lucidly discuss the need for counselor education programs to furnish instruction in multicultural counseling. Advisors should be engaged constantly in an objective evaluation of their interactions with ethnic minority students. It is an essential yet sometimes overlooked cornerstone to "functional advising" that academic advisors and counselors have both training and practical experiences in working with multicultural students (Lee, 1991).

Multicultural Competencies

Many concerned professionals (Ponterotto, Rieger, Barnett, and Sparks, 1994; Ridley, Mendoza, and Kanitz, 1994; Sue, Arredondo, and McDavis, 1992; Sue and Sue, 1990) have focused attention on the critical need for counselors to possess and utilize multicultural competencies. The appropriateness of this position clearly applies to advising. The specific competencies articulated by Sue, Arredondo, and McDavis (1992) can be understood in the context of three major classifications: attitudes, knowledge, and skills.

Advisors should be aware of the interactional dynamics between themselves and their advisees. This includes but is not limited to observing both the verbal and nonverbal actions of advisees. To be effective, advisors should be knowledgeable about their advisees' racial and cultural backgrounds, aspects of the presented advising concern, and the interaction between the two. A crucial aspect of advisor knowledge is the extent to which advisors are able to understand advisees rather than attempt to force them into an overgeneralized advising paradigm.

Developing multicultural competency skills is perhaps the biggest challenge confronting advisors. They should have the ability to understand their advisees' concerns and accurately articulate the issues their advisees raise. After the advising session, the advisee should be better informed, and in some cases more emotionally or psychologically relieved, than they were prior to being advised.

Advising International Students

The number of international students in American colleges and universities continues to increase. Stoynoff (1997) estimates that there are more than 450,000 international students attending colleges and universities in this country.

International students may present challenges to academic advisors that are distinct from those of ethnic minority students born in the United States. In addition to concerns related to academic programs of study, international students may present an array of unique issues, such as the following:

- Adjustment to sex-role expectations in the United States that are different from those in their native country (Hayes and Lin, 1994)

- Clashes between international students' native cultures and the culture of the United States (Sodowsky and Plake, 1992)
- Feelings of homesickness and alienation (Brinson and Kottler, 1995)
- Language communication difficulties (Barratt and Huba, 1994; Redmond and Bunyi, 1993)
- Legal and financial concerns of negotiating contractual obligations such as housing rental leases or automobile purchase agreements (Khoo, Abu-Rasin, and Hornsby, 1994)

Advisors should avoid any tendency to see international students as deficient on the basis of their cultural distinctiveness. An additional confounding consideration is that it is not unusual for international students to seek out their academic advisor "just to talk" because that is the person to whom they feel the closest. Kaul (1999) has astutely discerned that if international students are to make a successful transition from the academic environment in their native culture to the pervasive cultural environment found in the United States, advisors "need to make an effort to reach out to international students at frequent intervals and to be cognizant of the issues facing this vulnerable student population" (p. 14).

Recommendations

The authors recommend that academic advisors who work with ethnic minority students should implement the following interventions:

- When meeting with students either individually or in groups, identify and implement an academic program of study that is realistic given the rigor associated with the program selected and the student's nonacademic responsibilities. For example, it may be unrealistic for students to consider a major in engineering if they have not had the requisite mathematics courses in high school or are not willing to take remedial courses in college.
- Where indicated, students should be directed to resources where they can receive tutoring, study skills enhancement, and assistance with time-management concerns. It is not unusual for some ethnic minority students to experience difficulty completing course assignments due to ineffective time management. Similarly, these students may not know how to prepare effectively for college courses. A student who did not need to study in high school or merely needed to glance at assignments will find these habits counterproductive in college.
- Provide culturally sensitive advising for students in the context of academic curriculum and career expectations, and obtain commitments from ethnic minority professionals to advise students about the occupations they are considering. Ethnic minority students are in dire need of career professionals willing and able to be role models. By attaining professionals from similar ethnic

groups as mentors and role models, students are reaffirmed and may receive more realistic insights about their professional goals.

• Counseling ethnic minority students requires not only an understanding of the theoretical and practical traditions of the counseling profession, but also an appreciation of the dynamics of various cultures and the societal forces that impinge on mental health and well-being (Lee, 1991). Advising should be proactive and focus both on individual students and on their mastery of the academic environment.

• Facilitate colloquiums between students and faculty related to their perceptions of the campus environment. It is essential for students to feel that when they have concerns they will be heard by both faculty and administrators.

• Afford students an opportunity to realize a sense of accomplishment, and when something noteworthy has been accomplished, ensure that it is acknowledged (at both the undergraduate and graduate levels). When a student excels, it should be publicized. Public acknowledgment of academic achievement reinforces students' efforts and gives them an outlet other than sports in which to excel.

Evaluative Follow-Up of Interventions

The interventions provided by academic advisors and counselors are and should be varied. There is a paucity of information, however, on the efficacy of the interventions attempted (Lang, 1988). We believe that if the recommendations just listed are implemented, students will be more motivated to complete their academic curriculum and more likely to become academically and personally successful. The authors suggest that academic advisors should remain in contact with students at least one year beyond their graduation or discontinuance of a program of study. By engaging in this type of follow-up at three- or six-month intervals, advisors can adequately determine what interventions were effective and what new interventions may be required to improve the existing advising and retention processes.

Although they are not the focus of this chapter, we would be remiss if we did not acknowledge the importance of college administrators. College administrators must also be advocates of ethnic minority students. Advocacy cannot be limited to recruitment and admission. It must also include retention and graduation. Such advocacy will take the form of employing and assigning advisors who are committed to the graduation of ethnic minority students, and designating financial resources to student retention initiatives.

Conclusion

Colleges across the country are engaged in an intense effort to recruit qualified ethnic minority students. In large measure, the degree to which these students receive thoughtful and caring advisement is pivotal to ensuring that they graduate. We contend that it is the responsibility of the academic advisor to develop, in conjunction with the student, relevant interventions that make graduation for ethnic minority students a reality.

Additional research is needed to determine what specific components constitute effective advising and mentoring for ethnic minority students. We sincerely hope that the suggestions and practical experiences contained in this chapter will serve as a basis for further research endeavors.

References

Arbona, C., and Novy, D. M. "Career and Expectations of Black, Mexican American, and White Students." *Career Development Quarterly,* 1991, *39,* 231–239.

Atkinson, P. S., and Hord, I. L. "The Best System: Black Academic and Cultural Retreat. (Save the Children) Unpublished report, 1983.

Axelson, J. A. *Counseling and Development in a Multicultural Society.* Pacific Grove, Calif.: Brooks/Cole, 1993.

Baldwin, J. A . "African (Black) Psychology: Issues and Synthesis." In R. L. Jones (ed.), *Black Psychology.* (3rd ed.) Berkeley, Calif.: Cobb and Henry, 1991.

Barratt, M. F., and Huba, M. E. "Factors Related to International Undergraduate Student Adjustment in an American Community." *College Student Journal,* 1994, *28*(4), 422–436.

Brinson, J. A., and Kottler, J. K. "International Students in Counseling: Some Alternative Models." *Journal of College Student Psychotherapy,* 1995, *9*(3), 57–70.

Brown, T., and Rivas, M. "Advising Multicultural Populations for Achievement and Success." In M. C. King (ed.), *First-Generation College Students.* New Directions for Community Colleges, no. 62. San Francisco: Jossey-Bass, 1993.

Gibbs, J. T. (ed.). *Young, Black, and Male in America: An Endangered Species.* Westport, Conn.: Auburn House, 1988.

Green, M. F. *Minorities on Campus: A Handbook for Enhancing Diversity.* Washington, D.C.: American Council on Education, 1989.

Harris, S. M. "Psychosocial Development and Black Male Masculinity: Implications for Counseling Economically Disadvantaged African American Male Adolescents. *Journal of Counseling and Development,* 1995, *73, 279–287.*

Hayes, R. L., and Lin, H. "Coming to America: Developing Social Support Systems for International Students. *Journal of Multicultural Counseling and Development,* 1994, *22,* 132–140.

Johnson, S. D. "Toward Clarifying Culture, Race, and Ethnicity in the Context of Multicultural Counseling." *Journal of Multicultural Counseling and Development,* 1990, *18,* 41–50.

Kaul, A. "Acculturation Stress Among International Students in the United States." Manuscript submitted for publication, 1999.

Khoo, P.L.S., Abu-Rasin, M. H., and Hornsby, G. "Counseling Foreign Students: A Review of Strategies." *Counseling Psychology Quarterly,* 1994, *7*(2), 117–131.

Kunjufu, J. *Critical Issues in Educating African American Youth.* Chicago: African American Images, 1989.

Lang, M. "The Black Student Retention Problem in Higher Education: Some Introductory Perspectives." In M. Lang and C. A. Ford (eds.), *Black Student Retention in Higher Education.* Springfield, Ill: Thomas, 1988.

Lee, C. C. "Counseling African Americans: From Theory to Practice." In R. Williams (ed.), *Black Psychology.* (3rd ed.) Berkeley Calif.: Cobbs and Henry, 1991.

Lee, C. C., and Richardson, B. L. (1991). *Multicultural Issues in Counseling: New Approaches to Diversity.* Alexandria, Va.: American Counseling Association, 1991.

McPhee, S. A. "Addressing the Attraction of Minority Students on Predominantly White Campuses: A Pilot Study." *Student Affairs Journal,* 1990, *10,* 15–22.

Midgette, T. E., and Meggert, S. S. "Multicultural Counseling Instruction: A Challenge for Faculties in the Twenty-First Century. *Journal of Counseling and Development,* 1991, *70,* 136–141.

Neighbors, H. W., Jackson, J. S., Broman, C., and Thompson, E. "Racism and the Mental Health of African Americans: The Role of Self and System Blame. *Ethnicity and Disease,* 1996, *6,* 167–175.

Neville, H. A., Heppner, P. P., and Wang, L. "Relations Among Racial Identity, Attitudes, Perceived Stressors, and Coping Styles in African American College Students. *Journal of Counseling and Development,* 1997, *75,* 303–311.

Novels, A. N., and Ender, S. C. "The Impact of Developmental Advising for High-Achieving Minority Students." *NACADA Journal,* 1988, *8,* 23–26.

Outtz, J. M. "Higher Education and the New Demographic Reality." *Educational Record,* 1995, *7,* 65–69.

Pederson, P. *A Handbook for Developing Multicultural Awareness.* (2nd ed.) Alexandria, Va.: American Counseling Association, 1994.

Ponterotto, J. G., Rieger, B. P., Barnett, A., and Sparks, R. "Assessing Multicultural Counseling Competence: A Review of Instrumentation." *Journal of Counseling and Development,* 1994, *72,* 316–322.

Redmond, M. V., and Bunyi, J. M. "The Relationship of Intercultural Communication Competence with Stress and the Handling of Stress as Reported by International Students." *International Journal of Intercultural Relations,* 1993, *17,* 235–254.

Rendon, L. I. "From the Barrio to the Academy: Revelations of a Mexican American Scholarship Girl." In L. S. Zwerling and H. B. London (eds.), *First Generation Students: Confronting the Cultural Issues.* San Francisco: Jossey-Bass, 1992.

Richardson, R. C., and Skinner, E. F. "Helping First-Generation Minority Students Achieve Degrees." In A. M. Cohen (ed.), *First Generation Students: Confronting the Cultural Issues.* New Directions for Community Colleges, no. 82. San Francisco: Jossey-Bass, 1992

Ridley, C. R., Mendoza, D. W., and Kanitz, B. E. "Multicultural Training: Reexamination, Operationalization, and Integration." *The Counseling Psychologist,* 1994, *22,* 227–289.

Roper, L. D. "Getting Along with Non-Blacks on Campus." In R. D. Higgins and others, *The Black Student's Guide to College Success.* Westport, Conn.: Greenwood Press, 1993.

Sodowsky, G. R., and Plake, B. S. "A Study of Acculturation Differences Among People and Suggestions for Sensitivity to Within Group Differences." *Journal of Counseling and Development,* 1992, *71,* 53–59.

Stoynoff, S. "Factors Associated with International Students' Academic Achievement." *Journal of Instructional Psychology,* 1997, *24*(1), 56–68.

Strommer, D. W. "Advising Special Populations of Students." In M. C. King (ed.), *First Generation College Students.* New Directions for Teaching and Learning, no. 62. San Francisco: Jossey-Bass, 1993.

Sue, D. W., Arredondo, P., and McDavis, R. J. "Multicultural Counseling Competencies and Standards: A Call to the Profession." *Journal of Multicultural Counseling and Development,* 1992, *20,* 644–688.

Sue, D. W., and Sue, D. *Counseling the Culturally Different: Theory and Practice.* (2nd ed.) New York: Wiley, 1990.

Terenzini, P. T., and others. "The Transition to College: Diverse Students, Diverse Stories. *Research in Higher Education,* 1994, *35*(1), 57–73.

Upcraft, M. L. "Teaching and Today's College Students." In R. Menges and M. Weimer (eds.), *Teaching on Solid Ground: Using Scholarship to Improve Practice.* San Francisco: Jossey-Bass, 1996.

U.S. Bureau of the Census. "School Enrollment: Social and Economic Characteristics of Students, 1980." *Current Population Reports.* Washington, D.C.: U.S. Department of Commerce, 1981.

Wagner, J. B. "Financing my College Education: How Am I Going to Pay for It and Where Is the Money Coming From?" In R. D. Higgins and others, *The Black Students Guide to College Success.* Westport, Conn.: Greenwood Press, 1993.

Wilson, E. B. *The One Hundred Best Colleges for African-American Students.* New York: Penguin Books, 1993.

Wilson, T. D., and Linville, P. W. "Improving the Academic Performance of College Freshmen: Attribution Therapy Revisited." *Journal of Personality and Social Psychology,* 1982, *42,* 367–376.

Chapter Nine

Advising Students with Special Needs

Steven C. Ender, Carolyn J. Wilkie

One could argue that all students have certain predetermined needs and special characteristics that require specific attention from their academic advisor or from the college's advising system. However, in this chapter we describe five student populations that deserve, and in some cases are required by law to receive, special academic accommodations and advising services in order to maximize their potential for success in college: (1) honors students, or students with high academic abilities; (2) student athletes; (3) students with disabilities; (4) gay, lesbian, and bisexual students; and (5) underprepared or developmental student learners. We describe the general characteristics of each student population, their special academic advising needs, and advisor responsibilities in regard to each group.

In respect to all five populations, we advocate the need for an ongoing student-advisor relationship involving multiple content-focused contacts between the academic advisor and student. These contacts are described in terms of the criteria of establishing a developmental advising relationship. This relationship is defined and a developmental advising curriculum is introduced. The relationship among individual advisors, campuswide services, and advising centers designed to assist students in these populations is explored. The chapter concludes with a discussion about institutional readiness for and commitment to these special populations.

Developmental Advising

All advisors, and specifically advisors of special populations, must have a concept of the purpose and goals of an academic advising relationship. The students in the special populations described in this chapter have characteristics and advising needs that are different from other students on campus. For advisors to prepare for and address these needs, they must think about the nature of the advising relationship and its primary purposes. As a starting point, we focus on developmental advising as defined by Ender (1997):

> Developmental academic advising is a special advising relationship with students that both stimulates and supports their quest for an enriched educational experience. The relationship involves a systemic process of ongoing student-advisor interactions. It helps students achieve educational and personal goals by utilizing the full range of institutional and community resources. . . . Beyond course registration and scheduling, the specific themes of *academic competence, personal involvement,* and *developing or validating life purpose* become the content that the development advising relationship frames. Educators who implement developmental advising recognize and acknowledge that the advisor is the institutional representative most responsible for assuring that advisees know how to seek out the greatest possible benefits from higher education [p. 171].

The very nature of a developmental advising relationship—focusing on the three major themes of *academic competence, personal involvement,* and *developing or validating life purpose*—requires that the relationship between advisor and student be (1) ongoing and purposeful; (2) challenging for the student, but also supportive; (3) goal oriented; and (4) intentional as it maximizes the use of university resources. Effective advisors therefore provide both an *advising curriculum* and an *advising process* for the student to experience.

The Advising Curriculum

Many advisors consider the content or curriculum of an advising session to consist of issues such as course scheduling, registration, explanation of academic procedures, and degree planning. Although all of these issues are important, the developmental advisor focuses his or her attention more broadly on the student development themes of academic competence, personal involvement on campus, and developing or validating a life purpose.

Academic Competence. All of the students we discuss here, especially several represented by the five special populations, must demonstrate for themselves that they can be academically competent as college students. Without demonstrating and sustaining academic competence, students are forced to leave the higher education setting. Advisors must therefore make every effort to understand the academic readiness levels of their advisees and to know if there are any special circumstances that may affect students' ability to function intellectually—issues that may require specific academic accommodations or remedial curriculum demands. To address this area effectively, advisors should know each student's academic strengths and weaknesses. This is especially true for freshman advisees. Previous performance and courses taken in high school, formal test scores (SAT or ACT), and university or advanced placement test results are all important sources of information with which to begin the process of adequately advising students about curriculum choices that will maximize their ability to succeed academically.

Personal Involvement on Campus. The opportunity for students to be involved with other students, with staff and faculty, and with clubs, organizations, sports, preprofessional organizations, work-study jobs, campus governance, and cultural events are limitless on most college and university campuses. These cocurriculum offerings are important for students to engage in if they are to maximize their potential while enrolled in college. Many advisors ignore this area of discussion in their advising contacts with students. We believe this to be a mistake. Student involvement in campus life is an important retention factor (Astin, 1984) and is necessary for students' growth as they learn, practice, and refine their citizenship, work, and preprofessional skills.

Personal involvement is similar to academic competence in the sense that students function at a broad range of ability levels. Many students led active, involved lives while in high school. Others did not. Whereas some are extremely social, others are very shy. While some are overinvolved in nonacademic endeavors, others never leave their residence hall without prompting from a significant other. In this area, it is important for the academic advisor to assist advisees as they assess their level of involvement in campus activities and determine the correct mix of those activities with the demands of their academic curriculum.

Developing or Validating Life Purpose. Attending and graduating from college should lead to a meaningful outcome. For some advisees this means employment in their first professional position. Others go on to graduate school. Still others take some time to participate in other types of life experiences, such as joining the Peace Corps, traveling abroad, or taking some time off from the demands and pressures of the college environment. The point here is to assess life direction and purpose. The academic advisor should implement a discussion of this theme throughout the course of the advising relationship. Appropriate to this discussion are the student's interests and aptitudes, the relationship of the chosen academic major to various career paths, graduate school interests, lifestyle needs, and geographical preferences. The advisee should be encouraged to think about and plan his or her own life, and to think about the relationship of this plan to the academic curriculum.

The Advising Process

All three advising themes in the advising curriculum need consideration and attention at various times in the advising process. These themes provide the content of advising relationships. As we will show as we investigate the five special populations listed earlier, some themes require more attention than others at different matriculation points. All of these themes should be addressed within the context of a developmental advising relationship that is *ongoing and purposeful, based in an interpersonal relationship, goal oriented,* and both *challenging and supportive.*

Ongoing and Purposeful. The type of advising process we describe here cannot occur by meeting once a semester during the college's course registration period. This process consists of multiple contacts during the academic year. Each contact leads to another that is purposeful and planned. Assignments may be given based on the three advising themes discussed earlier. The advisor serves as the university representative as students develop academic competence, become involved on campus, and explore or validate their initial life purpose.

Based in an Interpersonal Relationship. If academic advisors are to deliver and monitor the content successfully, an interpersonal relationship between the student and advisor is essential. Trust and respect for one another must be established. Advisors may need to take some personal risks, sharing themselves and the methods they have utilized to explore and master the three themes they are now challenging advisees to explore. Advisors should consider themselves role models for their student advisees, emulating the life skills the students are exploring, learning, practicing, and refining.

Goal Oriented. Establishing and working on goals in all three theme areas is the cornerstone of the development advising relationship. Academic, personal, and life goals are important areas in which advisors must initiate discussion and assist advisees as they develop their plans for action. Specific goals within each area should be developed at some point during the advising relationship. At times more than one goal may be worked on simultaneously. The advisor serves as a monitor and guide as students work toward goal completion, offering additional suggestions about courses of action during debriefing sessions in which advisees describe their progress.

Challenging and Supportive. All of us in the business of advising college students know that although many students will be eager to learn and experience both intellectual and personal growth as a result of their work with us, many others will not be motivated to explore themselves and their college environment in meaningful and productive ways. To combat this reality, we believe, advisors should take the time to explain to their advisees the purpose of this special relationship and the expectations the advisor holds for them. Students should understand that the advisor will challenge them to develop and maintain academic competence, become personally involved (as time permits) with aspects of campus life, and begin the process of developing an initial life purpose that has some relationship to degree programs, personal interests, aptitudes, and lifestyle needs. Although this may be taken by some students to be somewhat of an ambitious agenda (and perhaps one in which they are not necessarily interested), they need to know that all areas are not pursued at one time and that they will pursue this agenda with the support, encouragement, and advice of the academic advisor.

Applying the Model with Special Populations

Even though we caution against stereotyping and overgeneralization, we do believe that many students in the populations we discuss here have similar characteristics and needs that provide a starting point for advisor-student interaction. We provide an overview of these characteristics for each population, and we discuss appropriate advisor responses within the context of the developmental advising relationship just presented. It is our belief that all students on campus can benefit from a developmental advising relationship, and that this is especially true for those in the following populations.

Honors Students

Danzig (1982) reports that honors programs have existed in colleges and universities since the 1920s. They were founded with the philosophy that academically talented students have scholarly and developmental needs that can best be addressed by coursework, living environments, and activities that are different from the usual college offerings (Gerrity, Lawrence, and Sedlacek, 1993).

A review of the literature by Gerrity, Lawrence, and Sedlacek (1993) regarding the demographics, attitudes, interests, and behaviors of honors and nonhonors freshmen reveals many interesting differences between the two groups. For example, they cite a report by Schroer and Dorn (1986) that concludes that gifted students experience a significant amount of career indecision and confusion due to their multiple talents and potentials. Also, honors students have higher expectations of college life, and when disappointments occur they often lead to sharp regret and cynicism (Robertson, 1966). Work by Mathiasen (1985) concludes that, compared to nonhonors students, honors students have a greater number of interests, participate in more extracurricular activities, are more prompt in completing assignments, report less procrastination, and use their study time more effectively. A study by Stephens and Eison (1986–1987) concludes that honors students show more intrinsic interest in learning and less interest in grades. Also, honors students have a more restricted perception of the range of good grades and are more likely to have an internal locus of control. Other studies (Blackburn and Erickson, 1986; Delisle, 1986) report that honors students have a tendency to be perfectionists and often place great pressure on themselves.

Gerrity, Lawrence, and Sedlacek (1993) conducted a rather large study of honors and nonhonors students. They report several findings that lend themselves to consideration by advisors of honors students. For instance, more honors students than nonhonors students had college-educated parents, and 40 percent of these parents had graduate degrees, compared to 26 percent of the nonhonors parents. This study found significant differences in the academic achievement of honors students compared to nonhonors students: 94 percent of the honors students compared to 54 percent of the nonhonors students had a B+ or better GPA in high school. In this study, 77 percent of the honors students ranked in the top 10 percent of their class, compared to 30 percent of the nonhonors freshman. This study also found that honors students had different motivations for coming to college. Of the honors students, 34 percent came to prepare for graduate school, compared to 16 percent of the nonhonors students.

Day (1989) offers additional insights into the unique characteristics of honors students. She reports that typical honors freshmen have excelled in high school, are creative, have an imagination that can play with ideas, see unusual concepts and connections, have a quick sense of humor, and can apply these abilities to problem-solving situations. The honors college student is task committed and is generally enthusiastic, determined, industrious, self-directed, goal oriented, and involved. Most have held one or more offices in student organizations.

The honors college student is an ideal candidate for a developmental advising relationship. Robertson (1966) recommends that an honors advisor know the interests and backgrounds of these gifted students and provide time for interaction beyond routine matters, to allow for discussion of ambitions and further study interests. Perhaps the greatest challenge for the advisor is determining, within the three content themes, where to focus attention, and the timeliness of these interventions.

Academic Competence. The issue of *academic competence* is not completely irrelevant in regard to this group of students. Of more concern in this area may be the academic expectations of the honors student. Failure to excel in all subjects (that is, to earn all A's) may be quite unsettling for this student. Also, classroom instructors who may not meet these students' expectations may cause the honors college student a certain degree of frustration and annoyance. Both of these issues and possible courses of action to combat problems in either area should be discussed early in the advising relationship. Also, the pressure to perform at high levels and the stress and anxiety associated with high expectations should be monitored. Many honors college freshman deal with considerable stress in the area of academic competence. High academic expectations from self and significant others (such as parents and honors college faculty) can be quite burdensome for these students. Academic advisors should attempt to teach students how to cope with these expectations, encouraging them to reach out for assistance if the stress levels become overbearing.

Personal Involvement. Most honors college students show high levels of involvement in student organizations while in high school and have expectations to continue to explore the new and expanded cocurricular offerings available on most college campuses. One conclusion of the Gerrity, Lawrence, and Sedlacek study (1993) was that honors students are more interested than nonhonors students in nonacademic activities, such as joining campus clubs. When working in this area, the advisor should caution honors students about the potential pitfalls associated with overinvolvement, especially during the first couple of semesters. Most honors curricula are demanding and time-consuming. The honors student will need time to adjust to these considerable academic challenges. This is not to suggest that these students should curtail personal involvement on campus altogether during their first year of college. However, they should be selective in their approach, or use the first year to explore potential opportunities prior to making a commitment to join.

Purpose. The third area, developing or validating life purpose, will in all likelihood provide the majority of work and challenge when advising an honors student. As stated earlier, these students have high expectations of themselves and varied interests. Over one-third of the students in the Gerrity, Lawrence, and Sedlacek (1993) study enrolled in college with the expectation of going on to graduate school. Also, students in this study were more likely to be interested in John Holland's occupational environments of Investigative and Realistic careers than nonhonors students, who were more evenly spread across all six of Holland's types. Gerrity, Lawrence, and Sedlacek explain that investigative jobs (such as scientist, design engineer, and physician) often require graduate or professional education. Among realistic occupations, engineering is a popular major for honors students.

Along with choosing demanding majors, many honors students participate in special honors curriculums, pursue dual majors, seek to study abroad, and are eager to take advantage of special course offerings, workshops, and cultural activities that relate to their academic and life interests. Undecided honors students require the additional challenge of sorting through their assorted interests and academic majors to choose a program of study that will lead to a purposeful life direction upon graduation from college.

Student Athletes

There are many impressions of today's collegiate athlete. Shriberg and Brodzinski (1984, p. 1) state:

> College athletes are simultaneously loved and hated, admired and despised. . . .
> We see them as saviors of the university for the revenue they create, and as
> pampered, spoiled brats for the benefits they receive. . . . We hear that large
> numbers do not graduate, yet research shows their graduation rate to be higher
> overall than that of non-athletes. . . . We see them as strong, mature, and confi-
> dent individuals, yet we often learn that they cannot perform in the classroom.
> Somewhere in the middle of all these images lies the real student-athlete.

Walter and Smith (1989) identify at least four unique differences when comparing student athletes to other students in general: (1) issues of time and energy devoted to their sport, (2) lower grades earned in high school, (3) less time for socialization on and off campus, and (4) a lifestyle that often involves living in a fishbowl-type atmosphere.

The first issue, time and energy devoted to athletic activity, is of critical importance if the academic advisor is to have some understanding of the life and lifestyle of an intercollegiate athlete. Most sports require a commitment of at least three hours a day, five to six days a week, fifty-two weeks a year. Becoming a college athlete at all levels of intercollegiate sports is a lifestyle commitment. Countless hours are spent becoming and staying fit, learning techniques, practicing, and actually competing in the sport. The energy demands are substantial and leave many athletes tired and depleted long before the primary demands of achieving and maintaining academic competence are finished for the day.

The second primary difference noted by Walter and Smith pertains to issues of academic competence and readiness to compete within the college's academic curriculum. They state, "Because some student athletes have earned significantly lower grades in high school and scored significantly lower on standardized tests, they have to work much harder than their peers to succeed academically" (p. 329). In effect, many athletes are underprepared academically and have fewer hours to devote to academics than their more competent peers. Added to that is the reality that sports competition and travel time often require athletes to miss class more than other students. Managing time is of critical importance to the academic success of the student athlete. Many times, however, the study time available is spent resting or sleeping due to the physical demands of the students' sports. Because of the combined time demands of the sport and academics, athletes have few hours to socialize and to become involved in their campus community in other ways. Many athletes are segregated into athletic residence halls and can become quite isolated from other students and easy access to campus programs.

The final differing characteristic identified by Walter and Smith pertains to the fishbowl atmosphere in which many athletes live. Because of their high visibility on campus and throughout the community, their behavior is often far more scrutinized and magnified than the behavior of other students. "Some athletes feel this pressure more than others, and may resort to unproductive social behaviors or substance abuse" (Walter and Smith, 1989, p. 329).

Academic Competence. When addressing the achievement of academic competence, advisors must avoid the tendency to stereotype or generalize student athletes as not academically motivated. Simons, Van Rheenen, and Covington (1999) point out that many of the qualities necessary for academic success are in most cases qualities that characterize college athletes. These include the ability to work hard, be self-disciplined, exhibit perseverance and determination, concentrate, and stay focused. All of these qualities are transferable to the academic arena. In most cases, female and nonrevenue athletes (such as tennis players or swimmers) seem more willing and able than revenue athletes (those who play football and men's basketball) to make this transfer. Revenue athletes seem less willing to make this transfer of qualities, showing an apparent lack of academic motivation.

In many cases the issue of academic competence will need considerable attention from the academic advisor, even though individual student athletes will have different academic abilities and aspirations. For freshman student athletes, the issue of academic readiness is of the utmost importance. Advisors should insist that university placement test results be available to advise student athletes in the proper sequence of skill-building courses (mathematics, English, and foreign languages). Also, course demands and semester curricula should be examined carefully. Advising student athletes to take on full academic loads (more than twelve or thirteen credits) during the semester that the athlete's sport is in competition places the student athlete at considerable academic risk. Specifically, during this time the student athlete is under considerable pressure and time restraints due to the demands of his or her sport. Semesters should be planned so that the more demanding courses and courseloads occur during the semester when the sport's competition season is not occurring. Often, due to the availability and sequencing of courses, athletes will by necessity have to attend summer school. Considerable attention should be given to both academic readiness and curriculum planning when advising a student athlete.

The student athlete's motivation to succeed academically should also be assessed. Many student athletes have a low sense of academic self-worth due to a history of academic failure and are not confident in their ability to succeed academically. This seems to be most true for male athletes, revenue athletes, and African American athletes, and especially true for African American athletes in revenue sports. Also, students with these motivational characteristics are more inclined than other student athletes to be committed to the athletic role and to believe that they are being exploited by the university (Simons, Van Rheenen, and Covington, 1999).

Students displaying or describing these motivational characteristics that often lead to academic failure need special attention from their academic advisor. Strategies to build academic competence and confidence need to be implemented. Students in this category need to understand the importance of education in their lives—now and in the future. Discussions regarding possible feelings of athletic exploitation need to be initiated and explored. The academic advisor, neutral to the athletic arena and department, is a natural university agent to pursue these discussions and possible courses of action with student athletes displaying low academic motivation.

Personal Involvement. As the academic advisor initiates discussions with student athletes regarding their personal involvement on campus, it is important to reemphasize how little time student athletes have at their disposal given both academic and athletic commitments. However, some commitments beyond athletics may help to strengthen the student athlete's overall sense of involvement on campus and reinforce membership within the academic community. Advisors should discuss possible sources of personal involvement, such as academic clubs, preprofessional opportunities, involvement in mentoring and peer advising for other athletes or children within the community, student organizations that may respond to the student athlete's interests beyond his or her sport, religious organizations, and other opportunities that match personal interests or professional aspirations. Student athletes should be encouraged to be selective as they assess possible avenues for personal involvement; however, the advisor should advocate some type of personal socialization and activity beyond the student athlete's sport.

Purpose. Developing or validating life purpose may present an area of challenge for academic advisors while working with some student athletes. Many such students at all levels of intercollegiate competition dream of a professional sport career. In fact, only 5 percent of high school athletes make college teams, and 1.7 percent spend at least one year on a professional sports team (Tucker, 1999). In other words, the overwhelming majority of college student athletes will need to prepare for professional careers outside athletics. This reality should be discussed early and often with student athletes. Meaningful careers require thoughtful planning; insights regarding work values, attitudes, interests and aspirations; and appropriate coupling of academic majors to career tracks.

The career planning process must be initiated early on in advising relationships with student athletes, if for no other reason than to provide for meaningful alternatives after professional sports, career-ending injuries, and abbreviated college athletic participation. Even though these rationales are important for only a miniscule fraction of student athletes, they may make enough sense to many students to give honest effort and personal attention to career interests outside sports.

Students with Disabilities

Section 504 of the Rehabilitation Act of 1973, Section 104.44 (a) of the original 1973 law, and the Americans with Disabilities Act (ADA), which was signed into law on July 26, 1990, require colleges and universities to make modifications to their academic requirements as are necessary to ensure that such requirements do not discriminate or have the effect of discriminating on the basis of handicap against a qualified handicapped applicant or student. "The provision of services to disabled students in postsecondary education places legal obligation on the disabled student (rather than parents), postsecondary institution, and sometimes the state vocational rehabilitation agency" (Frank and Wade, 1993, p. 26). The postsecondary institution has the obligation to inform students of the availability of academic adjustments and auxiliary aids, and disabled students have the obligation to identify and document their disabling condition or conditions and to request appropriate academic adjustments. Section 104.4

> explicitly prohibits denying a qualified disabled student the opportunity of full
> and equal participation and benefit, requires that the benefits given to disabled
> students are to be equal to and as effective as those given to others, and prohibits

the concept of separate but equal unless separation is necessary to provide equally effective benefits. . . . Discrimination is also prohibited by requiring post-secondary institutions to provide educational auxiliary aids to students with impaired sensory, manual or speaking skills" [Frank and Wade, 1993, p. 27].

In 1991, the U.S. Department of Education estimated that there were more than 200,000 postsecondary students with learning disabilities (LD) and that the number was increasing rapidly. However, Sitlington and Frank (1990) found that one year after graduation from high school only 6.5 percent of the 50 percent of students with LD who had enrolled in some type of postsecondary setting were still in school. At least two factors may account for this alarmingly low retention statistic, each having implications for the academic advisor. First, for many of these students, college is an initial experience in which personal responsibility and independence become critical. Whereas in high school, teachers, counselors, and parents assumed most of the responsibility for determining needs and accommodations, in the college environment students with LD are solely responsible for making their accommodation needs known (Synatschk, 1995).

Academic Competence. It is critical that advisors serving disabled students work to implement adjustment strategies to address the area of academic competence. Unlike high school, where supportive significant others (parents, teachers, and counselors) were engaged to ensure accommodations, in college the disabled student must assert himself or herself in this area. It is critically important that the advisor have access to documentation regarding the disability, and that he or she understand the accommodations that must be in place. Many students with learning disabilities require aids such as readers, note takers, extended testing time, and classroom adjustments. Without this documentation and recommended accommodations, advising will be limited at best.

The advisor must stress to these students the importance of personal assertiveness. Students must share their accommodation needs with their faculty. Often the advisor must also work with the student's faculty so they understand that it is their responsibility, at times, to modify their curriculum and educational methods to accommodate the needs of LD students. Because most faculty are untrained in these areas, and at times are unwilling to recognize their responsibility, the advisor must be willing to take an active role.

In many instances, reading comprehension, reading rates, written expression, visual processing, and short-term memory are the greatest areas of difficulty for LD students (Synatschk, 1995). Even though these impairments will be different for each LD student, it behooves the advisor when working in the area of academic competence to pay particular attention to course scheduling and curriculum planning. At times, academic schedules will need adjustment so that the student is not enrolled in a number of demanding reading or writing courses concurrently. Also, appropriate and timely assessment of critical academic skills (reading, writing, and mathematics) is necessary so that the sequencing of courses is handled appropriately. Students with learning and physical disabilities may need to be afforded priority scheduling so that appropriate courses can be obtained in locations that do not handicap them.

Personal Involvement. When working in the area of personal involvement on campus, the advisor should caution LD students that academic success may necessitate that they spend more time studying than their peers, that they establish study groups, attend class regularly, use enhanced note-taking strategies, tape lectures, and use tutors and enhanced study strategies (Synatschk, 1995). Not unlike student athletes, LD students may initially find little time for campus involvement, due to the increased demands of academic study and preparation. This issue should be discussed directly and early on with LD student advisees. Limited personal involvement during the first semester or two, until academic competence is documented, may be the best course of action. Exploration into campus activities of personal interest or preprofessional clubs and organizations is probably the best plan for beginning LD students. These students must learn to balance their personal freedom with the need to set personal goals, work on semester projects, and glean information from numerous sources, including class notes, texts, and library reference materials (Synatschk, 1995). It may take LD students more time than their peers to adjust to this balancing act.

Purpose. As advisors work with disabled students in the area of developing or validating life purpose, two important rules should be considered. First, advice and recommendations should be based on students' interests rather than on their limitations; second, counsel should be given based on evidence and not on supposition (Jarrow, 1996).

Most advisors, when working in this area, attempt to confirm that students' career interests and aspirations conform with their previous experiences, academic skills, talents, and knowledge of the career and the majors leading to successful preparation for it.

Jarrow (1996) reports that many students with disabilities are less mature in their career decision making than their nondisabled peers, often deciding to major in special education because their primary career role models were the special education teachers with whom they worked throughout their earlier schooling. Also, in a study by Hitchings and others (1998), fewer students with disabilities than students without disabilities reported reading career materials, completing career interest inventories, participating in job shadowing activities, having employment related to career fields, and participating in volunteer experiences. Many disabled students seem to have less mature career-decision attitudes than their peers without disabilities (Biller, 1988; Bingham, 1980; Fafard and Haubrich, 1981).

This information confirms that advisors must work actively and systemically when addressing the area of developing or validating life purpose. Undecided disabled students must be encouraged to complete career inventories, explore curriculum offerings, and participate in volunteer activities that match career and personal interests. Visits to and active participation in programs sponsored by the college's career services office should be encouraged by the academic advisor. Academic success is further enhanced if disabled students find majors that match their career interests. Determining appropriate career goals is essential in this process.

Gay, Lesbian, and Bisexual Students

The developmental tasks of creating a distinct identity and positive self-esteem can be especially long and complex for gay, lesbian, and bisexual (GLB) students. Troiden's (1988) retrospective study of GLB adults showed that there was a four- to five-year span between an individual's initial homosexual thoughts and when the individual acknowledged these homosexual thoughts to himself or herself. Many GLB students remain closeted either because of their own internalized homophobia or because they fear reprisal (Rhoads, 1997). For the same reasons, GLB students are referred to as the "invisible minority," largely indistinguishable from other students (Welch, 1996). Yet, the students themselves experience an intense feeling of "differentness" from their peers (D'Augelli, 1993).

GLB students often feel stigmatized and shunned by the same family, religious, and educational institutions that support others in their emotional struggles at this age (Ryan and Futterman, 1998). This problem is compounded because many GLB adolescents are in conflict about their identity and feel they must deny or conceal their feelings for fear of rejection by both social institutions and their peers (D'Augelli, 1992). Thus, GLB students are left to work through important developmental tasks without having the important sources of support that sustain others through the ordeal of achieving identity (Ryan and Futterman, 1998).

The primary challenges that characterize GLB students include

- Anxiety about being rejected, especially by peers, family, and perhaps teachers (D'Augelli, 1992; Sears, 1992)
- Accepting their own sexuality and self-worth (Ryan and Futterman, 1998)
- Learning to face and deal effectively with societal discrimination, such as in employment and housing, as well as from religious organizations, the health care system, and the insurance industry (Ryan and Futterman, 1998)
- Living in isolation and loneliness until they establish themselves within an affirming community (D'Augelli, 1992)
- Establishing positive interpersonal relationships (Besner and Spungin, 1995
- Learning to cope with the stress of social and emotional isolation and the stress associated with physical and verbal harassment (Walls and Evans, 1991)

Gay and lesbian adults are seven times more likely than others to be victims of crime (Obear, 1991), and these statistics are reflected in the college environment. Violence and verbal threats and harassment directed toward GLB students are high, especially in residence hall environments (Bourassa and Shipton, 1991). Walls and Washington (1991) contend that cultural norms that generally involve the role of the family or the church make the psychological challenges especially problematic for students of color, for whom relevant support networks are generally less available. The issues are compounded for GLB students of color, who are required to manage multiple levels of stigma (Slater, 1993).

The isolation experienced by GLB students in general may be especially intense for students who have not yet come out to others—a group that is most likely represented by students at the lower academic levels (D'Augelli, 1993). Ryan and Futterman (1998) assert that the isolation occurs on three levels: social, emotional, and cognitive. They explain that those students feel they have no one to talk to, are fearful of discovery, feel alone and different in virtually all social situations, feel a need to be constantly vigilant, experience emotional separation from meaningful others, and fear that same-sex friendships will be misunderstood. Cognitive isolation results from a lack of accurate information about homosexuality. The lack of appropriate information and role models causes the GLB student to build his or her understanding and identity on base stereotypes, with which he or she often has difficulty identifying (Ryan and Futterman, 1998).

For GLB teens, the constant stress, loneliness, and lack of role models and community result in significant levels of alcohol use (DeBord, Wood, Sher, and Good, 1998), depression and other mental health concerns (Mallon, 1992), and attempted suicide (Ryan and Futterman, 1998). Gibson's (1989) literature review indicates that GLB youth are up to three times more likely to attempt suicide than their heterosexual peers, and that GLB youth suicides may constitute up to 30 percent of all completed suicides. The frequency of suicide attempts has been questioned because of the use of convenience sampling (Durby, 1994), but the point remains that the GLB student faces considerably more psychological hurdles than the majority of other college students. For example, many GLB students face the real or imagined prospect that parents and others may cut off both personal and financial support once they learn that their child is gay. D'Augelli (1992) concluded, "At a time when accurate information and supportive experiences are critical to their development, young lesbians and gay men find few, if any, affirming experiences in higher educational settings" (p. 214).

Unlike with the other special populations discussed in this chapter, the advisor may not be aware that an advisee is gay, lesbian, or bisexual. By itself, GLB status is most likely not a relevant issue in the advising relationship. However, for many GLB students, the sense of aloneness is pervasive, and these students in particular need a strong, trusting relationship with an advisor, as well as with other campus professionals.

The process of building an identity not only as a young adult but also as a gay, lesbian, or bisexual person is an arduous one. In Cass's (1983–1984) Sexual

Identity Formation Model, six stages characterize the identity development process of GLBs. The process begins with becoming aware that one's thoughts, feelings, and behaviors are incongruent with one's assumptions of heterosexuality; progresses through comparing feelings with other gay people, becoming involved with a gay community, and accepting one's identity; moves on to becoming angry with heterosexist elements in society; and finally reaches an understanding that sexuality is just one part of a total identity.

Academic Competence. Especially if students are still in the process of gaining self-awareness or in the initial stages of coming out, the time and energy devoted to the process may well interfere with their achieving academic competence. The advisor should watch for warning signs such as frequent class absences, chronic procrastination, problems with concentration, lack of interest in academics, and sudden dislike of school (Besner and Spungin, 1995), and intervene by discussing the reasons for these behaviors. Advisors who are unaware of GLB issues and how to assist students directly may best provide assistance by listening to students' concerns in a nonjudgmental way and then providing referrals to appropriate campus or community personnel. The advisor should make a point of maintaining a strong monitoring relationship with the GLB student because it may take a substantial period before academics are a priority for such a student. Alternatively, perhaps the best course of action for the GLB student who encounters strong conflict with the GLB identity is to limit the academic courseload or even to withdraw from school until the issues are resolved.

Personal Involvement. The advisor may find that the GLB student is interested in participating only in organizations and programs with a GLB theme. If this is the case, the advisor needs to recognize that the student is progressing through Cass's (1983–1984) identity stages in a typical manner. There are skills, such as leadership and decision making, that the student could be encouraged to develop through participating in these organizations. The advisor may also encourage students who are active in GLB-related organizations to develop ways to educate the campus community about issues of importance to them.

Purpose. The advisor may have an especially important role to play in the GLB student's development or validation of life purpose. Gelberg and Chojnacki (1996) assert that "sexual orientation is inextricably connected to the career and life-planning processes. It affects career choices; the ways in which the job search is conducted; the development of work-related interests, values, experiences, and skills; the nature of personal and professional relationships; and the degree of stress experienced at work and at home" (pp. 4–5).

Research indicates that in comparison with heterosexual students, lesbians more readily identify career paths of interest; however, gay males encounter more difficulties than their heterosexual peers (Etringer, Hetherington, and Hillerbrand, 1990). The challenge may be based in part on the discrimination found in the military and in society's fear of gay men teaching and working in social service occupations (Jones, 1978), or it may be based in part on the belief that certain career paths are more appropriate for gay or lesbian students. It is the responsibility of the advisor to help students recognize whether they are limiting their career options because of such stereotypes.

A second critical role of the advisor is to provide information or a referral about individual lifestyles and the working environment. An important consideration is the impact of lifestyle disclosure on work relationships and career advancement. Other issues include identifying involvement in GLB organizations on resumes, the existence of domestic partner benefits, mandatory AIDS testing, geographic locations in relation to gay communities, partner relocation, and conflicts between public and private lifestyles (Hetherington, 1991). Helping GLB students to address these issues carefully before entering a profession is important in part because no national legislation exists to protect the rights of GLBs. One way in which this can be done is by referring students to GLB-related professional organizations. A listing of some organizations can be found in Gelberg and Chojnacki (1996).

Underprepared Students

Underpreparedness is a relative term referring to a student's ability to compete academically with other students attending the same institution. For example, a student who is underprepared to complete the curriculum of an Ivy League school may not be underprepared for a local community college. Underprepared students are often called *developmental education* students. As defined by Maxwell (1997), developmental education students are those whose "skills, knowledge, motivation, and/or academic ability are significantly below those of the 'typical' student in the college or curriculum in which they are enrolled" (p. 2).

Regardless of how underpreparedness is conceived at a particular institution, it has been a persistent concern in the history of American higher education, in large part because of the goal to democratize education (Cross, 1976). In the mid-1800s, preparatory departments offered tutoring and precollege courses as appendages to the regular college curriculum (Casazza and Silverman, 1996). The first remedial course in higher education was offered at Wellesley College in 1894 (Cross, 1976). Underpreparedness in reading, writing, and study skills was so pervasive at Ivy League schools in the early 1900s that remedial and developmental courses were established at Harvard, Yale, and Princeton (Casazza and Silverman, 1996). Many other colleges offered remedial and developmental courses in the 1930s and 1940s (Roueche and Snow, 1977). In the 1970s and 1980s, more holistic remedial and developmental programs were instituted and expanded throughout the country, often funded by federal or state grants. Many of these programs eventually took the form of learning assistance centers and focused on helping the underprepared student to adapt to the college environment and develop cognitive, psychosocial, and career skills (Enright, 1994). Developmental courses are now commonplace in higher education, with about 90 percent of two-year schools and 70 percent of four-year schools offering them

(Boylan, Bonham, Bliss, and Claxton, 1992). Levine and Cureton (1998) indicate that almost one-third of U.S. undergraduates have taken at least one developmental course.

Hardin's (1998) typology of developmental education students provides insight into some of their needs and characteristics. Seven types of students who may need developmental assistance are outlined: the poor chooser, the adult learner, the ignored student, English as a Second Language (ESL) students, disabled students, the user, and the extreme case.

The most common developmental student fits into the first category, the *poor chooser*. This group includes students who did not follow a college preparatory program in high school; once they are in college, they are at a disadvantage because of their lack of substantive background in math, science, and foreign languages in particular. Another group of poor choosers is students who dropped out of high school and are thus less prepared academically as well as conceptually for college. *Adult learners,* who may formerly have been poor choosers, are often in need of remedial or developmental assistance in college either because they lack skills or because their skills are rusty. *Ignored students* have learned to be passive learners, anonymous in the classroom. This group needs a better understanding of how learning occurs and how to act both responsibly and responsively in the academic environment. The developmental learning needs of *ESL students* are usually focused on literacy skills in the English language, although they may need assistance with test taking and time management. *Disabled students* are of two groups, the physically challenged and the learning disabled. Physically challenged students who are underprepared are usually so either because an accident or injury has caused a loss of previous knowledge or because they learned in a one-on-one situation and now need to learn to interact in a classroom. The underprepared learning disabled student often lacks self-confidence because of learning problems, helplessness, and frustration, especially in large lecture classes. The *user* attends college not to learn but to gain from the wider college experience or to avoid full-time employment. These students achieve the minimum grades necessary to remain in school, though they can often perform much better. They are often vocal about their dislike of requirements and policies. Finally, the *extreme case* is increasingly more common in higher education. This is a student burdened with such intense academic, psychological, or personal problems that success in college is impossible until the other issues are addressed successfully. They tend to be disruptive in class or in the residence halls. They may be homeless, violent, drug or alcohol abusers, or mentally ill. Advisors need to learn to identify these students as early as possible and refer them for appropriate professional services (Hardin, 1998).

Many of the characteristics of developmental education students cited almost thirty years ago by Pritchard and Blouschild (1970) hold true today. Those of us who have worked in developmental education recognize that in addition to weak academic skills in one or more areas, these students typically exhibit one or more of the following characteristics: low academic self-concept, unrealistic grade and career expectations, unfocused career objectives, extrinsic motivation, external locus of control, low self-efficacy, inadequate study skills for college success, a belief that learning is memorizing, and a history of passive learning. Because many developmental education students are first-generation college students, they are not likely to have a well-developed concept or vocabulary about higher education. In addition, they are not likely to seek academic or personal assistance (Astin, 1977). These characteristics require active intervention by the advisor if the underprepared student is to succeed in college.

Academic Competence. It is critical that the academic competence of the underprepared student be assessed and communicated to the student with a detailed plan developed to address the areas of academic need. Because the developmental student often has a naive conception of the importance of background skills and knowledge and tends to avoid registering for basic skills courses (Spann and McCrimmon, 1998), the advisor should be direct, emphatic, and prescriptive when designing the plan to overcome deficiencies. It is also important that the advisor understand the prerequisite skills for the courses in which the underprepared student may enroll.

A second important role of the advisor with regard to the theme of academic competence is to help the student develop an internal locus of control to understand that academic success follows in large part from specific actions on the part of the student. Students will need assistance from the advisor in setting long- and short-term goals and in developing and monitoring action plans to achieve those goals.

Third, underprepared students need frequent feedback about their progress and standing (Maxwell, 1997); it is therefore important that the advisor meet regularly with the underprepared student to discuss course progress. Because developmental education students often have inaccurate and unrealistic conceptions of their academic progress, advisors should require students to show evidence for their reports of their standing in each class. When necessary, the advisor should work with the student to develop a specific, written plan of action for improving academic performance. Minimally, this plan should include participation in academic support services and an analysis of the student's study skills.

Fourth, because the underprepared student is likely to have a negative self-concept with respect to the academic environment, it is important that the advisor provide the developmental student with positive and encouraging feedback when appropriate. Another strategy that the advisor could employ to assist the underprepared student to better achieve academic competence, particularly if the student is a first-generation college student, is to share information about operating in the college environment. For example, the advisor may discuss the importance of meeting application deadlines and of regular class attendance, ways to be an active learner, how expectations and requirements differ in high school and college, and ways in which the student may participate in class more actively. Underpreparedness may result from learning problems rooted in a learning disability, so the advisor should be alert for signs of such a disability, which may limit a student's success until it is diagnosed and the appropriate accommodations are implemented.

Personal Involvement. Within the area of personal involvement on campus, the advisor needs to alert underprepared students that they will need to spend more time on academic activities than many other students. As a result, they may need to limit their social involvement, at least initially, until they build a solid academic record. Because research indicates that campus employment for a limited number of hours is associated with higher retention and academic performance (Wilkie and Jones, 1994), students may be encouraged to obtain a work-study job on campus for a few hours a week. The benefits of such employment may include integration into the campus community, learning positive work habits, and developing relationships with professionals and other students. The advisor should also encourage the underprepared student to participate in enrichment programming to develop better understanding of areas important to a liberal education, such as politics, the fine arts, the environment, and other cultures, and of themselves.

Purpose. To help underprepared students in developing or validating life purpose, the advisor needs to recognize that many such students have a limited knowledge of career options, as well as an unrealistic understanding of the skills and abilities required to enter careers. The underprepared student should be encouraged to participate in career exploration courses, if they are available. Computerized career exploration programs can benefit the underprepared student, but follow-up from the advisor or referral to another professional is important so that the student better understands the prerequisite requirements. Just as important as the academic skills related to career opportunities are the personal qualities that students need to develop or enhance while in college. The underprepared student may not fully understand that skills such as timeliness, reliability, enthusiasm, and initiative are integral to both careers and life as an adult.

Special Populations and the Role of the Advising Center

Many of the special student populations addressed in this chapter are served through advising centers. Nationally, 54 percent of adult students, 63 percent of underprepared students, 54 percent of students with disabilities, 44 percent of honors students, and 41 percent of student athletes are served in some manner by university and college advisement or student services centers (Habley and Morales, 1998). For some students in these populations, special academic services are provided by centers and academic advising is performed by departmental faculty or staff advisors. Often this equates to dual advising, or an official advisor and an unofficial advisor. These dynamics can lead to potential problems and areas of conflict for the student advisee. These conflicts center on the coordination of effort, trust, and internal institutional transfers.

Coordination of Effort

As we have addressed, the unique needs and characteristics of many students in these special populations mandate the need for a developmental advising relationship that is goal oriented, ongoing, and curriculum based. An individual advisor must coordinate these efforts and this person should be the advisor of record. If a student is served within an advisement center, he or she should have one primary advisor who works to coordinate the efforts of the student in regard to the three content themes in the advising curriculum. Many academic and student services may exist within the center and the advisor should be the primary person to direct the student, through the results of an individual needs assessment and office interviews, to these special offerings. Problems and confusion can emerge for the student when multiple educators attempt to perform the role of the primary advisor.

Issues of Trust

If meaningful, ongoing, goal-oriented, curriculum-based advising is to occur, trust must be established and maintained between advisors and advisees. Often students served by advising centers are also served by multiple professional and peer advisors. These dynamics will make it difficult for the student advisee to feel confident and secure that a level of trust exists that will make it possible to share relevant information and formulate an ongoing plan in regard to the advising curriculum. Students in these populations need stability in their relationships with educators. Trusting relationships can occur within the context of advising centers if the student is assigned to one advisor and maintains an ongoing relationship with this educator.

Internal Institutional Transfers

Many students are advised at an advising center for one or two years and then transferred to a faculty member in their departmental major. Typically these students have demonstrated academic competence and are now fully engaged in their major area of study. Transfers to departmental faculty should be as seamless as possible. The original advisor best facilitates the handoff to a new advisor. Ideally, a personal introduction would be made. At the very least, students should be prepared to share their progress in regard to the advising curriculum and update the new advisor regarding current initiatives. Also, appropriate records and nonconfidential advising notes should be sent to the new advisor of record.

Institutional Readiness

The developmental advising model presented in this chapter is labor intensive, but we believe it is critical to the success of the special needs students we have discussed. An institution's readiness to implement such an advising model is demonstrated in three interrelated ways—through commitment, policies, and education.

Commitment. For the model to be effective in assisting students to be successful in college, a commitment to adopt the three-dimensional curriculum-based developmental advising model must occur on both the administrative and advisor levels. Because the model is highly personalized, it is both labor and time intensive. It will cost more to implement than a model focusing only on course scheduling concerns, because the advisor-student ratio must be lower in the developmental advising model. For most institutions, a decision will have to be made at the administrative level between appropriating resources for advising or for other priorities. A fundamental question that the institution needs to ask is whether the cost of implementing this model is offset by the benefits. Research indicates that required developmental advising can be an effective vehicle for increasing retention rates (Tinto, 1993). Many of the special populations we have discussed in this chapter are already at risk for dropping out of school because of lack of preparation, psychological problems, external pressures, or general adjustment issues, and they need the intensive assistance provided in this model.

Institutional commitment is also demonstrated through the administrative placement and reporting mechanism. Is there a professional responsible for directing or coordinating the model? At what level is this person hired? Does the director-coordinator have a direct line to a top-level administrator? Is the advising program an integral part of the institution and of the life of the student? What criteria are used to select advisors?

Another way in which institutional commitment is demonstrated is by the incentives offered for good advising. Is advising evaluated on a regular basis? Are criteria in place for choosing advisors? Is advising a factor in faculty-staff evaluations? Is it a factor in tenure and promotions decisions? Are funds available for research relating to advising? Is it the subject of colloquia? With what frequency is it discussed at the management level? Is there public recognition for high-quality advising?

The advisor's commitment to implement the model must also be clearly demonstrated through willingness to prepare for the role of developmental academic advisor. Prerequisite background knowledge and skills include a thorough understanding of developmental theory for both the traditional-age and adult student, familiarity with the literature on student success, an understanding of the unique needs for each population advised, a solid knowledge of campus and community resources, an understanding of career development theory and resources relating to career exploration, an awareness of the academic preparation required for various courses, and an understanding of the implications of assessment for achieving academic competence. The advisor's willingness to assume a developmental advising role is also demonstrated through networking with other professionals who will be instrumental to the advisees' success. For example, an advisor working through an advising center needs to establish a linkage with faculty in various academic departments, as well as with administrative staff in key offices such as financial aid, career services, and community services.

Policies and Procedures. Ideally, policies and procedures are linked to commitment. For the three-theme developmental advising curriculum to be effective, at a minimum institutions will need to adopt policies and procedures for placement testing and mandatory course placement, advisor training, and regular and frequent student participation. Tinto (1993) notes that effective developmental advising programs are integral to the institution and required of all students. Although we support the model for all students, we strongly encourage its implementation for at least the special-needs populations we have discussed in this chapter.

Education. For the model to be effective, it is critical that education occur at many levels. First, so that the model is supported at the top administrative levels, the relationship among college mission, retention, and developmental advising needs to be identified. That is, the top administrators need to educate themselves about the reasons for implementing the model. Second, the faculty must be educated about the rationale and design of the model and about the collaborative role they play in making the model work for students. Third, the core faculty or staff who will be the developmental advisors needs to be trained in the skills and knowledge listed previously. Fourth, the students themselves need to understand how they can benefit from the developmental advising relationship and what their responsibilities are in that relationship.

Conclusion

This chapter has presented an approach to academic advising for students in special populations that is curriculum based and process oriented. Many students with special needs require special attention and focus from their college. We believe that developmental advising is an approach that colleges and universities should embrace when designing advising programs for students with special needs. In fact, all students deserve and are entitled to the challenge and support of developmental advising. If this is not possible for all students, then students in special populations should receive first consideration.

References

Astin, A. W. *Four Critical Years.* San Francisco: Jossey-Bass, 1977.

Astin, A. W. "Student Involvement: A Developmental Theory for Higher Education." *Journal of College Student Personnel,* 1984, 25(4), 297–308.

Besner, H. F., and Spungin, C. I. *Gay and Lesbian Students: Understanding Their Needs.* Bristol, Pa.: Taylor & Francis, 1995.

Biller, E. F. "Career Decision-Making Attitudes of College Students with Learning Disabilities." *Journal of Postsecondary Education and Disability*, 1988, *6*(4), 14–20.

Bingham, G. "Career Maturity of Learning Disabled Adolescents." *Psychology in the Schools*, 1980, *17*, 135–139.

Blackburn, A. C., and Erickson, D. B. "Predictable Crises of the Gifted Student." *Journal of Counseling and Development*, 1986, *64*(9), 552–555.

Bourassa, D., and Shipton, B. "Addressing Lesbian and Gay Issues in Residence Hall Environments." In N. J. Evans and V. A. Walls (ed.), *Beyond Tolerance: Gays, Lesbians and Bisexuals on Campus.* Alexandria, Va.: American College Student Personnel Association, 1991.

Boylan, H. R., Bonham, B. S., Bliss, L., and Claxton, C. S. "The State of the Art in Developmental Education." Paper presented at the First National Conference on Research in Developmental Education, Charlotte, N.C., Nov. 1992.

Casazza, M. E., and Silverman, S. L. *Learning Assistance and Developmental Education: A Guide for Effective Practice.* San Francisco: Jossey-Bass, 1996.

Cass, V. C. "Homosexual Identity: A Concept in Need of Definition." *Journal of Homosexuality*, 1983–1984, *9*(2–3), 105–126.

Cross, K. P. *Accent on Learning.* San Francisco: Jossey-Bass, 1976.

Danzig, A. B. "Honors at the University of Maryland: A Status Report on Programs for Talented Students." University of Maryland, 1982. (ED 243 358)

D'Augelli, A. R. "Teaching Lesbian/Gay Development: From Oppression to Exceptionality." In K. M. Harbeck (ed.), *Coming out of the Classroom Closet: Gay and Lesbian Students, Teachers, and Curricula.* New York: Harrington Park Press, 1992.

D'Augelli, A. R. "Preventing Mental Health Problems Among Lesbian and Gay College Students." *Journal of Primary Prevention*, 1993, *13*(4), 245–261.

Day, A. L. "Honors Students." In M. L. Upcraft and J. N. Gardner (ed.), *The Freshman Year Experience.* San Francisco: Jossey-Bass, 1989.

DeBord, K. A., Wood, P. K., Sher, K. J., and Good, G. E. "The Relevance of Sexual Orientation to Substance Abuse and Psychological Distress Among College Students." *Journal of College Student Development*, 1998, *39*(2), 157–168.

Delisle, J. R. "Death with Honors: Suicide Among Gifted Adolescents." *Journal of Counseling and Development*, 1986, *64*(9), 558–560.

Durby, D. D. "Gay, Lesbian, and Bisexual Youth." In T. Crescenzo (ed.), *Helping Gay and Lesbian Youth: New Policies, New Programs, and New Practices.* Binghamton, N.Y.: Harrington Park Press, 1994.

Ender, S. C. "Developmental Advising." In M. Houland, E. Anderson, W. McGuire, D. Crockett, T. Kaufmann, and D. Woodward (eds.), *Academic Advising for Student Success and Retention.* Iowa City: The Noel Levitz Center for Enrollment Management, 1997.

Enright, G. "College Learning Skills: Frontierland Origins of the Learning Assistance Center." In M. Maxwell (ed.), *From Access to Success: A Book of Readings on College Developmental Education and Learning Assistance Programs.* Clearwater, Fla.: H & H Publishing, 1994.

Etringer, B. D., Hetherington, C., and Hillerbrand, E. "The Influence on Sexual Orientation of Career Decision Making: An Initial Investigation." *Journal of Homosexuality*, 1990, *19*(4), 103–111.

Fafard, M., and Haubrich, P. A. "Vocational and Social Adjustment of Learning Disabled Young Adults: A Follow-Up Study." *Learning Disabled Quarterly,* 1981, *4,* 12–130.

Frank, K., and Wade, P. "Disabled Student Services in Postsecondary Education: Who's Responsible for What?" *Journal of College Student Development,* 1993, *34*(1), 26–30.

Gelberg, S., and Chojnacki, J. T. *Career and Life Planning with Gay, Lesbian, and Bisexual Persons.* Alexandria, Va.: American Counseling Association, 1996.

Gerrity, D., Lawrence, J. F., and Sedlacek, W. "Honors and Nonhonors Freshmen: Demographics, Attitudes, Interests, and Behaviors." *NACADA Journal,* 1993, *13*(1), 43–52.

Gibson, P. "Gay Male and Lesbian Youth Suicide." In M. Feinleib (ed.), *Preventions and Interventions in Youth Suicide.* (DHHS Publication No. ADM89-1623). Washington, D.C.: Government Printing Office, 1989.

Habley, W. R., and Morales, R. H. "Advising in Advising Offices or Centers." In W. R. Habley and R. H. Morales, *Current Practices in Academic Advising: Final Report on ACT's Fifth National Survey of Academic Advising.* National Academic Advising Association Monograph Series, no. 6. Manhattan, Kans.: National Academic Advising Association, 1998.

Hardin, C. J. "Who Belongs in College?" In J. L. Higbee and P. L. Dwinell (eds.), *Developmental Education: Preparing Successful College Students.* Columbia, S.C.: National Resource Center for the First-Year Experience and Students in Transition, 1998.

Hetherington, C. "Life Planning and Career Counseling with Gay and Lesbian Students." In N. J. Evans and V. A. Walls (eds.), *Beyond Tolerance: Gays, Lesbians and Bisexuals on Campus.* Alexandria, Va.: American College Student Personnel Association, 1991.

Hitchings, W., and others. "Identifying the Career Development Needs of College Students with Disabilities." *Journal of College Student Development,* 1998, *39*(1), 23–32.

Jarrow, J. E. "The Americans with Disabilities Act, Students with Disabilities, and the Role of the Academic Advisor." *NACADA Journal,* 1996, *16*(2), 6–10.

Jones, G. P. "Counseling Gay Adolescents." *Counselor Education and Supervision,* 1978, *18,* 144–152.

Levine, A., and Cureton, J. S. "What We Know About Today's College Students." *About Campus,* 1998, *3*(1), 4–9.

Mallon, G. P. "Counseling Strategies with Gay and Lesbian Youth." In K. M. Harbeck (ed.), *Coming out of the Classroom Closet: Gay and Lesbian Students, Teachers, and Curricula.* New York: Harrington Park Press, 1992.

Mathiasen, R. E. "Characteristics of the College Honors Student." *Journal of College Student Personnel,* 1985, *26*(2), 171–173.

Maxwell, M. *Improving Student Learning Skills.* Clearwater, Fla.: H & H Publishing, 1997.

Obear, K. "Homophobia." In N. J. Evans and V. A. Walls (eds.), *Beyond Tolerance: Gays, Lesbians and Bisexuals on Campus.* Alexandria, Va.: American College Student Personnel Association, 1991.

Pritchard, R. W., and Blouschild, B. *Why College Students Fail.* Hahwah, N.J.: Funk & Wagnalls, 1970.

Rhoads, R. A. "Implications of the Growing Visibility of Gay and Bisexual Male Students on Campus." *NASPA Journal,* 1997, *34*(4), 275–286.

Robertson, J. H. "The Superior Student: Characteristics, Aspirations and Needs." In J. W. Cohen (ed.), *The Superior Student in American Higher Education.* New York: McGraw-Hill, 1966.

Ross, J. M. "Transitions, Triggers, and Return to College: No Simple Solution." *Journal of College Student Development,* 1988, *29,* 112–118.

Roueche, J. E., and Snow, J. J. *Overcoming Learning Problems: A Guide to Developmental Education in College.* San Francisco: Jossey-Bass, 1977.

Ryan, C., and Futterman, D. *Lesbian and Gay Youth.* New York: Columbia University Press, 1998.

Schroer, A.C.P., and Dorn, F. J. "Enhancing the Career and Personal Development of Gifted College Students." *Journal of Counseling and Development,* 1986, *64*(9), 567–571.

Sears, J. T. "Educators, Homosexuality, and Homosexual Students: Are Personal Feelings Related to Professional Beliefs?" In K. M. Harbeck (ed.), *Coming out of the Classroom Closet.* New York: Harrington Park Press, 1992.

Shriberg, A., and Brodzinski, F. R. *Rethinking Services for College Athletes.* San Francisco: Jossey-Bass, 1984.

Simons, H. D., Van Rheenen, D., and Covington, M. V. "Academic Motivation and the Student Athlete." *Journal of College Student Development,* 1999, *40*(2), 151–161.

Sitlington, P. L., and Frank, A. R. "Are Adolescents with Learning Disabilities Successfully Crossing the Bridge into Adult Life?" *Learning Disability Quarterly,* 1990, *13,* 97–111.

Slater, B. R. "Violence Against Lesbian and Gay Male College Students." *Journal of College Student Psychotherapy,* 1993, *8*(1,2), 177–212.

Spann, M. G. Jr., and McCrimmon, S. "Remedial/Developmental Education: Past, Present, and Future." In J. L. Higbee and P. L. Dwinell (eds.), *Developmental Education: Preparing Successful College Students.* Columbia, S.C.: National Resource Center for the First-Year Experience and Students in Transition, 1998.

Stephens, J., and Eison, J. A. "A Comparative Investigation of Honors and Non-Honors Students." *Forum for Honors,* Fall-Winter 1986–1987, pp. 17–25.

Synatschk, K. "College-Bound Students with Learning Disabilities: Assessment of Readiness for Academic Success." *LD Forum,* Summer 1995 (http://www.ldonline/ldin_depth/postsecondary/ldforum_assess.html).

Tinto, V. *Leaving College: Rethinking the Causes and Cures of Student Attrition.* (2nd ed.) Chicago: University of Chicago Press, 1993.

Troiden, R. R. "Homosexual Identity Development." *Journal of Adolescent Health,* 1988, *9,* 105.

Tucker, C. "Striking Down of Tough Academic Standards Will Hurt Black Athletes." *Philadelphia Inquirer,* Mar. 13, 1999, p. 16.

U.S. Department of Education. "Thirteenth Annual Report to Congress on the Implementation of the Education of the Handicapped Act." Washington, D.C.: U.S. Department of Education, 1991.

Walls, V. A., and Evans, N. J. "Using Psychosocial Development Theories to Understand and Work with Gay and Lesbian Persons." In N. J. Evans and V. A. Walls (eds.), *Beyond Tolerance: Gays, Lesbians and Bisexuals on Campus.* Alexandria, Va.: American College Student Personnel Association, 1991.

Walls, V. A., and Washington, J. *"Becoming an Ally."* In N. J. Evans and V. A. Walls (eds.), *Beyond Tolerance: Gays, Lesbians and Bisexuals on Campus.* Alexandria, Va.: American College Student Personnel Association, 1991.

Walter, T. L., and Smith, D.E.P. "Student Athletes." In M. L. Upcraft and J. N. Gardner (eds.). *The Freshman Year Experience.* San Francisco: Jossey-Bass, 1989.

Welch, P. J. "In Search of a Caring Community: Group Therapy for Gay, Lesbian and Bisexual Students." *Journal of College Student Psychotherapy,* 1996, *11*(1), 27–40.

Wilkie, C. J., and Jones, M. "Academic Benefits of On-Campus Employment to First-Year Developmental Education Students." *Journal of the Freshman Year Experience,* 1994, *6*(2), 37–56.

Chapter Ten

Advising Students in Transition

George E. Steele, Melinda L. McDonald

tran•si´•tion, n [L. Transitio] *1. Passage from one state, stage, subject,*
or place to another; change.
—*Webster's Collegiate Dictionary* (1983)

There are three phases to transitions: endings, neutral zones, and beginnings (Bridges, 1980). An ending occurs at the point of beginning something new. Students entering college for the first time are beginning a new life phase. While this movement is a new beginning, it also signals an end to a previous situation (such as their high school experience or previous college experience). In this new environment, students confront a different set of rules, regulations, norms, and expectations. They may lack direction and appear confused about themselves in relation to the environment during this period of adjustment. Many students question whether coming to college was the right choice for them as they struggle with fitting in and balancing academics with other activities. This neutral zone or "moving-in" process (Schlossberg, Lynch, and Chickering, 1989) is frequently uncomfortable for students and can extend until they become familiar with the institutional setting, the academic demands of higher education, and their place among their peers. Advisors work every day with students who are going through transitions. Recognizing and understanding the different stages of transitions and the impact they have on students is key to improving interventions in academic advising.

This chapter focuses on advising four types of students in transition: undecided students, major-changers, transfer students, and adult students. Undecided students represent a significant portion of freshman who begin college each year. In addition to dealing with the transition of moving in and adjusting, these students also need assistance with both academic and career exploration. Major-changers are students with advanced hours who may not be making progress toward a major or who have been denied admission to a selective program. This group also includes students who have delayed the major and career exploration process. Similar to undecided students, major-changers need to address academic and career decision making. However, because these students have advanced hours and may have already selected an academic major that did not work out for them, the major-changing transition may be more complex and intense than the undecided transition.

When changing institutions, transfer students are signaling the end of their identity with one university and the beginning of a new identity with a different university. This transition affects transfer students' existing social relationships, academic and career goals, and expectations of academic performance. Adult students also need to face the ending of former self-perceptions, responsibilities, and expectations as they learn to modify roles and balance school with work and family.

This chapter is divided into four sections, each of which addresses one of these groups of students in transition. Each section describes the characteristics that distinguish that group and how their needs may differ from those of the student population in general, and provides advising approaches, practical suggestions, and models for working with that particular student population.

Undecided Students

Sooner or later we all have to ask the question, What do I want to be when I grow up? Some students find it easier to answer this question than others. Those who have experienced difficulty because they are "unwilling, unable, or unready to make educational or vocational decisions have been referred to as *undecided* in the research" (Gordon, 1995, p. x). The fact that this is a highly studied group of college students is understandable within the context of transitions. After all, many traditional-age college students are asking this question as they move from adolescent to adult roles. This is the time in life when a great deal of energy is focused on defining self and addressing the future. With the multiple possibilities of academic and career options ahead of them, combined with the forces of internal and external pressures, undecided students are certainly a group in transition.

Characteristics of Undecided Students

The question of why some students are decided while others are undecided about academic and vocational choice while in college has been the subject of research for many decades (Gordon, 1995). Many noted researchers have offered suggestions (Holland, 1973; Osipow, 1983,). Other researchers have explored specific issues in trying to assess the differences between decided and undecided students (Apple, Haak, and Witzke, 1970; Kimes and Troth, 1974; Serling and Betz, 1980; Taylor and Betz, 1983; Zytowski, 1965). In recent years the focus of the research has shifted to defining subtypes of undecided and decided students (Newman, Fuqua, and Minger, 1990; Savickas and Jorgourna, 1991). This approach is characterized by use of multiple variables to help identify clusters of students who share similar characteristics. These studies offer promise because they help provide a unique way of grouping undecided students for specifically designed interventions based on their personality characteristics and decision-making abilities.

The literature comparing types of undecided and decided students helps advisors consider how needs may vary within this population (Gordon, 1995, 1998). An advantage of using the undecided subtype perspective is that it can help focus the development of interventions and training as well as the evaluation of program services. A disadvantage of this approach is that few students match subtypes exactly and individual attention must still be given to each student. However, the subtype perspective can assist advisors in determining a student's unique profile.

Gordon (1998) reviewed fifteen studies that investigated subtypes of decided and undecided students. She proposes seven subtypes—three decided and four undecided—whose defining characteristics are discussed here, along with possible advising considerations.

Very decided. These students feel good about themselves, believe that they have control over their lives, and see themselves as making good decisions regarding their future. Although they are capable of implementing choices or making plans, it may still be necessary for advisors to review the exploration process with them.

Somewhat decided. These students have some doubts about their decisions and have higher levels of state and trait anxiety and lower levels of self-clarity, decisiveness, and self-esteem. They may have made premature choices because of external pressures. By taking time to encourage these students to explore their concerns, advisors can in the long run help them confirm their original choices or identify a well-grounded alternative.

Unstable decided. These students exhibit high goal instability, a high level of anxiety, and a lack of confidence in their ability to perform adequately. They may also experience ambivalence about their choices and believe that when a decision has been made there is no reason to seek help to confirm or change their direction. Advising strategies would include discussing students' career development history along with the goal of improving their decision-making skills.

Tentatively undecided. These students feel comfortable with themselves, have a strong sense of personal esteem, and are more vocationally mature. They may exhibit a vocational direction and are often intuitive decision makers. They do not perceive barriers to achieving their goals and are confident that a decision will be made when it feels right. Advisors can help these students establish a plan to explore and discuss the relationship of values to work and nonwork tasks, and concerns about commitment.

Developmentally undecided. These students are dealing with the normal developmental tasks involved in the major and career decision-making process. They need to gather pertinent information about themselves and the world of work and develop decision-making skills. They may have multiple potential, that is, they may be interested and competent to succeed in many areas. Advising strategies would include traditional psychoeducational and career planning interventions.

Seriously undecided. These students have low levels of vocational identity, self-clarity, and self-esteem. They have limited knowledge of educational and occupational alternatives and may be looking for the "perfect" choice. They may be seeking occupational information to support that choice. In addition to utilizing traditional psychoeducational and career planning interventions, advisors may need to refer these students to personal counseling due to the scope of their problems.

Chronically indecisive. These students have excessive anxiety that permeates many facets of their lives. They are often distressed, unclear about their career options, and dependent on others' assistance and approval when making decisions. Advisors may need to refer these students to long-term counseling rather than begin academic and career advising with them.

Advisors can draw on a variety of similar advising techniques and resources to assist many of these students. The second phase of a transition is a time of emptiness or unintelligible patterns and a lack of direction (Bridges, 1980). Clearly, some decided and undecided students may have the same transitional characteristics. The sensitive advisor recognizes that even some declared students can benefit from some of the advising strategies and resources developed for the undecided student population.

Advising Approaches for Undecided Students

Many advising strategies and resources can be used with different types of undecided students. A clear example is the general assistance that students in many of the subtypes need in the academic and career exploration process. Gordon's (1998) synthesis illuminates the need to integrate the academic and vocational choice processes. Although administratively academics and career may be considered separate concerns, many students do not make such fine distinctions. Many see the choice of major and occupation as one. A unified academic-and-career advising approach may be more important to this group of students compared to other groups.

The Exploration Process. The central advising task in working with undecided students is helping them with the exploration process. Gordon (1992) proposed a model for this process that includes four components:

- *Self-knowledge:* Addresses the need for the assessment of personal interests, abilities, and values, as well as goal setting
- *Educational knowledge:* Includes an understanding of the value of different levels of educational programs, academic majors, curricula, academic skill development, and credentialing or licensure
- *Occupational knowledge:* Addresses career development and job-seeking skills such as writing resumes and cover letters and interview techniques; job exploration and preparation activities, such as co-ops and

internships; assessing occupational information, such as entry-level expertise, occupational task identification, job marketability, salary ranges, and the physical demands of the job

- *Decision-making knowledge:* Addresses the integration of self-knowledge with educational and occupational information, the influence of decision-making styles, the acquisition of decision-making strategies, and approaches to goal implementation

The goal of this model is to provide a framework to help students gather the kind of information needed to make realistic and satisfying choices. The Major and Career Exploration Web site [http://www.uvc.ohio-state.edu/capsheets/tmcefc.html] developed in University College at The Ohio State University provides an example of how this model can be used to integrate resources to aid students in both an advising and instructional way.

Subtypes and the Exploration Process. Advising students using this model of exploration raises some important issues when considering the proposed subtypes:

- Different subtypes will need more emphasis on and assistance with specific components of the model.
- The exploration process is not necessarily linear.
- The role of the advisor is to help students recognize where they are in the process and to provide structure when needed.
- Using literature on the subtypes helps advisors focus on those students who are "unwilling, unable, or unready" to engage in the exploration process (Gordon, 1995, p. x).

The last point emphasizes that for a variety of reasons individual decided and undecided students might not be ready to engage in active exploration (Chickering and Reisser, 1993). Understanding the characteristics of different types of students helps advisors focus on possible advising approaches. For example, some tentatively undecided students might be unwilling to explore because they do not want to deal with issues of commitment. Some unstable decided students may not be ready to explore because even though they have made a decision, their goals are unstable and they are highly anxious about their choice. One critical issue to address when working with some of the undecided subtypes is that they may not be ready or they may be reluctant to start any aspect of exploration. In these situations, it is probably good to remember the Chinese proverb, "All long journeys begin with one step." Helping students determine where they are in the process and encouraging them to take a few small steps might lead to a degree of success that can be built on.

Incorporating the tools of subtype literature and exploration models into advising can enhance our understanding of undecided students. These tools are not meant to stand in the way or interfere with the establishment of an open and honest dialogue with students, but they can be used to support and challenge undecided students as they engage in the exploration process.

Major-Changers

Major-changers constitute a large segment of the undergraduate student population on college campuses today. Previous research on this group of students has estimated that between 50 to 75 percent of students change their major at least once before graduation (Foote, 1980; Noel, 1985; Titley and Titley, 1980; Titley, Titley, and Wolff, 1976). Helping students move through a major-changing transition requires patience, advanced-level helping skills, and knowledge of college student development and career development theories. This portion of the chapter address the reasons that students change their majors, and suggests advising approaches that may be useful in working with this group of students.

Reasons for Changing Majors

There are a variety of reasons why students change majors. Lack of information, outside influence, developmental issues, and academic difficulties are the main categories that provide an explanation for this frequently occurring phenomenon.

Lack of Information. Perhaps the most common reason for changing majors is lack of information (Kramer, Higley, and Olsen, 1994; Pierson, 1962). Students are exposed to a limited number of subject areas at the high school level and are often overwhelmed by the number and variety of majors an institution offers. Similarly, students entering college are knowledgeable about a small number of occupations. They also lack information about the major and career decision-making process. They may come from high schools that did not provide career planning or decision-making assistance (Lewallen, 1993). These students may have chosen a major based on inaccurate information or just to choose something, without knowing the steps for deciding on a major.

A key element in the decision-making process is self-information. Often students have not explored their interests and are unaware of their abilities, skills, and values. Decision-making style frequently plays a role in changing majors. According to Coscarelli (1983), spontaneous decision makers tend to change their minds frequently, moving from one major to the next without gathering pertinent information. Conversely, systematic decision makers tend to choose a major and persist, even when faced with information that may indicate incongruencies between them and their chosen major. In the extreme, neither style is productive and can lead to either unrealistic or uninformed major choices.

Outside Influence. Some students change majors because their original choice was not their own. Parents, family members, and friends influence students to follow particular academic paths (Gordon and Polson, 1985). Doing what others recommend is sometimes viewed as easier than taking the time to engage in the exploration process. Students change majors when they realize that the major someone else has chosen for them is not interesting or is too difficult.

Developmental Issues. Not every student is ready to engage in the major and career decision-making process in the freshman year. Chickering and Reisser (1993) have outlined seven developmental tasks that traditional-age students (ages seventeen to twenty-three) work on during their college years. According to their theory, upon entering college students begin working on the first three developmental tasks (developing competence, managing emotions, and developing autonomy) simultaneously. It is not possible, however, for some students to work on all three of these tasks at the same time. They spend a great deal of time dealing with the social demands of the university and questioning whether or not they belong. Therefore, making an initial choice of a major may not be as important as other developmental issues. For these students, a serious choice of a major is delayed until other developmental tasks are completed. Adult students may revisit some of these tasks as they adjust again (or for the first time) to college demands.

Academic Difficulty. Some students change majors because they have been having academic difficulty in premajor or major course work. Poor academic preparation or an unrealistic determination of abilities may play a part in such students changing their majors (Gordon and Polson, 1985). Students may be unaware that college coursework requires a higher level of skills and abilities than high school. As a result, it may not be possible for some students to succeed in certain fields of study. Students who are not making academic progress toward or who are denied admission to selective academic units constitute a large number of major-changers. More and more academic units are employing enrollment management to limit the size of certain programs, such as business, health sciences, education, journalism and communication, and computer science. Students enrolled in these programs may have gone through a well-planned decision-making process but were not aware of the competitive nature of the major or had unrealistic expectations about their chances of entering the program.

To facilitate movement through this transition, major-changers need accurate, up-to-date information about majors, including completing prerequisite coursework and other requirements for entry. Current occupational information needs to be provided as well so that these students have a clear understanding of their career options. Many students need to reexamine their interests, abilities, skills, and values in relation to both major and occupational information.

Advising Approaches for Major-Changers

Advisors who work with major-changers need to have general knowledge about the majors offered at their institution, as well as information about options outside these institutions. Students denied admission to certain programs may want to transfer to another institution to pursue their original choice of major and may not be interested in exploring alternatives. Advisors also need to understand the relationship between major and career information and have knowledge of the career planning and job search processes. Students who are changing majors in their sophomore and junior years are also exploring career-related experiences and need help with resume writing and interviewing. Knowledge of career services offices, career events, and workshops is essential to providing good academic advising to this population.

Students who are denied admission to selective programs present a variety of emotions, including anger, disappointment, confusion, and anxiety. These students experience tremendous loss in realizing that they will not be able to reach their goals. According to Schlossberg and Robinson (1996), a *nonevent* is an event that does not happen. For these students, being denied entrance to their program of choice becomes a nonevent in their lives. Schlossberg and Robinson describe the *Dream-Reshaping Process* to help individuals cope with nonevents. This process has tremendous applicability to students who do not gain access to their programs of choice. The phases of the process are described here and applied to the advising process.

• *Acknowledging* that a dream has not been fulfilled is the first step in the dream-reshaping process. The goal of advising at this initial stage is to establish rapport and assess students' issues, concerns, and coping strategies. Listening to students and allowing them to tell their story in a supportive and nonjudgmental environment is essential. It is also important to explore students' support systems and determine who they have told (parents, friends, and so on). For some students the advisor is the first person they have talked to about the denial. Acknowledging the loss and giving students the opportunity to verbalize the event and the impact it is having on them helps them to understand fully the reality of their situation.

• *Easing nonevent stress* that comes from the loss of a dream can bring relief, especially if the emotional reactions were uncomfortable. The goal of advising at this stage is to process feelings resulting from rejection and to discuss support services. Advisors need to encourage expression of feelings, such as anger, disappointment, loss, anxiety, confusion, and blame. Validating and clarifying these feelings helps students understand that their feelings are justified. Advisors need to provide information about alternatives advising and how the program and resources can assist students in setting goals. Advisors also need to be positive about the change process and optimistic in relation to students' situations (past, present, and future).

• *Refocusing* involves letting go of old expectations and reframing the nonevent. At this stage, the advising goal is to assist students in reassessing their initial choice of major and in establishing a link between their previous and future choices. Strategies to accomplish this goal include exploring students' motivation for selecting their initial major or career, introducing and discussing the idea that there are other options (alternative majors) worth considering that fulfill criteria they have identified as important, and determining where the student is in the decision-making process. Some students may have already started to think about other majors to pursue, while others are not ready to explore alternatives.

• *Reshaping* the future is done by identifying new dreams or fresh visions. Possible options at this stage are "holding onto a dream, modifying the dream, or letting it go completely" (Schlossberg and Robinson, 1996). The advising goal in relation to reshaping involves helping students analyze their current academic situation and establish a new plan for success. Advising strategies at this stage consist of reviewing students' academic records and having them discuss their academic strengths and limitations; reexamining self-information in relation to major and career information; referring to resources, such as specific Web sites, advisors in academic units of interest, career services offices, employers, and so on; and helping students to integrate self, major, and career information and implement their new choice. Some students may choose to hold onto their dream and reapply to the program of study from which they were denied. Other students may modify their plan by applying to the same program of study at different institutions. Still others are ready to move on and let go of their dream completely. These students have chosen other majors that are realistic and attainable and have developed new dreams for the future.

Changing majors is a difficult transition for students. Advisors working with this population need to feel comfortable with expression of feelings and be knowledgeable in determining the difference between disappointment and depression. Some students may benefit from personal counseling to help them cope. Most students simply need information about alternative majors and the decision-making process. Providing support and having an understanding of what students are experiencing as they move through a major-changing transition are the keys to helping this group of students become successful.

Adult Students

Over the last twenty-five years the number of adult students in higher education institutions has grown dramatically. Adult students are those who are twenty-five years old and older and enrolled either full-time or part-time in undergraduate, graduate, or professional programs of study. College enrollment data as of fall 1995 indicate that adult students constitute 42.6 percent of all college students (U.S. Department of Education, 1998). Although adult students will continue to be an important population on college campuses, the number of adult students enrolling in institutions of higher education is expected to decrease slightly over the next ten years (Gerald, 1998).

Characteristics of Adult Students

Currently most adult students are enrolling in colleges and universities to resume programs of study; few adult students are enrolling in college for the first time. This trend is the result of a slow reversal that began in the late 1960s, when the majority of adult students in college were first-time undergraduates. Adult women constitute a larger segment of the undergraduate population than adult men. This difference suggests that traditional roles may still be operating to some degree, causing some women to delay educational pursuits until after raising a family (Nordstrom, 1989).

Adult students return to higher education for a variety of reasons. Two surveys conducted in the mid-1980s suggest both career motivations (advancement or change) and personal motivations (to increase knowledge or earn a degree) (Nordstrom, 1989; Sewall, 1984). According to Knox (1980), adult learners experiencing a life-change event were more likely to enroll in college. Similarly, a state of transition (Schlossberg, 1984, 1987; Schlossberg, Lynch, and Chickering, 1989) has also been found to influence adults in returning to a learning environment. Transitions may be prompted by structured events (such as divorce or early retirement) or by a nonevent, such as the realization that a long-awaited job promotion is not going to happen. These events act as catalysts for change, prompting individuals to evaluate their situations and determine what is needed to take the next life-enhancing step.

Much of the research on adult students compares the characteristics of this special population to the characteristics of students entering college directly from high school. Richter-Antion (1986) found that relative to traditional-age students, nontraditional students had a greater sense of purpose, stronger consumer orientations, and multiple non-school-related commitments and responsibilities; lacked an age cohort; and experienced limited social acceptability and support for their student status. The majority of adult students tend to be commuters (Benshoff, 1993) who have active family and work roles. Appling (1991) found that many older students were parents and a significant number of these were single parents. Hughes (1983) found that adult students tend to be employed, married, and have families. As a result of these multiple commitments, adult students may have difficulty balancing family, work, and education, and determining which area of their lives is most important. Time constraints prevent adult students from spending more time on campus. Conversely, traditional students tend to have limited commitments and are more campus-focused than adult students.

Adult students and younger adult students have also been compared on the basis of their approaches to learning (Hughes, 1983). Adult learners tend to be motivated intrinsically rather than extrinsically, to question why they need to learn something, and to be ready to learn things that can be applied to real-life situations (Knowles, Holton, and Swanson, 1998).

Adult students prefer a more informal approach to learning in which work and life experiences are integrated. Other characteristics that have been used to describe adult students include achievement oriented, highly motivated, and relatively independent; lacking in study and communication skills and the ability to succeed in an academic setting; and being uncertain in dealing with authority (Aslanian, 1996; Benshoff, 1993; Cross, 1980; Krager, Wrenn, and Hirt,

1990). Younger adult students tend to be more familiar with the formal learning process and therefore are more successful in courses taught by instructors who rely on traditional teaching methods.

It can be argued that adult students have a different set of concerns than younger adult students—concerns that require more specialized services. Several authors (Byrd, 1990; Hughes, 1983; Martin, 1988; Rawlins, 1979) have suggested the following services to meet the needs of adult students: separate registration, advising, and orientation services; adequate parking; child care; more evening, weekend, and summer course offerings; assistance with financial aid and housing; information services and communication networks; social networking and support; educating university faculty and staff about the needs of nontraditional students; and increased students' awareness of and access to personal, academic, and career counseling services.

Advising Approaches for Adult Students

Adult students benefit most from advising approaches that take into consideration their unique needs and special circumstances. Coursework and academic advising that are delivered conveniently, expediently, and cost-effectively can impact the adult learner's decision to enroll in an institution of higher learning.

Distance Learning. Offering courses through distance learning provides adult students who live in rural or remote areas with access to coursework without leaving their communities or even their homes. For adult students who have children, who work, or both, these modes of delivering coursework save both time and money and in many cases make a difference in whether or not they enroll in institutions of higher learning. Similarly, at more and more colleges and universities, admissions, registration, and financial aid services are being handled on-line as opposed to in person. On-line resources, such as those provided by libraries, allow students to do research from their homes instead of traveling to campus.

Evaluating Credits. Many adult students have had their educations interrupted by career or family changes that have involved relocating. Electronic systems, such as Course Applicability System (CAS), that allow students who have taken coursework at one institution to see how their credits will transfer to another institution have a tremendous affect on the adult student population. Similarly, there is a need for consistent policies about how coursework taken more than five years earlier is viewed by universities. Adult students get frustrated when told that previous coursework cannot be evaluated because course numbers or course content has been changed, or when previous coursework is ignored altogether. Colleges and universities would enhance their services to the adult student if they had policies in place to determine how dated coursework is to be evaluated. In addition, the number of institutions that give college credit for work experience is growing. The opportunity to receive college credit for knowledge and skills acquired in an occupation is very appealing to working adult students.

Delivery of Academic Advising. In working with the adult student, the academic advisor needs to be both flexible and adaptable. In responding to the adult student, advisors may need to move outside the traditional office setting where advising has typically been conducted with students in person. Academic advisors are handling more and more questions by e-mail than ever before. Helping adult student advisees through e-mail or on the telephone provides additional methods for helping that may also involve policy adjustments. Procedures (such as dropping courses or withdrawing from the university) that have always been completed in person need to be revised. Video advising may bridge the gap for those students who need person-to-person contact but are unable to get to campus to meet with an academic advisor. These means of communicating and dispersing information, as well as changes in traditional service delivery, are vital in serving and retaining the adult student.

Advisor as Advocate. In working with adult students, academic advisors may be called on to play the role of student advocate. Academic advisors may need to promote separate orientation sessions or seminar courses for adult students so that support groups can be created among this population. Many adult students need academic success skills, such as time management and test-taking strategies. In addition, many of these students have doubts about their ability to handle academics after being away from learning and studying for a number of years. Discussing these issues and encouraging the use of resources among students with similar concerns is an advantage. Adult students may feel threatened or inadequate in discussing these concerns with younger adult students. Similarly, "bridge" courses that are designed for adult students returning to the university provide an opportunity for these students to take coursework with other adult students. This can be especially beneficial in the first quarter or semester, as adult students make the transition back into a college setting.

Adult students attending colleges and universities present a unique and complex set of needs to student services and to academic advising in particular. Academic advisors need to be knowledgeable about developmental issues throughout the life span in order to work effectively with these students. Advising programs that incorporate flexible policy with innovative technology will be effective in providing services to the growing number of adult students on college and university campuses.

Transfer Students

Student transfer from one institution to another is a defining characteristic of American higher education today (King, 1994). A significant portion of students attending higher education institutions will transfer sometime during their academic stay. There are many reasons why students transfer. Some students start their education at a two-year institution with the intention of transferring to a four-year institution. The Center for Community Colleges reported that over an eight-year period in twenty states and at more than four hundred institutions, 20 percent of community college students transferred each year in order to complete their baccalaureate degrees (Cohen and Sanchez, 1997).

Students follow the two-year to four-year institution enrollment pattern for a variety of reasons: financial considerations, geographic proximity, availability of remedial coursework, or admission standards (Rifken, 1996). Other students follow different transfer patterns. Some students transfer due to poor institutional fit, because the educational opportunities or the social environment of the current institution is not congruent with the student's expectations, abilities, future plans, academic performance, or comfort level. Still other students, drawn by the desires and needs of lifelong learning, take advantage of our nation's diverse educational arrangements by engaging in higher education even after they have achieved their initial degrees. All of these scenarios share one common element: students will be making some significant changes in their lives because they will be transferring from one institution to another.

Characteristics of Transfer Students

The transition that transfer students experience is sometimes called "transfer shock" (Cantrell and others, 1996; Kraemer, 1996). Students who are unprepared for transfer shock may become discouraged and drop out before obtaining their desired educational goal.

Transfer students are a very diverse group with many different needs. Generalizations are therefore made at the risk of contradiction. As advisors know, it is important to understand the uniqueness of any student's prior experience. However, all transfer students face the critical issues of either uncertainty over course transferability or clarification of articulation agreements. On these issues, transfer students seek and need the greatest amount of assistance (Harbin, 1997).

In addition, transfer students also share characteristics with other student groups discussed in this chapter and elsewhere in this book. They can be undecided-transfer students, adult-transfer students, or minority-transfer students. Sensitive advisors recognize that such combinations increase the need to provide additional help to these students, as well as specialized programs and resources to serve them adequately.

Advising Issues for Transfer Students

Creating successful and satisfying transfer experiences requires a strong partnership between students and the institutions involved. Gernand (1992) offers suggestions for students transferring from one institution to another that embrace three stages: pretransfer, transfer, and posttransfer. Gernand's model identifies a transitional process and hence serves as an excellent model for categorizing academic advising issues and services. It helps to explain the potential breadth of experience that encompasses transfer shock. Not only is it important for students to plan their transfer, but it is also important for them to evaluate the progress they are making in their new environment.

Pretransfer Phase. This phase helps students consider and plan new beginnings. It is characterized by raising issues of transfer awareness, helping students locate relevant transfer resources, and encouraging them to prepare for transfer by developing positive academic, social, and personal habits. Following are some pretransfer advising issues:

- Clarify the current institution's curricular options and relationships to possible careers.
- Help students with academic and career exploration and assessment of their academic abilities.
- Help students clarify transfer articulation agreements that exist between institutions and assist them as they prepare to document existing coursework in case it needs to be evaluated for transfer credit at the new institution.
- Encourage students to develop greater skills in those subject areas in which they have the greatest difficulty and to develop their academic study and time management skills.
- Assist students with exploring the personal, social, and financial costs of attending another institution, along with the interpersonal and financial support they might receive.

Transfer Phase. In this middle phase, students acquire relevant and necessary information so that decisions about their transfer are based on fact. This is often when students feel they are without support. Cooperation between institutions in this stage can serve as a safety net. Institutions should be sensitive to students' feelings of emptiness, confusion, and lack of direction. In this phase, helping students complete the following tasks is critical:

- Examine the majors at different institutions to make sure they are of interest to students.
- Identify contact people at the institution to which they are transferring, such as admission and financial aid counselors, academic advisors, and faculty members.
- Locate and use resources that clarify course transfer and articulation agreements.
- Know the procedures for application and acceptance to the new institution, including deadlines that need to be met.
- Address the social and emotional issues associated with transfer.
- Address financial issues and resources at the new institution.
- Assess students' academic abilities as they consider new majors.
- Establish long-term goals and evaluate new information as it applies to these goals.

Posttransfer Phase. Posttransfer advising issues are those special needs that transfer students have as they matriculate at their new institution. The new institution should be aware of these needs and provide services and programs to meet them, including the following:

- Help students link to necessary academic support services.
- Help students develop a sense of belonging; encourage them to join student organizations, clubs, or intramural activities.
- Help students find living arrangements.
- Help students monitor and review their financial situations.
- Help students monitor their time management and school-, work-, and social-life commitments in their new environment.
- Assign the transfer student an academic or faculty advisor who is familiar with transfer issues.
- Develop and organize ways of providing these services in a comprehensive and effective fashion, such as through specially designed orientations, survey courses, use of peer advisors, or mandatory advising during the first quarter of enrollment.

King (1994) identifies five factors that discourage or prevent students from transferring: (1) academic and articulation barriers, (2) inadequate support systems, (3) bureaucratic barriers, (4) age-related impediments, and (5) racial and ethnic concerns. Academic advising can play a critical role in ameliorating the effects of these factors on transfer students. The broad perspective on the advising transfer process that includes pretransfer, transfer, and posttransfer helps provide an effective means of addressing these issues for students starting on their new journey.

Conclusion

The transition process is a time of considerable unease and instability with perhaps the only certainty being that people's reactions to an event or nonevent will change over time for better or worse (Schlossberg, Lynch, and Chickering, 1989). Academic advisors have an opportunity to influence student reactions to events and nonevents and the journey through the transition process. This chapter focused on four groups of students who experience transitions while in college: undecided students, major-changers, adult students, and transfer students. Each of these four groups approaches transition in unique ways. Working effectively with these populations requires not only an understanding of the transition process, but also how group and individual differences and developmental issues influence the process. Core helping skills, accurate information about academic majors and institutional policies and procedures, and flexibility are essential in helping these students realize their goals. The advising strategies presented in this chapter provide a framework for helping students in each of the four populations move successfully through the transition process and establish new beginnings.

References

Apple, V., Haak, R., and Witzke, D. "Factors Associated with Indecision About Collegiate Major and Career Choice." *Proceedings, American Psychological Association,* 1970, *5,* 667–668.

Appling, R. N. *Nontraditional Students Attending Postsecondary Institutions: Congressional Research Service Report for Congress.* Washington, D.C.: Library of Congress, 1991.

Aslanian, C. B. *Adult Learning in America: Why and How Adults Go Back to School.* Washington, D.C.: Office of Adult Learning Services, The College Board, 1996.

Benshoff, J. M. "Educational Opportunities, Developmental Challenges: Understanding Nontraditional College Students." Paper presented at the Association for Adult Development and Aging Conference, New Orleans, La., Nov. 1993. (ED 363 842)

Bridges, W. *Transitions: Making Sense of Life's Changes.* Reading, Mass.: Addison-Wesley, 1980.

Byrd, S. R. "Perceptions of Barriers to Undergraduate Education by Non-Traditional Students at Selected Non-Public, Liberal Arts Institutions in the Mid-South." Paper presented at the Annual Conference of the Mid-South Educational Research Association, New Orleans, La., Nov. 1990. (Ed 331 407)

Cantrell, E. D., and others. *Meeting the Needs of Rural Students Through Distance Advising: The Role of Transfer Guided in Three Measures of Student Success.* ERIC, 1996. (ED 394 782)

Chickering, A. W., and Reisser, L. *Education and Identity.* (2nd ed.) San Francisco: Jossey-Bass, 1993.

Cohen, A., and Sanchez, J. *The Transfer Rate: A Model of Consistency.* Los Angeles: Center for the Study of Community Colleges, 1997. (ED 409 953)

Coscarelli, W. C. *Manual for the Decision Making Inventory.* Columbus, Ohio: Marathon Consulting, 1983.

Cross, K. P. "Our Changing Students and Their Impact on Colleges: Prospects for a True Learning Society." *Phi Delta Kappan,* May 1980, pp. 627–630.

Foote, B. "Determined and Undetermined Major Students: How Different Are They?" *Journal of College Student Personnel,* 1980, *21,* 29–43.

Gerald, D. "Projections of Education Statistics to 2008." [http://www.nces.ed.gov/pub98/pj2008/p98c02.html]. July 1998.

Gernand, R. (ed.). *The College Handbook for Transfer Students, 1993.* New York: College Board Publications, 1992. (ED 347 948)

Gordon, V. N. *Handbook of Academic Advising.* Westport, Conn.: Greenwood Press, 1992.

Gordon, V. N. *The Undecided College Student: An Academic and Career Advising Challenge.* (2nd ed.) Springfield, Ill.: Thomas, 1995.

Gordon, V. N. "Career Decidedness Types: A Literature Review." *Career Development Quarterly,* 1998, *46*(4), 386–403.

Gordon, V. N., and Polson, C. "Students Needing Academic Alternative Advising: A National Survey." *NACADA Journal,* 1985, *5,* 77–84.

Harbin, C. "A Survey of Transfer Students at Four-Year Institutions Serving a California Community College." *Community College Review,* 1997, *25,* 21–40.

Holland, J. "Vocational Guidance for Everyone." *Educational Researcher,* 1973, *3,* 9–15.

Hughes, R. "The Non-Traditional Student in Higher Education: A Synthesis of the Literature. *NASPA Journal,* 1983, *20,* 51–64.

Kimes, H., and Troth, W. "Relationship of Trait Anxiety to Career Decisiveness." *Journal of Counseling Psychology,* 1974, *21,* 277–280.

King, M. "Enhancing Transfer." *NACADA Journal,* 1994, *14,* 1, 4–7.

Knowles, M., Holton, E., and Swanson, R. "The Adult Learner." Houston: Gulf, 1998.

Knox, A. B. *Teaching Adults Effectively.* San Francisco: Jossey-Bass, 1980.

Kraemer, B. "Meeting the Needs of Nontraditional Students: Retention and Transfer Studies." Paper presented at the 101st Annual Meeting of the North Central Association, Chicago, Ill., 1996. (ED 395 603)

Krager, L., Wrenn, R., and Hirt, J. "Perspectives on Age Differences." In L. V. Moore (ed.), *Evolving Theoretical Perspectives on Students.* New Directions for Student Services, no. 51. San Francisco: Jossey-Bass, 1990.

Kramer, G. L., Higley, B. H., and Olsen, D. "Changes in Academic Major Among Undergraduate Students." *College and University,* 1994, *69,* 88–98.

Lewallen, W. "The Impact of Being 'Undecided' on College Student Persistence." *Journal of College Student Development,* 1993, *34,* 103–112.

Martin, J. Y. "Meeting Nontraditional Students Halfway." *Journal of College Student Development,* 1988, *29,* 369–371.

Newman J. L., Fuqua, D. R., and Minger, C.. "Further Evidence of the Use of Career Subtypes in Defining Career Status." *Career Development Quarterly,* 1990, *39,* 178–188.

Noel, L. "Increasing Student Retention: New Challenges and Potential" In L. Noel, D. Levitz, and Associates, *Increasing Student Retention.* San Francisco: Jossey-Bass, 1985.

Nordstrom, B. "Non-Traditional Students: Adults in Transition." ERIC, 1989. (ED 310 686)

Osipow, S. H. *Theories of Career Development.* (3rd ed.) Englewood Cliffs, N.J.: Prentice-Hall, 1983.

Pierson, R. "Changes of Majors by University Students." *Personnel and Guidance Journal,* 1962, *40,* 458–461.

Rawlins, M. E. "Life Made Easier for the Over-Thirty Undergrads." *Personnel and Guidance Journal,* 1979, *58*(2), 139–143.

Richter-Antion, D. "Qualitative Differences Between Adult and Younger Students." *NASPA Journal,* 1986, *23,* 58–62.

Rifken, T. (ed.). *Transfer and Articulation: Improving Policies to Meet New Needs.* New Directions for Students Services. no. 96. San Francisco: Jossey-Bass, 1996.

Savickas, M. L., and Jorgourna, D. "The Decision Scale as a Type Indicator." *Journal of Counseling Psychology,* 1991, *38,* 85–90.

Schlossberg, N. K. *Counseling Adults in Transition.* New York: Springer, 1984.

Schlossberg, N. K. "Taking the Mystery out of Change." *Psychology Today,* 1987, *21*(5), 74–75.

Schlossberg, N. K., Lynch, A. Q., and Chickering, A. W. *Improving Higher Education Environments for Adults: Responsive Programs and Services from Entry to Departure.* San Francisco: Jossey-Bass, 1989.

Schlossberg, N. K., and Robinson, S. P. *Going to Plan B: How You Can Cope, Regroup, and Start Your Life on a New Path.* New York: Simon & Schuster, 1996.

Serling, D., and Betz, N. "Development and Evaluation of a Measure of Fear Commitment." *Journal of Counseling Psychology,* 1980, *37,* 91–97.

Sewall, T. J. "A Study of Adult Undergraduates: What Causes Them to Seek a Degree?" *Journal of College Student Personnel,* 1984, *25*(4), 309–314.

Steele, G. E., and McDonald, M. L. "Major and Career Exploration." [http://www.uvc.ohio-state.edu/capsheets/tmcefc.html]. April 1999.

Taylor, K., and Betz, N. "Application of Self-Efficacy Theory to the Understanding and Treatment of Career Indecision. *Journal of Vocation Behavior,* 1983, *22,* 63–81.

Titley, W., and Titley, B. "Initial Choice of College Major: Are Only the 'Undecided' Undecided?" *Journal of College Student Personnel,* 1980, *21,* 293–298.

Titley, R., Titley, B., and Wolff, W. "The Major-Changers: Continuity or Discontinuity in the Career Decision Process?" *Journal of Vocational Behavior,* 1976, *8,* 105–111.

U.S. Department of Education. "The Nation: College Enrollment by Age of Students, Fall 1995." *Chronicle of Higher Education Almanac,* Aug. 28, 1998, p. 18.

Webster's Ninth New Collegiate Dictionary. Springfield, Mass.: Merriam-Webster, 1983.

Zytowski, D. "Avoidance Behavior on Vocational Motivation." *Personnel and Guidance Journal,* 1965, *43,* 746–750.

Chapter Eleven

Integrating Academic Advising and Career and Life Planning

Betsy McCalla-Wriggins

In surveying college freshmen, Alexander Astin and his colleagues discovered that one of the main reasons that students come to college is "to get a better job" (Astin, Parrott, Korn, and Sax, 1997). To get that better job, they need a degree. A specific degree is required for some jobs, but for other positions, any degree is appropriate.

Even with this better job as a goal, many students entering colleges and universities do not come with carefully thought-out academic and career goals. Several studies have estimated that between 20 and 50 percent of students entering college are undecided about their academic major and career (Gordon, 1995). In addition to this group, many other students become major-changers during their college years (Steele, 1994). Developmentally, many traditional-age college students are not ready to make these decisions.

Students who are trying to make decisions about a major, a career, or both need assistance with answering some very basic questions. What are their interests, skills, values, and goals? Obtaining these answers can lead a student to making appropriate decisions; however, institutional structures often require students to go to different people and offices to get help. For example, at one public university with approximately six thousand students, the career development office and the office of academic advising were located in two different buildings separated by a grassy quad. Change-of-major and undecided students meeting with academic advisors would ask the question, "What careers can I pursue with a degree in [fill in the blank]?" Students were then referred across the quad to the career development office for information about careers relating to different majors and if necessary to take self-assessment inventories. Once students had decided on some career options and possible related majors, they would then ask the career counselor, "What courses do I need to take to get a degree in [fill in the blank]?" The student was then sent back across the quad to see the academic advisor. Unfortunately, many times the students did not make that short walk between the two offices. Although the professionals were operating within the parameters of their job functions, students were not being well served.

Students and faculty in advising relationships may have similar experiences. Although they are experts in their discipline and program, faculty advisors may not feel adequately prepared to assist students with the whole realm of career development and employment issues. Providing both faculty and professional advisors with the skills, tools, and system to assist students with both academic advising and career and job search counseling demonstrates an integrated approach to making these very important decisions.

This chapter identifies and addresses issues to consider in the integration of these two functions, and the benefits of this integration for students, faculty, and the campus community.

Review of Theories

In Chapter Two, the role of developmental theory in academic advising was presented. Here, selected career development theories are reviewed. These theories have been grouped into five classifications: trait and factor, developmental, personality-based, social learning, and economic and sociological (Isaacson and Brown, 1993).

Although individual advisors develop their own approaches to helping students integrate major and occupational information, many find Holland's (1985) personality types and Super's (1990) developmental concepts easy for college students to understand.

Holland states that people express their personality through their choice of vocation. He identified six personality classifications as well as similar categories for occupations. These six classifications are realistic, investigative, artistic, social, enterprising, and conventional. The theory suggests, for example, that a person with a *realistic* personality type will be most compatible with and satisfied in an occupation and work environment that value and display realistic characteristics. The *social* person will opt for occupations that embody social characteristics, and so on.

A number of instruments have been developed to assess individual career preferences. The Self-Directed Search and the Strong Interest Inventory are two instruments that identify the predominant types of vocational personalities and environments based on John Holland's theory of career choice (Holland, 1985). The three-digit Holland code derived from these instruments provides a good starting point for exploring careers.

Super's life-span approach is a developmental theory. He believes that people differ in their abilities, personalities, needs, values, interest, traits, and self-concepts. All of these unique characteristics then qualify people for a multitude of occupations. Satisfaction with both work and life depends on the extent to which individuals can find adequate outlets for their abilities, needs, and so on. This satisfaction may and probably will change as the person moves through different stages of life (Super, 1990).

For example, Super describes five life stages that have an impact on career choice. The *growth* stage includes both physical and psychological growth, which have direct bearing on a person's self-concept. A person's awareness that an occupation will be an aspect of life begins the *exploratory* stage. In the *establishment* stage, the individual actually has work experiences, and aspects of the occupation are brought into the self-concept. During the *maintenance* stage, the individual is concerned with enhancing the satisfying components of the occupation and changing those parts that are less rewarding. The *decline* stage is where the person is more concerned with keeping the job; it ends with retirement.

Elements of Career Planning

Once a theoretical framework is established, the basic elements of career and life planning, self-assessment, career exploration, reality testing, and job search need to be understood.

Self-assessment is the starting point and foundation for making appropriate major and career decisions and is frequently the area in which students find the greatest challenge. They are afraid of making a "wrong" decision and do not understand that making no decision is in fact a decision. What do students need to know about themselves in order to make wise academic and career decisions?

Richard Bolles, in his book *What Color Is Your Parachute?* (1999), offers a comprehensive approach to self-assessment. He defines a career as an occupation plus a field. The occupation is *what* a person will do. Bolles's approach to discovering *what* is to identify the person's gifts, talents, and favorite transferable skills, in priority order. It does not matter where these skills were acquired; it does matter that the person enjoys using them.

The *where* is the field where a person wants to use the skills. This involves identifying favorite subjects, fields of interest, geographic preferences, preferred working conditions, and the kind of data, people, and things the person most enjoys.

Helping students clarify their values is another important part of the self-assessment process. When individuals understand and can articulate what they believe in and what they want to work toward, an important step has been made. However, if a person fails to engage in these components of self-assessment, they have no foundation on which to make academic and career decisions.

Self-assessment is followed by career exploration. With thousands of different occupations listed in the *Dictionary of Occupational Titles* and with more being created each year, finding the "right" position can be overwhelming. The information that students gain through self-assessment provides them with specific criteria with which to evaluate the various options. Using those criteria as a measuring stick when researching different occupations helps students to narrow down, eliminate, and select occupations for further exploration. They can then focus on options that connect best with their skills, interests, and values.

After students make a tentative career or occupational choice, their next step is to do some reality checking. This involves getting some hands-on experience in the chosen area. Internships, field experiences, part-time and summer jobs, and volunteering are all valuable options for seeing what a job is really like. This experience usually has one of two outcomes. It can reaffirm that the tentative choice was an accurate one, give the student greater incentive to complete the preparation necessary to gain entry into the field, and provide important experience and contacts in the field. If the experience is very different than what was hoped for, the student may eliminate that option and begin to explore other fields.

Once a firm decision has been made about which career and occupation to pursue, then the last stage, marketing and the job search, begins. This stage includes writing a resume, identifying and developing contacts, planning and implementing a job search, and preparing for the interview. If students have completed the prior steps in the career decision-making process, they will be able to complete the career objective component on their resume. Those students who have not taken an active role in the career decision-making process are now confronted with the basic yet critical self-assessment issues.

Once an effective resume is available, the next step is establishing and developing contacts, or *networking.* Attending professional meetings, joining clubs related to areas of interest, and setting up informational interviews are just a few ways to make these important connections.

Establishing a plan for identifying organizations that have opportunities is the next step. Again, with so many options this is often an overwhelming part of the process. The difficulty is compounded by the career and job resources now available on the Internet. The first step, however, is to develop a plan and make a commitment to spend time on this process. The person who said "Getting a job is a job" was absolutely correct. The more time a person can commit to job search activities, the sooner that person will probably obtain meaningful employment.

The final piece in this career and life planning process is having a successful interview that results in a job offer. Often people leave to chance what happens in the interview. Thoroughly preparing for the experience is the key. The interviewee must know not only what he or she can offer to the employer, but also why the organization is right for that individual. Conducting extensive research on the organization and participating in several mock interviews are two activities known to make a difference.

Although these activities have been described sequentially, the process is not necessarily so for students. They may move back and forth in accomplishing the tasks listed in Wes Habley's (1984) Advising Process/Intervention Model.

Depending on where students enter the model, faculty and professional advisors need to understand how to help them accomplish the tasks that will allow them to make wise and informed academic and career decisions.

Integrating the Academic Advising and Career Development Functions

Integrating academic advising and career development activities on campus can take many different forms. There is no one right way, and each institution must determine what is best for the organization, its culture, and its students. However, one place to begin is to look at the similarities and differences between the two functions.

Similarities

Faculty and staff who provide academic advising and career counseling all need to possess and demonstrate several key functional skills: listening, counseling, communicating, referring, researching, challenging, and supporting.

Listening is the first and foremost skill in both of these areas. Unless the individual is able truly to listen to what the student says and does not say, the interaction will not be productive and it will be very difficult to establish a positive, trusting relationship.

Counseling skills are also essential. Faculty and staff must ask appropriate questions, restate what the student says, and clarify the issues. This is true whether the student comes with a career, major, or personal issue that is having an impact on the student's decision-making ability.

No one can be expected to have all the information needed to help all students, so *referral* skills are important. Depending on the issue, a student may be referred to other resources either on or off campus, or to print, video, or electronic resources. This can sometimes be a major challenge, particularly if personal issues appear to be interfering with the student's ability to make a decision. Unless the faculty member, professional advisor, or career counselor is also a trained psychologist or therapist, it is usually best to call the campus counseling center and support the student in making an appointment and speaking with a professional there.

Feeling stuck, powerless, and helpless prevents many students from making decisions. Faculty and staff therefore need to help students *research*, identify, and evaluate their options. This can give students a sense of control, which can lead to an increased ability to make decisions.

Challenging and supporting skills are important in all phases of the advising and career development process. When students' behaviors are not consistent with their words or when their resources are not sufficient to meet their goals, it is important to challenge them. At the same time it is critical to demonstrate to students that they have support as they explore issues and options. This skill of challenging and supporting is an art that requires both facts and intuition.

Faculty and professional staff also use a variety of communication skills on a daily basis. Speaking, writing, making presentations, facilitating small groups, and persuading various groups to work collaboratively are essential skills for all members of the college community.

Creating an environment that is conducive to learning is also very important when faculty, professional advisors, and career counselors interact with students. Opportunities for "teachable moments" can occur all over campus and in many different settings.

In addition to the functional skills just discussed, faculty advisors, professional advisors, and career counselors at the same institution share a common body of knowledge. This includes information about the college or university, general policies and procedures, and support services that are available to assist students, as well as academic majors and degree options.

Differences

In addition to having a theoretical background, individuals preparing to provide career counseling need to learn about occupations, the job search, and the job market. One of the major challenges in this area is that information is not static. With technology and the explosion of electronic resources, changes are occurring even more rapidly and will probably continue to increase.

Being knowledgeable about all careers is an impossible task for any one person. Therefore, to be effective, faculty and staff must learn how to use key resources that organize occupations according to data, people, skills, majors, interests, personality type, and so on.

Another body of knowledge essential in this process is information related to the job search. Searching for a job incorporates the basic components indicated earlier: resume and cover-letter writing, researching an organization, developing a portfolio, preparing for an interview, gaining career-related experience, planning volunteer and organizational activities to explore career options, networking with professionals, and utilizing the Internet in the job search. In addition, some career fields have different expectations in this process.

Being aware of the employment market and employer expectations is also essential in career development. The employment market varies somewhat by year and by region of the country, but employer expectations seem to be rather consistent. Helping students to understand and develop the skills that employers want is a key to student success. An excellent resource for obtaining both national and regional data on these two areas is the National Association for Colleges and Employers.

Another major difference between advising and career counseling is the number of choices students have and the multitude of ways they may achieve their goals. When helping a student select a major, the choices are finite and limited to the majors offered at that institution (assuming that the student does not want to or cannot transfer). There are also usually prescribed ways to obtain a degree in a specific major. The student may have options within the general education and elective components, but the path to the degree has definite parameters.

In working with a student making a career decision, the choices are much more extensive and the path to a particular career may be quite varied. For example, a person with practically any degree can become very effective and successful in marketing and sales. In this career, being successful depends more on personal characteristics than on a specific degree. However, to gain entry into the field of pharmaceutical sales, a degree in biology or chemistry would certainly be advantageous.

On the flip side, if a student wants to be a computer programmer, there are a limited number of degrees that will prepare the individual for that career. However, if a person wants to get into the computer field in general, there are many paths to that goal. One example illustrates this point. Computers fascinated a student majoring in music education. Even though he completed his degree in music education, during his free time he learned everything he could about computer hardware, volunteered to get experience and to enhance his technical skills, and took computers apart and put them back together to understand how they worked. Upon graduation he was hired as a computer specialist, not as a music teacher, in a school system. The skills he developed on his own and the fact that he had a degree got him the right job.

Another difference is that most people make academic decisions about a degree once or perhaps twice in their lives. Career decisions, however, are made much more frequently and sometimes are made out of necessity rather than by choice. It is suggested that people will make three to six career changes during their lifetime, and this does not include job changes within a career field (Bolles, 1999).

As more nontraditional students return to school, faculty and staff need to understand adult development issues because they will encounter people in many different situations. Moving, getting downsized, having limited advancement opportunities, and being part of a merged organization are all reasons that people make job or career changes. What does this mean for those working with adults making career choices? Bolles (1999) describes the task as helping people find their mission in life. This definition ties directly back to helping people identify their values, skills, and interests. John Crystal, a noted career expert, once said that the best way to find out what a person wants to do is to ask him. What Crystal was suggesting is that many people know what their dream is; they just need support in rediscovering, uncovering, or gaining confidence in their ability to achieve it.

Developing Skills and Competencies in Career and Life Planning

For those who want to develop skills and competencies in career development, there are a number of options to consider. First, the individual must have an understanding of career development theory. Next, joining and becoming active in professional associations is an excellent way to obtain knowledge, establish contacts, and keep up-to-date with changing trends. Many of these organizations schedule regional, national, and sometimes local workshops or conferences specifically dedicated to career and life planning issues. They also have journals that incorporate articles on this topic.

Another way to develop skills and competencies is through reading books and publications. Local libraries and major bookstores have whole sections dedicated to career choice and the job search. Professional associations are also excellent resources for reference materials.

Utilizing the Internet is yet another way to gain information. Using key words such as *careers, occupations,* and *jobs* will direct the user to literally thousands of sites.

Taking self-assessment inventories is a very personal way to learn about tools used in the career development process. The Strong Interest Inventory, the Myers-Briggs Type Indicator, the Self-Directed Search, and the Career and Occupational Preference and Educational Survey are instruments that help individuals identify their interests, values, skills, and related majors and occupations.

Some specific computer programs that are used at various colleges and universities across the country are Discover, from American College Testing, and SIGI-Plus, from Educational Testing Service. Both programs are interactive and take a person through a series of career decision-making modules.

Finally, another way to gain competence is to collaborate and cooperate with colleagues on campus.

Integrating Academic Advising and Career Resources

Integration can occur both informally and through a formal approach. The informal option can occur independently of the structure and culture of the organization. The only ingredient necessary is the willingness of the faculty and staff who provide academic advising and career counseling. Informal collaborations are limited only by the imagination of the parties involved.

Faculty-Staff Collaborations

The liaison concept offers faculty and staff many opportunities to work together. Faculty and professional advisors who serve as departmental or college liaisons to career services ensure the flow of information both to and from the academic departments. Having career service staff serve as liaisons to departments and colleges also provides opportunities for information exchange. Both models enhance and make explicit and visible the connection between the two functions.

When faculty, professional advisors, and career counselors work together to collect and disseminate employment data about graduates from different majors, opportunities are created to begin or continue conversations about the connection between advising and career life planning. This information can be extremely helpful not only to students in the major but also to undeclared and prospective students at the institution.

Inviting faculty and staff to the respective groups' staff or department meetings is another approach that supports integration. Career counselors find it very helpful to hear discipline-specific information directly from faculty in those academic departments. Likewise, faculty may learn of new career resources and employer contacts that can be shared with their majors.

Advisement coordinator and support staff breakfasts also foster integration. Faculty and professional advisors can be invited to the career resource center once each semester. New policies and procedures, programmatic changes, and special career and advising events, as well as other information that has an impact on academic and career assistance to students, can be shared at these meetings. This is also when the career staff can reinforce the offer to come into classrooms and make career and job search presentations.

Similar topics can be covered at a breakfast for the support staff. Because these individuals are often asked advising- and career-related questions, it is important that they be kept informed of where students can receive help and what types of assistance are available.

Setting up a luncheon meeting with faculty and professional advisors, recruiters visiting campus, and career counselors provides yet another opportunity to dialogue about the integration of academic advising, discipline-specific knowledge, and career options. The more information these three groups of people can share, the more helpful they can be to students.

Special Events and Activities for Students

When faculty invite career staff into classes to describe the services available to students and to incorporate self-assessment activities into freshmen seminars, students begin to see how academic and career decisions are related. Requiring essays on career options in basic composition classes, using career sites on the Internet as a way to teach computer literacy, and incorporating job search strategy information and assignments into senior capstone seminars are some specific examples of how faculty can integrate career planning into the student's academic experience.

Organizing programs for alumni to speak to majors about different career paths and options helps students, faculty, and professional advisors identify how majors and careers may or may not be directly related. Including alumni who have attended graduate school helps students gain valuable insights and information about even more options.

A career and major expo is another program that demonstrates integration. Faculty in each department identify alumni who are in various career fields related to that major. These alumni, along with faculty from all the departments in the college or university, depending on the size of the institution, come together in a designated place for a specified period. The career services staff, which has coordinated the event, publicizes the activity to all students, but especially to premajors or undecided students. The faculty share information about their academic program, and alumni tell students about how they got their jobs, what they do, what kind of preparation is needed, and additional skills and experiences that will make students more competitive.

Providing experiential learning opportunities such as cooperative education programs, internships, and field experience courses is another way to help students integrate academic and career planning. These courses provide a real-life environment in which students can check out career options and see firsthand how academic and career decisions are interrelated.

Resources and Materials

Cooperatively developing electronic resources on both academic and career-related topics provides assistance for the entire college community. However, once these resources have been developed, ways need to be identified to help faculty and professional advisors, career counselors, and students learn how to use them. Brown-bag lunches in a "smart" classroom with time afterwards in a computer lab is one way to help individuals learn to use and explore these valuable tools.

Developing printed materials for students to use in academic and career decision making is an excellent way to initiate or enhance connections between those faculty and staff who are providing academic advising and career counseling. Students find handouts about what they can do with a major in particular fields valuable in exploring options.

Other examples of cooperatively developed projects include newsletters, radio shows, videotapes, Web pages, orientation programs, parents programs, and so on. Again, the possibilities are limitless.

Steering Committee and Advisory Board

A campus steering committee is another way for the institution to make explicit the need for and importance of integrating academic and career advising. Representatives from the faculty, advising staff, career staff, and student body act as an advising body to identify current practices, develop models, and make recommendations to enhance and support campuswide academic and career advising. When this committee reports to the vice president's level, credibility is enhanced and the explicit value of this integration is emphasized.

Some career centers have also established an advisory board that includes representatives of all the stakeholders: students, faculty, professional advisors, employers, and other staff. This board differs from the steering committee in that it focuses on issues from a career service and employment perspective. Faculty and professional advisors provide valuable input in this board's conversations and also receive information that can be shared with students.

When institutions make the commitment to integrate the two functions in a more formal way, many approaches can be effective.

Faculty and Staff Located in Colleges and Offices

In some institutions, career counselors are actually assigned to the different colleges. These people are physically located in the colleges and they develop areas of expertise related to those academic majors. Because of their physical proximity, these career counselors are much more visible to everyone in that college. This situation also facilitates those very important, informal, in-the-hall conversations with faculty, staff, and students. When the individual counselor is invited to department meetings on a regular basis, the integration of academic and career advising is reinforced.

Another option is to locate faculty liaisons in advising units that may or may not be connected to career service units. Faculty who have a great interest in working with undeclared or undecided students provide both academic and career information to these students. Faculty usually are appointed, selected, or chosen, or they volunteer, for a specific period. This provides the opportunity for a number of faculty to participate and to gain additional knowledge about career resources that they can then take back to their department. The career and advising staffs also have the benefit of that particular faculty member's expertise. Again, the connections between academic and career decisions are reinforced.

Physical Proximity of Units

Another approach is to locate the advising unit, if there is one, and the career service unit close to or next to each other. In this case, the organizational and reporting structures remain untouched, but students find it easier to take advantage of both services. In addition, the physical proximity also encourages and fosters collaboration between the staffs from the two units.

Reporting Structures

Another option is to have the two units remain separate but report to the same individual. This can provide more directed, purposeful collaboration between the advising and career service units. It also makes more explicit the institution's position that the two functions are connected.

Another model is to have all functions in one unit reporting to one director. Individuals continue to have distinct responsibilities, but they collaborate on joint projects. A variation is to identify one or two services that all professional staff provide while keeping the other responsibilities separate and distinct.

In all these models, collaboration can occur in many forms. Workshops, Web pages, computer systems, and academic and career resources can all be jointly developed and shared. The possibilities are truly endless.

Total Integration of Resources

The last model presented in this chapter is perhaps the most radical. It is the total integration of the academic advising and career service units. In this model all staff report to one director and their responsibilities include both developmental academic advising and career and job search counseling. It is important to state up front that this is without a doubt the most challenging model to implement. This model does not imply that academic advising is more important than career development, or vice versa. They are both equally important as is evidenced by their different but complimentary professional associations, bodies of knowledge, and theories.

Identifying, acknowledging, and addressing the following issues is crucial to a successful total integration of the academic advising and career service units. There is no one right way. Each institution must look at its organizational structure, history, culture, politics, and overall goals in making decisions on each issue.

First, *What is the mission of the new unit?* What specific target populations will it serve? To whom will it report? How will both professional and support jobs change? How will issues of equality and parody be addressed? Who will be in charge and how will that person be selected? Each individual must have a clear job description and know how each person in the unit fits into the overall picture.

Next, *What kind of training will be needed?* Equally important, and often not addressed, is *What resources will be committed so that each staff member will be trained and prepared to function efficiently in this new unit?* Shadowing and observing are low-cost options, but time to attend workshops, seminars, and professional meetings and to read particular books and professional journals is essential. Scheduled time to process and discuss new information is another crucial component.

Another critical area to address is *How do people feel about this new structure, unit, and way of operating?* It is important to include everyone in the process, to get their input and ideas, but it may not be possible to obtain consensus. Therefore, the person in charge must be willing to make the final decision. In doing this, it is important to identify the feelings, often not expressed, of those experiencing the merger.

Career counselors often fear that they will make a mistake in advising students about what courses to take. They translate that into the student having to stay in school an extra semester, which means a significant additional cost. Professional advisors moving into the career counseling area feel overwhelmed with the amount of career information that exists and with the lack of a specific prescribed path to meeting a career goal. What they tend to do is focus on the differences instead of on the similarities discussed at the beginning of this chapter. Interestingly enough, when new staff join an integrated center, they see more of the similarities. They see the two processes as part of the whole and move from one to the other in a seamless fashion.

Another area to address is the physical space of the unit. If possible, moving to a new space that has been designed with both functions in mind is ideal. The psychological aspect of moving into another group's space or having to share space with the "intruders" can have an impact on the way the individuals perform.

Another consideration is the name of the new unit. This can have a significant impact on how the office is perceived by students, faculty, staff, and employers. Using focus groups of various stakeholders to test out different options can be very enlightening and can also create support for the initiative.

Once the new unit is operational, some other issues may surface. When combining the two units, the number of personnel and dollars in the budget usually remain the same. However, there can be the perception that the personnel and nonsalary resources have been increased, and therefore there can be a tendency to give the unit more responsibility without increased resources. One way to help avoid this situation is to publicize continually to all constituents, through as many means as possible, all the services provided to the stakeholders. Enlisting the support of faculty, employers, student clubs and organizations, and other administrators is another way to reinforce the message to the individuals allocating resources.

Another major factor that has a great impact on the success of these more formally integrated models is how people are assisted in the process of dealing with change. Having outside facilitators work with the groups, creating opportunities for social interaction outside the work environment, and organizing retreats off-campus are just some examples of ways to help people manage these very important issues of change.

As is evidenced by the many examples presented here, integration of academic advising and career life planning can take many different shapes and forms. There is no one right way. Each institution can create a variety of unique opportunities for faculty and professionals to collaborate in providing academic and career advising to their students.

Advantages of the Integrated Approach

One of the major reasons to consider the integration of academic advising and career life planning is that this approach demonstrates the four educational quality principals. These concepts can be used as a measure of effectiveness and efficiency when serving students (Education Commission of the States, 1995).

The first principle, *student-centeredness,* is clearly evident in these integrated models. Students receive assistance with selecting a major, choosing a career, identifying internships to gain exposure in a career field, and then learning skills for the job search from one resource. Questions from *What courses are required for a specific major?* to *What career options are consistent with my values and interests?* are all part of a continuing decision-making process. Faculty and professionals in these models see students throughout their college career and are focused on helping them acquire the information they need to make appropriate decisions.

Integrating these two functions that complement and support each other demonstrates the second principle, *efficiency and integrity of operation.* It is more efficient and effective for faculty and professionals to work in an environment where they influence and have a great deal of knowledge of the academic and career decision-making process of their students. Because so many policies and procedures affect so many functions, having faculty and professional advisors involved in this entire process provides the opportunity to intervene when a policy or procedure may not be serving students.

The third principle, *commitment to good practices,* includes high expectations for delivery of student services, as well as high expectations for students to participate in the service. At institutions with these integrated approaches, the first time that professionals and faculty advisors interact with students, clear expectations are established. The ongoing process is clearly explained and constantly reinforced.

The fourth principle, *quality management practices,* is also evident in these integrated models. Establishing a clear set of goals with ongoing processes for assessment and improvement is critical for effective delivery of services to students.

One advantage of the totally integrated unit is that it enhances and contributes to the professional development of all staff in the unit. Each person has a greater variety of job functions, contact with more and different stakeholders, interactions with students from freshman through senior year, projects with greater diversity, technological expertise with wider applications, involvement in all phases of academic and career decision-making activities, and more professional development options and opportunities.

All of these approaches also provide the opportunity for establishing more connections throughout the institution. By establishing these connections, faculty and professional staff become much more aware of each other as resources and are more apt to support each other. Taking a proactive approach to building and enhancing these relationships definitely has a significant payoff for everyone, but especially for the students.

Conclusion

As indicated throughout this chapter, the major goal of both developmental advising and career life planning is to help students in the process of making appropriate academic and career decisions. Academic decisions are just one part of the career life planning process. Faculty and professionals assisting students with these issues work from a foundation of common knowledge and skills. By creating a variety of ways in which they can share information and learn from each other, a synergy is developed, and this positive energy affects all their interactions with students. They are able to assist students in the total process and in a holistic manner. The result is that students, faculty, and staff understand and experience these activities as a natural and integrated process.

References

Astin, A. W., Parrott, S. A., Korn, W. S., and Sax, L. J. *The American Freshman: Thirty-Year Trends.* Los Angeles: Higher Education Institute, University of California, 1997.

Bolles, R. N. *What Color Is Your Parachute?* Berkeley, Calif.: Ten Speed Press, 1999.

Education Commission of the States. *"Making Quality Count: A Report for the ECS Chairman's 'Quality Counts' Agenda in Higher Education."* Denver, Colo.: Education Commission of the States, 1995.

Gordon, V. N. *Advising Undecided First-Year Students.* In M. L. Upcraft and G. L. Kramer (eds.), *First-Year Academic Advising Patterns in the Present, Pathways to the Future.* Monograph no. 18. Columbia: National Resource Center for the Freshman Experience, University of South Carolina, 1995.

Habley, W. R. "Integrating Academic Advising and Career Planning." In R. B. Winston Jr., T. K. Miller, S. C. Ender, T. J. Grites, and Associates, *Developmental Academic Advising.* San Francisco: Jossey-Bass, 1984.

Holland, J. L. *Making Vocational Choices: A Theory of Vocational Personalities and Work Environments.* (2nd ed.) Englewood Cliffs, N.J.: Prentice Hall, 1985.

Isaacson, L. E., and Brown, D. *Career Information, Career Counseling and Career Development.* Needham Heights, Mass.: Allyn & Bacon, 1993.

Steele, G. E. *"Major-Changes: A Special Type of Undecided Student."* In V. Gordon (ed.), Issues in Advising the Undecided College Student. Monograph no. 15. Columbia: National Resource Center for the Freshman Year Experience, University of South Carolina, 1994.

Super, D. E. "A Life-Span, Life-Space Approach to Career Development." In D. Brown, L. Brooks, and Associates, *Career Choice and Development: Applying Contemporary Theories to Practice.* (2nd ed.) San Francisco: Jossey-Bass, 1990.

Part Three

Organization and Delivery of Advising Services

T he quality of an institution's advising program must rest on the foundations of organization and service delivery. Not only do students and parents expect a degree of educational planning support, but also external constituencies such as accrediting agencies, legislative bodies, and public interest groups demand that higher education become both more efficient and more effective. Increasing emphasis has been placed on organizing (reorganizing) our institutions to focus on student learning and to provide quality services that meet the needs of an increasingly diverse student body. In the face of these imperatives, advising services must be organized around a series of program goals and objectives that are clearly related to the institution's mission, and the delivery of services as well as the information systems that support those services must focus on the identification and achievement of student educational outcomes. This section of the handbook provides a template for planning and delivering an academic advising program.

In Chapter Twelve, Eric R. White builds a rationale for and provides examples of the mission, goals, and objectives of the advising program. White affirms that a quality advising program is built on clearly defined goals and objectives that are integrally tied to the institution's mission statement. In addition, he suggests that it is not sufficient for an institution to develop a set of advising goals and objectives. Rather, he believes that each unit that provides advising services must develop its own goals and objectives.

Although many observers of academic advising programs have suggested that organization models are institutionally idiosyncratic, Celeste Pardee, in Chapter Thirteen, provides a framework for understanding several principles that help us to grasp how advising programs are organized. She provides descriptions, explores patterns of use, and looks at both the positives and negatives of seven organizational models categorized as centralization, decentralization, or shared responsibility models.

Just as there is no single best way to organize a campus advising program, Alice G. Reinarz, suggests in Chapter Fourteen that there is no single type of individual best equipped to deliver advising. It should be noted that although faculty continue to be dominant in the delivery of advising, many campuses have augmented and in some cases supplanted faculty advising through the use of professional advisors and counselors as well as peer and paraprofessional advisors. Reinarz traces both the scope of involvement and the strengths and limitations of each advisor type, suggesting that programs that focus on the diversity of student needs may indeed implement advising programs featuring delivery by multiple types of advisors.

Chapters Fifteen and Sixteen review the important considerations necessary to deliver academic advising. In Chapter Fifteen, Charlie L. Nutt discusses the skills essential to delivering one-to-one advising. He focuses on the development of listening, questioning, and referral skills as the most important attributes of the advising relationship. He also reviews the critical steps an advisor should take in planning and preparing for the advising session, the content and process of the session, and the follow-up required after the session is completed.

In Chapter Sixteen, Nancy S. King underscores the important role of group delivery of academic advising services as a strategy to extend and augment advising services. King provides a solid rationale for using group advising programs. But the bulk of the chapter focuses on the incorporation of advising services in orientation programs, first-year seminars, and learning communities, and the use of group advising to augment individual advising provided to student subpopulations.

Although advising is essentially a person-to-person activity, the future of academic advising clearly rests on the degree to which technology can be deployed to increase both the efficiency and the effectiveness of advising programs. In Chapter Seventeen, Michael E. McCauley reviews macro applications of technology that support the advising program. Among these applications are degree audit systems, transfer articulation models, touch-tone registration, and systems that assist the advising office and advisors in managing appointments and maintaining advisee records.

Remy R. Sotto, in Chapter Eighteen, lends credence to the adage that the future is now in her review and discussion of the ways in which the delivery of advising may be accomplished through the use of technology. She provides an excellent overview of both synchronous and asynchronous methods that utilize text, audio, and video media to support advising. In addition, Sotto reviews the advantages and disadvantages of using technology to deliver advising and provides readers with key considerations on the use of technology.

Because the use of data to inform student decisions is a cornerstone of quality advising, Chapter Nineteen by Thomas J. Grites provides a comprehensive review of assessment instrumentation that supports the delivery of academic advising. Grites organizes the chapter according to various stages of student development, both chronologically and developmentally. He also provides examples of some of the most commonly used student reports. He concludes the chapter with a series of important observations on the choice and use of assessment instruments.

Chapter Twelve

Developing Mission, Goals, and Objectives for the Advising Program

Eric R. White

Advising programs, more often than not, are established to fill a very pressing need. Throughout the nation's colleges and universities, the need for students to be provided with quality academic advising programs is as critical as ever. With a burgeoning number of majors available on college campuses, an increasingly complex and rapidly shifting work environment at hand, and a dizzyingly extensive array of out-of-class educational experiences to choose from, college students are demanding more and better advising.

When a college or university cannot satisfactorily meet this demand, students are rarely reluctant to express their dissatisfaction with a school's advising program. In a climate where students often view themselves as customers both of the advising program and of the institution in general, and where dissatisfaction can lead to students leaving an institution (and consequently taking their tuition dollars with them), the necessity to develop coherent and purposeful advising programs is paramount.

It is therefore incumbent upon every advising program—at the university level, at the college or school level, and at the departmental level—to develop a mission statement that includes goals and objectives. The approach to such a task can be found in the Academic Advising Standards and Guidelines of the Council for the Advancement of Standards in Higher Education (CAS), last published in revised form in 1997 (Miller, 1997). These standards and guidelines, approved by the National Academic Advising Association (NACADA), a member of the CAS consortium, provide the basis for developing an appropriate mission statement.

There are many rationales for developing such statements and for periodically revisiting statements that already exist. Without such statements to provide the purpose for advising programs, the very existence of such programs and services can be challenged. No longer can advising programs and services be provided simply because it seems like the right thing to do. Such an approach can leave an advising program vulnerable to severe criticism for operating without a clear sense of purpose and may even lead to program elimination. With accountability a major focus in higher education, no advising program should operate without knowing what it is about and where it fits into the institution's panoply of offerings.

Likewise, the very activity of developing mission statements along with goals and objectives can be a potent source for the professional development of advisors. The chance to examine the very nature of an advising operation is an invaluable opportunity to engage advising staff in one of the most fundamental of professional tasks. Although disagreements may arise and various (and perhaps widely disparate) advising philosophies may be promulgated, such activity allows for meaningful discourse, and when approached with openness and appreciation for multiple viewpoints, consensus can be achieved.

Having a mission, goals, and objectives also allows for the assessment process to work more effectively. Without such a statement, assessment, if it can be conducted at all, would be an empty exercise. Certainly in a climate where financial support for higher education from all constituencies is critical, the ability to assess one's effectiveness is vital. The existence of a mission, goals, and objectives thus provides the basis for the assessment of an advising program. The ability to know when goals have been met and when the mission of the program is being fulfilled cannot be underestimated. On the basis of thorough assessments, advising programs can more readily justify their existence and make their cases, especially when resources are limited and need to be allocated sparingly and judiciously.

When beginning the process of developing an advising mission statement, the most logical place to look is at the institutional mission statement. It is within the context of the total institution that advising programs operate; thus there is a critical need to be consistent with the overall philosophy of the institution. Institutions of higher education may serve students in very different ways and may serve very different kinds of students. How a college or university goes about defining its mission depends on many factors. Institutions with religious affiliations may maintain strong ecclesiastical ties and may approach the education of their students differently than either independent private or publicly funded institutions. Schools serving a traditional-age population may approach the education of students quite differently than schools where the student population is much older than the traditional-age cohort. Schools serving a diverse student population may define their mission quite differently from schools dedicated to serving a more homogeneous population.

Institutional Mission

Whatever the mission of the institution, it must drive the development of the mission statement for advising. Basically, the first rule to observe is to make sure that the mission of the advising program is consistent with that of the institution.

For example, if the institution is committed to a basic core curriculum that guarantees that students will study the arts, humanities, social sciences, natural and physical sciences, quantification and computer applications, communications, and health and wellness concepts, then the advising program must incorporate into its activities approaches that can facilitate an appreciation of these subject areas. In addition, an effective advising program might include approaches to help students see the interconnectedness between the various components of an institution's core curriculum.

Advising programs in schools that place a heavy emphasis on preparing students for the world of work would naturally include a stronger emphasis on career development than an advising program at a very traditional liberal arts school, where the education itself might be seen as the most basic component of workforce preparation. Colleges that encourage students to examine and practice their spiritual and religious beliefs should have advising programs reflecting such attitudes.

Mission of Advising

Once the mission of the institution has been determined, developing a consistent advising mission statement is the next task. No matter at what level of the institution the advising program operates, it must prepare this statement and see that it is recorded in official documents and ultimately implemented.

Basically, the majority of advising program mission statements acknowledge that the primary purpose of any advising program is to assist students in the development and implementation of their educational plans. Included within the mission statement might be a statement of beliefs about students. NACADA's Statement of Core Values (National Academic Advising Association, 1995) can serve as a source of reference for the development of such statements, or the entire NACADA statement might be adopted as part of the advising mission. The teaching and learning culture of the institution might also help to delineate the belief structure of the advising program. For example, at Pennsylvania State University it is acknowledged that advising is part of the teaching and learning continuum and that there is a synergism between classroom instruction and academic advising. Because Penn State provides an enrollment unit for the undecided student, it is recognized that such students do exist, that they can be accommodated with appropriate interventions, and that they can learn about themselves and their relationship to the curricular options available within an advising context.

In preparing mission statements, it is critical to look to the value system of the institution and to the advisors who will be working with the students. Values to be espoused might include ensuring that an advising program provides opportunities for students to assess their interests and academic abilities, encouraging the fullest intellectual development of students, and providing an environment in which students can learn about the full array of educational opportunities available to them.

While some mission statements may be short, others might be expanded to include the thirteen components included in the CAS's Academic Advising Standards and Guidelines (Miller, 1997). At a minimum, mention of the nature of the advising program to be offered and of the type of leadership and organizational structures required would be appropriate. Whatever approach is taken, measures should be taken to ensure that there is consensus as to how the advising program will operate. Agreement should extend not only to the advisors providing the programs and services, but also to the upper-level administration. Within the CAS Standards and Guidelines, all the necessary components of an advising system are detailed, starting with the mission of advising and moving to the programmatic elements; the nature of the leadership; the management and organizational model; the human, financial, and physical resources necessary; the legal and ethical responsibilities inherent in the advising practice; the relationship of advising to other campus and community activities; commitment to equal opportunity, access, affirmative action, and diversity; and finally an assessment and evaluation imperative.

When an entire institution needs to revise its advising program or establish one, then it is important that the internal governance organization be involved in the process, especially if faculty are providers of advising. To a great extent, those who provide the advising must own the mission statement. Operating from a framework of acceptance can be ensured when those who provide the programs and services are those who take an active role in the development of the mission statement and its accompanying goals and objectives.

For example, Penn State's faculty senate saw a need to update previous advising policies that had been developed in the 1970s. As a result, the senate initiated the most recent revision to its statement on academic advising, acknowledging the concept that ultimately academic advising is a relationship between student and advisor, between student and institution, and between advisor and institution. Within each of these relationships, various responsibilities are inherent. Likewise, certain implicit ideas about the delivery of coherent advising programs required articulation. First of all, it is recognized that in a large, complex institution an organizational model for the delivery of advising must be developed. Senate legislation called for the development of appropriate informational systems, especially electronic media, to support both advisors and students in the advising endeavor; a comprehensive training program; and the implementation of strategies to accommodate the special advising needs of all students in the institution. The implementation of a recognition and reward system for advisors and a multifaceted assessment model was required. Finally, it was acknowledged that focus should be placed on first-year students (an approach supported by the advising literature) and that academic advisors must be readily available to meet the needs of those students.

All of these policies were developed within a mission framework of the institution that acknowledged a reliance on the latest technologies to support learning endeavors, a commitment to addressing the diverse needs of the student body, an organizational structure and philosophy that reflected the needs of the clientele, and an overarching concept that although all students would be assigned a primary advisor, all personnel in the institution were ultimately part of the advising system and should act accordingly.

In the development of mission statements, any unit with the responsibility for delivering advising programs and services can refer to the CAS's Academic Advising Standards and Guidelines (Miller, 1997). These standards and guidelines are available on the Internet at the NACADA Web site [www.ksu.edu/nacada].

All components of the Academic Advising Standards and Guidelines, when addressed within the context of an institutional mission, ensure the establishment of a well-functioning academic advising program. It is critical that every unit on campus that provides academic advising create its own mission statement. For example, a large institution with many schools and colleges within its structure should develop advising mission statements for each unit. It could be expected that a college of business administration might have somewhat different advising outcomes for its students than a school of fine arts. Yet both statements should clearly reflect the institutional mission.

Likewise, if an institution recognizes the need to advise exploratory and undeclared students in a separate unit, then the mission statement of such a unit would call for different outcomes than an advising unit that advises students who have already declared majors. If an institution structures its advising system so that students in certain categories, such as student athletes, honor students, or underrepresented students, are served by separate advising programs, it would be expected that the mission statements of such units would reflect the unique advising needs of the clientele.

Even a relatively small homogeneous institution with a single educational purpose might find that one advising mission statement would not suffice. Ultimately the vast majority of students graduate after declaring majors and it is assumed that each major might expect different advising outcomes for its students. It might be possible for an institution to choose to focus on a single broad mission statement, a situation that is more likely at small homogenous institutions with less complex missions. Whether an institution has many advising mission statements or just one, the expectation is that the mission statement clearly reflects the mission of the institution.

Expectations of Advisors and Advisees

A significant component of any mission statement is a set of expectations for advisors and advisees. Without expectations, confusion results. Indeed, some of the greatest complaints about advising appear to arise out of the differences between what students want from advisors and what advisors believe they should be providing. In relationships where these expectations are not synchronous, misunderstanding and dissatisfaction readily occur. Consequently, the absence from the mission statement of expectations for both advisors and advisees would leave a very unfinished document.

There are numerous approaches to defining these expectations. Without a doubt, those who are charged with providing advising must have a stake in delineating the expectations of advisors, while students should be provided with the opportunity to state not only what they expect from advisors, but also in which areas they will take responsibility. An example of an expectation statement from the Penn State advising policy follows (Pennsylvania State University Faculty Senate, 1997):

> Both advisors and advisees share responsibility for making the advising relationship succeed. By encouraging their advisees to become engaged in their education, to meet their educational goals, and to develop the habit of learning, advisors assume a significant educational role. The advisee's unit of enrollment will provide each advisee with a primary academic advisor, the information needed to plan the chosen program of study, and referrals to other specialized resources. The college or department also will monitor the progress of its advisees towards satisfactory completion of all graduation requirements and inform students of their status each semester. Advisees in turn will routinely contact their advisors each semester and will assume final responsibility for course scheduling, program planning, and the successful completion of graduation requirements.
>
> The Academic Advisor's Role is to:
>
> 1. Help the advisee to understand the academic and administrative processes of the university and the nature of its academic programs. The advisor also seeks to understand each advisee's particular concerns affecting academic progress. The advisor neither grants nor denies administrative approval for particular academic actions.
>
> 2. Help the advisee to understand the expected standards of achievement and likelihood of success in certain areas of study.
>
> 3. Discuss the educational and career objectives suited to the advisee's demonstrated abilities and expressed interests. The advisor helps the advisee to understand the relationships among the courses, programs, undergraduate research opportunities, internships, study abroad programs, and other academic experiences provided by the university.
>
> 4. Help the advisee to plan a course of study and give advice about courses and the adjustment of course loads. The advisor will inform the advisee about the prerequisites for subsequent courses in the advisee's program.
>
> 5. Refer advisees to other resources when appropriate.
>
> 6. Participate in the advisor training sessions provided by each college or department to keep informed and current.
>
> The Advisee's Role in the Academic Advising Process is to:
>
> 1. Acquire the information needed to assume final responsibility for course scheduling, program planning, and the successful completion of all graduation requirements.
>
> 2. Seek the academic and career information needed to meet educational goals.

3. Become knowledgeable about the relevant policies, procedures, and rules of the university, college, and academic program.

4. Be prepared with accurate information and relevant materials when contacting the advisor.

5. Consult with the advisor at least once a semester to decide on courses, review the accuracy of the audit, check progress towards graduation, and discuss the suitability of other educational opportunities provided by the University.

Statements such as these articulate expected behaviors. However, simply developing and publishing such statements is only the beginning of ensuring that quality advising is occurring. It is imperative that students be introduced to these expectations and to the notions of academic advising as early as their first orientation to their chosen college or university.

Likewise, those who are expected to provide advising, be they faculty or staff, should be given copies of these expectations, or in an era of electronic media, told where such statements are located on the institution's Web site. As part of any training program, the existence and rationale for such statements must be presented. Only with such an approach can those who are responsible for seeing that successful academic advising programs are provided find that they can reduce the discrepant attitudes that often develop between students and advisors.

Although academic advising primarily addresses the student's educational experience within the context of a total collegiate experience, and acknowledges that many factors influence the student's success or failure in the collegiate environment, an advising mission statement may include additional elements as appropriate to the institution and to the unit responsible for providing advising. For example, an institution in which a great many students go on to graduate or professional schools may include within their mission the notion of encouraging and facilitating this process. Two-year institutions may indicate that one of their advising goals is to send as large a percentage as possible of their graduates to baccalaureate degree–granting schools. Liberal arts colleges might express within their advising mission notions of the relationship of a liberal arts education to the world of work and of the expected outcomes of a liberal arts education. The advising mission statement of schools with significant enrollments of students who will pursue work immediately upon graduation will have a different emphasis. Schools with sectarian ties may acknowledge these relationships and stress the significance of such ties to the educational outcomes of their students.

The importance of the mission statement, then, is to provide advisors with the foundation from which they will conduct their work. More often than not, it is during an advising session that the mission of an institution can be explained to a student. Sharing this mission is particularly appropriate when students find themselves questioning either their goals or their reasons for attending such an institution. When a mission statement for advising clearly identifies what is expected to be accomplished in advising, then the needs of both students and the institution can be served. Advising and its concomitant mission statement thus provide the vehicle for an advisor to articulate the goals of a particular school, its values, and how a student might find a place within such an environment.

When such mission statements are not readily available to the advisor, a major component of the advising endeavor is left untended, often reducing advising to the role of burdensome adjunct to the registration process.

Goals for Advising

While advising is predicated on the mutual responsibilities of advisor and student within the institution and on the institution's support to ensure that successful advising occurs, the final determinant of any student's program of study and of how students use the educational opportunities available to them ultimately rests with the students. Nonetheless, advising mission statements should include some variation of the following goals:

The development of suitable educational plans. This goal provides the foundation for much of the advising endeavor. With the assistance of an advisor, students can craft an educational experience that meets their needs, is consistent with the goals of the institution, and uses as many of the educational opportunities available to students as possible.

Clarification of career and life goals. Because all students move from college to other experiences, an important goal of advising is to assist in that transition. Students should be assisted in examining their values, their purpose for being in higher education, the relationship between education and the world of work, and ultimately how they see themselves as lifelong learners.

Selection of appropriate courses and other educational experiences. The selection of courses is the most readily identifiable activity of academic advising. While course selection and the registration process drive many of the procedural aspects of how academic advising is conducted, the ultimate value of course selection is in the timing and purpose of courses and in understanding why courses are in the curriculum in the first place. It is within this context of course selection that the values and culture of an institution can be transmitted to students. When an institution has a rich and coherent general education or core curriculum, the opportunity to explore the vast array of educational opportunities open to students should not be missed. In addition, students need to be aware of the entire array of experiences provided by the institution. For example, is an internship or cooperative program appropriate? Should a student consider a study-abroad opportunity? How can a research opportunity with a faculty member enhance a student's experience? What is the role of service learning for a particular student? Should a student consider living in an interest house or perhaps expand his or her studies through a student exchange program? A viable advising planning process must take into account all of these aspects. To enable this process to occur, the advising planning process must not only provide advisors with the necessary information and referral resources, but also provide students with the understanding that advising extends beyond the mere scheduling of courses once a semester.

Interpretation of academic requirements of the institution. Institutions of higher education in America contain a vast and complex arrangement of majors, minors, academic emphases, options, interdisciplinary and general degrees, and self-designed degree programs. Many large institutions are now offering more than two hundred majors. In addition to majors, most institutions require a general education or core curriculum. In most cases, especially at schools with a distributive approach to general education, there is a lengthy list of courses from which students can choose. To a certain extent the certifying of a degree is the assurance that a student has met all of the institutional requirements. This can mean a minimum number of credits in everything from biological sciences and mathematics to the arts, communication, and health and wellness. In addition, requirements for writing across the curriculum and for diversity and other cultures, and specific requirements determined by external accrediting agencies may be included in curriculum requirements.

The advisor's role is to know and interpret these requirements to the students. This is often accomplished with the aid of electronic degree audit systems and through specially produced check sheets. The amount of time students take to complete a degree often depends on how they make their way through the maze of requirements. While the ultimate responsibility for the completion of the requirements rests with the student, advisors who are unaware of requirements, who misinterpret them, or who provide outdated information may be subject to criticism for being poor advisors or, if the advice given contradicts institutional practice or policy, may find themselves involved in litigation.

Making students aware of all the available resources that enhance their education. In addition to the formal courses that students take and the academic experiences that are provided outside the classroom, advisors need to be aware of support resources available on campus that can assist students. For example, a student with a psychological issue may need a referral to the campus mental health center. Students who may need supplemental instruction or tutoring also need to be referred to such resources. Advisors must thus know that these resources exist, how to identify students who might need such resources, and how to make a referral in an appropriate manner.

Evaluation of student progress toward their degrees. For many students and their families, the rising costs of higher education mean that time spent in school is also money spent, and more time in school is also potentially less time as a wage earner. The time it takes a student to earn a degree is of course the individual student's decision. However, many factors determine the length of time to graduation: the number of credits required in a particular field, the number of credits scheduled each semester, the number of courses passed each semester, changes of major, and the number of withdrawals that a student might opt for either as part of a regular procedure or as part of a formal petition process for a retroactive action. Thus the advisor works with the student to determine what an appropriate time line might be and how it might best be accomplished, pointing out that any variation from the plan may result in lengthening a student's time to degree.

Developing decision-making skills. Much of academic advising involves the making of decisions. Students constantly ask, Should I change my major? If I do, how much time will it take to complete a new major? What are the consequences of dropping a course? If I study abroad will I earn credits for the experience or will it delay graduation? Is that delay worth it? Should I choose a minor in addition to a major or maybe take two minors? How about a dual-major program? Should I consider graduate or professional school immediately after graduation or work for a few years? What kind of work does a particular major prepare me for? How many credits should I schedule this semester? If I stay with this many credits each semester, will I graduate on time? How an advisor deals with these questions determines the relationship between student and advisor. Yet these questions should be dealt with in a context that purports that one of the most important outcomes of advising is facilitating the student's decision making. Not only are these skills necessary during the collegiate years, but students will be constantly facing decisions. How students are assisted in making academic decisions may provide the basis for whether or not they are able to make additional reasonable decisions in their lives.

Helping students become independent learners. Higher education does not end with the completion of one or two degrees. Rather, in a rapidly changing educational and work environment, a habit of continuing to learn in various settings must be cultivated. The goal of advising is to help students see past the choice of a major or the completion of degree requirements. Students need to understand that once they commit themselves to higher education, they need to remain learners throughout their lives. This is not only to benefit themselves and to enrich their lives, but it will also be required to achieve the level of career to which they aspire.

Collection of data about students' educational needs, their history in the institution, and how these data might affect institutional decisions and policies. The goal of any advising program is not only to serve the students directly, but also to learn as much about the students as possible. This includes surveying students as they enter the institution or the unit, providing advising, and determining what the students need from the advising system and whether the advising system meets those needs. An examination of how students progress academically through the institution or program can also inform institutional practices. Such analysis may also lead to the revision of advising policies.

If, for example, an advising model that used faculty as advisors at the major level discovered that students were not satisfied with this approach, an appropriate response might be to look to other models, such as hiring a professional advisor. Another response might be to determine whether faculty feel they are having a difficult time staying current on all institutional policies. Although additional training and informational meetings could resolve this concern, the employment of a professional advisor to handle these aspects of advising may also be appropriate.

An analysis of how students respond to their educational experience could lead to program enhancements such as the development of freshman seminars, capstone courses, courses on writing and speaking across the curriculum, or computer literacy requirements. All of these potential programmatic alternatives may be informed by the continued assessment of students' experiences.

Program Criteria

To determine if an advising program is consistent with its mission goals and objectives, it is important to look for the following criteria. Although these statements are important beginning points for the development of effective advising programs, their ultimate value lies in how a program is implemented.

First, an advising program must be intentional and coherent; that is, it must not be delivered ad hoc and it must be coherent in structure and purpose. Advising programs should also operate from some theoretical basis or bases that advisors understand. The department itself should look to its own curriculum to provide such a basis. It might be reasonable to assume that a psychology department could deliver its advising based on some theory of human development, while a philosophy department might approach the education of its students from a humanistic framework focused on the human condition and how students want to tell their stories.

Any advising program that does not take into account the demographic characteristics of its clientele will find itself floundering and mired in unsatisfactory responses to its services. Adult learners may need to be served by different office hours than traditional ones and might respond more to and use electronic communications when they cannot come to campus. Women students studying in fields that are dominated by men may require different advising interventions. Students with disabilities need an advising program that is responsive to their particular needs, one that accepts the student's circumstances.

All advising programs need to operate from the assumption that learning both inside and outside the classroom should be promoted, and they need to accept the premise that learning occurs within the context of an advising session. Students need to craft experiences that will stretch them intellectually, that will take them farther than they had gone before they entered higher education. Students will need to see not only the value of higher education to their lives, but also why a nation needs a college-educated workforce.

Regardless of curriculum, the purpose of broader criteria for advising is to ensure that students experience activities that help them communicate clearly, that ensure that they can work both collaboratively and independently, and that develop an appreciation of cultural and aesthetic diversity. Students also need to be provided with experiences that help them make realistic self-appraisals—

appraisals that can lead to satisfying educational and life experiences—while at the same time continuing to clarify their values about the nature of their education, their lifestyles, and their careers.

Ultimately, advising programs can flourish only when advisors have access to all relevant information about the students served and when all students are given opportunities to meet with advisors on a regular basis and in an in-depth manner. The mission of any advising program is to serve the students, and consequently how these students are to be served should be taken into account. While caseload is often a resource issue, knowing what the mission of the advising unit is might help to determine appropriate roster sizes. Two essential features should also determine caseloads: the types of students who are being seen, and the amount of time an advisor has available for advising. First-year students who are undecided typically need more advising time than seniors in majors. Faculty advisors, with classroom teaching, research, and service obligations, cannot handle the same-size roster that professional full-time advisors have.

The synergism, then, between mission statements in which the goals and criteria of an advising program are recorded and the implementation of such a program should be a strong one. This connection allows not only for the implementation of an advising program but also for the continued evaluation and assessment of advising practices when guided by the mission. Should the mission of the institution change, should the student body change or the types of providers of advising change, then mission statements should be reexamined. This is a continual process. If done systematically and involving all constituents, then quality and effectiveness can be guaranteed.

References

Miller, T. K. (ed.). *The Book of Professional Standards for Higher Education*. Washington, D.C.: Council for the Advancement of Standards in Higher Education, 1997.

National Academic Advising Association. "NACADA Statement of Core Values of Academic Advising." *NACADA Journal*, 1995, *15*(1), 5–7.

Pennsylvania State University Faculty Senate. "Advising Policy." [http://www.psu.edu/ufs/policies/32–00.html]. Aug. 1997.

Chapter Thirteen

Organizational Models for Academic Advising

Celeste F. Pardee

An advising program cannot be developed, assessed, and improved without considering its organizational context. When the need for change in academic advising is identified by students, advisors, or administrators, that need is frequently related to organization. Concerns about the organizational framework of services have been documented since the early American College Testing (ACT) National Surveys of Academic Advising (Habley, 1988). In their 1990 survey of NACADA members, Creamer and Creamer (1994) found that a third of the respondents had orchestrated recent change projects in academic advising in either administration or organization.

A distinction should be made here between the organizational *context* (characteristics of the institution or unit that create a specific environment) and the organizational *structure* (a framework for delivering services that is closely tied to the organizational context) of the advising program. It is not possible to examine the organizational structure separately from the organizational context, because the structure necessarily reflects those factors that are unique to the setting of the advising program (Habley, 1983). Therefore, both structure and context are addressed in this chapter.

An organizational model is the formalized way in which advising services are structured for delivery to students, not only at the institutional level but also at the campus, college, or department level. The organizational structure of advising should not be confused with the delivery system—the persons who deliver advising services. *Who* advises is the topic of Chapter Fourteen.

It is also important to distinguish the organization of the components that constitute an advising program (that is, the internal elements) from the organizational structure of the program—its external form and scope. Effective advising programs include a variety of components (such as mission statement, advising coordinator, system of recognition and rewards, sufficient advising resources, training, and evaluation, to name only a few). Improved organization of advising services may entail the addition of components or the redesign of components that were not functioning well. Frank (1988, 1993) suggests that an effective program evolves over time in a series of phases, illustrated by what she calls the Integrated Model of Advising Program Development. As a need surfaces within or outside the system and exerts pressure for change, the model suggests ways that the program services or structure may be altered to address the need. The Integrated Model provides a framework for progressive change that can be adapted to the circumstances of the unit or institution. This chapter focuses not on the internal components but on the external organizational structure of advising. The information provided here will be most relevant to administrators with responsibility for developing or revising an advising system for an institution, campus, college, or department.

Central to the selection of an appropriate organizational structure is the institution's mission statement, which should include a philosophy on academic advising. This statement provides a basis for assessing the various organizational models. Congruence between the institution's mission and organization of advising is key to the successful delivery of advising services (Glennen, 1995). Likewise, a functional organizational structure will contribute to the achievement of the institution's mission and goals.

This chapter defines three kinds of organizational structures, along with seven specific organizational models for academic advising; it examines the application of institutional models at the college, campus, and department levels; it discusses variables that affect the selection of an organizational model; and it explores the related issues of effectiveness and goal achievement of the organizational model.

Institutional Models of Academic Advising

Although the organizational structure of advising differs from one institution to the next, Habley (1983) determined that organizational patterns exist and that certain structures are more apt to be found at similar types of institutions. A basis for comparison and categorization lies in the degree of centralization. In a *decentralized* organizational structure, advising services are provided by faculty or staff in their academic departments. Even though overall coordination of advising may be centralized, advisors are accountable to their respective departments, where the advising activity takes place. A *centralized* organizational structure consists of an administrative unit, usually an advising center, with a director and an advising staff housed in one location. In some programs, however, the administration is centralized and the advising staff are in multiple locations. More commonly, advising services are *shared* between a central administrative unit and faculty or staff in academic departments. On a continuum from centralization to decentralization, there is considerable variability in the shared category: from a sequential system in which students move from an advising center to a department advisor, to a parallel system where students are served by both the advising center and the department advisor throughout their college career. Inherent in each system are strengths and weaknesses.

The organizational structure of advising includes coordination of the program, which may be centralized (such as with a vice president or dean of academic affairs) or decentralized (such as with directors of advising offices or divisional deans). Thus, within an institution it is possible for the coordination of advising to be centralized but the delivery of advising services to be decentralized. The discussion of institutional models in this chapter addresses both aspects of organization: program coordination and the location of the delivery system.

Decentralized Models

Two of the organizational models identified by Habley (1983, 1988; Habley and McCauley, 1987) are structurally decentralized: the Faculty-Only Model and the Satellite Model.

Faculty-Only Model. All advising is done by faculty in their department offices. This is the only model that defines those who deliver advising. Students with majors are assigned to a faculty member in their discipline. Undecided students are distributed among either faculty in the liberal arts, faculty who volunteer to assist undecided students, or faculty with lighter advising loads. This model has several benefits, including low direct cost and the proximity of advising services to classes that students take within their academic department. For further information about the benefits and weaknesses of the Faculty-Only Model, see Chapter Fourteen.

Satellite Model. Advising is provided by central offices in each of the academic subunits at the institution (such as colleges within a university or campuses of a multicampus community college). Each satellite advising office serves students with majors in that college or school. In some institutions, students are served by the college advising office from their initial enrollment until their graduation. Alternatively, the satellite office may refer students to a faculty advisor's office when they have completed certain criteria. Undecided students are frequently advised by the staff of a university college office until they declare a major.

Maintaining several central advising offices is more costly than the Faculty-Only Model, because centers require space, operating funds, and professional and support staff. Duplication of services is a budgetary issue. An added weakness of the Satellite Model is that undecided students or major-changers may experience a difficult transition when changing from one advising center to another in which services differ (Gordon, 1992). Nonetheless, the satellite system offers the advantages of autonomous administration, location in the college or school of the student's major, and the capability of responding to those majors' needs and of offering advising services to students throughout the day. Each decentralized office is usually staffed by professional advisors, including specialists for students with unique needs.

Role of the Coordinator. The coordinator of advising in a decentralized system may have little direct oversight of faculty or staff dispersed in department offices. Advising is usually one of many concerns of the administrator. The Fifth ACT National Survey on Advising revealed that the most common title used in decentralized models is vice president for academic affairs (Habley, 1997). In the Faculty-Only Model, faculty are generally supervised by the department head, who reports to an academic dean. Typically, a coordinator in central administration oversees the development of advising policy, establishes training and evaluation systems, and provides advising manuals and newsletters. But when advising is not a formal part of the tenure and promotion process, and the advising coordinator has no authority over the delivery of services, there is no incentive for faculty to participate in training or to devote a specified time to advising.

Coordination of advising is equally challenging with the Satellite Model, in which college deans or center directors have autonomy within their subunit (King and Kerr, 1995). Because the satellite offices tend to operate in isolation, the campus coordinator should establish a council or committee of deans and directors of all subunits. In this council, policies and procedures would be reviewed, problems would be identified and resolved, and a referral system would be established whereby students could find help in other areas when needed. Although the advising coordinator in central administration has little direct involvement with the advising function, he or she may be responsible for providing resources and opportunities for professional development for advisors campuswide.

Pattern of Utilization. The 1997 ACT National Survey of Advising revealed that 28 percent of the respondents from 754 institutions, most of which were smaller two-year and four-year institutions with fewer than five thousand students, identified the Faculty-Only Model. The Satellite Model, cited by 6 percent of the total, was associated with larger four-year institutions with more than ten thousand students. At some larger institutions, a combination of these decentralized models existed (Habley, 1997).

Centralized Models

Only one of Habley's models meets the criteria of a centralized organizational structure: the Self-Contained Model. In this model, all academic advising of students, from orientation through graduation, is provided from a central administrative unit. The dean or director of the unit oversees all advising functions for the institution (Habley, 1983, 1988; Habley and McCauley, 1987).

This model has several advantages: trained staff, consistent quality of advising, no duplication of services, easy accessibility, and on-site supervision of advising services. Students with special needs, such as undecided students or freshmen, may be served more effectively at a central location. The center is, however, more expensive to staff and operate than a model based on faculty and staff advisors in their departments. Unless faculty are released from their departments to work part-time at the advising center, students lose the expertise of faculty and the faculty-student interaction that the advising role promotes (King and Kerr, 1995). Another potential problem arises from a growing enrollment—the advisee load may become unmanageable for professional staff (Crockett, 1982). Sometimes the centralized model exists in conjunction with other student services, such as counseling, academic support services, or career services. The Fifth ACT National Survey on Advising indicated that the most common title of the coordinator in the Self-Contained Model is director of counseling (Habley, 1997). Where these services are combined, counseling staff may be cross-trained with advising staff to ease the advising load and better serve undecided students (Gordon, 1992).

Role of the Coordinator. When the advising structure is centralized, the dean or director is more involved with the advising function and direct supervision of staff, even if the staff includes faculty assigned to the center. The coordinator is responsible not only for setting advising policies but also for implementing those policies. The unit administrator also has more control over training, evaluation, and support programs. Clearly administrative tasks are more easily managed when the organizational structure is centralized.

Pattern of Utilization. The ACT Fifth National Survey on Advising indicated that the Self-Contained Model, found at 12 percent of the 754 institutions, was predominantly at two-year colleges. The use of the self-contained model has seen a noticeable decline, however. (Habley, 1997).

Shared Models

There are four Habley models with structural characteristics of both centralized and decentralized systems: the Supplementary Model, the Split Model, the Dual Model, and the Total Intake Model. In each of these models, the advising function is divided between department advisors (faculty or staff) and staff in a central administrative unit (Habley, 1983, 1988; Habley and McCauley, 1987). Most of the advantages and potential weaknesses of these organizational models have been identified by King and Kerr (1995).

Supplementary Model. All students have department advisors. The advising office serves the department advisors by providing resources, such as advising information systems, handbooks on policies, and training on advising techniques. For students, it typically operates as a referral source for advising or other support services on campus. The administrative unit might process a student's petition, evaluate transfer credit, or finalize a degree audit, but decisions about the student's program rest with the department advisor.

This model has an advantage over the Faculty-Only Model in that it offers a certain degree of coordination and a consistent quality of administrative support services. It frequently functions as a clearinghouse for advising information. However, because decision making rests with the department advisor, advising staff in the central office may lack credibility. A drawback of the Supplementary Model is that students with special needs may not be well served.

Split Model. Initial advising of students is divided between department advisors and staff in a central office. For example, students with majors may be assigned to faculty in their major department while students without majors are assigned to staff in an advising center. Advising center staff have authority for monitoring and approving academic transactions for students up to a point (such as when students declare a major), at which time the students are referred to department advisors. Additionally, the advising center may serve the department advisor in a capacity similar to the capacity served by the center in the Supplementary Model—as a clearinghouse on advising information and as a referral source for students with petition issues or academic difficulties. The Split Model is applicable when the administration determines that a subgroup—such as undecided or exploratory students, underprepared students, student athletes, or premed or prelaw students—could benefit from special advising services.

This model has the advantage of offering high-risk students the additional advising support needed to improve their chances for academic success. Students still benefit from developing advising relationships with faculty or staff in their major department. However, students in transition from the center to a faculty advisor may experience a difference in accessibility, advising skills, and commitment.

Dual Model. Students have two advisors to guide them through their degree program: a department advisor for the major, and a staff member in a central office for general education issues, college policies, and academic procedures. Undecided students are served at the central office until they declare a major, at which time they acquire a department advisor as well. The division of advising responsibilities approximates fifty-fifty. Both advisors monitor and approve the student's graduation plan.

The Dual Model has some of the strengths of centralized and decentralized organizational structures. Potential problems with this model lie in the definition of advising and the communication of responsibilities. Unless there is frequent and clear communication among the advising staff and students, department advisors may not be clear on the boundaries of their jurisdiction, and students may not understand which advisor can help them in a given situation. Thus the success of the Dual Model depends on effective coordination of the campuswide system.

Total Intake Model. Initial advising of all students is conducted in a central advising unit. This might be a university college, an office of undergraduate services, a counseling center, or a freshman-year center. When students meet specific criteria (such as completion of a certain number of units, achievement of a certain grade point average, fulfillment of general education requirements, completion of premajor courses, or some combination thereof), they are referred to the academic subunit of their major for advising on the remainder of their academic program. The advising center may have responsibility for curriculum and instruction; for development and enforcement of academic policies, depending on reporting lines (that is, academic affairs or student affairs); or for both.

Like the Dual Model, the Total Intake Model realizes the best aspects of trained staff, central access, and economy of scale for a portion of the advising function, balanced with the resources offered by advisors in their academic departments. The structure of shared responsibilities is sequential in the Total Intake Model, as opposed to simultaneous in the Dual Model. This reduces the amount of student confusion connected with the Dual Model. Care needs to be taken when students shift to department advisors that their advising needs continue to be met. Likewise, department advisors need to know that students have been adequately prepared to begin their chosen major.

Role of the Coordinator. When the organizational structure is one of shared responsibility, the coordinator of advising is usually the dean or director of the central advising unit (Habley, 1997). Besides supervising the staff and overseeing the advising services of the unit, the administrator may also be responsible for advising the institution on policy and procedure decisions. The challenge with the shared models is coordination between the academic departments and the advising center. Training programs, advising resources, and campuswide evaluation of advising are typically under the auspices of this advising administrator. But selection of department advisors and of the recognition and reward system, and supervision of the faculty or staff, usually rests with the academic subunit (that is, the department head). This limitation in the role of the coordinator is a potential weakness of any of the shared models.

Pattern of Utilization. The 1997 ACT National Survey on Advising showed that 54 percent of 754 institutions employed one of the shared organizational structures. The Split Model was most typical, cited by 27 percent of the respondents, with a relatively even distribution among smaller (fewer than 5,000 students), midsize (5,000 to 9,999 students), and larger (10,000 or more students) institutions. This model is the structure of choice at both two-year and four-year public institutions. The Supplementary Model (used at 20 percent of the schools surveyed) was employed at small to midsize institutions (both two-year and four-year), more of which were private rather than public. Used at only 5 percent of the surveyed institutions, the Total Intake Model was more common at four-year public institutions, regardless of size. The Dual Model, identified by only 3 percent of the respondents, was associated with small to midsize four-year institutions (Habley, 1997).

Although there are patterns in the use of each model, the data cannot be used for predictions. For example, the 1997 survey revealed that the Self-Contained and Split Models were more likely to be employed at two-year public colleges. However, community colleges have successfully implemented all models. Leymaster's (1989) survey of two-year colleges indicated a similar pattern but also found that two-year colleges focusing on technical programs were more likely to use the Faculty-Only Model, and that colleges with fewer than two thousand students were more likely to use the Faculty-Only Model but colleges with more than 60 percent part-time students tended to use the Split and Self-Contained Models. Jefcoat's (1991) research on the organization of advising at rural community colleges showed a different pattern than at urban colleges; the most frequently used models on rural campuses were the Faculty-Only, Split, and Supplementary Models. Obviously many variables influence the application of a certain model at a given institution. After analyzing data from five national surveys, Habley (1997) concluded that it is impossible to identify the common traits of institutions that employ any one of the models. Regardless of type and size, institutions have applied nearly all of the organizational models.

Applications at the College, Campus, and Departmental Levels

Each of the organizational models found at the institutional level exists on a smaller scale at the college, campus, and departmental levels. Thus more than one model may be employed at an institution, particularly at large universities and community colleges. For example, the Satellite Model may best describe the advising structure at a large public university. However, each college or school at the university may establish a different advising structure in keeping with a unique set of variables. Similarly, a community college with multiple campuses may employ a different model on each campus.

Microsystems may be found at the department level within colleges of a university, especially those with a large number of majors. For example, the Total Intake Model may be used effectively in one department while the Self-Contained Model is more efficient in another. The model of choice for one subunit may not be suitable elsewhere on the same campus. What may evolve at a large institution is a conglomeration of models functioning at different levels of the hierarchy, a situation that can be very confusing for students, particularly those who change colleges only to find themselves lost in a different organizational web. The advising coordinator at the institutional level must construct a complimentary mesh of organizational models that are appropriate for the delivery system of each academic subunit and that effectively meet students' needs for advising.

The following examples illustrate how the three kinds of organizational structures are applied at the college, campus, or department level.

Which organizational structure is suitable for the growing number of distance education students? Curry (1997) tackled this research question in his study of academic advising practices in distance education programs. His survey of institutions offering distance baccalaureate degrees revealed that the decentralized models, Faculty-Only and Satellite, were most frequently used for the distance program on the main campus of small institutions. Large institutions were more likely to use the Self-Contained Model for the distance education advising function. Curry concluded that program size is a factor in the selection of a certain model but overall there is no best organizational model for distance programs.

Institutions with a university college or a college of undergraduate studies may effectively employ a centralized structure, the Self-Contained Model. An advising office serves the majority of freshmen, whether they are undecided or decided on a major. The advising staff includes not only professionals trained to assist undecided students in the major-exploration process but also staff or faculty trained to advise in specific major fields. Gordon (1995) points out two advantages of this structure within a university college: (1) undecided students may explore options along with those who have chosen majors, without feeling separated from their peers; and (2) students who have made a tentative choice of major may change majors in this structure, with few bureaucratic obstacles.

Advising centers were created in the early 1970s at each of the ten academic colleges at Brigham Young University (BYU), after a pilot project demonstrated that application of this model resulted in improvement in the quality of advising services. Each center included faculty in addition to professional advisors (Spencer, Peterson, and Kramer, 1982). From the institutional perspective, this is an example of the Satellite Model, but at the college level it exemplifies centralization of the advising function. Institutionally, coordination at BYU was centralized under the dean of admission and records.

A centralized model of advising on the department level was advocated by Johnson and Sprandel (1975), who presented a case study of an undergraduate advising center for English majors at Michigan State University in 1967. While a faculty member and a graduate assistant in the center handled all official academic advising functions for the six hundred majors, other faculty in the department served as mentors.

A variety of shared models that divided advising between staff in a central office and faculty members in the departments were identified by Bens (1995) in three faculties (that is, colleges or schools) at the University of Alberta, Canada. Although the structure was similar in the selected faculties, the proportion of advising responsibilities assumed by faculty members differed from one academic unit to the next; for example, the proportion was greater in the Faculty of Agriculture, Forestry, and Home Economics than in the Faculty of Education.

Dinoto (1991) studied the organization of advising in six academic disciplines at selected land grant universities with enrollments of at least ten thousand students and found a correlation between the type of intellectual activity in the selected disciplines (among other factors) and the department's organization of advising. Her study indicated that the Split Model was perceived as an effective structure for psychology, English, and mechanical engineering, but the Total Intake Model was a better fit for physics at these institutions.

Variables That Affect Selection of an Organizational Model

To determine an appropriate organizational structure for the delivery of advising services at the institutional, college, campus, or department level, multiple variables must be considered. Examination of these factors is necessary whether a new structure is designed or an existing structure is altered in response to a problem or need. The success of a certain model depends on the *degree of fit* between the model and the institutional culture (Habley and Morales, 1998a). Relevant variables fall into the following categories: institutional characteristics, student characteristics, faculty characteristics, scope and structure of the advising program, and philosophy and goals of advising.

Institutional Characteristics

The institutional type (two-year or four-year), governance (public or private), number of campuses, and enrollment are some of the most visible variables that influence the organization of advising services. Larger size, for example, is associated with centralized systems that usually evolve in response to economies of scale and efficiency, but advising centers are not necessarily more effective (Hines, 1984). Institutional policies are important factors, including the mission (such as purpose, emphasis on teaching versus research, and level and rigor of educational offerings) and admission criteria (open to all versus highly selective). The curriculum may also have an impact on the choice of an organizational model. Such elements as types of program (liberal arts, technical, or professional), program selectivity (limited space or advanced-standing requirements), and the complexity of the institutional or college program requirements (sequencing of courses, specificity of general education requirements, and amount of flexibility in substituting or waiving requirements) affect the extent that centralization or decentralization of advising is practical. Even the number of institutional or college policies and procedures is a factor, because this affects whether an advisor must approve certain academic transactions, such as changing a major, withdrawing from a course, or taking a course overload. When there are myriad rules and regulations, there is a greater need for professional advisors to interpret and apply the rules, which leads to a highly structured centralized or shared advising system (Habley, 1988).

Another consideration is the amount of resources allocated by the institution or college in support of advising functions. The human, physical, and technological resources that are available may determine the degree of centralization that is possible. At first glance, a decentralized system may appear more economical, but the costs of a reduced teaching load inherent in the Faculty-Only Model are carried in college and department budgets (Crockett, 1982).

Student Characteristics

The choice of an organizational structure depends on the advising needs of the students. Attributes of the student population include ethnic and cultural diversity, proportion of first-generation students, proportion from urban versus rural locations, proportion of underprepared versus honors students, and proportion of transfers, natives, and reentry students. As the diversity of the population increases, so does the need for a centralized or shared model to meet those needs. Beyond the student profile at the point of admission, enrollment patterns must also be examined. What is the proportion of distance learners, the proportion of lower-division versus upper-division or graduate students, the proportion attending day classes versus evening and weekend classes, and the proportion of part-time versus full-time students? As the number of part-time and evening and weekend students grows, access to advising becomes an issue, and this need is met more easily with a centralized model than with a decentralized model.

The proportion of students in residence halls relative to the number of commuters can also affect the organizational structure of advising services. For example, if the campus is primarily residential, advising centers could be established in residence halls (the Satellite Model) (Hines, 1984). The proportion of declared and undeclared majors is another variable. If the population includes a high number of undecided students or premajors, a centralized or shared advising structure is more desirable. If, however, more students have declared majors, they can be dispersed throughout the institution and efficiently advised by faculty or staff in their respective departments. Regardless of the model selected, administrators should ensure that the system addresses each student's unique needs.

Faculty Characteristics

Faculty affect the organization of advising. The organizational structure depends on the availability, competence, and willingness of individuals to perform the advising function. The role of faculty is to a certain extent determined by their contract conditions and job description. Collective bargaining agreements and faculty contracts may limit which organizational options are possible (Crockett, 1982). The formal institutional context dictates the advising responsibilities that are designated to administrative units and to faculty, the time and resources allocated for faculty advising, and the rewards and recognition that reinforce the advising component. If promotion and tenure depend primarily on research and publications, the greater will be the need for a centralized or shared advising structure. The success of a decentralized model requires a tangible demonstration that advising has priority, such as releasing faculty from teaching and research to participate in advising and the training it entails. The absence of a formal administrative structure in support of faculty advising can jeopardize any organizational model that depends on faculty—even if department heads and deans promote the importance of advising (Holmes, Clarke, and Irvine, 1983).

With respect to individual faculty members, those who are interested in advising, who are aware of students' needs, and who are willing to develop the skills to address those needs will be an asset to a faculty-based advising system (King and Kerr, 1995). Thus, at all levels the organizational structure must be conducive to an efficient process of selecting and retaining advisors. To ensure quality advising, the structure should also facilitate evaluation of individuals and programs (Habley, 1983). Although the most meaningful rewards from advising are intrinsic, salary increments and consideration in promotion decisions are significant incentives for faculty to participate (Habley and Morales, 1998a). Certainly the extent of faculty involvement determines whether the Faculty-Only Model is an organizational option. In fact, faculty attitudes and behavior influence the success of all but the Self-Contained Model.

Scope and Structure of the Advising Program

The scope of the advising program is the level at which it is administered, that is, at the institutional, campus, college, or departmental level. The broader the scope of the program, the more difficult it is to change the organizational structure. Even at the departmental level, the scope of the program consists of a number of other factors. Dinoto (1991), in her research on the organization of advising in selected academic disciplines, examined the number of upper-division majors in the department, the ratio of advisors to students, the number of full-time faculty in the department, the percentage of resources devoted to advising, and advising in relation to other department priorities. Advising program coordination can involve just as many factors. In a study of Catholic colleges and universities, Wong (1986) found that the larger the enrollment, the more decentralized the coordination was in comparison with smaller institutions. The advising coordinator may operate a central advising unit with relative autonomy but may have little authority over department advisors at the college or department level.

The structure of the administration reflects key organizational behaviors, the values of top administrators, and the evolution or context of the institution. As a single variable, administrative structure does not lead to a certain advising structure, but it may indicate the priority given to academic advising and the resources that might be allocated to support advising staff and services (Hines, 1984). Reporting lines affect the degree of oversight and coordination of the advising function. Other responsibilities may restrict the amount of time the coordinator can devote to advising issues. Whether advising is relegated to the division of academic affairs or student affairs may mean the difference between budget increases or cutbacks. This variable also affects who delivers advising services—faculty or staff.

The complexity of the advising program is a significant variable in the organization of services. Complexity results from need determined by the institutional culture for specialists to meet students' needs. At larger institutions, students' advising needs are frequently met by many specialists: freshman advisors, general education advisors, honors advisors, learning disability advisors, academic support advisors, career services advisors, prehealth-profession advisors, residence hall advisors, student athlete advisors, and graduation services advisors, in addition to the major advisor. The multiplicity of staff who are engaged in the advising function (sometimes with the title of counselor or specialist) may create confusion for students who had one guidance counselor in high school. In contrast, smaller institutions tend to combine advising services with other student services, such as counseling or career development, resulting in generalists (Koerin, 1991). Along with the expectation that advisors become specialists comes the assumption that faculty cannot be wholly responsible for advising. As the number of specialists increases, the greater is the need for a centralized or shared advising model.

Philosophy and Goals of Advising

What is academic advising? The structure of advising rests on how the institution defines the process. If it is narrowly defined as a series of procedural tasks (such as course selection, registration, and degree audit), the organizational model might look considerably different than if advising is defined as a developmental process in which goals are set and an educational plan is created (Koerin, 1991). For the model to be effective, all faculty and staff who participate in advising must subscribe to a similar philosophy, one that addresses not only the advisor's role but also the student's. Variables related to the philosophy include responsibilities of the advisor and the student, the degree to which advising is mandatory or voluntary, accessibility of advising, and whether advisors are to be proactive or intrusive.

An organizational model should be chosen that can help the institution or unit accomplish its goals. Both the goals and objectives of the advising program should be clearly articulated in a written policy statement, along with the priority of advising with respect to other institutional, college, or departmental goals. By considering advising goals in this context, administrators can make decisions about the allocation of human and physical resources. If the institution has accepted the core values of the National Academic Advising Association (Glennen and Vowell, 1995) or the academic advising standards established by the Council for the Advancement of Standards in Higher Education (Miller, 1997), these guidelines will provide a starting point for developing an appropriate organizational structure.

Effectiveness of the Organizational Model

It is difficult to assess the effectiveness of an organizational model apart from the advising program in its entirety. Such indicators of effectiveness as student retention, student satisfaction, and student use of advising services all reflect a combination of program components, not the structure of the delivery system alone. When students, staff, faculty, or administrators notice a problem with the advising program, they seldom isolate the organizational structure as the source. The best means for evaluating the effectiveness of an organizational model is through a self-assessment or an assessment by an outside consultant with expertise in this area. For more information on program assessment, refer to Chapter Twenty-Three.

A number of researchers have conducted surveys to determine the relationship between the seven organizational models and program effectiveness. Habley (1988) first examined this relationship using the 1987 ACT National Survey. Based on respondents' answers to a series of questions, he applied an effectiveness rating to each model. Although a superficial conclusion from this exercise was that the Self-Contained Model was the most effective overall, Habley realized that this model was effective only within a particular institutional context. Ivery (1992) tested this finding by surveying students and administrators at three Colorado institutions representing different organizational models: Faculty-Only, Self-Contained, and Split. Her study revealed that students rated the Faculty-Only Model as very effective in meeting their needs, but administrators reported that model as the most ineffective in meeting students' needs. Ivery's study illustrates the discrepancy between administrators' and students' perceptions of the models. Jefcoat's (1991) conclusion about the level of effectiveness of organizational structures employed at rural community colleges is that all models can perform equally well in meeting the basic requirements of an advising program.

The diversity found in the use of organizational models suggests that there is no one best model. All are potentially effective for the delivery of advising services, depending on the organizational context. Habley (1997) sees evidence that more institutions are adopting models that combine the strengths of decentralized models with those of centralized models. Given the array of institutional, faculty, student, and program variables that affect the structure of advising, it makes sense to employ a model in which responsibility for advising is shared between a central unit and faculty or staff in academic departments. The proportion of faculty and professional advisors, along with the degree of centralization in an integrated structure, will differ at each institution. For example, the centralized office may be at the institutional, college, or departmental level (Hines, 1984).

Some researchers have argued that there is indeed an ideal model based on institutional type. King (1993) has proposed that the Total Intake Model exemplifies the best features for community colleges, whereas the Dual Model is more advantageous for four-year institutions (King and Kerr, 1995). Both models utilize faculty and professional advisors to best advantage with respect to students' academic progress. Additionally, King (1995) has recommended the Total Intake Model on the basis that it ensures effective supervision and coordination of advising services.

An effective system hinges on an arrangement in which students can see a logical relationship among the individuals and divisions involved with advising, and in which those individuals and divisions can interact effectively. Holmes, Clarke, and Irvine (1983) suggest that an institutional framework for advising should be established to bring all participants into a coherent sequence of steps in which advisors can make smooth referrals among programs. No matter which of the models based on shared responsibility is employed, this is a challenge for the coordinator of advising. The coordinator's role is to foster a networked, collaborative advising system and to monitor how the system functions and develops. Tukey (1996) has proposed that the monitoring process should include a feedback function (that is, assessment and planning) that enables the coordinator to stay abreast of system changes.

The key to constructing an effective organizational structure that can be efficiently coordinated is to match the model not with an institutional type but with a particular institution. The exact configuration of advising is determined from the mix of variables that make the institution unique. Unfortunately, there is no equation that incorporates all the variables to determine an appropriate model for a particular institution, college, or department. Thus the advising administrator's goal is to take relevant variables into account and to select a model with the intent of optimizing its strengths and minimizing its weaknesses.

The commitment to implement a new organizational structure or alter an existing structure must come from the upper administration. The transition to a new organizational structure requires sustained administrative support to overcome institutional barriers, supply the necessary budget, and make complementary policy changes (Koerin, 1991). To neutralize any resistance, administrators should include personnel affected by the new structure in the planning and implementation stages. If the negotiation process is a collaborative effort that includes faculty, staff, and students, changes in advising will be more readily accepted (Glennen, Farren, Vowell, and Black, 1989; Frost, 1991). Nothing less than a campuswide effort will lead to a successful structural change.

Conclusion

The goals of the organizational model, at any level of the institution, should support the attainment of goals for the advising program as a whole. If a purpose of the advising program, as proposed in the CAS Standards and Guidelines (Miller, 1997), is to assist students with the development of educational plans in keeping with their life goals, then the organizational structure should facilitate this as well. Even more critical to the structure of advising are the goals for the institution as stated in its mission statement. The structure of the advising program should reflect the institutional mission and contribute to the achievement of institutional goals. When the organizational structure of advising is not aligned with that of the institution, the needs of its students, and its stated purpose, the advising program will be ineffective and inefficient. The particular arrangement of institutional, faculty, student, and program variables at each institution or subunit leads to the diversity of organizational models in evidence at colleges and universities.

An appropriate structure, whether centralized or decentralized, should promote open communication and interaction among those who deliver advising services and those to whom advisors are accountable: students, administrators, and the community supporting the institution. If the delivery system integrates features of centralized and decentralized structures, combining the expertise and skills of faculty and professional advisors, clear communication channels are essential. An organizational chart showing all personnel with advising roles and clearly delineating their responsibilities and reporting lines should be distributed to both advisors and students. A diagram of the organizational model would eliminate duplication of services among advising personnel and reduce confusion about advising specialists among students. In addition, an effective organizational structure would facilitate the coordination of advising, which encompasses written policies and procedures for advisors, expectations for performance, decision-making and conflict resolution guidelines, accountability systems, and recognition and reward avenues (Miller, 1997).

An effective organizational model is the framework for a successful academic advising program. The advising program crosses many institutional boundaries and affects almost all students. Because of its pervasiveness, the organizational structure of advising warrants close scrutiny. Of the models identified in this chapter, the best one for an institution is so well integrated that it blends into the structure of the institution, yet the framework for advising is so clearly outlined that advisors and students know how to operate within the structure to best advantage.

References

Bens, S. L. "Undergraduate Academic Advising in Selected Faculties at the University of Alberta." Unpublished master's thesis, Department of Educational Policy Studies, University of Alberta, 1995.

Creamer, E. G., and Creamer, D. G. "Planned Change Projects in Academic Advising: A NACADA Research Grant Report." *NACADA Journal*, 1994, *14*(1), 43–45.

Crockett, D. S. "Academic Advising Delivery Systems." In R. B. Winston Jr., S. C. Ender, and T. K. Miller (eds.), *Developmental Approaches to Academic Advising*. New Directions for Student Services, no. 17. San Francisco: Jossey-Bass, 1982.

Curry, R. F. "Academic Advising in Distance Education." Unpublished doctoral dissertation, School of Education, College of William and Mary, 1997.

Dinoto, D. M. "A Study of Variations in Undergraduate Academic Advising Processes by Academic Discipline and Organizational Structure of Departments." Unpublished doctoral dissertation, College of Education, Florida State University, 1991.

Frank, C. P. "The Development of Academic Advising Programs: Formulating a Valid Model." *NACADA Journal*, 1988, *8*(1), 11–28.

Frank, C. P. "An Integrated Model of Academic Advising Program Development." *NACADA Journal*, 1993, *13*(1), 62–73.

Frost, S. H. *Academic Advising for Student Success: A System of Shared Responsibility.* ASHE-ERIC Higher Education Report, no. 3. Washington, D.C.: School of Education and Human Development, George Washington University, 1991.

Glennen, R. E. "Obtaining Presidential Support for Advising." In R. E. Glennen and F. N. Vowell (eds.), *Academic Advising as a Comprehensive Campus Process.* National Academic Advising Association Monograph Series, no. 2. Manhattan, Kans.: NACADA, 1995.

Glennen, R. E., Farren, P. J., Vowell, F., and Black, L. "Expanding the Advising Team." *NACADA Journal,* 1989, *9*(2), 25–30.

Glennen, R. E., and F. N. Vowell (eds.). *Academic Advising as a Comprehensive Campus Process.* National Academic Advising Association Monograph Series, no. 2. Manhattan, Kans.: NACADA, 1995.

Gordon, V. N. *The Undecided College Student: An Academic and Career Advising Challenge* (2nd ed.). Springfield, Ill.: Thomas, 1995.

Gordon, V. N. *Handbook of Academic Advising.* Westport, Conn.: Greenwood Press, 1992.

Habley, W. R. "Organizational Structures for Academic Advising: Models and Implications." *Journal of College Student Personnel,* 1983, *24*, 535–540.

Habley, W. R. "The Organization of Advising Services." In W. R. Habley (ed.), *The Status and Future of Academic Advising: Problems and Promise.* Iowa City, Iowa: American College Testing Center, 1988.

Habley, W. R. "Organizational Models and Institutional Advising Practices." *NACADA Journal,* 1997, *17*(2), 39–44.

Habley, W. R., and McCauley, M. E. "The Relationship Between Institutional Characteristics and the Organization of Advising Services." *NACADA Journal,* 1987, *7*(1), 27–39.

Habley, W. R., and Morales, R. H. "Advising Models: Goal Achievement and Program Effectiveness." *NACADA Journal,* 1998a, *18*(1), 35–41.

Habley, W. R., and Morales, R. H. (eds.). *Current Practices in Academic Advising: Final Report on ACT's Fifth National Survey of Academic Advising.* National Academic Advising Association Monograph Series, no. 6. Manhattan, Kans.: NACADA, 1998b.

Hines, E. R. "Delivery Systems and the Institutional Context." In R. B. Winston Jr., T. K. Miller, S. C. Ender, and T. J. Grites (eds.), *Developmental Academic Advising.* San Francisco: Jossey-Bass, 1984.

Holmes, D. R., Clarke, J. H., and Irvine, C. A. "Organizational Change and the Improvement of Faculty Advising." *NACADA Journal,* 1983, *3*, 21–29.

Ivery, E. F. "College Student Satisfaction with Academic Advising: The Influence of Advising Models and Student Characteristics for Traditional and Adult Learners." Unpublished doctoral dissertation, Graduate Interdisciplinary Degree Program, University of Northern Colorado, 1992.

Jefcoat, H. G. "The Organization of Academic Advising Services in America's Rural Community Colleges." Unpublished doctoral dissertation, School of Education, University of Mississippi, 1991.

Johnson, J., and Sprandel, K. "Centralized Academic Advising at the Department Level: A Model." *University and College Quarterly,* 1975, *21,* 17–19.

King, M. C. "Advising Models and Delivery Systems." In M. C. King (ed.), *Academic Advising: Organizing and Delivering Services for Student Success.* New Directions for Community Colleges, no. 82. San Francisco: Jossey-Bass, 1993.

King, M. C. "Organizational Models and Delivery Systems for Faculty Advising." In G. L. Kramer (ed.), *Reaffirming the Role of Faculty in Academic Advising.* National Academic Advising Association Monograph Series, no. 1. Manhattan, Kans.: NACADA, 1995.

King, M. C., and Kerr, T. J. "Organizing and Delivering Academic Advising for First-Year Students." In M. L. Upcraft and G. L. Kramer (eds.), *First-Year Academic Advising: Patterns in the Present, Pathways to the Future.* Monograph Series, no. 18. Columbia: National Resource Center for the Freshman Year Experience and Students in Transition, University of South Carolina, 1995.

Koerin, B. B. "Improving Academic Advising: Strategies for Change." *NASPA Journal.* 1991, *28*(4), 323–327.

Leymaster, M. J. "A Study of Two-Year College Academic Advising Programs." Unpublished doctoral dissertation, College of Education, Ohio University, 1989.

Miller, T. K. (ed.). *The Book of Professional Standards for Higher Education.* Washington, D.C.: Council for the Advancement of Standards in Higher Education, 1997.

Spencer, R. W., Peterson, E. D., and Kramer, G. L. "Utilizing College Advising Centers to Facilitate and Revitalize Academic Advising." *NACADA Journal,* 1982, *2,* 13–23.

Tukey, D. D. "Academic Advising as a Multisystem, Collaborative Enterprise." *NACADA Journal,* 1996, *16*(1), 6–13.

Wong, T. D. "The Organization, Delivery, and Evaluation of Academic Advising Systems in Selected Catholic Colleges and Universities in the United States." Unpublished doctoral dissertation, Department of Educational Leadership, Miami University, 1986.

Chapter Fourteen

Delivering Academic Advising

Advisor Types

Alice G. Reinarz

An often heard stereotype is that institutions of higher education are recalcitrant to change. Individuals outside of academia are frequently amazed and frustrated by the culture in higher education. In fact, many of the foundational principals of education have, with good reason, been defended and reaffirmed for centuries. Yet although these guiding philosophies are stable, there are many changing elements inside and outside the academy that affect advising. Many who have been significantly involved in academic advising in the recent past have come to realize that diversity among students and among institutions is driving change in advising programs. It is imperative for academic advisors and administrators to recognize and utilize these institutional and student changes as opportunities.

The delivery of academic advising has evolved rather rapidly in the recent past. Although most institutions of higher education continue to depend primarily on faculty advisors, other advising roles have emerged to address the evolving needs of students and institutions. Advising delivery must be evaluated, and potentially adapted, through the lens of changing needs. This chapter describes the academic advisor types on which delivery systems depend.

Chancellor Robert M. Berdahl, chief academic officer of the University of California at Berkeley, a research institution, says, "It is necessary for the academic advising structure to be flexible. The pool of advisors ought to have varied expertise and experience to accommodate transitions in student needs" (Berdahl, 1995, p. 9). This call for flexibility and mixture of skill types is pronounced as advising systems are responding to institutional changes and evolving student expectations.

Institutional Changes

Clearly, various types of institutions, including research universities, public and private colleges, and community and junior colleges, are evolving in different ways. The differing missions of institutions will affect faculty and staff, including those in academic advising. These differences are essential in selecting the advisor types (such as faculty, full-time professional, counselor, or paraprofessional) for the academic advising model.

Because of changes in students in recent decades (such as socioeconomic status, age, ethnicity, and high school preparation), many institutions are working to meet the advising needs of working and commuting students, who often are more mature in age than traditional students and who may have a variety of goals for their educational experience. It is impossible to assess educational outcomes (academic advising elements) or persistence for these students relative to the parameters for affluent, well-prepared, traditional-age students who are not working (or who are working only a modest number of hours). Accommodating a variety of student subpopulations presents particular challenges for academic advisors.

Many institutions (particularly those that are significantly dependent on tuition dollars) are concerned with recruitment and retention of undergraduates. Even colleges and universities that are highly selective must be concerned with attracting particular cohorts of students. There is competition for students, and the reputation of the institution relative to services such as academic advising is particularly relevant.

In spite of competition for undergraduates among many institutions, particular students are extremely eager to gain admission and be successful in certain colleges and universities. Because of the opportunities afforded after acceptance, however, the preparation, motivation, and decisions of individual students will determine whether they graduate and when. Academic advisors are often the persons with whom undergraduates have a continuing relationship during their undergraduate experience, and as such they may have a key role in successful student navigation of complex academic choices.

Given the current financial climate, students are providing substantial funds to pursue their educational goals. Particularly those using loans will need to be mindful of their investment and will often have high expectations that the institution and their advisor are meeting their needs. Another important economic factor is that many institutions are investing tremendous sums in the technology they use for student records, registration by computer and on the Web, computerized degree audits, and electronically available (that is, simultaneously shared among various advisors) academic advising information.

At present, a variety of relatively new opportunities for education and training are changing the landscape of higher education. Many corporations are maintaining their own programs to train their employees. There are also rapidly growing "virtual universities" that appeal to particular students' needs. It will be interesting to follow the development of models for academic advising in these new educational formats.

Expectations of Students

Parallel to the changes affecting institutions are changes in students' expectations of advising, which are often higher than in the past. Students may have a variety of complex needs (such as work requirements, family responsibilities, personal development issues, and shifting goals) and the advising delivery model and individual advisors must be able to accommodate in order to sustain continuing academic advising relationships with these students. Again, depending on the students' concerns, advisors need to have different strengths and weaknesses to meet students' particular needs. The undergraduate population therefore markedly influences the choices that institutions make among delivery systems and advisor types.

Many first-year students are quite frank with academic advisors about their ultimate goal to enhance their chances of finding a job. Whatever their career plans, these students may view the undergraduate experience as primarily enhancing their professional success. In these cases, the academic advisor must work with students to make choices that prepare them to be educated citizens with an appreciation of learning, as well as to be competitive in an employment arena.

Academic advisors may often be surprised and occasionally be offended by what they view as a "consumer" approach to higher education. It is important to understand that current students (and the families of traditional-age undergraduates) simply have expectations that can be traced to the present economic and social environment. These students' attitudes may be particularly shocking to new advisors. Undergraduates vary considerably, of course, in their reasons for being in an educational institution in the first place. Various cohorts (such as preprofessional, honors, international, and disabled students, and athletes) may find a particular advisor type to be an easy match.

At many institutions, significant opportunities outside the classroom format are available to students. Programs for undergraduate research, volunteer activities, study abroad, and internships are attractive and must be publicized. Advisors can play a key role in maximizing the undergraduate experience by explaining these options.

Depending on the student, the family may or may not be significantly involved in academic decisions. At some institutions, other family members may be active participants along with students in programs such as orientation. In these instances, the academic advisor must adapt to the increased complexity of the circumstances.

At present, prospective and current students make comparisons among institutions on the basis of the significant information they find on the Internet. The availability of increased academic information does not diminish the importance of an advising relationship, however, and in fact may open up additional time for valuable discussions that extend beyond factual curriculum information. Some individual advisors, and some advisor types, may be more resourceful than others in utilizing these additional opportunities.

Academic Advisor Types

Information obtained from American College Testing's (ACT) Fifth National Survey of Academic Advising (Habley and Morales, 1998a) demonstrates that different types of institutions (such as research, four-year, two-year, public, or private) utilize a variety of academic advising delivery models. These models, described and evaluated on their program effectiveness by Habley and Morales (1998b), provide choices for administrators who must develop or maintain the academic advising infrastructure at the institution. Habley and Morales (1998b, p. 39) state that "the key factor in the success, or lack thereof, of an advising model resides in the degree to which there is a fit between the model and institutional culture." In 1991, Frost (1991) suggested that academic advising should be a shared responsibility that makes use of the combined resources of all members of the academic community. Additional data reported in ACT's Fifth National Survey show "movement toward the organization of advising services in which responsibility is shared between faculty advisors and staff advisors and counselors" (Habley and Morales, 1998a, p. 62). Awareness of these trends and of current institutional and student needs provides important contexts for decisions about who should deliver advising and about how resources should be applied to deliver optimal advising services.

King (1988) provides a useful template for comparing the strengths and limitations of all advisor types. She explains several parameters in which to frame these comparisons, including access and availability to students, priority placed on academic advising, knowledge of the field of study and curriculum, knowledge and experience in student counseling roles, credibility with faculty and staff peers, cost to the institution, and training requirements. All of these elements must be considered because no single advisor type can deliver quality advising to the increasingly diverse student population. King also argues for a delivery model that draws together the strengths of multiple advisor types.

Faculty Advisors

Many institutions depend solely on faculty to deliver advising. In the most recent decade, however, data cited by Habley and Morales (1998a, p. 13) show a "noticeable decline in the use of the faculty-only model across all institutions (from 35% to 28%)." Campuses that rely most on this model are private two-year and four-year institutions (Habley and Morales, 1998a). To maintain an accurate overview of advising delivery systems, however, it is important to appreciate possible implementation models for faculty advisors, including campuses where all faculty advise, where faculty are given release time for advising, and where advising coordinators are located within academic departments. As with other advisor types, the evolution of these institutions' advising systems has been dictated by their unique faculty culture and student expectations.

Faculty members provide many advising services exceptionally well. They are most able to answer discipline-specific questions and have the greatest understanding of course content and curriculum rationale in their own areas. Faculty are excellent resources for students who are considering a particular field, and they have insights on graduate schools and professional opportunities. Because availability and competition vary in both graduate programs and the workplace, faculty are well suited to advise students in considering their goals.

In their mentoring relationships, faculty may develop rapport with students both inside and outside the classroom. Such rapport is a significant contribution to the undergraduate experience for students (Lagowski and Vick, 1995). Many faculty are eager to work with students who are making key academic, personal, and career choices. These mentoring relationships may provide an attractive counterpoint to formal instructor-student interactions. Both faculty and students report that they enjoy conversations outside the realm of graded, classroom-specific work. Moreover, faculty involvement in any advising function lends their prestige and credibility to the enterprise.

Faculty members who enjoy advising often place a high personal priority on the role and give generously of their time and talent. Depending on the institution, the reward for this commitment varies significantly. On many campuses, recognition of faculty for advising is sadly limited. This lack of recognition, when coupled with competing demands for faculty time, may indeed lead some faculty to place less emphasis on advising. Because of these circumstances, it may be possible to involve only faculty who choose to be advisors (such as volunteers, tenured individuals with fewer time demands from research and scholarship, and instructional staff with released time), which is generally preferable to expecting all faculty members to advise.

A reliable and sensible organization is necessary for students to have access to faculty advisors. For example, some advising programs may coordinate schedules so that undergraduates know when and where to find their advisor. Even with appropriate infrastructure, however, faculty advisors must balance their advising time demands with their teaching and scholarship, which may affect both their interest in advising and their availability to students. This constraint is a greater concern at times of the year when many students simultaneously are eager to meet with their advisors.

Experience and ability to counsel students in nonacademic problems varies considerably among faculty advisors. With increasing diversity in student populations comes increasing complexity in the personal problems students may present to faculty advisors. Although all faculty advisors should not be expected to deal directly with students' personal problems, it is essential that they be informed about support services that are available to deal with student concerns that the faculty member is personally unprepared to address. An additional concern of faculty advisors lies in the increasing complexity in curriculum and in policies and procedures. Because many faculty advise a moderate number of students, they are not equipped to respond to issues that are entangled by institutional policies and procedures. As in situations involving personal concerns, faculty advisors must be supported by services provided by other individuals or offices on campus.

Some administrators argue that an advantage of faculty advising is that it involves only indirect costs because the institution is already paying faculty salaries. Yet because faculty time must be allotted like any other resource, there are costs associated with faculty advisors. It must also be pointed out that direct costs associated with low-quality faculty advising may in the long run actually result in significant direct costs to the institution. At some types of institutions, however, student expectations for frequent and continuing interactions with faculty may be an overriding consideration in justifying the costs of a faculty advisor model.

Full-Time Staff Advisors

In recent decades, the number of full-time advisors in higher education has increased dramatically. This is a role that is just coming of age. It is no surprise that most institutions (and executive officers) have recognized the importance of full-time advisors because of the unique value they provide in the delivery of effective academic advising.

ACT's Fifth National Survey of Academic Advising revealed that "one of the most consistent trends traceable through all five ACT surveys of academic advising is the continuous growth in the percentage of institutions reporting the existence of an advising office" (Habley and Morales, 1998a, p. 63). The same survey also reports that "in just 18 years the percentage of campuses with advising centers has nearly tripled to 73% in 1997" (p. 63). Describing and evaluating the organizational models, Habley and Morales (1998a, 1998b) explain that all models other than Faculty-Only Model (see Chapter Thirteen) depend in some way on an office or unit with specific responsibilities for academic advising. Staffing in these units depends heavily on full-time advisors.

These advisors have definite strengths in contributing to an effective advising system. Foremost, they are committed to the role and choose to work with students in an advising relationship. Their enthusiasm and expertise can be coupled to an infrastructure that provides continuing availability and, with reasonable advisee loads, reliable and regular access for students. Many student contacts can be handled as one-on-one appointments, telephone conversations, small-group topical discussions, and ever-increasing e-mail correspondence.

Some advising professionals are recruited from backgrounds in counseling, social work, education, or higher education administration. Many have received training (student developmental theory, for example) as part of their education to prepare them for the advising role. Other professional advisors are drawn from disciplines represented by the advising unit and are educated in the liberal arts and sciences.

In a large office, it is particularly beneficial to find a group of advisors with a mosaic of these educational backgrounds because their shared knowledge and experience make for an exceptionally well-rounded staff. With appropriate training, professional advisors are able to address student problems and respond to discipline-specific questions. Their continuity in advising allows them also to learn about and remain up-to-date on complex curriculum and policy information. It is also important to note that, particularly on large campuses, individual academic departments are utilizing full-time advisors to meet the advising needs of their students.

The cost to the institution for utilizing advising professionals varies with campus location and advisor credentials. The credibility of staff advisors among faculty and other noninstructional staff depends on campus culture. It is important for administrators to seek input from or involve staff advisors directly in academic decisions and curriculum committees. Liaison arrangements or forums that bring together faculty advisors and professional advisors are also useful to promote mutual understanding and respect. Time invested in these relationships pays large dividends in effective referrals. Topical meetings involving both staff and faculty advisors can be used for information sharing and for exchanging advising strategies.

The weaknesses of full-time staff advisors relate most often to an individual's lack of teaching experience and involvement in the disciplines. If staff advisors have insufficient time to visit classes and interact with faculty and other colleagues, their information can become disconnected and dated. Advising administrators must be sensitive to these factors and ensure that advisors have appropriate professional development opportunities.

Counselors

Among two-year colleges, only 19 percent of public and 33 percent of private institutions rely exclusively on the Faculty-Only Model (Habley and Morales, 1998a). In other delivery systems, junior and community colleges frequently utilize counselors to provide academic advising. The strengths and limitations of using counselors, as described by King (1988), to deliver advising services are comparable to those associated with professional advisors. One difference, however, relates to the high priority of professional counselors to provide psychological and career services. Among counselors' strengths are general accessibility to students, and knowledge about curriculum and policies. Because counselors may be asked to fulfill roles in addition to academic advising, however, it is possible that their advising time may be diluted by these other functions. King (1993, p. 145) suggests that "advising may be given a low priority among the variety of tasks that counselors perform."

Peer Advisors and Paraprofessionals

Carefully selected and trained peer advisors (undergraduate students) and paraprofessionals (such as graduate students, practicum students, and individuals hired during peak advising times) are used principally at four-year public colleges (Habley and Morales, 1998a). At many institutions, peer advisor roles are limited to involvement in support roles in orientation or in residence halls while at other institutions additional advising responsibilities are assigned by advising offices. Undergraduate and graduate students' strengths in advising derive from their opportunities to relate easily to advisees because they often share some of the same problems. Because they are less mature and experienced than professional advisors, however, peer advisors must be carefully trained and supervised so they do not exceed their limits. For example, students may have strong opinions about certain professors, courses, or majors, but they must not share inappropriate biases. Peer advisors and paraprofessionals are less costly to the advising operation than professional advisors, however, and are often eager for the salary and experience the positions provide. In appropriate roles, undergraduate and graduate student advisors have energy, creativity, and perspective that can be exceedingly valuable to the advising enterprise.

Evolution of an Advising Delivery System

As an academic advising system evolves, administrators may choose to shift personnel and resources from one advisor type to another. It is apparent that various advising functions can be accomplished effectively by several types of advisors. These changes are affected by the institutional culture as well.

Adaptation to Change

Although some faculty advisors have the commitment and skills to adapt readily to changing student demographics and expectations, many advising units are depending more often on professional advisors or counselors to respond to shifting delivery needs. The primary focus on academic advising by full-time advisors and counselors suggests that they are most likely to have the accurate, timely information and the enhanced training that will enable them to work optimally with large groups of students with various, changing needs. They may, as a group, utilize new technology to support advising more readily than faculty advisors who have many competing responsibilities.

Reflection of Student Needs

Particularly during their first contact with an institution, students must be educated about the various advisors on whom they will ultimately depend. It will not be unusual for a first-year undergraduate at many institutions to utilize differently the advising help of faculty mentors, full-time professional advisors, counselors, and peer advisors. Some of these relationships may be formalized while others will be informal. As they negotiate with the institution, many students develop intuition about getting information and help from a variety of resources. Many of these students share this savvy with their peers. Unfortunately, many students also share information that is inaccurate. As they must in their postcollege life, undergraduates can maximize their educational experience with the assistance of the many persons from whom they will seek advising.

On large campuses, the various advisor types must connect in an integrated network of complementary services. This is particularly challenging for inexperienced advisors on a large decentralized campus with a complex infrastructure. To the extent possible, administrators should encourage the creation of networks, either formal or informal, of advisors from units across the campus. In addition, membership in the National Association for Academic Advising (NACADA) is a valuable resource for advisors. Meetings (national and regional) and print and video resources provide the information that advisors need. Membership in a campus advising group (some of which are affiliated with NACADA) is a useful opportunity for advisors in the institution to become personally connected in a professionally meaningful way.

Complementary Strengths of Advisor Types

In a research university, full-time professionals may be the principal advisors in units that work with specific cohorts of undergraduates. The breadth of knowledge and experience of these advisors, coupled with their continuing availability, may position them ideally to work with undeclared students, for example. By contrast, a faculty mentor may ideally advise students who have declared a particular major and who have many discipline-specific questions. In this same institution, peer advisors may frequently work with students in parts of summer orientation, in residence halls, or as members of the advising office staff, where relevant experience and peer status are enormously valuable. Because of the large undergraduate population at many research universities, it is especially easy to see the value of an advising delivery system that utilizes a variety of advisor types.

In four-year colleges and universities, a professional advisor may work with students who have general questions, but a faculty advisor frequently has a continuing relationship with students throughout their undergraduate experience. Particularly if the institution has a low student-to-faculty ratio, out-of-class mentoring by faculty may be a key element in attracting students.

At two-year colleges, models in which counselors provide multipurpose academic and career advising are likely to be found.

In any institution, peer advisors and paraprofessionals can effectively amplify the availability of information. They are often best able to connect with students who feel most comfortable with persons near their own age. The key is keeping the peer advisors and paraprofessionals adequately trained and supervised and connected to appropriate referral units.

Conclusion

Because of rapid social and technological change, advisors and administrators must view academic advising as a holistic service to students. Outstanding academic advising can never be limited to impersonal rote signing of course requests. The institutional culture (and the executive officers responsible for allocation of resources) must understand and value effective advising. The diversity of students and institutions must drive a continuing evolution of advising delivery systems. A mosaic of advisor types with a variety of backgrounds and experience appears to provide maximum flexibility to respond to these changes.

References

Berdahl, R. M. "Educating the Whole Person." In A. G. Reinarz and E. R. White (eds.), *Teaching Through Academic Advising: A Faculty Perspective.* New Directions for Teaching and Learning, no. 62. San Francisco: Jossey-Bass, 1995.

Frost, S. H. *Academic Advising for Student Success: A System of Shared Responsibility.* ASHE-ERIC Higher Education Report, no. 3. Washington, D.C.: School of Education and Human Development, George Washington University, 1991.

Habley, W. R., and Morales, R. H. (eds.). *Current Practices in Academic Advising: Final Report on ACT's Fifth National Survey of Academic Advising.* National Academic Advising Association Monograph Series, no. 6. Manhattan, Kans.: National Academic Advising Association, 1998a.

Habley, W. R., and Morales, R. H. "Advising Models: Goal Achievement and Program Effectiveness." *NACADA Journal,* 1998b, *18*(1), 35–41.

King, M. C. "Academic Delivery Systems." In W. R. Habley (ed.), *The Status and Future of Academic Advising.* Iowa City, Iowa: American College Testing Program, 1988.

King, M. C. (ed.). *Academic Advising: Organizing and Delivering Services for Student Success.* New Directions for Community Colleges, no. 82. San Francisco: Jossey-Bass, 1993.

Lagowski, J. M., and Vick, J. W. "Faculty as Mentors." In A. G. Reinarz and E. R. White (eds.), *Teaching Through Academic Advising: A Faculty Perspective.* New Directions for Teaching and Learning, no. 62. San Francisco: Jossey-Bass, 1995.

Chapter Fifteen

One-to-One Advising

Charlie L. Nutt

Academic advising at its very best is a supportive and interactive relationship between students and advisors. Susan Frost, in *Academic Advising for Student Success: A System of Shared Responsibility* (1991), states that this relationship is important for three reasons: "(1) advising, unlike most out-of-class activities, is a service provided to most students; (2) advising provides a natural setting for out-of-class contacts with faculty to occur; and (3) advising involves intellectual matters, the most important area of concern for students"(p. 10). Often the one-to-one relationship between the student and advisor is the only opportunity a student has to build a personal link with the institution; it thereby has a profound effect on the student's academic career and on the student's satisfaction with the institution. Chickering and Gamson (1987) state that frequent faculty-student contact is the most important factor in student motivation and involvement and can provide students with the support needed to get through the hard times and keep working toward academic success. Therefore, it is clear that the value of the one-to-one academic advising relationship to students' success cannot be underestimated.

Necessary Interpersonal Skills

The one-to-one relationship is often not developed, due to advisors' lack of clarity about the skills and competencies that are vital to the effectiveness of such academic advising. Advisors must of course have clear knowledge of the academic programs and curriculum requirements at their institutions. One of students' most stated expectations of an advisor is the ability to give accurate and correct academic guidance. However, effective communication is also key to the one-to-one academic advising relationship. Unfortunately, advisors find it easy to revert to being the "teller" or the "expert" in the relationship, focusing primarily on the information they have to deliver to the student. Instead, advisors must be aware that one-to-one academic advising must be built on shared communication, which requires a different set of skills than those required in a one-way communication, including communication skills, questioning skills, and referral skills.

Communication Skills

Communication skills are perhaps the most important set of skills needed by advisors in building relationships with their advisees. Yet these are often the skills most overlooked in advisor training or development programs. Advisors must understand that listening effectively to both what their advisees are saying and what they are not saying is an essential communication skill in creating an environment of trust in the advising relationship. The communication skills that advisors should demonstrate are as follows:

1. *Establishing and maintaining eye contact with students.* Students must feel they have the undivided attention of their advisors if they are to communicate openly and honestly on issues of concern. In addition, maintaining eye contact with students can enable advisors to pick up on nonverbal clues that students may be giving that contradict their words.

2. *Avoiding the inclination to interrupt students with solutions before students have fully explained their ideas or problems.* Advisors often fall quickly into the "savior mode" instead of giving students the chance to express themselves fully, resulting in communication becoming only one-way.

3. *Being aware of body language.* Students can tell immediately whether an advisor is listening or not by the body-language message the advisor sends. Shuffling papers, allowing for distractions such as telephone calls, and facing away from the student are all nonverbal clues that the advisor is more interested in the daily routine than in the advising session. Advisors should also be aware of the body language of their students. Students can portray many feelings through their body language that they would never express openly. Folded arms, nervous gestures, slouched posture, or physically turning away from the advisor are all examples of body language that may indicate feelings of anger, frustration, or depression.

4. *Focusing on the content of students' words.* Advisors must listen to the words and phrases that students use in conversation. They must be sure they understand clearly the facts of the issues or problems being discussed. It is important that advisors ask leading or probing questions if necessary to be sure they have understood distinctly the content of the conversation.

5. *Focusing on the tone of students' words.* Listening is paying attention to both what is being said and what is not being said. Often the tone of students' words or their facial expressions are more important than what they are saying.

Advisors should listen carefully to students' voice levels or the distinctions they make in order to pick up on issues of major concern. In addition, tone of voice can often indicate to advisors a student's state of mind or well-being.

6. *Acknowledging what students are saying through verbal and nonverbal feedback.* This may include simply nodding one's head or responding to students with "yes" or "I see."

7. *Reflecting on or paraphrasing what students have said.* After students have finished talking, advisors must demonstrate that they have been listening by repeating back in their own words what students have said. This provides students with the opportunity to clarify what they have said and to correct any misunderstandings.

Questioning Skills

In addition to having good listening skills, advisors must become adept at using questioning skills. Learning how to ask questions effectively in order to assist students is vitally important in the one-to-one advising relationship. The key to effective questioning is to focus the questions on the concerns of the student and not on the concerns of the advisor. Advisors must develop skills in using both open-ended and closed-ended questions. Open-ended questions are invitations to students to talk more openly about concerns or issues without feeling as if the advisor is setting the agenda of the session. One strategy for using effective open-ended questions is to phrase them in terms of the student's needs, wishes, or desires; that is, instead of asking, "How can I help you?" or "What can I do for you today?" ask the student, "What do you want to talk about today?" or "What issues do you have about next semester?" Such questions will begin to help students understand that their role in the advising process is as important as their advisor's role. A simple method for developing the skill of using open-ended questions is to ask, "Can this question be answered in three words or less?" Closed-ended questions are best used to gather factual information only. Although it is often important to ask such questions in order to be sure that the facts are gathered, they can also serve to foreclose on dialogue instead of extending the conversation. Advisors must be aware of the types of questions they are asking because questions are clues to students that advisors are truly interested in the students' feelings and concerns. Open-ended questions indicate interest in the student; closed-ended questions indicate interest in only the facts.

Referral Skills

Last, to develop a one-to-one advising relationship with students, advisors must use referral skills. Effective referral skills depend on an advisor's listening and questioning skills because the first step in referring a student is to determine the student's problems and issues. Advisors often make the mistake of referring students on the basis of the advisor's own feelings or views rather than clearly listening to the students or asking effective questions to determine what the students' problems or issues may be. When this is the case, students may see such referrals as only a method of getting them out of the advisor's office instead of as genuine desire to assist students in the best way possible.

The first and possibly most important step in effective referrals is for the advisor to explain clearly and in an open manner why the student should seek assistance from another source. The advisor and student must have jointly determined the problem for which assistance is needed and then formulated a plan of action that includes the referral. Demonstrating effective referral skills requires advisors to have a clear understanding of the services available on campus and in the community. In addition, advisors will be able to explain the type of assistance the student needs as well as the qualifications of the persons or agencies to whom the student is being referred. Advisors should take the time to visit and become acquainted with all areas of the campus that can support their students in order to be effective in the referral process.

An effective referral always includes the name, location, and if possible, telephone number and e-mail address of a contact person at the office or agency to which the student is being referred. To increase the likelihood of a successful referral, the advisor should assist the student by scheduling the appointment or by walking the student to the appropriate office. Finally, effective referrals include following up with students on the referrals and assistance they have received. If the situation warrants, the advisor should contact the student shortly after the appointment to discuss the referral and to determine if the student needs additional assistance. In other instances, the outcome of the referral can be discussed in the next advising session. Failure to follow up indicates to a student that the referral was not important or that the advisor is not interested in the student's progress.

Developing the interpersonal skills of effective listening, questioning, and referral is vital for advisors in order for one-to-one academic advising to be successful. Although it is important for advisors to know the academic programs or requirements or the curriculum of the institution, such knowledge alone will not provide students with the level of academic advising they need for success in their academic careers.

The One-to-One Academic Advising Session

Having knowledge of the institution's programs and requirements and developing effective interpersonal skills for communicating and assisting students are only part of the successful one-to-one academic advising relationship. The advising session or interview with the student is vital to the advising process. Often the best intentions and well-developed skills of advisors are overshadowed by their lack of attention to the advising session itself. The advisor must clearly understand the essential components of the advising session: planning and preparing for the session and the content and process of the session.

Planning and Preparing for the Advising Session

The area in which most advisors fall short is planning and preparing for the advising session. The first step in planning is to understand that for many students scheduling an appointment with an advisor is something they may not do without the advisor taking some proactive measures. Successful advisors include the initiation of contact as a vital component of their work. Communicating with advisees on a regular and consistent basis is the first step they take when planning for advising sessions. This communication may take the form of personal letters, telephone calls, postcards, or e-mail messages. Communication begins early in the advisor-advisee relationship and continues until students have reached their educational goals. The communication might be to invite the students in for a session, to congratulate them on some success, academically or personally, to check on their academic progress, or simply to keep in touch. Whatever the method of communication or the purpose behind it, the goal is to establish ongoing contact as the basis for a quality relationship.

Second, planning for an advising session with an advisee involves the advisor learning as much as possible about the student. The advisor reviews academic history, test scores, educational goals, and other information sources that might be available. An important source of information is advising notes from previous sessions. These notes are invaluable in helping to set the agenda or content of an advising session. They can also be used to remind the advisor of things that still need to be accomplished by either the advisor or the advisee. Advising notes are also extremely important if an institution has an advising center model in which students see different advisors for each session. An advisor must have the advising notes from the previous advisor in order to conduct an effective advising session with the student. In addition, many advisors send questionnaires to advisees for them to complete and return prior to their first advising session in order to get a clear picture of the students, their academic and personal strengths and weaknesses, and their goals. This step is not only done before the initial advising session, however. A successful advisor reviews the information on his advisees prior to all scheduled advising sessions.

Third, although spur-of-the moment advising sessions or advising-in-the-hall sessions are a part of the college environment, advisors should be proactive in stressing to students the importance of scheduling appointments in advance in order to provide the advisor with ample time to plan effectively for each session. This scheduling itself takes careful preparation. The advisor must have a clearly designated schedule for advising sessions that should be communicated to students each academic term. Again, this can be done through written communication, telephone calls, or e-mail messages as well as by posting a schedule on the advisor's door or in his or her office area. Appointment scheduling encourages students to plan and prepare for the advising session. If students must make appointments, they are less likely to walk in at the last minute expecting the advisor to make their decisions or solve their problems. Instead, they will arrive ready to play an active role in the advising session. However, this approach also requires advisors to have the courage and fortitude to reschedule appointments for drop-in students instead of dropping everything at the last minute to see a student. An advising session in which neither the advisor nor the student has had an opportunity to plan and prepare is limited in its productivity.

Fourth, the advisor must plan for uninterrupted time with the students during the advising session. Telephone calls should be put on hold or the phone should be taken off the hook. Adequate time should be allowed for each appointment so that a student does not feel rushed. Also, the schedule should allow time for the advisor to make notes and take care of other actions that result from the advising appointment. In the busy environment of higher education institutions today, this is likely the most difficult part of planning for advising sessions. However, the effectiveness of any advising session is seriously jeopardized by not planning carefully to avoid interruptions, which suggest to the student that the session is not an important activity.

To provide every student with a quality advising session, it is clearly the responsibility of the advisor to plan and prepare adequately. Although this may be the most time-consuming step, it sets the tone for all sessions and can determine whether a session is successful or not.

Content and Process of the Session

Once the session has been scheduled, the advisor then focuses on the session itself—on its content and process. It is desired that all advising sessions have a clear purpose when they are scheduled so that the advisor and the student both understand what will be discussed and can move into the content of the session smoothly. It is also clear, however, that in colleges today this is not always possible. Therefore, the advisor must focus on the session content on the basis of prior planning and preparation, while at the same time be sensitive to the student's concerns.

The first component of any advising session is developing or quickly reestablishing rapport with the student. While developing rapport is critical to the success of the initial advising session, it must also be done for each subsequent session. Although advisors may wish to jump quickly into the content of sessions, they must first take time to greet students by name and make them feel comfortable. This can be done by asking general questions about their well-being, family, or classes or by reviewing the content of the previous advising session. This component underscores the importance of planning and preparing for the session because an advisor must be familiar with students' backgrounds and goals in order to initiate rapport. Students must be made to feel comfortable at the beginning of each advising session if they are to work collaboratively with the advisor on the topics or issues addressed during the session. Many advisors often overlook this step, but it can truly make the difference between a successful session and an unsuccessful session.

It is important that advising sessions have a clear agenda or flow in order to be effective in assisting students. First, the advisor and student should discuss the previous advising session. This is the time to discuss the results of any referrals, the outcome of any actions taken, and the student's academic progress since the last session. The advisor and advisee then move to the purpose of the current advising session. It is essential that both parties be clear about the primary purpose of the session as well as look at any secondary or underlying issues. Next is discussion of the issues or concerns that the student has brought to the advising session. This is when the advisor's interpersonal skills will be most important. For example, the student may state that the purpose of the session is to discuss withdrawing from a class, but on the basis of the student's body language, tone, and facial expressions the advisor may determine that the issue is much more than withdrawing; instead, it may actually be financial problems, family problems, or other issues. It is also important during this stage in the advising session to discuss the issues and concerns of the advisor, which may range from academic policies and regulations to academic difficulties of which the advisor has been made aware by the advisee's instructors. Finally, the advisor should carefully conclude the advising session by taking time to summarize the discussion that has taken place and to outline any plans of action that have been developed. During the session, the advisor should make all appropriate referrals and assist the student in setting a time line for accomplishing any goals or plans. By failing to do this, an otherwise successful advising session may accomplish very little for the student or the advisor.

Conclusion

The successful one-to-one advising relationship can be a major factor in a student's decision to remain in college and be academically successful. One-to-one advising relationships must first be built of the advisor's development of the interpersonal skills of communication, questioning, and referral. During the advising session, advisors must use these interpersonal skills to assist their students. It is the advisor's responsibility to keep the conversation moving and on target; this may include carefully asking open-ended questions and focusing on analyzing students' verbal as well as nonverbal clues. Advisors must avoid the tendency to out-talk students by allowing them time to discuss issues before responding. The advisor must also focus on accepting students' attitudes and feelings about an issue; students recognize when advisors do not value their problems and concerns, and next time they will not be as willing to be honest and straightforward in the advising session.

Advisors must recognize the importance of planning and preparing for an advising session and then follow a clear plan of flow during the session. This flow must include a clear look at previous sessions, discussion of the present issues and concerns, and a distinct summary and follow-up plan for future actions and sessions. It is clear that one-to-one advising provides students and advisors with the opportunity to build lasting and valued relationships that will positively affect students' academic performance and satisfaction with the institution.

References

Chickering, A. W., and Gamson, Z. F. "Seven Principles for Good Practice in Undergraduate Education." *AAHE Bulletin,* 1987, *39*(7), 3–7.

Frost, S. H. *Academic Advising for Student Success: A System of Shared Responsibility.* ASHE-ERIC Higher Education Report, no. 3. Washington, D.C.: George Washington University, School of Education and Human Development, 1991.

Chapter Sixteen

Advising Students in Groups

Nancy S. King

Although individual advising is generally acknowledged to be ideal for the delivery of advising programs, there are situations in which one-to-one advising is not needed or may not be possible. Indeed, at times group advising is not only necessary but can also be quite effective in enhancing and augmenting advising services. In addition, innovative group advising methods may offer retention value by connecting students with both their peers and an advisor. It is important to note that many of the underlying principles of developmental advising theory still apply in group advising. Grites (1984, p. 221) notes that a group advisor, such as a classroom teacher, "facilitates discussion, suggests alternatives, and answers specific questions; this is developmental advising at its peak."

Whether advising individuals or a group, it is critical that the advisor view advising as a student-centered process. As Frost (1991, p. 16) points out, developmental advising "contributes to students' rational processes, environmental and interpersonal interactions, behavioral awareness, and problem-solving, decision-making and evaluation skills." In individual advising situations, the advisor and the student share responsibility. Likewise, in the group advising process the advisor and the students share responsibility. Furthermore, the developmental model of including exploration of life, educational, and career goals in addition to making referrals and giving accurate information is relevant for group as well as individual advising. The hallmarks of a successful one-to-one advisor—knowledge, accessibility, and a caring attitude—are characteristics of the successful group advisor as well. In fact, one might well make the case that these attributes are also typical of effective classroom teachers.

Crookston (1972, p. 12) defines teaching as any experience that "contributes to individual growth and that can be evaluated. The student should not be a passive receptacle of knowledge, but should share responsibility for learning with the teacher." When group advising is done well, the advisor is indeed teaching. Classroom instructors increase their effectiveness as they master various teaching techniques and as their understanding of various learning styles and student development theories increases. In much the same way, academic advisors are more effective in both individual and group advising when they expand their knowledge of advising techniques and developmental theory. For example, understanding Chickering and Reisser's (1993) seven vectors of college students' developmental tasks allows advisors to see more clearly the direct connection between advising and three of these vectors (Gordon, 1988, p. 109):

- Developing competence, or increasing the intellectual, physical, and social skills that lead to the knowledge that one is capable of handling and mastering a range of tasks
- Developing autonomy, or confronting a series of issues, leading ultimately to the recognition of one's independence
- Developing purpose, or assessing and clarifying interests, educational and career options, and lifestyle preferences and using these factors to set a coherent direction for life

An advisor who is knowledgeable about student development theories can assist students in developing competence, autonomy, and purpose in advising groups that augment individual contact between advisors and students.

Reasons for Using Group Advising

There are many incidences when group advising may be desirable. From a practical standpoint, there are situations in which individual advising is simply not a viable option. For example, when the number of students to be served far outweighs the number of available advisors, group advising becomes an alternative that can work. This is particularly true in cases of oversubscribed majors or at peak advising times. The University of Toledo's College of Business, for example, faced the question of providing advising services with a student-to-advisor ratio of one to fifteen hundred. Their solution was group advising (Santovec, 1996).

Serving large numbers of students with a limited pool of advisors is but one of the challenges many campuses face in providing advising services. Some student populations have special time restraints, and group advising sessions can be a viable solution. For example, nontraditional commuters who are balancing jobs and family responsibilities with school frequently cannot connect with their advisor at a mutually agreeable time. However, giving these students the option of a group session may assist both the student and the advisor in addressing the time pressures that are so prevalent among today's students and advisors.

Not only is group advising a valuable way to meet the challenges of numbers and time, but it can also be an extremely efficient and effective means of sharing important information. Rather than repeating the same information again and again—an exercise that may very well become tedious and time-consuming for the advisor—using groups can enable advisors to convey important information to several students at the same time, thus freeing advisors to spend their one-to-one advising time addressing individual needs. There are several categories of information that can be shared quite well in a group format, including giving instructions about the registration process, course selection, and policies and procedures; offering general career-planning advice; and providing a framework for selection of a major. For example, many institutions offer a variety of group sessions in which students may gain information about degree requirements, options for programs of study, and career opportunities for a particular major. By attending several of these "major sessions" students are in a better position to make informed choices about a program of study. Ideally, representatives from the administration, faculty, and students from each of these majors would be available at these information sessions.

Perhaps the most compelling reason for using groups to advise relates to the establishment of peer groups. Unquestionably, peers exert a powerful influence on student success, especially in the critical first year. Peers play a vital role in how students view themselves and in the connection they make with the institution. In addition, peers influence students' attitudes toward academic goals and values. By creating advising groups, the advisor becomes, in Rice's (1989, p. 326) view "an agent for social change whose primary task is to engineer ways for students to interact with student peer groups and faculty." Commuter students, who typically find it more difficult than residential students to establish peer group relationships, will especially benefit from an advising group.

Methods of Delivering Group Advising

The methods of delivering group advising vary widely. Many options already exist on most campuses or can be easily developed.

Orientation Program

For most students, the first introduction to campus life comes during new-student orientation. Because one-to-one advising may not be feasible for all orientation sessions, advising groups are often used. According to American College Testing's (ACT's) Fifth National Survey of Academic Advising (Habley and Morales, 1998), group advising during orientation or registration is used by about a third of institutions and is by far the most dominant form of group advising currently being used. These small group meetings can serve to inform students about the curriculum, assist them in planning a first-semester schedule, and introduce the basics of the registration system. Peer advisors and orientation leaders make excellent facilitators to lead these group sessions. New students are likely to pay attention to a peer, especially if this person has received training as a group facilitator. Transfer students present some unique problems and can benefit from an orientation to the institution separate from the new students. Many of the transfer students' questions can be answered in a group advising session prior to their meeting one-to-one with advisors to address their individual situations.

The Freshman Seminar and Group Advising

Another excellent venue for group advising is the freshman seminar course. The instructor for this class usually serves in the dual role of teacher and mentor. Because a great deal of the course content is clearly related to advising goals, the freshman seminar instructor serves as an informal advisor. In some freshmen seminar programs, the instructor is also formally assigned as the academic advisor. Topics frequently covered in a freshman seminar include setting goals; developing study skills and effective time-management skills; exploring individual interests, aptitudes, and career options; introducing students to all of the resources of the institution; encouraging student involvement in out-of-class activities; examining the purpose of higher education; and encouraging student growth in all of the dimensions of wellness. Because many of these topics are definitely part of a developmental advising model, using the freshman seminar as a forum for advising is a logical and effective strategy. Certainly the class sessions can be supplemented by individual meetings with the instructor or advisor, but the group setting becomes a valuable avenue for group advising. In the process of group discussions about these advising issues, students not only gain information but also learn from one another. In sharing their questions and common experiences, a sense of group identity begins to develop that is important to the success of the class.

Advising and Learning Communities

A method that is receiving a great deal of interest is the freshman interest group (FIG) or learning community. The FIG at the University of Oregon, established in 1982 by the Office of Academic Advising and Student Services, is a prototype of a learning community (Love and Tinto, 1995). The FIG program at the University of Washington is another example of such a program (Love and Tinto, 1995). Groups of about twenty students are enrolled during their first term in a cluster of three courses that are linked by a common theme. The FIG members also participate in meetings that are facilitated by a junior or senior peer advisor. One of the major advantages of learning communities and FIGS is the social interaction they afford among peers both inside and outside the classroom. In the opinion of Love and Tinto (1995, p. 85), "of special importance at large institutions, learning communities allow students to aid each other with one of the key points of transition—learning their way around campus and meeting people."

As Bennett (1999) points out, academic advisors are uniquely qualified to be key players in the learning community. Bennett identifies six functions in the design and implementation of learning communities that can benefit from the expertise and participation of advisors: making decisions about the structure of the learning community, especially as they relate to curricular concerns; assisting students with the selection of an appropriate learning community; selecting peer leaders; helping to administer the program; teaching a student success seminar as a component of the learning community; and helping to identify the support needs of both students and faculty in the community. Because advisors are in an excellent position to assist students in making connections within the institution, their participation in the learning community can contribute to the success of the program.

Advisors do play a key role in many learning communities. At La Guardia Community College's New Student House (Love and Tinto, 1995), three faculty members and one advisor teach a group of students who are divided into three course sections. The advisor meets with the group in a seminar format and the advisor and faculty members meet regularly to discuss student progress. The advisor uses the group to administer and interpret learning skills tests, to teach study skills techniques, and to advise students for registration the following term. These learning communities afford opportunities for students to establish relationships and to gain insight into strategies that will help them successfully navigate their college experience and plan for their futures.

Advising in Residence Halls

Learning communities can be especially useful on commuter campuses as a way of helping students establish meaningful connections with their peers. At residential institutions, however, the structure naturally exists for creating advising groups. According to Schein (1995, p. 120), the residence hall environment offers a possible solution to "the problem of introducing the life-skills approach that developmental academic-advising theory advocates. This setting has great potential for supporting interaction between students and advisors. It also facilitates group advising in an environment where peer-support is already built into the participants' social structure." For this to work, however, there must be intentionally designed advising interventions. Some institutions have located advising offices within residence halls; others have set up schedules for advisors to meet with groups at specified times during the week or have advisor-on-call systems in place.

Senior Capstone Courses

Although advising groups like FIGS are especially helpful for freshmen making the important transition into college, they are also useful for seniors. Senior capstone courses, for example, offer advisors the opportunity to assist students with another important transition—from college to the world of work. The instructor for a senior capstone course, like the freshman seminar instructor, can serve not only as instructor but also as advisor and mentor. Student sharing of concerns and excitement about their impending graduation creates a supportive environment for successfully navigating this transition. Bringing in alumni and individuals from various careers to serve in an advisory role for the group also assists students in preparing to move into the next phase of their lives. In much the same way that juniors and seniors may serve as peer mentors in the freshman seminar, these alumni and individuals from various careers can help prepare seniors for their transition from college into their careers.

Group Advising for Special Populations

Other methods for delivering group advising include providing group experiences for specific populations of students who may have special needs. For example, many institutions have successfully used regular group meetings to address the needs of students on probation. Such groups are frequently led by counselors, faculty, or professional advisors. Group meetings with these students have several purposes. First, the advisor or group leader helps students to understand the common reasons that lead to students being placed on probation. The objective is to help students achieve some self-understanding and accept responsibility for their actions. However, the advisor should also assist the students in developing success strategies that will enable them to succeed. Self-esteem issues are important in these groups because students who are in academic difficulty often feel down on themselves. Getting to know others in the group is beneficial; students realize that they are not alone, that others are facing similar challenges. The interaction among the students in the group can be a vital contributor to their building self-esteem and setting achievable goals. The advantages of a probation group far outweigh any stigma that may be attached to a group composed of students in academic difficulty.

Another population that may well benefit from group advising is honors students. Although these are high-achieving students, they too can benefit from interaction with peers who are also part of the honors program. Coming together to discuss coursework, to establish a sense of camaraderie, and to meet informally with a faculty member or advisor adds value to the in-class honors experience. The same advantages of group meetings also hold true for other populations. Students with disabilities, members of minority groups on campus, international students, and adult learners can all benefit from frequent group meetings that serve not only as a means of information sharing but also to help students establish relationships with their peers.

Two other populations that lend themselves quite naturally to group advising are students in oversubscribed majors and undeclared students. From a practical standpoint, group advising for students in oversubscribed majors helps to alleviate the logistical problem of providing services for large numbers of students. Using groups to provide information can supplement individual sessions while enabling students to meet with fellow students who share their program of study.

Advising groups can also be established for students who have not decided on a major. In addition to providing opportunities for them to explore available options and receive assistance in the decision-making process, these groups provide a means for advisors to deliver noncognitive assessment that focuses on interests, values, and motivation. The groups also reassure undecided students that they are not alone in their confusion about a major and career direction.

Perhaps more important, groups can be established for students who fail to be admitted to the major of their choice. Knowing that other students also face making alternative plans can be reassuring to students who are denied admission to their first-choice major. In addition, the advisor can work with these students to help them explore viable options, gather relevant information, and make informed decisions about other possible majors. Having this help available may prevent a student's leaving the institution in discouragement.

A variation of group advising that works well with certain populations is the chat room. (See Chapter Eighteen for additional uses of technology.) Following a group meeting, participants may continue to interact electronically. Chat rooms offer students ongoing contact with other group members and the advisor. Students may provide reactions to and insights on past group discussions or pose questions or topics to discuss at the next meeting. These "virtual" groups are a way for students who are initially reticent about asking questions or offering their opinions in meetings to become involved in the discussion. They also provide a way for students to post questions and replies as they occur to them. As dependence on technology in advising grows, we can expect to see an increase in chat rooms that are extensions of advising groups.

Keys to Successful Group Advising

For an advising group to be fully effective, the advisor needs to be aware of strategies for successful group facilitation. First, introductions and icebreakers are critical to establishing a climate in which students feel comfortable. Winston, Boney, Miller, and Dagley (1988) caution that icebreakers, which are designed to alleviate anxiety, are frequently misused. Their purpose is not solely to provide entertainment; rather, they should be directly related to the group's goals and they should promote a feeling of identity with the group. Other keys to facilitating a successful advising group include learning the names of all the group's members and using them frequently, establishing a climate of trust and respect between the advisor and the students and among the group members, and avoiding having one group member dominate the questions and discussion.

The advisor should also be aware of some of the same cautions that apply to one-to-one advising meetings. The advisor should begin the group by discussing the broader purpose of advising as a means of assisting students in establishing appropriate and meaningful educational plans. After helping students understand this primary goal, the advisor may then move to more specific questions related to course scheduling or major requirements. The advisor should avoid supplying all the answers and instead encourage students to think for themselves. Advisors certainly need to give guidance in the decision-making process, but their overarching goal is to assist students in making informed choices and taking responsibility for their decisions. A group in which the advisor lectures to the students is clearly less effective than a situation in which a give-and-take discussion takes place between group members and the advisor, in which the advisor acts in more of a coaching role. One of the characteristics that effective advisors share with successful coaches is the ability to motivate and encourage. College life, especially when combined with job and family responsibilities, can be stressful. A group advisor can be an excellent sounding board for students to help alleviate some of their stress and confusion.

Group advisors also need to be aware of the importance of collaborating with other areas of the campus. It is equally important for both one-to-one and group advisors to be familiar with all of the resources of the institution and to make appropriate referrals when necessary. To refer students correctly, advisors must not only be knowledgeable about all available resources but also be skilled at reading group members' needs. For example, if a student is having difficulty relating to other members of the group or seems particularly withdrawn, the advisor should follow up with the student outside the group and perhaps make a referral to the counseling center.

Assessment of Group Advising

As with all advising services, assessment is a necessary component of group advising. Certainly group advisors should be consulted for their perception of their groups' effectiveness and of their role in the advising process. The coordinator or administrator in charge of the program should conduct both formative and summative evaluations. Formative evaluation is ongoing. Determining the group's effectiveness while it exists allows for changes and midcourse corrections that will improve its value for students. Information can be collected informally through either written or oral feedback from group members. In contrast, summative evaluation, which is generally more formal, occurs at the conclusion of the group's experience and focuses on the outcomes and on final judgments about the efficacy of the group. Administrators may use the summative evaluation to make decisions about the group's effectiveness and to make decisions about continuing the program. Both formative and summative evaluations are important in assessing the value of group advising.

Conclusion

Assessment of the feasibility of group advising should consider the interests of three major campus constituencies—administrators, faculty, and students. Each of these constituencies has a vested interest in group advising services. From an administrative perspective, advising groups are related to retention because they connect students to a peer group and a mentor. These connections are invaluable in establishing a student's sense of belonging to the institution, a critical factor in retention. In fact, peers seem to be the most important contributors to institutional fit (Bean, 1985). Faculty (and the majority of advising is delivered by faculty) can relate to the value of group advising with regard to time issues. Because of the multiple demands of teaching responsibilities, research, and other institutional commitments, many faculty view group advising as an efficient use of their time. They may also be led to see the analogy between teaching in the classroom and teaching in an advising group. Finally, students who participate in group advising appreciate the opportunity to interact with peers as well as with an advisor. The feeling of not being alone is a powerful by-product of the group experience.

While it is true that the relationship established between an advisor and advisee most naturally develops during an ongoing one-to-one advising process, there is a definite place for group advising in an institution's overall advising program. When group delivery of advising services is done well, these groups can indeed aid retention, ease a faculty member's advising load, and enhance and supplement students' advising experiences.

References

Bean, J. P. "Interaction Effects Based on Class Level in an Explanatory Model of College Student Dropout Syndrome." *American Educational Research Journal,* 1985, *22*(1), 35–64.

Bennett, J. W. "Learning Communities, Academic Advising, and Other Support Programs." In J. Levine (ed.), *Learning Communities: New Structures, New Partnerships for Learning.* Monograph Series, no. 26. Columbia, S.C.: National Resource Center for the First-Year Experience and Students in Transition, University of South Carolina, 1999.

Chickering, A. W., and Reisser, L. *Education and Identity* (2nd ed.). San Francisco, Jossey-Bass, 1993.

Crookston, B. B. "A Developmental View of Academic Advising as Teaching." *Journal of College Student Personnel,* 1972, *13,* 12–17.

Frost, S. H. *"Academic Advising for Student Success: A System of Shared Responsibility."* ASHE-ERIC Higher Education Report no. 3, Washington, D.C.: George Washington University, School of Education and Human Development, 1991.

Gordon, V. N. "Developmental Advising." In W. R. Habley (ed.), *The Status and Future of Academic Advising: Problems and Promises.* Iowa City, Iowa: American College Testing Program, 1988.

Grites, T. J. "Techniques and Tools for Improving Advising." In R. B. Winston Jr., T. K. Miller, S. C. Ender, and T. J. Grites (eds.), *Developmental Academic Advising.* San Francisco: Jossey-Bass, 1984.

Habley, W. R., and Morales, R. H. (eds.). *Current Practices in Academic Advising: Final Report on ACT's Fifth National Survey of Academic Advising.* National Academic Advising Association Monograph Series, no. 6. Manhattan, Kans.: National Academic Advising Association, 1998.

Love, A. G., and Tinto, V. "Academic Advising Through Learning Communities: Bridging the Academic-Social Divide." In M. L. Upcraft and G. L. Kramer (eds.), *First-Year Academic Advising: Patterns in the Present, Pathways to the Future.* Monograph Series, no. 18. Columbia: National Resource Center for The Freshmen Year Experience and Students in Transition, University of South Carolina, 1995.

Rice, R. L. "Commuter Students." In M. L. Upcraft and J. N. Gardner (eds.), *The Freshmen Year Experience: Helping Students Survive and Succeed in College.* San Francisco: Jossey-Bass, 1989.

Santovec, M. L. (ed.). *Making More Changes.* Madison, Wisc.: Magna, 1996.

Schein, H. "University Residence Halls in the Academic Advising Process." In R. E. Glennen and F. N. Vowell (eds.), *Academic Advising as a Comprehensive Campus Process.* National Academic Advising Association Monograph Series, no. 2. Manhattan, Kans.: National Academic Advising Association, 1995.

Winston, R. B., Boney, W. C., Miller, T. K., and Dagley, J. C. *Promoting Student Development Through Intentionally Structured Groups.* San Francisco: Jossey-Bass, 1988.

Chapter Seventeen

Technological Resources That Support Advising

Michael E. McCauley

Prior to the early 1970s, record keeping by academic advisors was essentially accomplished manually. With pen, pencil, or typewriter, advisors listed each student's name, address, and identification number on an advising folder. The student's academic information, standardized test scores, course placement test scores, special program designations, intended majors, and so on were recorded by hand on forms within the folder. Additionally, limited student profile information such as the courses and number of high school semesters completed in mathematics, English, and foreign language were noted by the advisor.

Advisors monitored student progress toward completion of a specified educational objective (major) on a program checklist, recorded transfer course equivalents, and kept track of individual student exceptions (course substitutions, waivers, and so on) manually, usually on preprinted forms. Advisors memorized complex and ambiguous academic regulations (for example, courses may be used only once to satisfy a general education requirement and may be used again to satisfy a major or minor requirement but may not be used to satisfy both major and minor requirements) and academic policies (course repetition, maximum hours of pass-fail credits, residency requirements, cross-listed courses, and so on). Although cumulative grade point averages were calculated on the transcript, advisors were frequently forced to calculate grade point averages in the various components of a specific degree program (general education, professional courses, upper- or lower-division courses, major requirements, and so on) either manually or with a calculator. The scheduling of advising appointments was done exclusively by hand, and notes on individual advising sessions with advisees were also recorded manually.

These necessary and vital advising tasks were time-consuming and labor-intensive. Significant time was expended by the advisors and clerical support personnel executing these duties, which kept advisors from utilizing their time in more substantive contacts with advisees.

The change of focus from prescriptive to developmental academic advising and changes in the management of information led to a transformation of advising. Dolence and Norris (1995, p. 14), in their monograph *Transforming Higher Education,* state that "American higher education in the twenty-first century will provide a spectrum of choices for learners, ranging from the truly traditional to the totally transformed. These choices will be exercised by individual learners, faculty, researchers, and practitioners in their daily work." For advisors, this transformation began in the 1970s with the expanded use of the personal computer and the establishment of the National Academic Advising Association (NACADA). Since 1982 the capacity and power of the personal computer have increased nearly 25 percent while the costs of hardware and software have decreased by 4 percent. During the same period, the cost of human resources increased by 75 percent (Kramer and McCauley, 1995). Thus, the use of information technology in the form of increasingly powerful computer hardware and software has the potential to permit advisors to do more for less cost.

Shortly after the creation of NACADA, the focus of academic advising shifted from prescriptive to developmental. The organizational structures of advising programs were redesigned and advising was made the joint responsibility of faculty and professional advisors. On many campuses, advising centers were created to support the primary and supplemental advising needs of students. These centers actually augmented the advising performed by faculty, a shift that continues today (Habley and Morales, 1998). Additionally, the American College Testing Program (ACT) began to collect and disseminate information on all aspects of advising in their national surveys on academic advising. These data have been used as benchmarks for advising program development and as a basis for advising program standards.

At about the same time, the information age emerged in higher education. Computerized student record databases were developed, as were computerized course masters (course offerings and availability of class space), files, and registration systems. Development of automated degree audit, transfer course equivalency, electronic notebook, appointment calendar, and student profile systems followed over the next two decades.

Implementation of these systems dramatically reduced the time advisors expended in record-keeping chores, and paved the way for a more developmental focus for advising. The current trend is for these mainframe or client server applications to migrate to the World Wide Web, and for the various components of student information systems to be integrated to permit easy retrieval of accurate and comprehensive academic and student data.

Each of the aforementioned computerized systems should be examined to illustrate how they contribute to the support of developmental advising concepts. For the most part, these systems, if properly developed and maintained, manage various types of information vital to advisors accurately and comprehensively. By doing this, these systems liberate the advisor from time-consuming, labor-intensive, and redundant activities.

Degree Audits

Simply stated, an automated degree audit matches completed coursework with sets of degree-program requirements, tracking student academic progress from declaration of a major to completion of a degree. In addition to assessing the progress of completed coursework, the system applies various university policies and regulations—such as those related to residency, course repetition, and pass-fail—in an automated fashion, negating the need for advisors to intervene manually. Further, some degree-audit systems equate transfer credit to local institution courses and provide for exception record data (course substitutions, waivers, and individualized requirements).

Automated degree audits became prevalent in colleges and universities in the past decade, but they had their beginning in the early 1960s, with the "Bingo Sheet" created at Purdue University. In 1968, Georgia State University introduced its Programmed Academic Curriculum Evaluation (PACE) degree audit, followed by North Carolina State's table-driven system in the early 1970s. Brigham Young University released its Advising by Computer reporting system in 1978, and in 1984 Miami University (Ohio) implemented its Degree Audit Reporting System (McCauley and Southard, 1996). Other institutions that subsequently developed degree-audit systems on their respective campuses include Southern Methodist University, Texas A & M University, and Clemson University.

Because of the potential profitability of degree-audit systems, several software firms entered the marketplace, some with a degree-audit module incorporated within a student information software package. Among these corporate vendors are Campus America, CARS Information Systems, Computer Management & Development Services, Computing Options Company, Datatel, Degree Navigator, Iron Soft, Peoplesoft, Quodata Corporation, Software Research Northwest, and SCT Corporation (McCauley and Southard, 1996).

According to the most recent ACT survey on academic advising, among the departmentally based advising units, 48 percent of the faculty advisors are routinely provided with computerized degree audits as informational reference materials. Similarly, 31 percent of advisors of centralized advising units are routinely offered degree audits as an academic reference (Habley and Morales, 1998).

Because the academic advisor is frequently the university official who interprets complex academic requirements, enforces a multiplicity of academic policies and regulations, and communicates changes to academic programs, it is crucial that the degree audit be capable of executing many diverse transactions. Using the degree-audit system enables institutions to achieve many vital and important objectives.

First and foremost, a properly developed and implemented audit system can significantly reduce the amount of advisor time expended in the clerical duties typically associated with the advising enterprise. The degree audit accurately reports student progress toward completion of degree requirements and does so comprehensively, consistently, and in a timely manner. These systems provide for instant feedback from clientele, whether the users are students, faculty, administrators, or support personnel. Degree audits enhance advisor morale and effectiveness by reducing the likelihood of litigation typically associated with advising and by virtually eliminating the perfunctory, redundant record-keeping chores. Also, degree audits can provide a comfortable academic environment for students by clearly and concisely reporting progress toward graduation, proper course choices, and minimum grade point average stipulations.

Some degree-audit systems have the capacity to support tasks peripheral to the typical advising functions. In some institutions, degree-audit systems assist with management of course offerings, monitor "four-year guarantee" compacts, evaluate academic honors (cum laude, summa cum laude, magna cum laude, Phi Beta Kappa), and execute the complex National Collegiate Athletic Association (NCAA) Division 1 and 2 Continuing Academic Eligibility Compliance Checks. Many degree-audit systems improve the accuracy of some transcript information, especially with cross-listed courses and converted courses (for which the prefix or number has been changed) as well as course repetition policies.

Finally, these systems provide a fiscally prudent way to accomplish vital and necessary advising tasks. Reducing the labor-intensive aspects of the advising function by using an effective and efficient degree-audit system demonstrates fiscal responsibility in an era of constrained budgets and downsized operations (McCauley and Southard, 1996).

In order for degree audits to be of paramount support for academic advising, the systems must possess a large number of diversified features. These features, when invoked with little or no manual intervention, save students and advisors time in monitoring academic progress and interpreting academic policies. One mandatory feature permits students to shop for alternative curricular choices. This "major-shopping" feature particularly assists students who have not yet decided on an educational program, as well as those who wish to supplement a major with a minor, an option, or a specialization area.

The audit should be available to clients in both on-line and batch modes, and it should reflect real-time data. Audits produced via batch runs and distributed to students at a later time may not reflect data that have changed since the initial run. Thus, it is imperative that an on-line system providing up-to-the-minute information be available to the advisor.

Degree audits assess degree program progress by evaluating courses according to the number of courses completed, the number of credit hours completed, the minimum grade earned, the minimum grade point average achieved, and the best grades earned from a group of courses used to satisfy a requirement. The system must correctly identify cross-listed courses, repeated courses, repeatable courses, and converted courses and apply them appropriately to each requirement, without manual intervention by the advisor or a school official.

All components of a degree program must be clearly identified and monitored correctly. University requirements (such as minimum credit hours, minimum grade point average, and residency policies) as well as general education, upper- or lower-division, college- or department-specific, professional school (licensure), major, and minor requirements must be evaluated collectively and correctly.

A critical feature of a computer-assisted advising degree-audit system is the treatment of individual exceptions such as course substitutions, course or credit-hour waivers, and so forth. Caution should be exercised when making exceptions, and exception-tracking procedures must be in place to ensure the academic integrity of the report.

Few individuals other than advisors recognize that two types of course substitution exceptions—global and individual—exist. A global course substitution treats the substituted course in the same manner every time the course appears on the audit. An individual course substitution permits a course to be substituted only once. Security is the primary issue with exceptions, and external as well as internal auditing of exception entries are necessary.

By providing accurate and comprehensive curricular information, the degree audit supports academic advising. It promotes a feeling of ownership in the student and requires the student to engage in decision-making activities. It relieves the advisor of record-keeping duties so that appropriate time can be expended assisting the student with the developmental aspects of academic advising.

Computerized Transfer Course Equivalency Systems

Transfer students tend to be one of the best retention risks in higher education today. These students usually have one or two years of college experience, are more mature, and have often determined an educational objective. Even though transfer students possess these attributes, the transfer process on most college and university campuses remains time-consuming and cumbersome, and requires numerous contacts, visits, and personal discussions before reaching closure.

According to the most recent ACT national survey on academic advising, 70 percent of all the departmentally based advising units that responded engage in advising transfer students, and 24 percent of these departments evaluate transfer credit. Similarly, in institutions with centralized advising offices, 31 percent of these offices engage in the evaluation of transfer credit (Habley and Morales, 1998). Indeed, determining course equivalents and articulating the transfer of degree programs are primary responsibilities of advising personnel in many schools.

Although most two-year and four-year institutions are actively involved with transfer students, many have not automated the process of equating courses or articulating programs. From the time prospective transfer students inquire about transferring to when they enroll in the proper courses is frequently several weeks or months.

Of the steps between initial inquiry and enrollment (admission, evaluation of courses, application of courses to a major, and seeing an academic advisor prior to registration), evaluating courses tends to take the greatest amount of time. Some institutions have created computerized systems to assist in making the transfer process smoother.

These transfer course equivalency systems are designed to reduce the time expended by transfer credit evaluators and to provide consistent and accurate course equivalency data for all students (regardless of the number of institutions attended). The systems provide a vehicle from which students can "shop" for the school that offers the most expedient route to degree completion, thus providing more time for meaningful exchanges among students, faculty members, and advisors. Additionally, these systems can reduce the likelihood of litigation, which is frequently associated with transferring because of inaccurate information, incomplete information, or information delivered in an untimely manner.

Although transfer systems have been in place for some time, they tend to rely on printed course-equivalency booklets that are frequently outdated and not systematically maintained. Some schools have computerized these booklets for advisors to view on-line, but currency of information remains a problem. With these systems, most courses are reduced to a single-course-to-single-course equivalency, even though the relationship may not be accurate in all instances. Advisors recognize that some course equivalents differ depending on the educational objective selected by the student. Thus many courses could have more than one course equivalent.

In addition to equating a single course to a single course, multiple courses to a single course, a single course to multiple courses, and multiple courses to multiple courses, a comprehensive, computerized transfer course equivalency system can address many more transfer issues that advisors see as routine. Sensitivity to the term and year in which a course was completed, credit-hour compatibility between the transferred course and its equivalent, and choosing the "best" equivalent when multiple courses equate to the same course are but a few examples (McCauley and Southard, 1996).

Some institutions award separate grades for course components (one grade for the lecture portion and one grade for the laboratory exercises), while other schools combine both components and award only one grade. A system that can combine the components of a course and calculate a "weighted average" is one that can be of great value and service to the advisor (or transfer evaluator or departmental official), especially if the grade for one component is below the minimum acceptable grade.

Linked to an automated degree audit, a transfer course equivalency system can provide vital and valuable curricular information for transfer students. It is possible to generate a degree audit that references courses in which students can enroll at their current institution until the transfer is completed. In other words, community college students bound for four-year institutions can compare requirements at both schools and maximize the applicability of their course choices. Thus transfer students can be better prepared, possess a more comprehensive understanding of curricular requirements, and be more satisfied with the transfer process.

In addition to the obvious support a computerized transfer course equivalency system provides for students and advisors, this application, when transported to a World Wide Web environment, can enhance the recruitment of transfer students. Admissions counselors welcome such a system to support their efforts in the highly competitive transfer-student marketplace.

By and large, transfer systems support advising by providing accurate, comprehensive transfer course equivalency information to transferring students, which permits advisors to have more time for meaningful exchanges with these students. Reducing the concern for litigation related to the transfer process and providing reference course data for curricular planning purposes has brought about better-prepared transfer students, which is likely to improve retention and stabilize campuswide enrollment.

Touch-Tone Telephone Registration Systems

Although not administered directly by academic advising operations, registration is an advising-related function. For decades, suffering through long registration lines was a major inconvenience for students, and for advisors. Closed classes, time conflicts, classroom locations, and so forth were frequently factors to be considered in the course-selection process. Alleviating advisor involvement in registration and eliminating registration lines were two primary goals for registrars and advisors.

In 1984, Brigham Young University, in cooperation with Apple Computer, pioneered the Touch-Tone telephone voice-response registration system. The objectives were to eliminate long registration lines, provide immediate feedback on the status of a course, and produce real-time enrollment information to departments, registration administrators, and academic support services personnel. This concept was soon used on the Georgia State University campus and has become a staple on most college campuses today (Bell, 1996).

For a Touch-Tone telephone registration system to work effectively and efficiently, colleges must design the system to relate to typical users and future users. Creating the script (to ensure the flow of the call covers all aspects of registration), determining the vocabulary (consisting of two parts: the phrase or continuous flow of speech and the variable or caller-specific data), and identifying the functional specifications (such as call length, system length in hours, standard time-outs, and error handling) must take place in the system-design phase of development. A data transaction format (computer screen displays, interactive voice response, or both) must be created, followed by the scripting of each plausible transaction with concise yet informative messages. Other elements that should be addressed are the determination of student access (who, when, and how) and how to pace the accessibility of individuals to the voice-response environment, in both the advanced registration and add-drop periods. Finally, much attention should be devoted to security concerns, to make certain that the person accessing the system is in fact the person whose records are made available (Bell, 1996).

Typical features of Touch-Tone registration systems for students include initial registration exercises and subsequent course adds and drops. Student-centered systems tend to provide immediate alternative section-availability data when the system encounters a closed class or time-conflict situation. Additionally, these systems can be conveniently accessed from residence hall rooms, apartments, home, or the workplace, and they can be modified to link with financial aid, billing, grade reporting, and transcript information. Interactive Voice Response (IVR) features that benefit departments include departmentally controlled course enrollment adjustment transactions, and flexibility to establish enrollment priorities. Also, real-time enrollment data and the reporting of course-section status enhance the system's ability to offer the number of seats needed and requested by students. Automated degree audits offer appropriate course-selection information, and IVR registration systems permit students to register for the appropriate courses. Thus, the registration data reviewed by departmental administrators is more likely to be valid, which leads to the offering of courses that students need and want.

Interactive voice-response registration systems do indeed reduce the time advisors are engaged in the registration process. However, only when these systems alert departments that more seats are needed, and when they provide a vehicle from which departments can make adjustments to section offerings, do they address the problems of closed classes and long registration lines. Transforming long lines into busy signals does not accomplish the desired results, but providing valid registration data to departments, on the basis of which they may act appropriately, greatly improves student satisfaction with the registration process (Bell, 1996).

In the same light, some institutions have utilized on-line registration applications, thus enabling students to register for classes via a computer terminal. Instead of a voice response, students receive registration information via a computer monitor, and instead of using the telephone keypad, data entry is done by computer keyboard. Other schools are building Web interfaces to their on-line registration systems, permitting students to register for classes via the World Wide Web. Registration can thus occur at any site from which a student can access the Web.

Computerized Appointment Calendar Systems

A more recent application that is both mainframe and personal-computer based is the electronic appointment calendar. Designed to permit students themselves to schedule appointments with their advisors, this innovation reduces the amount of time that clerical support personnel expend in making advisor appointments. These advising support individuals can therefore be assigned more productive responsibilities. Making their own appointments fosters a feeling of ownership among students in their advising interview, and the advisor is afforded more advance time to prepare for the advising session. Brigham Young University has developed a Web-based calendar system, while Ball State University utilizes a telephone-based system in which students call one number to schedule an appointment with any advisor in the advising center.

An electronic appointment calendar system simply permits students to make their own advising appointments and provides an opportunity to capture additional information that may be helpful to the advisor. For instance, some systems ask the student to identify the nature of the appointment, such as selecting a course for an ensuing registration (fifteen minutes), changing a curricular objective (thirty minutes), dropping or adding a course (ten minutes), and so forth, then assigns the appropriate amount of time for the specified appointment.

These systems may also be used to produce statistical data on the number of appointments per advisor or for all advisors collectively, and data on the nature of the appointments. Collating and reporting these data can help structure in-service advisor-development meetings and provide information from which to identify topics for advisor training sessions.

Electronic Advisor Notebooks

The electronic advisor notebook is a system that permits advisors to monitor the myriad information associated with a student advising session. The two major purposes are to provide the advisor with an automated storage device in which to record individual advising contacts and the content associated with each contact, and to provide a historical basis for collecting and disseminating information to enhance the advising processes.

The contact portion of the system indicates who was seen, why, when, and by whom. The system also specifies what advice or information was shared and what academic actions were recommended or completed. Storing these data provides an opportunity for advisors and administrators to analyze the demand for and delivery of advising as well as the advising paths followed by students from college to college, department to department, and across the institution and its branch campuses. The information gathered, in addition to improving planning, staffing, and training efforts, can be utilized to describe the many types of activities that occur in individual advising sessions and the complexity and subtleties associated with such activities (Division of Undergraduate Studies, 1996).

Typical content information captured by successful and efficient electronic notebook systems ranges from pre-admission through postgraduation discussions. The Pennsylvania State University, a pioneer in this automated support application, provides codes for advisors that describe forty-five distinctly different content areas. Among these numerous and varied content areas, one would find discussions about academic difficulty, change of major, curricular choice, degree-audit interpretation, course selection and drop-add, study abroad, financial aid, mentoring, and study skills development. Other content areas focus on scholarship opportunities, test interpretation, transfer-credit acceptability and applicability, as well as referrals, reenrollment, reinstatement, and withdrawal from a course or from the school. The referral content code reports not only that a referral was made but also the specific office or agency to which the student was referred, such as bursar, disability services, minority affairs, faculty member, dean's office, career development services, honors program, or veterans affairs. The Penn State system identifies more than thirty such campus offices and agencies. Institutions with multiple campuses could also provide a campus location code to specify which campus was providing which services. Other codes identify a student's failure to keep an advising appointment, which differs from the code that reflects an appointment that has been cancelled or rescheduled by either the advisor or the student (Division of Undergraduate Studies, 1996).

The electronic notebook system supports advising by providing a repository for information on individual advising appointments and allows advisors to follow a plan of action that they have suggested or recommended. Similar to the electronic calendar system, the electronic notebook system collects and reports data on the volume of contacts; whether in person or by phone, mail, or e-mail; the content of appointments; and the suggested or recommended disposition of the advice offered. Knowing this information enhances planning efforts and advisor training.

Automated Student Profile Systems

Pertinent high school information has long been desired and frequently used by advisors. However, most secondary school data focuses on grades and on the number of semesters completed in specific disciplines (such as English, mathematics, social studies, and sciences). Additional high school information that is not routinely recorded but that is important for advisors includes involvement in cocurricular and extracurricular activities, self-assessed knowledge level in some subjects, and subjects in which college-level tutoring might be necessary. These types of information are particularly important to the advisor during the first few semesters of attendance.

It is well documented that involvement in various aspects of college life enhances success in the classroom and is vital to student persistence. Possessing information that assists the advisor in referring students to various support services such as study skills development, tutoring, and career exploration, and suggesting involvement in cocurricular and extracurricular activities, often enhances university retention efforts.

Conclusion

At the fingertips of advisors today are powerful computer devices and sophisticated software that are more economical to acquire than earlier versions. Advisors have long complained about overwhelming client loads, too many varied responsibilities, and insufficient time to accomplish the student developmental tasks associated with advising. Significantly reducing, and in some instances eliminating, the traditional record-keeping chores of the advisor while providing more accurate and comprehensive information leads to the availability of more time to devote to student developmental interaction.

Indeed, as advising has changed in the past twenty years to focus more on developmental advising, information technology has played and will continue to play a primary role in affording time for these developmental activities. Degree audits, transfer-course equivalency, Touch-Tone telephone registration, and electronic calendar and notebook systems incorporate information technology into the mainstream of the advising enterprise.

With academic advising being perceived as an information-giving responsibility, the role of technology to support these activities is paramount in providing comprehensive and accurate information and in providing time for advisors to engage in professional and developmental activities.

References

Bell, M. M. *Transforming Academic Advising Through the Use of Information Technology.* National Academic Advising Association Monograph Series, no. 4. Manhattan, Kans.: National Academic Advising Association, 1996.

Division of Undergraduate Studies. "Freshman Academic Information Support Advisor Contact User's Guide." University Park: Pennsylvania State University, 1996.

Dolence, M. G., and Norris, D. M. *Transforming Higher Education: A Vision for Learning in the Twenty-First Century.* Ann Arbor, Mich.: Society for College and University Planning, 1995.

Habley, W. R., and Morales, R. H. (eds.). *Current Practices in Academic Advising: Final Report on ACT's Fifth National Survey of Academic Advising.* National Academic Advising Association Monograph Series, no. 6. Manhattan, Kans.: National Academic Advising Association, 1998.

Kramer, G. L., and McCauley, M. E. *Academic Advising as a Comprehensive Campus Process.* National Academic Advising Association Monograph Series, no. 2. Manhattan, Kans.: National Academic Advising Association, 1995.

McCauley, M. E., and Southard, J. *Transforming Academic Advising Through the Use of Information Technology.* National Academic Advising Association Monograph Series, no. 4. Manhattan, Kans.: National Academic Advising Association, 1996.

Chapter Eighteen

Technological Delivery Systems

Remy R. Sotto

Technology has transformed our world from the Industrial Age to the current Information Age—and indeed the Information Age is quickly transitioning to a Learning Age in which learning has become more accessible through the technology of communication and computers. Whether through reading, watching, or doing, information is being communicated, thus increasing our personal database of knowledge. Never before has information been so accessible and available. Through technology, individuals can witness events that are happening not only around the planet but also in galaxies in faraway parts of the universe. Information can be easily communicated back and forth between a remote village and thousands of people around the world. Technology is also transforming higher education from a teaching institution into a learning system.

This transition to the Learning Age has provided academia with the opportunity to develop new learning models, to shift from curriculum-centered to learner-centered education. Students are looking for alternatives, a variety of choices, and flexibility in meeting their educational goals. Students today have a broad range of options, including taking courses through technology-driven education systems such as the Internet. They are also able to receive college degrees without setting foot on the physical campus of their graduating institution. As academia transforms to serve the needs and demands of students, so too must academic advising.

The challenge for advising centers is to provide high-quality service to students who choose technology-delivered courses. Electronic access to student records, on-line registration, degree audits, and computerized evaluation of articulation are some of the enhancements that student services are making to meet the demands of the Learning Age student.

Advising delivered through technology is most beneficial for distance learners, defined here as students taking courses provided through alternative delivery systems. It is worth noting that advising provided through technology is not limited to distance learners. Traditional on-campus students may prefer to utilize electronic means to access information and services. However, technology may be the distance learner's only source of academic advising.

The tools that advisors used in the 1970s to serve distance learners were postal mail, telephone, and even citizen band radios. In the 1980s, desktop computers started to emerge, but even if advisors had access to them, few knew how to use them effectively. The 1990s brought on the explosion of accessibility to computers, the Internet, and innovative technology in education. The tools of the past are still being used today, but computers and the Internet are dominating as the technology of choice to deliver academic advising, especially to distance learners.

Technology in Person-to-Person Advising

One of the most important aspects of academic advising is the relationship developed in one-to-one, person-to-person sessions. Even though advising delivered through technology is not quite the same as being in the same office, some delivery systems are providing the next best thing.

Synchronous Advising

Synchronous advising that is delivered through technology can be defined as same-time, same-pace, different-place, person-to-person advising. The advising session can occur through a variety of media, as illustrated in Exhibit 18.1. The most common form of person-to-person advising is over the telephone. Most students have access to a telephone and there is a familiar comfort level for both advisor and advisee. As computers and the Internet continue to become more accessible, higher education institutions are also utilizing electronic Internet-based tools to communicate with their students.

The advantage of synchronous technology is that the advising sessions are live, or real-time. Whether the technology used in the advising session is video, text, or audioconferencing, the advisee is able to receive immediate feedback in an interactive discussion with an advisor. Advising is a people-oriented function and no matter how the communication is delivered, it is reassuring to both advisor and advisee to have some sense of human contact.

Videoconferencing

Videoconferencing (VC) provides the closest experience to an in-the-same-office advising session. It provides the advisor and advisee with both video and audio communication. A VC advising session provides both students and advisors with a greater sense of being together than other forms of technology. Because they are able to see each other, the advisor can look for visual cues from the advisee

Synchronous	2-way video/ 2-way audio	1-way video/ 2-way audio	2-way audio	1-way video & audio	1-way audio	Text
Videoconferencing—Desktop	x					
Videoconferencing—IITV	x					
Internet Chat Conferencing						
Audioconferencing			x			
Video Phone	x					
Whiteboard Conferencing						x
Telephone			x			
Fax						x
Interactive Classrooms	x					
Broadcast—Television		x[a]		x		
Broadcast—Radio			x[a]		x	
Broadcast—Satellite		x[a]		x		

EXHIBIT 18.1. Synchronous Technology Used to Deliver Academic Advising.

[a] Combined with telephone call-in or voice interactivity

Note: This is technology that was available in April 1999.

and the advisee can associate a face with the institution. Most VC systems today allow for text communication either through chat windows or by sharing files and documents. Advisors are able to share student records, department requirements, transfer guides, and other text information. The advisee can print out the information at his or her location and use it for future reference. The video aspect can also resolve security issues; the advisee can show his or her picture ID for verification before any personal material is shared and discussed.

Colleges today are using videoconferencing in a variety of ways, including for course delivery, recruitment, teacher-student conferences, tutoring, exam proctoring, and group collaboration. The uses of VC specifically in student services can be direct person-to-person advising, mentoring, presentations to groups, and student orientations.

The most economical VC systems are Internet-based, such as Microsoft's Net-Meeting and White Pine's CU-SeeMe. The quality of the video and audio transmission depends on the "traffic" in the Internet connection. The advantage of Internet-based videoconferencing is that there are low operational communication costs and anyone who has an Internet connection and the appropriate hardware and software can videoconference. Internet-based VC systems are especially beneficial for distance learners located far from the college campus. The Internet also makes videoconferencing available internationally. For these students, attaching a face to the advising session provides a sense of connectedness even from afar. The disadvantage of Internet-based VC systems is that the quality of the transmission can be herky-jerky, although the software is improving to eliminate the disadvantages.

The more sophisticated VC systems have direct communication lines between the sites. These systems can range from full studio-quality classrooms to desktop computers. The advantage of these systems is the high quality of video and audio transmission. There is little interruption of the communication between advisor and advisee. The disadvantage is that the communication may be limited to the sites that are connected. These VC systems also require large bandwidth communication lines, which translates into ongoing operation costs.

Computer Chat and Computer Audioconferencing

Computer chat conferencing allows the participants to send text messages simultaneously over the Internet. Computer audioconferencing adds the ability to talk over the Internet. Computer chatting and audioconferencing can be done one-on-one or among a group of people. Software such as PowWow (http://www.tribal.com), CU-SeeMe (http://www.whitepine.com), Microsoft NetMeeting (http://www.microsoft.com), and Netscape CoolTalk (http://www.q5.com) allows individuals to chat or audioconference. ICQ software (http://www.icq.com) provides conferencing in the chat text mode only.

Advising Using Instructional Delivery Systems

The use of technology to deliver advising has also followed in the footsteps of instructional delivery systems. Broadcasts over cable TV, radio, and satellite have been used for years to deliver instructional courses, and academic advising is now taking advantage of these media. Orientations and student information sessions are broadcast accompanied by live telephone interactivity or instructions for interactive telephone voice response. CD-ROMs, videotapes, audiotapes, and computer disks that contain academic advising information can be sent to individual students, high schools, academic institutions, and community organizations. Interactive classrooms can be used to deliver group or individual advising. By utilizing technology to deliver instruction, academic advising can tap into potential existing resources to deliver advising services.

Asynchronous Advising

Asynchronous person-to-person advising that is delivered through technology can be defined as anytime, anypace, anyplace advising. Electronic mail (e-mail), video mail (v-mail), and voice mail are examples of the communication technology used in asynchronous advising. Exhibit 18.2 highlights some of the asynchronous delivery systems.

E-Mail and V-Mail

The use of e-mail advising has grown with the increased use of the Internet. A student can send a text message at any time of the day and receive a personal answer at a later time. It is also possible to send voice and video messages. V-mail can provide a more personal touch by connecting a voice and face to the

Asynchronous	2-way video/ 2-way audio	1-way video/ 2-way audio	2-way audio	1-way video & audio	1-way audio	Text
World Wide Web pages				x	x	
E-mail (electronic mail)				x[a]	x[a]	
V-mail (video mail)				x		
Internet cybercast		x[b]		x	x	
Listservs						x
E-mail advising newsletters						x
Internet bulletin boards						x
Kiosks				x		
Stand-alone computer—CD-ROM, etc.				x		
Videotapes				x		
Audiotapes			x[b]		x	
Telephone infolines					x	

Exhibit 18.2. Asynchronous Technology Used to Deliver Academic Advising.

[a] With attached files

[b] Combined with telephone call-in or voice interactivity

message. There are, however, security issues that need to be considered when providing information through electronic media such as e-mail, fax, and voice mail. Institutions are requiring notarized release forms and passwords to be on file before any personal advising takes place.

Technology in the Self-Help Advising Age

In the Information and Learning Ages we have been discovering new ways to access information and services. In a sense, technology is providing a tool that fosters the developmental advising process and promotes students' responsibility for their academic careers. Through technology, academic advising information and services are readily available anytime, anypace, and anyplace. Students are becoming better informed about basic academic information and are thus giving advisors the opportunity to provide more detailed, in-depth advising when they meet face-to-face.

World Wide Web

The most active and prolific use of technology to deliver academic advising is through the World Wide Web (WWW). Exhibit 18.3 lists some features that are available anytime, anyplace, and anypace. Advising through the WWW is self-help advising. Students may interact with databases and their personal profiles,

Basic Services—Text Information

> Policies and procedures
>
> Frequently asked questions
>
> Address, building location, room number
>
> Phone numbers
>
> Hours of operation
>
> Name and/or e-mail contact
>
> Links to other resources
>
> Assessment or practice tests

Midlevel Services

> On-line forms—applications, requests for information
>
> Search capability
>
> Order forms (such as for textbooks)
>
> Audio and/or video

Advance-Level Services

> Web registration
>
> Degree audit
>
> Schedule planner
>
> Articulation and transfer evaluation
>
> Access to student records and profile
>
> Grade point average calculator
>
> Interactivity with student profile
>
> Artificial intelligence

EXHIBIT 18.3. Advising on the World Wide Web.

but there is no one-to-one interaction. Most higher education institutions have WWW home pages that provide, at the minimum, basic information about the institution. College catalogues, schedules of classes, policies and procedures, addresses, phone numbers, and so on are readily available at the click of a mouse. Institutions that have the resources are developing interactive Web pages. On-line applications, request forms, and the capability to search for information are appearing on more college Web sites. The most sophisticated college Web pages provide on-line registration, degree audits, electronic evaluation for articulation, schedule planners, grade point average calculators, and artificial intelligence, all based on a student's personal profile.

Through the Web, advising information is being delivered via *cybercasts*. Cybercasts are live or stored video and audio presentations. Students can download and view advising information in a multimedia format. The student must have hardware and software that are capable of viewing the cybercasts. Text versions of cybercasts can also be made available.

Anyone who has been on the Web has found a plethora of easily accessible and readily available information. Yet many of us who have been on the information superhighway have also gotten lost as we have wandered around the Web. Looking for information and not finding it can be time-consuming and frustrating. To make the search for academic advising information and services more convenient for students and advisors, college's are creating *virtual advising centers.* A virtual advising center is a central point of electronic access to advising services and information. Web links both within and outside the college are organized so that students and advisors can quickly find information about student services.

Virtual kiosks are another way of providing academic advising information. Virtual kiosks are touch-screen information centers that integrate access to the Web with text or multimedia information stored on the local computer's hard drive. Virtual kiosks are centrally located where students gather, such as at campus student centers. Sophisticated virtual kiosks and virtual advising centers enable interactivity with the college's databases, allowing students to register for classes, calculate degree audits, and change personal information.

Advising over the Internet

In addition to obtaining advising services over the Web, students can also find listservs, e-mail newsletters, and electronic bulletin boards on the Internet. Listservs and e-mail newsletters are accessed via e-mail accounts and do not require Web browsers. Advisors can mass distribute information about upcoming events, calendar deadlines, and other timely tidbits. E-mail newsletters can provide students with helpful articles, including study hints, note-taking guides, and test-taking tips. Listservs provide students with opportunities for interchange with other students and college staff. Lively discussions on hot topics can provide a sense of group connectedness. Electronic bulletin boards provide students with a means of viewing announcements and posting messages. Examples of innovative uses of advising on the Internet can be found at Academic Advising Resources on the Internet (http://www.psu/dus/ncta/linkacad.hmt).

Advantages and Disadvantages of Using Technology to Deliver Advising

Some advantages of using technology to deliver advising are convenient access, accuracy of information, and timeliness of feedback for both the provider and the student. Through the Internet, information and services can be accessed from around the globe. Students can be home on vacation and register for their classes on-line or through Touch-Tone telephone. They can electronically file financial aid information and get a response back within a week. They can ask their advisor questions by e-mail at 2:00 A.M. and the advisor can answer the next day. Advisors can meet with students who live miles away through video-conferencing and then meet with other students face-to-face without leaving the advisors' offices. Advisors can assist students who are requesting career information by simply researching over the Internet. These are just a few examples of the convenience and timeliness of technology-delivered advising.

Another advantage is that some students prefer the anonymity of technology. They feel bolder in expressing their thoughts, fears, and concerns when they do not have to meet face-to-face with their advisor. If it were not for the access the Internet provides, they may not receive the information they need. The Internet gives these students an avenue for gathering information and for taking responsibility for their academic careers.

There are, however, some disadvantages. Notwithstanding technical difficulties, the person-to-person relationship is different via technology. Though videoconferencing is closest to the student and advisor being in the same place, the advisor-student interaction does not have the same sense of contact and connectedness as in the in-person conference. Can rapport be built and a sense of personality exhibited through technology? Absolutely! This has been demonstrated many times with text-based listservs such as ACADV, the National Academic Advising Association's electronic network started in 1989, which now boasts a membership of more than 2,400 higher education professionals.[1] This network provides a means for academic advisors around the world to communicate their thoughts, feelings, and ideas regarding their profession. The members of the listserv have acquired a sense of their fellow contributors' personalities and styles through lively discussions. Yet we all still wonder who the folks are behind those typed messages. In general, students tend to relate better when they see their advisor as a living, breathing person and not an automated, typed response.

Issues of Technology-Delivered Advising

Advising delivered through technology is still an issue of the haves and the have-nots for both the student and the institution. Technology requires computers, Internet connections, phone access, and televisions. Not all students have these resources and not all institutions can provide advising using sophisticated technology.

There is also the issue of serving students who have disabilities. Institutions should consider the accessibility of their Web designs and of the services they provide through technology. The World Wide Web Consortium, or W3C, provides Web accessibility guidelines through its Web Accessibility Initiative. These guidelines can be accessed at http://www.w3org/WAI/GL.

Conclusion

As the Learning Age continues to advance, advisees, advisors, and administrators must adjust "the way we do business." In addition to the financial commitment of computers, connections, and software, training is an integral part of this adjustment. Workshops and information sessions on electronic access to student services must be provided for advisees, on campus, in dorms, or over the Internet. Administrators must provide professional development programs and release time so that advisors can become more proficient in serving their students via technology. Institutions must market all their electronic access so that students are aware of what is available to them.

A whole new campus culture of virtual colleges is being spawned from the influence of technology in higher education. To meet the challenge of serving the virtual colleges, academic advising is providing easier access, alternative approaches, and innovative practices. Video advising, e-mail advising, and virtual advising centers are being implemented to serve distance learners. Advisors are creatively developing better ways to establish the human connection for students in this virtual world. As new technological resources evolve, institutions continue to learn, adjust, and find new ways to deliver academic advising. The Learning Age provides an opportunity for use to continue to expand and share our knowledge. After all, we are providers and promoters of lifelong learning.

Notes

1. To join the National Academic Advising Association's electronic network (ACADV Listserv) send an e-mail to < Listserv@Listserv.nodak.edu >, no subject, with the following message on the first (and only line): subscribe ACADV [first name, middle initial, last name].

Other Resources

Dolence, M. G., and Norris, D. M. *Transforming Higher Education: A Vision for Learning in the Twenty-First Century.* Ann Arbor, Mich.: Society for University and College Planning, 1995.

Kramer, G. L., and Childs, M. W. (eds.). *Transforming Academic Advising Through the Use of Information Technology.* National Academic Advising Association Monograph Series. no. 4. Provo, Utah: Brigham Young University Press, 1996.

Syllabus Press. *Syllabus: New Directions in Education Technology.* < http://www.syllabus.com >.

T.H.E. Institute. *T.H.E. Journal: Technological Horizons in Education.* < http://www.thejournal.com >.

Chapter Nineteen

Using Assessment Instruments

Thomas J. Grites

This chapter provides academic advisors with a set of tools that can assist them in their efforts to maximize their students' educational planning. The approach to using these tools is presented in a chronological fashion, that is, from the student's admission to the institution (as a first-time college student, not a transfer student) through graduation, and even beyond.

The assessment instruments described in this chapter include primarily those that are available from national testing companies and other resource organizations. The instruments have been selected by the author. They are not the only ones available, but they are representative of the various areas in which assessment tools might be used by academic advisors. Clearly other commercial instruments are available, and many institutional instruments have been designed, implemented, and used effectively to enhance the advising process on those campuses. Such efforts should continue.

This review identifies the significant characteristics of these assessment instruments, which should be reviewed for use at the various stages of students' development, both chronologically and developmentally. Institutions that desire to develop their own instruments will have a template of concepts, structures, formats, and processes on which to base their own assessment design efforts.

Admissions Instruments

Except for the community college sector of higher education, nearly all colleges and universities require their entering first-year students to submit standardized test scores from the American College Testing Program (ACT) or from the College Board's Scholastic Aptitude Test (SAT). Along with other information, these scores are used to predict the student's academic success at the institution and therefore to determine whether or not the student should be admitted.

Included with the basic score reports provided by the testing companies are various sets of information that provide a wealth of additional resources to the student's academic advisor once the student arrives on campus. These documents contain a wide range of self-reported information that the advisor might use to determine the student's potential need for academic assistance, for career planning, and for campus involvement.

The ACT College Report provides normative, predictive, and self-reported data that can be used to compare individual students to others to determine the likelihood of their success in college (see Exhibit 19.1). The categories of information include the following:

- Predictions of overall grade point average (GPA) for broad fields of study and for specific selected (freshman-level) courses
- Personal characteristics that might affect students' performance, such as their preference for the institution attended, their certainty about their educational and vocational choices and plans, and their recognition of any special academic needs or deficiencies they might expect to encounter
- Previous participation and levels of performance in extracurricular activities and academic subjects
- Additional demographic characteristics such as ethnicity, religious preferences, and native language

A special feature of this report is the World-of-Work Map (Exhibit 19.2), which indicates categories of the general types of career options the student seems to prefer. The student's score, based on the ACT Interest Inventory completed at the time of test registration, is mapped according to four basic "Career Families" (working with data, people, things, or ideas). Within each of these Career Families, or combinations of them, broader programs of study and specific college majors are suggested for the student to consider.

The SAT Program's College Report (Exhibit 19.3) provides a more concise version of the information provided by the ACT report. The SAT report includes self-reported data about the student's academic background and performance in the broader curricular areas of the college curriculum—for example, the arts, the social sciences, the natural sciences, and mathematics. The report also includes the student's educational and vocational plans, his or her preferences for the type of institution attended, identification of expected needs and services, and both previous and anticipated participation in extracurricular activities and programs, as reported on the Student Descriptive Questionnaire.

A unique feature of the SAT testing program is the SAT II: Subject Tests. Students who have taken these additional exams in specific content areas (for example, writing, literature, languages, mathematics, science, or history) have their scores reported on the College Report as well.

ACT COLLEGE REPORT

		SOC. SEC. NO.:	392-11-1999		TYPE OF TESTING:	NATIONAL
TRACY ARTHUR C		DATE OF BIRTH:	08/22/82	MALE	DATE TESTED:	10/99
7852 W 46TH ST		PHONE NUMBER:	303 468-7982		YEAR OF H.S. GRAD.:	2000
WHEAT RIDGE CO 80033						

H.S. ATTENDED: 067-890 WHEAT RIDGE SR HS 9505 W 32ND AVE WHEAT RIDGE COLORADO 80033

SCORES AND PREDICTIVE DATA (See ACT User Handbook)

TESTS AND SUBSCORE AREAS	TEST SCORES (1-36)	SUBSCORES (1-18)	NORMS (% AT OR BELOW SCORE) COL-BND		TESTS AND SUBSCORE AREAS	TEST SCORES (1-36)	SUBSCORES (1-18)	NORMS (% AT OR BELOW SCORE) COL-BND	
			NATL	LOCAL				NATL	LOCAL
ENGLISH	24		76	75	READING	25		75	72
Usage/Mechanics		13	80	80	Soc. Studies/Sci.		10	50	46
Rhetorical Skills		12	74	72	Arts/Literature		14	79	78
MATHEMATICS	17		31	28	SCI. REASONING	18		31	25
Pre-Alg./Elem. Alg.		09	37	35					
Alg./Coord. Geom.		10	57	55					
Plane Geom./Trig.		08	25	20	COMPOSITE	21		56	52

NAT'L NORMS BASED ON RECENT H.S. GRADUATES TESTED AS JRS OR SRS ON NATIONAL TEST DATES. OTHER NORM GROUPS IN USER HDBK.
LOCAL NORMS REPORTED ONLY IF INSTITUTION PARTICIPATES IN ACT RESEARCH SERVICES.

OVERALL GPA PREDICTIONS

NAME OF GROUP	% S. PGPA	PROB ≥ C
EDUCATION	91	89
BUSINESS ADMIN	74	72
LIBERAL ARTS	74	81
ENGINEERING	41	32
ALL FRESHMEN	75	80

SPECIFIC COURSE PREDICTIONS

NAME OF COURSE	% S. GRADE	PROB ≥ C
FRESHMAN ENGLISH	89	72
COLLEGE ALGEBRA	15	18
HISTORY	86	82
CHEMISTRY	59	68
PSYCHOLOGY	79	89

ADMISSION/ENROLLMENT DATA

	COLLEGE CODE	CHOICE	STUDENT BODY COMP.	ENTRANCE DATE	FULL-TIME	TYPE OF STUDENT	U.S. CITIZEN	RESIDENT OF ABOVE STATE	PHYSICAL/LEARNING DISABILITY	VETERAN	COLLEGE CREDIT	HOUSING PLANS
	9521	1ST	CO-ED	FALL 00	YES	DAY	YES	YES	–	NO	NO	RESID HALL

COLLEGE SELECTION ITEMS BY RANK ORDER

	TYPE	CHOICE	LOCATION	COST (MAX. TUITION)	SIZE	FIELD OF STUDY	OTHER FACTOR
	FOURTH	FIRST	FIFTH	SECOND	THIRD	FIRST	SEVENTH
	PUB 4-YR	SIXTH	COLORADO	2,000	5-10,000		

EDUCATIONAL AND VOCATIONAL PLANS

EDUCATIONAL MAJOR	HOW CERTAIN	DEGREE OBJECTIVE	PROF LEVEL	SELF-ESTIMATE OF COLLEGE G.P.A.
POLITICAL SCI/GOVERNMENT	FAIRLY SURE	PROF LEVEL	FIRST	3.0-3.4

FIRST VOCATIONAL CHOICE	HOW CERTAIN	SECOND VOCATIONAL CHOICE
LAW	VERY SURE	INTERNATIONAL RELATIONS

SELF-REPORTED HIGH SCHOOL INFORMATION

YEAR H.S. GRAD. OR EQUIVALENT	SIZE OF SENIOR CLASS	TYPE OF SCHOOL	PERCENT SAME RACE AS STUDENT	TYPE OF PROGRAM STUDIED
2000	200-399	PUBLIC	90%	COLL PREP

SELF-REPORTED RANK: TOP QTR **AND AVERAGE:** 3.0-3.4

YEARS CERTAIN SUBJECTS STUDIED AND ADVANCED PLACEMENT IN HIGH SCHOOL

	ENGLISH	MATH	SOCIAL STUDIES	NAT'L SCIENCES	SPANISH	GERMAN	FRENCH	OTHER LANGUAGES	BUSINESS/COMMERCIAL	OCCUP VOC
YEARS:	4	4	3	3	1	1	0	0	1	1
GRADES:	–	4	3	3	1					

ADVANCED PLACEMENT IN H.S.	LANG.	SELF-REPORTED ADEQUACY OF H.S. EDUCATION
YES NO	YES NO	EXCELLENT

SPECIAL EDUCATIONAL NEEDS AND INTERESTS

INDICATED NEED FOR HELP WITH:

WRITING	READING	STUDY SKILLS	MATHEMATICS	ENGLISH	PERSONAL CONCERNS	FRESHMAN HONORS COURSES	INDEPENDENT STUDY	CREDIT BY EXAMINATION
N	N	N	N	N	N	N	N	N

INDICATED INTEREST IN:

EDUCATIONAL OR VOCATIONAL PLANS	MATHEMATICS	ENGLISH	SOCIAL STUDIES	NATURAL SCIENCES	ROTC	ENGLISH	MATHEMATICS	SOCIAL STUDIES	NATURAL SCIENCES	FRENCH	GERMAN	SPANISH	OTHER LANGUAGES
Y	N	N	N	N	N	N	N	N	N	N	N	N	N

ADVANCED PLACEMENT IN:

H.S. EXTRACURRICULAR ACTIVITIES AND COLLEGE EXTRACURRICULAR PLANS

	INSTR. MUSIC	VOCAL MUSIC	STUDENT GOVT.	PUBLICATIONS	DEBATE	DEPT. CLUBS	DRAMATICS	RELIG. ORG'S	RACIAL-ETH. ORG'S	INTRAMURAL ATHL.	VARSITY ATHL.	POLITICAL ORG'S	RADIO-TV	FRAT./SORORITY	SPECIAL INTEREST	SERVICE ORG'S
HIGH SCHOOL	Y	N	Y	Y	Y	Y	N	Y	N	N	Y	Y	N	N	N	N
COLLEGE	Y	N	Y	Y	Y	Y	N	N	N	Y	N	N	N	N	N	N

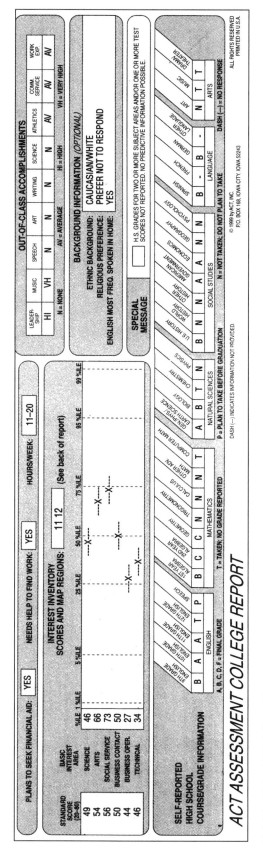

Exhibit 19.1. ACT College Report.

Copyright ACT, Inc. Used by permission.

World-of-Work Map (2nd Edition)

Working with Data

Region 3 — C. Records and Communications

Region 4 — Financial Transactions, D., E., Distribution and Dispatching

People and Data — Region 2 — A. Marketing and Sales, B. Management and Planning

Data and Things — Region 5 — F. Business Machine/Computer Operation, G. Transportation Technologies

Region 1 / Working with People — U. Education and Related Services, V. Social and Government Services

Data / People / Things / Ideas (center)

I. Agriculture and Natural Resources, H. Crafts and Industrial Technologies — Region 6 / Working with Things

Region 12 — T. General Health Care, S. Applied Arts (Written and Spoken)

N. Medical Specialties and Technologies — Region 7

Q. Applied Arts (Visual), M. Engineering and Related Technologies

People and Ideas — Region 11 — R. Creative/Performing Arts, P. Social Sciences

O. Natural Sciences and Mathematics — Region 9

Ideas and Things — Region 8

Region 10 — **Working with Ideas**

Map Regions:

How to Use the Map:

1. Find your map regions in the Interest Inventory section on the reverse side of this report and enter them in the box above. (If "Region 99" is reported, your activity preferences did not indicate particular map regions to explore.)

2. Find your region numbers on the map and circle them. Note the work tasks (working with People, Things, Data, Ideas) shown for your map regions. Then, look over the Career Families in or near the regions you circled.

3. If you wish to consider college majors related to those Career Families, see the list to the right. If you wish to consider job options, ask for ACT's Career Family List, which lists 170 jobs by Career Family. It appears on the back of your Student Report and in ACT's counselor/advisor materials.

CAUTION! Map regions (like other test scores) are estimates. They provide suggestions, not decisions. Also, your **interests** and **abilities** may differ. Both need to be considered in career planning.

Exhibit 19.2. ACT World-of-Work Map (partial reproduction).

SAT PROGRAM

COLLEGE REPORT

PUBLIC UNIVERSITY 6666

Student ID

Name	Jane L. Henderson					Social Security No.	123-45-6789

Address	761 Valley Forge				Valley Forge		PA 00032

Report Date	1/15/2000	Sex	F	U.S. Citizen	Yes	First Language	English

Birth Date	06/15/82	EPS Market	PA-35	County	Cook

H.S. Grad.	Jun 2000	Ethnic Group	Black		Phone Number	222-333-4444

Current Grade Level	Senior	Religion	Baptist

Latest Scores   Test Date: December 1999

SAT I: Reasoning Test	Score	Score Range	Percentiles College-bound Seniors National	State
Verbal	R550	520-580	64	68
Mathematical	R540	510-570	59	65

R = Recentered score (test dates on or after April 1, 1995)
See reverse side for information.

Summary of Scores

SAT I: Reasoning Test

Test Date	Grade Level	Verbal	Math	Reading	Vocabulary	TSWE
Dec 99	12	R550	R540			
May 99	11	R460	R500			

Verbal Subscores[1]

SAT II: Reasoning Test

Test Date	Grade Level	Test 1	Score	Reading	Listening	Usage/Prof.	Test 2	Score	Test 3	Score
Nov 99	12	Chinese Lst	R570	53	57	61				
Nov 98	11	French Lst	R580	60	54					

Listening Subscores[1]

[1]Not all test have subscores

Student Reported Data (as reported on SDQ 11/99)

Educational Background

Courses	Years	Honors	Average Grade	Course Work and Experience
ARTS AND MUSIC	4	Yes	A	Acting/Play production, Dance, Drama
ENGLISH	4	Yes	B	Amer Lit, Comp, Grammar
FOREIGN LANGUAGES	2		B	French
MATHEMATICS	4+	Yes	A	Algebra, Geometry, Trigonometry, Calculus
NATURAL SCIENCES	2		B	Biology, Chemistry
SOCIAL SCIENCES	4		A	U.S. History, Other
COMPUTER EXPERIENCE				Programming, Math
Grade Point Average	B+	Class Rank		Second tenth

Years of High School and Community Activities		Officer/ Award	Years
Academic honor society	9, 10, 11, 12	Yes	Basketball
Art activity	11, 12	Yes	Field
Dance activity	12		hockey
Religious activity or org.	10, 11, 12	Yes	Softball
Theater activity	12		Squash
Part-time job	12		Tennis

Student's Plans

Degree Goal	Bachelor's
First Choice of Major	Economics
Certainty of 1st Choice	Very Certain
Other Majors Listed	Dramatic Arts Art (painting, drawing, sculpture) Engineering/Engineering Technologies
Requested Services	Educational planning Part-time job
Preferred College Characteristics	Type: 4 yr. Public, Private Size: More than 20,000 Setting: Medium size city Dist. from home: Undecided Other: Coed, On-campus housing
College Programs and Activities	Art Dance Drama/Theater
Advanced Placement or Exemption Plans	Art, Math

High School Data

Information Provided by	Central High School		333222
Address	4800 Center Street	Phone Number	111-222-3333
	Philadelphia, PA 12345	Senior Class Size	500–749
Location	Large City	Honors Courses Are Offered?	Yes
Type	Public	Number of AP Courses Offered	7
Percent of Seniors Going to College	60–69	Units to Graduate	15

Score Analysis Data

	Type of Question	Number of Questions	Estimated Percentile College-bound Seniors
VERBAL	Critical Reading	40	75
	Analogies	19	25
	Sentence Completion	19	55
MATH	Arithmetic and Algebraic Reasoning	43	55
	Geometric Reasoning	17	65

SAT I score analysis data based on most recent test (form code QQ)
For more information, refer to the reverse side, or consult the Guide.

48550-03768/DI1-930608

HENDERSON   LAST NAME

JANE   FIRST NAME

L   MI

F   SEX

06/15/82   BIRTH DATE

123-45-6789   SOCIAL SECURITY NUMBER

Exhibit 19.3. SAT Program College Report.

Reprinted by permission of Educational Testing Service and the College Entrance Examination Board, the copyright owners.

The two reports just described provide a wealth of opportunities for advisors to facilitate an early positive advising experience. Clearly the basic test score data provide clues to the expected academic success of the student. The self-reported data indicate the student's strength and commitment to achieving personal success in college, as well as areas in which support and assistance may be needed.

It is obviously to the advisor's advantage to have these profiles available in advance of the first meeting with the student. By reviewing this breadth of information in advance, the academic advisor can begin to "know" the student before the initial meeting, target areas of the student's plans to question or confirm, and begin to formulate an appropriate educational planning strategy for the student.

It is rather obvious how much of the information provided in these profiles might be used. Students who have achieved low academic performance scores and have indicated no interest in scientific areas of study will not likely indicate that engineering is a strongly preferred program of study. Such consistency would be expected.

However, it is the inconsistencies or incompatibilities that the advisor must seek to identify in these profiles. Students who indicate a strong preference or commitment to an academic major but who do not have the test scores to support anticipated success in that major or who indicate that they need additional help in educational planning demonstrate such incompatibilities.

The student who indicates the need for financial and study skills assistance but who also intends to be involved in several school activities will likely need the advisor to clarify the academic expectations of the institution relative to those needs and desires.

Ironically, even the most successful students frequently need to reassess their achievements and expectations, and the academic advisor can facilitate this review as a preventive measure, especially in very competitive institutions or programs. Those students who have experienced only success in their academic and personal lives and who might suddenly find themselves only average present one of the most difficult challenges to academic advisors. By reviewing these profiles to identify the "superstars," advisors are better able to foster supportive relationships with these students if they fail to meet their own (and others') expectations.

In brief, an array of information about students is available to academic advisors even before the students set foot on the campus. Better preparation at this early stage will serve only to strengthen the advising relationship and promote student growth and development in the future.

Course Placement Instruments

Although the role of academic advisor has recently evolved into that of educational planner, facilitator, and confidant, one of the primary functions of advisors is still to assist students in the selection of courses. Such selection extends throughout the student's college career but is most critical at the time of initial enrollment. Students, their parents, their advisors, and the teaching faculty all desire to have the students enrolled in courses in which they are likely to succeed. A variety of instruments are available to aid advisors in the initial course selection and placement of first-time students.

The score reports from the two major testing companies described earlier also contain information that is designed to assist in initial course placement. The ACT College Report includes actual test score data reported in broad academic categories (English, mathematics, reading, and science reasoning) along with both national and local norms for each category. Several specific skill subscores and a composite score are also reported. In addition, this report includes student self-reported information on the number of years various subjects were taken, the grades received in those subjects, and estimates of their previous academic achievement and preparation for college study. If the advisor's institution subscribes to the additional course placement service, then predictions of success in specific courses at that institution are also shown.

The SAT College Report also shows raw score data, including national and state norms in the primary academic skill areas (verbal and math), along with the subject test scores, if these tests were taken. This report includes self-reported data on the average grades in seven course areas (arts and music, English, foreign languages, mathematics, natural sciences, social sciences, and computers; the latter is a recent addition). The report also includes self-estimates on the overall high school GPA and the class rank.

In addition to these basic score reports, both companies offer separate assessment packages that are specifically designed for appropriate placement of students, especially in basic skills courses. These instruments have primarily been used in two-year community and technical colleges to determine preparedness for college-level work in the areas of reading, writing, and mathematics.

ACT offers the ASSET and COMPASS assessment instruments. ASSET is a paper-and-pencil version that is utilized primarily in two-year colleges and is typically administered to a group. COMPASS uses a computerized adaptive testing format and applies to both two-year and four-year institutions. ASSET includes options for advanced testing in mathematics and for study skills and career skills, and an interest inventory. COMPASS also provides diagnostic scores to identify specific areas of skill deficiency. Both instruments can be integrated with each other, as well as with the data from the respective admissions instrument (see Exhibits 19.4 and 19.5).

The College Board provides Computerized Placement Tests (CPTs) as one component of its ACCUPLACER system (see Exhibit 19.6). The CPT scores are based on proficiency statements that enable each institution to examine students' potential success in courses requiring the academic skills demonstrated in the tests.

Another component of the ACCUPLACER system that is beneficial to academic advisors is the Computerized Placement Advising and Management Software (see Exhibits 19.7 and 19.8). This component utilizes such additional information as student background information, institutional data, and the student's intended major field of study.

Browning, Elizabeth A.   MCKINLEY COLLEGE   05/09/96
4105 Michael, Iowa City IA 52243   800-555-1212

A. BACKGROUND: 021-49-2333, born 01/18/69; diploma 1985, Mason City HS, Mason City IA;
   have not attended after HS; Univ. of Iowa; not a veteran; English is first language.

   PREVIOUS COURSE/YEARS COMPLETED/LAST GRADE REPORTED
   High school—No courses reported
   After high school—No courses reported

B. PLANS: program/major—Education (very sure); enroll Fall 1994, 12 credits, day classes;
   career goal—Education (very sure); planning 4-yr. degree; transfer to 4 yr. coll./univ. (Univ. of
   Iowa); attending for general reqmts; plans 2-yr. degree; work 1-10 hrs./wk.; expects grades of
   B to A-; info released to postsecondary institution only.

C. HELP REQUESTED   CAMPUS RESOURCES RECOMMENDED
   Financial Aid   Y   Financial Aid Office, Admin. Bldg., Rm. 309 (338-2246)
   Finding Work   M   Employment Office, Farley Bldg., Rm. 34 (338-9935)
   Reading Skills   M   Learning Center, Walker Bldg., Rm. 116 (336-1234)
   Writing Skills   Y   Learning Center, Walker Bldg., Rm. 120 (336-1234)
   Math Skills   M   Tutoring Center, Ford Bldg., Rm. 443 (335-1467)
   Major/Career   M   Student Development Center, Floyd Bldg., Rm. 100 (335-1555)
   Health Problem   Y   Student Health Center, Walker Bldg., Rm. 200 (336-1500)
   Commuter Info   Y   Student Development Center, Floyd Bldg., Rm. 85 (335-1456)
   Day Care Info   Y   Child Care Center, Wilson Bldg., Rm. 100 (335-1258)

D. MCKINLEY COLLEGE FACULTY COURSE PLACEMENT RECOMMENDATIONS

MEASURE	SCORE	COURSE INFORMATION FOR: Education Test Form: B2
Writing Skills	40	English 1, Written Expression, for associate degree and transfer to other colleges.
Reading Skills	30	Enroll in RDG 98, College Reading (required) to increase your strength and speed. When this is completed successfully, you may enroll in courses such as psychology, biology, or similar courses which require college-level reading skills.
Numerical Skills	36	Math 30 followed by Math for Teachers (Math 109). Talk with advisor if uncertain about choice.
Study Skills	195	Study Dev 1 will review study skills techniques to help you succeed in classes.
Subscores:		MTE: 37 RT: 41 TCN: 37 UIR: 40 PTE: 40
English Essay	35	Composition Placement: English 1, Written Expression.

E. ADDITIONAL INFORMATION
   Interested in part-time work in school settings? See our placement office (109 Walker Hall) for
   leads on before- and after-school jobs with local schools. A listing of transfer requirements for
   Education students is also available in the Education Department (145 Johnson Hall).

F. LOCAL ITEMS: 1.C 2.A 3.D 4.B 5.E 6.C 7.B 8.A 9.A 10.B

G. ADVISOR: James Arnold, 339-3526, Wilson Bldg., Rm. 106
   Ask about our new DISCOVER computerized guidance system to help you explore your
   options (no charge, but appointment required; Student Development Center, Rm. 100). Let us
   know how you plan your success here at McKinley College. We're glad you're here.

Please keep this copy with you for use in advising discussions.

Exhibit 19.4. Sample ASSET Student Advising Report.

Name: Williams. Francis L.   ID: 111–11–0566
Address: 1515 Elm Street Our Town, MI 37209
Test Date: 05/17/99   Test Session: 4   Location: Station 1

Student Background and Educational Plans

English first language:	Yes	HS GPA:	B- to B (2.5–2.9)
Type of HS certificate:	HS diploma	High school:	North High School
Employment hours:	16–20 hrs weekly	Ed plan:	Four-year degree
Considering transfer:	Four-yr coll/univ	Transfer school:	Central State Univ.
Previous credits:	6	# Credits planned:	12
Program choice:	Accounting		

Local Demographic Item(s)

Last mathematics course: Elementary Algebra
Time of last math course: 6–10 years ago
Travel to campus: 11 or more miles each way

Help Requested by Student

Financial aid	Financial Aid Office, Walker Building, Rm 309, 338–2246
Reading skills	Learning Assistance Center, Walker Building, Rm 116, 336–1234
Study skills	Learning Assistance Center, Walker Building, Rm 116, 336–1234
Choosing major/career	Career Development Center, Walker Building, Rm 100, 335–1456

Choice of Programs

Welcome to the Accounting Program at Central Community College. Our goal is to help you build new business and computer skills, which will help you succeed in gaining and progressing in your preferred career in the accounting field. Page 42 of the Catalog describes the program and required courses in detail. Mr. Rod Thompson and Ms. Sherry Williams are the program advisors for accounting students (offices located in Room 55 in Johnson Hall; phone 555–1234). Call for an appointment to discuss course planning, graduation requirements, four-year degree transfer opportunities, part-time job opportunities, job placement services, and salary information for CCC Accounting Program graduates.

Assessment Results and Related Recommendations

Administration mode:	New Student Placement Test (Mathematics, Reading, Writing)	
Placement group:	Accounting Program Recommendations	
Demographics Time:	3:20	Total time: 1:18:08

Mathematics Placement Information

Placement Test:	Score	Time	Note
Pre-algebra	69	7:45	Starting Domain
Algebra	37	14:55	Placement Domain

Mathematics Placement Recommendation: Your Algebra score indicates that you are eligible to enroll in Math 90, Elementary Algebra. However, with some additional brush-up work before the start of the next term, you may regain enough skills to be eligible for the next higher course. To work on rebuilding your Elementary Algebra skills, use the Elementary Algebra Textbook or the Elementary Algebra Review program on the computers in the CCC Learning Assistance Center. You may then complete the Placement Test again after you have finished your review to see if you have gained the strengths you need to be eligible for the Intermediate Algebra course. Intermediate Algebra is the final math prerequisite before College Algebra, a required course for the Accounting degree.

Algebra Diagnostic Test Results: 4:38

Substitution	65	Setting Up Equations	35
Exponents	75	Polynomials-Factorization	76

Algebra Diagnostic Recommendation: Your score on the problems involving Setting Up Equations indicates that you need additional brush-up work in this area. To build your skills in this area, study and work through Chapters 3 and 4 in the Elementary Algebra Textbook by Johnson (available in the book store) or use Part 3 of the Elementary Algebra Skills Review Program on the computers in the CCC Learning Assistance Center (no charge; open 8 am to 7 pm, Monday-Friday). When you have finished this review, complete the Mathematics Placement Test again to see if you are then eligible for entry into the next higher course required in your program of study.

(Additional results and recommendations for Reading and Writing Skills appear on page 2).

Exhibit 19.5. Sample COMPASS Student Advising Report.

Student ID; 112121112

First Name: MICHAEL

Last Name: MANN

Middle Initial: M.

Student DOB: 01/01/1975

Major Name: Dramatic Arts

College Name: College of Testing

Advisement

Please pick up a copy of your test report at the printer by the door. Then proceed to Oak Hall for freshmen orientation.

Scores

Test	Date	Score	Percentile
Sentence Skills	09/29/1999	90.8	58

Placements

English 100A

Background Information

1 Sex
    Response: Male
2 English First Language
    Response: Yes
3 Studied Algebra in High School
    Response: Yes

Exhibit 19.6. Sample CPT Student Score Report

Used by permission.

Two unique features of ACCUPLACER are that it is the only assessment placement system available through the Internet and that it also is available in audio and Braille formats.

Other Instruments

Various higher education systems have developed their own course placement instruments, especially for determining students' preparedness for college-level work. Some examples of these are the California State University's Entry Level Math Test and English Placement Test, the City University of New York's Freshman Skills Assessment Program, and the state of Texas's Academic Skill Program. Although the state of New Jersey no longer requires its Basic Skills Placement Test, the College Board has used this instrument to conduct score comparability studies for its CPT scores, described earlier.

Certain other standardized tests have been used for course placement purposes as well, although they were not necessarily designed for that purpose. These include the College Board's Advanced Placement (AP) program of courses and tests for high school students, as well as its College Level Examination Pro-

Student ID: 130301330

First Name: MARY

Last Name: MARTIN

Middle Initial: M.

Student DOB: 01/01/1985

Major Name: Radiobiology

College Name: College of Testing

Scores

Test	Date	Score	Percentile
Arithmetic	09/29/1999	58	52

Placements

Arithmetic 100

This class will include Geometry and Measurement

Background Information

1   Sex
    Response: Female
2   English First Language
    Response: Yes
3   Studied Algebra in High School
    Response: Yes
4   Major Field of Study
    Response: Null

Exhibit 19.7. Sample CPAMS Placement Report

Used by permission.

gram (CLEP), the Regents College Examinations, and the Test of English as a Foreign Language (TOEFL), published by the Educational Testing Service. The AP, CLEP, and Regents Examinations are intended to assess achievement in specific subject areas so that college credit might be awarded; the TOEFL Exam is used mainly to determine admission for international students, but it might also dictate the need for students to be placed in English as a Second Language courses.

Finally, transcripts from other institutions can be used to determine appropriate course placements for transfer students.

Institutions that use course placement instruments normally have already established specific criteria for the results. Indeed, the more extensive standardized instruments provide such criteria either by denoting specific competencies demonstrated in a range of scores or by providing specific course recommendations based on research conducted locally. Therefore, many course decisions are already made for the student and the advisor.

The role of the academic advisor in this situation is clearly one of clarification, support, and monitoring of the student's progress. Students need to understand their relative strengths and weaknesses in the various academic skill areas, and the advisor is in a position to explain these in a nonthreatening and supportive way. As the academic term progresses, the advisor has a responsibility to review

Lastname	Firstname	Student ID	Exnum	Test Date	Alge	Rd	Ss	Arit	Clm
Martin	Mary	130301330	42770	19990929	–	–	–	57.96	–
Mann	Michael	112121112	42785	19990929	–	–	90.77	r	–

ALGE:Elementary Algebra
RD:Reading Comprehension
SS:Sentence Skills
SNMN:Sentence Meaning   Download Now!
ARIT:Arithmetic
CLM:College-Level Math
LGUS:Language Usage
RESK:Reading Skills

Back

The College Board

Exhibit 19.8.   Sample CPAMS Score Roster
Used by permission.

the student's progress in current courses in order to assist in planning future course selections, academic majors, and other related activities.

Another significant role for the advisor is to review the balance of course selections and workloads beyond the course placements already determined. Unless the assessments described earlier mandate the student into a full slate of courses, other course choices will need to be made. The academic advisor is familiar with the institutional environment in which the student must exist and is able to suggest courses that will complement those that have been otherwise required.

The primary goal of both the student and the advisor is student success. In many cases, course placement decisions have already been made in an attempt to ensure this success, but a strategic intervention by an alert academic advisor might well be the single factor that culminates this success.

Early Intervention Instruments

In recent years, much emphasis has been placed on the importance of a meaningful first-year experience in helping students to optimize their collegiate opportunities and success. Improved orientation efforts, freshman seminar and academic success courses, and yearlong colloquia, symposia, and guest lecturers have characterized many of these programs.

All of the information made available through the admissions and course placement assessment instruments might also be used extensively in a first-year experience program. A variety of other instruments have also been used in such programs. Five such instruments are described here. Each represents a different type of approach, intervention, or expected outcome. Several of these instruments focus on the assessment of noncognitive variables in determining student success.

The College Student Inventory

The College Student Inventory (CSI) is the essence of the comprehensive Noel-Levitz Retention Management System (RMS). This questionnaire contains 194 items that represent nineteen different scales that are reported in five broad categories (academic motivation, social motivation, general coping skills, receptivity to support services, and initial impression).

Results are reported in two formats, one for the student and one for the advisor. The Student Report contains a set of specific recommendations for achieving success and both a graphic representation and a narrative description of four of the broad categories just listed. The Advisor/Counselor Report (see Exhibit 19.9) contains the same graphic representation and includes the fifth category and the Summary of Academic Motivation, which identifies the student's potential difficulties and proneness to drop out.

A third report, the RMS College Summary and Planning Report, is generated for broader institutional planning but is not likely to be made available for individual advisor use.

The CSI Advisor/Counselor Report provides specific recommendations for each student, all of which have been reported on the Student Report as well. Clearly these suggestions provide a framework on which to establish helpful relationships with students.

The RMS Advisor's Guide describes possible strategies to employ with students, including focusing early on the positive areas indicated, establishing sources for improvement, and enacting appropriate follow-up behaviors by both the student and the advisor.

Another use of the CSI data during interactions with students is for advisors to identify institutional deficiencies, inaccuracies, obstacles to success, and other characteristics that might impede student learning, satisfaction, and development on a large scale. Advisors should then initiate actions that will serve to remedy these situations.

The Myers-Briggs Type Indicator

The Myers-Briggs Type Indicator (MBTI) is one of the most frequently used personality assessments used with college students. Its combination of brevity and utility makes it attractive in many collegiate settings.

College Student Inventory™
Advisor/Counselor Report

Jane C. Doe, Freshman
Female, Age 22, ID#000000021
Demonstration University
June 1, 1999

Instructions

This is a report of Jane's results based on the College Student Inventory. Please give her a thorough explanation of her student copy. If you agree with the recommendations, gently encourage her to follow them. When possible, try to make the arrangements yourself as a way of reducing motivational barriers. But avoid attempting any psychological counseling if not professionally trained for such work. Above all, be sure to protect the confidentiality of the present report. Please see the RMS Advisor's Guide for more details.

Summary of Academic Motivation[1]

Summary scores are expressed on a stanine scale:
9 = very high, 5 = average, and 1 = very low

Dropout proneness 7
Predicted academic difficulty 4
Educational stress 4
Receptivity to institutional help 6
For greater detail, see Motivational Assessment

Motivational Assessment	Perc. Rank	Very low		Ave		Very high
Academic Motivation		VL	L	A	H	VH
Study habits	14	x				
Intellectual interests	14	x				
Academic confidence	69				x	
Desire to finish college	91					x
Attitude toward educators	2	x				
Social Motivation						
Self-reliance	36		x			
Sociability	79				x	
Leadership	68				x	
General Coping						
Ease of Transition	98					x
Family emotional support	2	x				
Openness	96					x
Career planning	8	x				
Sense of financial security	79				x	
Receptivity to Support Services						
Academic assistance	18	x				
Personal counseling	91					x
Social enrichment	76				x	
Career counseling	71				x	
Initial Impression[1]	31		x			

Internal Validity   Excellent

Specific Recommendations for Jane

The strength of each recommendation is indicated by its priority score (0 = low, 10 = high):

a. Discuss an unwanted habit with counselor 8.5
b. Get help in selecting an occupation 8.3
c. Discuss the qualifications for occupations 8.3
d. Get help in meeting new friends 8.2
e. Discuss emotional tensions with counselor 8.2
f. Discuss family problems with counselor 8.0
g. Discuss job market for college graduates 7.9

Notice

To protect the student's privacy, she should be allowed to recover and remove this report at any time.

Student Background Information

High School Academics

Senior Year GPA	**B + average**
Class size	**1–49**
Program	**Commercial**
Perceived Stds.	**Average**

Noncredit activities

Athletics	
Fine Arts	**yes**
Leadership	**yes**
Misc. Groups	**yes**
Oral Expression	**yes**
Science	
Written Expression	**yes**

Family Background

Native language	**English**
Racial origin	**White**
Mother's education	**H.S. diploma**
Father's education	**H.S. diploma**
Marital status	**Single, no plans**
Miles from family	**10–50**

Admissions Test Scores

ACT Composite	**27–30**
SAT (V + M)	**n/a**

College Experience

Housing	**Own apt./house**
Degree sought	**Master's**
Plans to study	**15 hrs./week**

Other Indications[1]
Desires to transfer

[1]This information is not shown on the student's copy.

Noel-Levitz
Iowa City, Iowa

Exhibit 19.9. College Student Inventory Advisor/Counselor Report.

The MBTI questionnaire indicates a student's preferences for interacting with the environment and for making decisions. Four polar scales (extraversion-introversion, sensing-intuiting, thinking-feeling, and judging-perceiving) are used to describe the student's preferences. An individual's score is represented by a four-letter combination of interacting preferences. Each combination is described by the characteristics associated with the four separate poles (Gordon and Carberry, 1984; Murray, 1984).

The scores and characteristics are not value-laden, that is, extraverted students are not judged to be better than introverted ones, those who solve problems intuitively are not considered better than those who do so more systematically, nor are those students who show little emotion deemed inferior to those who show much.

Knowledge of students' views of the college environment and how they process information to make decisions can aid the academic advisor in fostering the human aspect of the advising process. Coupling this awareness with knowledge of the institution; of its academic rigors, requirements, and resources; and of each student's background, abilities, and interests can help the academic advisor bring a multidimensional and dynamic element to the advising relationship.

Specifically, knowledge provided by the MBTI can assist advisors in helping students choose appropriate academic courses, programs, and majors; in challenging some students to reassess their decisions; and in identifying students' interpersonal strengths and weaknesses.

The Learning and Study Strategies Inventory

The Learning and Study Strategies Inventory (LASSI) is both a diagnostic and a prescriptive tool for improving student success. This seventy-seven-item self-scored instrument yields scores on ten academic success scales (attitude, motivation, time management, anxiety, concentration, information processing, selecting main ideas, study aids, self-testing, and test strategies). The scale names are self-explanatory in what they assess.

The ten scale scores are plotted on a profile sheet that displays the student's percentile rank in each success category and in comparison to national norms. The brevity, ease of administration, self-scoring, and immediate visual results offer an efficient instrument that can be used in a variety of campus success programs. A computerized version (E-LASSI) is also available (Weinstein, 1987).

Institutions using this instrument typically administer it to groups in orientation programs, college success courses, or periodic academic skill development workshops. Some institutions use the LASSI as both pre- and postmeasurement for determining programmatic, course, specific intervention, or individual student success. It is also possible for advisors to administer the LASSI to individual students when appropriate.

The LASSI helps the academic advisor to assist students who demonstrate deficiencies in learning strategies or study skills. Using it as a diagnostic instrument, the advisor can help the student identify potential reasons for performance in certain courses, especially when that performance is worse than expected. Such results are appropriate for use with both developmental students and skills-proficient students who might be aspiring to apply to certain graduate or professional schools later in their undergraduate careers.

Using the LASSI as a prescriptive instrument, the advisor can assist the student in targeting the severest deficiencies and in developing a plan to identify appropriate campus and community services that might foster improvement. In some areas the advisor will be able to provide direct assistance.

The Developmental Advising Inventory

The Developmental Advising Inventory (DAI) was originally developed through a research grant from the National Academic Advising Association. This instrument is based primarily on Chickering's (1969) vectors of young adult development, but it can also be used with nontraditional-age students. The DAI exhibits nine dimensions (intellectual, life planning, social, physical, emotional, sexual, cultural, spiritual, and political), each of which contains fifteen items. The original model has been expanded to reflect research on gender, diversity, and ethnicity issues.

The scores on each of these dimensions are presented in a wellness wheel format that displays either a relatively smooth or an out-of-balance, bumpy wheel, symbolic of the student's expected path to success in college (see Exhibit 19.10). In addition, students indicate their general satisfaction with their development on each item, as well as whether they would like to discuss the item with their advisor. A Goal Planning Schedule is included as part of the instrument (Dickson and McMahon, 1991).

The DAI has both group and individual applications and has recently been more directly linked to the academic curriculum. The recent application purports either the integration of a student development curriculum with the objectives and courses of the general education curriculum at the institution, or a separate curriculum. The separate curriculum might even result in a cocurricular major (for example, leadership development) with its own core of student development growth activities and a certificate of completion (Dickson, Sorochty, and Thayer, 1998).

The DAI Advisor's Guide suggests a series of five individual advising sessions totaling more than three hours, plus the student time to take and score the instrument between the first two sessions (Dickson and McMahon, 1988; Dickson and Thayer, 1993). Because this type of commitment is probably unrealistic for most individual advisors, especially faculty, group administrations and applications are more likely to be used. The most common administrations are in first-year seminar courses, residence hall units, Greek chapters, and learning resource centers.

Individual advisors should be aware that such an instrument is being used on the campus and should certainly take advantage of the data generated by it. The DAI Advisor's Guide also describes potential uses in the overall academic

Instructions

Plot the value on each spoke which corresponds to your score for that dimension. Then connect the plotted points on each spoke with the curved lines to see what your wheel looks like. The Yes-No boxes represent your satisfaction with the scores. This may help you decide which spokes you would like to improve.

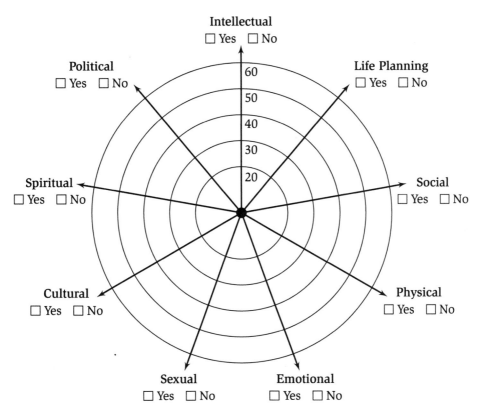

Exhibit 19.10. Developmental Scoring Wheel.

advising context, including for educational programming (with other campus resources), for career development (from choice of major through graduation), for utilization of the general education curriculum (skill development, the integration of disciplines, and the development of discipline-based assignments that include broader student development objectives), and to foster lifelong learning in both the intellectual and the social contexts of postcollege growth and development (Dickson and McMahon, 1991). A student guide is also now available with this instrument.

These uses reflect the essence of the (developmental) academic advising process, and data from an instrument such as the DAI serve to facilitate a productive advising relationship.

The Non-Cognitive Questionnaire

The Non-Cognitive Questionnaire (NCQ) is a twenty-three-item instrument that yields high and low scores on eight noncognitive variables (positive self-concept or confidence, realistic self-appraisal, understands and deals with racism, preference for long-range goals over short-term needs, availability of strong support person, successful leadership experience, demonstrated community service, and knowledge acquired in a field). The NCQ includes two items on educational expectations, eighteen Likert-type items on expectations about college and self-assessment, and three open-ended items on goals and accomplishments (Sedlacek, 1987).

The NCQ has been especially useful in the prediction of student persistence, and even GPAs, for African American minority students. One of the most significant findings in the research using this instrument is that it is most predictive of early academic success, as well as persistence, when used as a supplement to the traditional academic success predictors, such as ACT and SAT scores, rather than using the latter exclusively (Tracey and Sedlacek, 1987).

The bulk of the research on the NCQ has been on African American students. However, the NCQ has also been used successfully with a variety of nontraditional students, including international students, Hispanic students, and student athletes, as well as female students (Sedlacek, 1991; Boyer and Sedlacek, 1988; Fuertes and Sedlacek, 1995; Sedlacek and Adams-Gaston, 1992; Ancis and Sedlacek, 1997).

Clearly, academic advisors who have access to such scores as those shown on the NCQ are able to identify students whose attrition potential is high. Advisors can then intervene to suggest programs and services that would compensate for these negative variables.

All students come to campus with a set of noncognitive variables that can impede or enhance their success. It is incumbent upon the academic advisor to recognize the potential influence of these variables, to assist the student in efforts to compensate for or complement them, and ultimately to integrate these variables into the student's total undergraduate experience to enhance success.

The instruments described in this section provide the academic advisor with assessment tools that reflect the nonacademic skills and characteristics necessary for college success. The use of these instruments complements those that reflect the student's cognitive abilities.

Several other instruments that are designed to facilitate career development in students are also used in early intervention programs. These include the ACT DISCOVER and the Educational Testing Service's SIGI+ systems. These are described in Chapter Eleven of this book. The reader is encouraged to review these systems as well in order to maximize student development through the use of assessment instruments in academic advising.

Ongoing Assessment Tools

Although the instruments described in the previous section can be readministered as the student progresses in class standing, most of the standardized assessment instruments that are used in the academic advising process concentrate on the student's early experiences at the institution. Once a student has adapted, adjusted, and acclimated to the new environment, in terms of both academic learning and social integration, advisors must rely on their own institutional assessment mechanisms to gauge their students' progress and success. These tools include the following:

- Midterm, final, and cumulative grade reports
- Academic notices of warning, probation, or dean's list
- Computerized (or other) degree progress audits
- Results from portfolio reviews, rising-junior exams, and applications to restricted programs
- The advising interview

Advisors routinely receive the information obtained from the first three items and should certainly know how to interpret and use this information accordingly. Portfolio reviews and other measures that are used to determine admission to restricted programs can present either a positive or a negative advising encounter. Finally, each advising session provides an opportunity for the advisor to gather additional data about students and to provide additional information to them.

The states of Texas and Florida use their skills tests as ongoing assessments. Two-year community and junior college students must pass or demonstrate proficiency in all areas of the respective tests in order to earn an associate's degree. The Texas Academic Skill Program was mentioned earlier in the chapter. In Florida, students who do not earn an associate's degree must still pass in all areas of the College-Level Academic Skills Test or meet specific proficiency alternatives in order to earn a baccalaureate degree. The skill areas include writing an essay, English language skills, reading, and mathematics. In addition, all students must show evidence of writing a minimum of 24,000 cumulative words over the course of their program of study in order to graduate.

Two specific examples of ongoing assessment devices are worthy of mention. One provides an academic assessment; the other provides an extracurricular effort.

The ACT Collegiate Assessment of Academic Proficiency

The Collegiate Assessment of Academic Proficiency (CAAP) is an outcomes achievement measure geared to the end of the sophomore year. The instrument includes individual test modules in writing skills, reading, mathematics, science reasoning, and critical thinking, which are the skill areas typically targeted in the general education curriculum of most institutions. Because the modules are separate, institutions can select which ones to use, when to test, and whom to test; that is, the instrument can be tailored to the needs and overall assessment scheme of the institution.

Results of the tests are reported both for individuals and, in the aggregate, for the institution (see Exhibit 19.11). They can be used as pure outcomes measures of those skills that have been achieved by the end of the sophomore year. They can also be used as value-added outcomes measures, if the same test was given to the same students upon entry to the institution. In those institutions where the ACT was used for admission, the CAAP can be used as the direct value-added measure. It might also be used to estimate a student's likely success in certain upper-division academic work.

Obviously the academic advisor uses the results of this instrument in accord with the intent of the assessment program, be that to improve specific outcomes criteria over time or to predict future academic success. The specific advice provided or the advising strategy employed depends on the positive or negative results of the assessment.

Certain scores will confirm the student's choice of academic major; others will suggest that the student needs to reassess the intended major. Some scores will indicate minimal academic improvement since the student entered the institution, which could suggest a need for stronger motivational strategies. Still others might identify a deficiency in a specific skill area, in which additional coursework would be suggested.

In brief, academic skill assessments provided at the relative midpoint of the student's college career can provide a significant review of past performance and a preview of future success. The academic advisor is a pivotal force at this critical point in a student's undergraduate career.

The Student Development Transcript

The Student Development Transcript is not an assessment instrument per se; that is, it does not generate specific score results. Rather, it is a dynamic document that reflects the student's ongoing performance or involvement in growth and learning activities that are corollary and supplemental to the academic achievements normally recorded on academic transcripts. Examples of these activities are specific skill development workshops, wellness programs, human relations seminars, or community volunteer work.

Brown and Citrin (1977) suggest three possible formats for the student development transcript: (1) an experiential checklist that contains a variety of specific activities or experiences in which the student has participated (for example, attended a computer workshop or was elected to a student office); (2) a competency-based checklist that indicates performance and achievement levels (for example, has raised $1,200 in a fundraising effort for a sorority chapter); or (3) a portfolio of accomplishments, such as an award for service or a listing in the credits of a student theatrical production. A variety of adaptations and other reporting formats are possible, depending on the institution's goals, resources, and expected outcomes of such an effort.

Whether or not the student development transcript is formally adopted and structured by the institution, individual academic advisors can suggest the concept to their students. The cumulative record of involvement and achievement

CAAP
The Collegiate Assessment of Academic Proficiency
Student Report

Identification

Name	TIP , B
Student ID	
School Name	MI COLLEGE
School Code	22
Test Date	08/1999

For more information on the CAAP Student Report, please see the *CAAP Student Report Interpretive Guidelines*

Background Characteristics (self-reported)

Sex	Female	Cumulative GPA	3.01 – 3.50
Birthdate		Academic Major	Business
Ethnicity	White/Caucasian	Enrollment Status	Full-Time
English First Language	Yes	Enrolled as Freshman	Yes
Educational Level	Freshman	Educational Plans	Return to this school

Test Scores

Objective Test	Test Scores (40-80)	Subtest Scores (5-25)	% of local students at or below score*	% of students nationally at or below score
Writing Skills				
Usage/Mechanics				
Rhetorical Skills				
Mathematics	58		58	59
Algebra		15	71	64
Reading	65		70	67
Arts/Literature		19	89	91
Social Studies/Sciences		16	53	47
Critical Thinking	67		76	83
Science Reasoning	68		98	95

Writing (Essay) Test	(1-6)			
Composite		N/A		
Essay 1				
Essay 2				

* Figures are based on the students at your institution who took the same test(s).

Exhibit 19.11. The Collegiate Assessment of Academic Proficiency Student Report.

beyond the formal classroom is difficult to recall and re-create at the time of graduation, so students should be encouraged early in their experience to begin keeping such a record.

In addition to simply accumulating dates, events, and types of activities, this kind of transcript might enable advisors, through periodic review, to identify shortcomings in students' total collegiate experiences that could be rectified through future involvement. Advisors might suggest other activities that would provide students with additional learning experiences related to their chosen majors or anticipated careers. Still other reviews might stimulate students to seek out new resources or even develop resources of their own (for example, tutoring assistance, security escort services, or study groups).

The student development transcript provides both a self-assessment strategy for students and a method of demonstrating their achievements in areas outside their academic curriculum.

All of these instruments, reports, and processes provide the academic advisor with information that reflects students' growth and development well beyond their entrance into the school. The advisor who integrates a combination of these academic, social, and personal data into the overall advising process will provide students with a composite self-assessment and self-reflection, as well as a well-developed and realistic plan for future career, community, and personal success.

Graduate and Career Advising

Students desire and expect their college experiences to provide them with skills and opportunities for future employment. Many will aspire or be required to pursue a graduate or professional school education upon their graduation. The focus of the academic advisor's role changes at this point, as students near the graduation threshold.

By the end of the junior year, students and advisors have utilized many of the assessment instruments discussed in this chapter to determine appropriate degree programs. Students have begun to realize and assess their own potential for future success, whether in the workplace or in advanced academic study. For those who plan the latter, the assessment cycle begins again as a new set of instruments faces them.

Academic advisors of upper-division students enrolled in their academic disciplines are expected to have specific knowledge about the job and career opportunities and graduate school expectations in those disciplines. Score results from the following instruments provide further opportunities for addressing specific advising issues.

Graduate and Professional School Examinations

Admission to most graduate and professional programs is based on a combination of factors, including various calculations of GPAs, written essays, letters of recommendation from various sources, previous work or volunteer experiences, personal interviews, and standardized test scores. Some programs explicitly require minimum scores, similar to the pattern used in course placement exams at the undergraduate entry level; others use a range of standardized test scores that is weighted with some combination of the other factors noted earlier.

Most academic advisors are familiar with the examinations that are preferred or required in their disciplines or related fields of advanced study. The most common of these exams are the Graduate Record Examination, for most discipline-oriented programs; the Graduate Management Admission Test, for business-related programs; the Law School Admission Test (LSAT), for legal studies; the Medical, Dental, or Veterinary Admissions Tests, for those health-related programs; and the Praxis Examination Series for the licensure of public school teachers.

The initiative to obtain academic advising assistance on the basis of these test scores might rest solely with the student, because advisors do not always routinely receive these scores. When such scores are received, whether directly or through the student, the academic advisor has the opportunity to engage in substantial career (or indeed life) planning with the student.

Obviously, high scores or scores meeting minimal cutoff criteria are relatively easy to use. The advisor's role is congratulatory and to acknowledge the student's success. This is not to say that all students with such scores will obtain their first-choice postgraduate options, but the advising goals are clearly positively directed.

Students who receive lower scores present a different role for the advisor to play. This role is even more significant than the one advisors play for first-year students still adjusting to college life. This role helps students adjust to "real" life. Two strategies seem to evolve in this situation, depending on the relative merit of the score achieved; a combination of the two strategies described is also appropriate.

One strategy is to help the student accept his or her scores and decide whether to retest, assess which programs are more appropriate or realistic, or reconsider certain postgraduate or even career plans. The role is one of support and encouragement, which has (it is hoped) been maintained throughout the advising relationship with the student.

The second strategy is also one of support and requires review of the student's overall strengths and weaknesses according to the additional admissions criteria mentioned earlier. The advisor might determine that an improved essay, additional or stronger letters of recommendation, or additional practical experience in a field might be appropriate to balance the score and strengthen the student's overall application. The possibility of a delayed application might also be discussed.

The receipt of such test scores can stimulate student reactions that range from disappointment and depression to extreme euphoria. The academic advisor must be prepared for this full range of results and reactions and must be capable of employing different advising strategies, perhaps within the same hour.

Other Self-Assessment Resources

Most institutions provide a variety of support systems and programs that serve to enhance postgraduate plans and applications. Discipline-oriented clubs and organizations provide students with further insights into the discipline itself through guest lectures, field trips, workshops, and conferences. Career centers frequently offer workshops on resume writing, interviewing skills, and portfolio development, in addition to specific job and career fairs. The explosion of Internet and World Wide Web resources provides a unique opportunity for students to better assess their skills and abilities, especially in job seeking. These electronic resources provide not only instant availability to information about jobs worldwide, but also significant insight into the range of skills, characteristics, and expectations required of future employees. Early recognition of this insight affords students the time and opportunity to build their expertise accordingly.

The role of the academic advisor in making use of these resources is simply awareness, encouragement, and referral. Students might not readily appreciate or acknowledge the value of many of their extracurricular or cocurricular activities. Often they are too focused on academic performance (and social integration). The advisor's credibility and suggestions can provide the impetus for students to take early advantage of these resources. Participation in such programs contributes to students' self-assessment, which can be discussed, verified, and modified with the advisor.

Clearly the most traumatic time for college students is their arrival and entry into the college environment. Their uncertainty, apprehension, confusion, and surprise all demonstrate the need for well-developed student support programs across campus. The academic advisor is both a provider of direct support to the student and a catalyst for helping the student use other resources as well.

The next most traumatic time for college students, however, is when they are about to leave this environment to which they have adjusted, especially as graduates (rather than because of attrition). To leave the safe, comfortable environment of the campus presents yet another adjustment. The academic advisor's knowledge, information, challenge, and support of students at this critical point might well be the most significant of the entire relationship. This time of transition cannot be taken lightly or for granted; it certainly cannot be ignored.

Strategies for Using Assessment

Different advising strategies exist that enable advisors to utilize the types of assessment instruments described in this chapter, as well as other information and materials available on the local campus. Three such strategies are briefly described as follows:

1. *Skills strategy:* Because the full range of assessment instruments described in this chapter includes assessment of academic and workplace skills, students must demonstrate certain levels of proficiency in many of these areas. The advi-

sor can assist students in recognizing the need for writing, speaking, research and analysis, organization and leadership, interpersonal, and quantitative reasoning skills in the constantly changing workplace, and in selecting course, program, and cocurricular options that promote these skills (Grites, 1983).

2. *Course and curriculum strategy.* Grites and Colijn (1989) offer a strategy for course selection that yields multiple benefits, lessons, and skills from each course that is used to fulfill curricular requirements. This strategy includes, in addition to nurturing the skills suggested in the previous paragraph, the fostering of global awareness, the use of independent study courses as a mode of learning, internships, international study, additional concentrations or minors, and the development of understanding of organizations and contexts. Grites and Colijn suggest a checklist format to record and visualize how each course can or should result in multiple benefits.

3. *Human capital strategy.* This strategy is based on economic principles, is geared toward the workplace environment, and refers to any condition that increases a worker's productivity. Shaffer (1997) describes various types of investment in human capital, including many of the job-transferable skills listed in the previous paragraph. He further describes the ability to learn quickly (reducing the learning curve), to advance learning continuously (lifelong learning), and to accept geographic mobility.

Another aspect of human capital that is especially relevant for today's college students is their investment in good health practices. Alcohol abuse (for example, binge drinking), drug experimentation or addiction, and unsafe sexual practices reduce a person's human capital, especially because these practices are not likely to change significantly just because a student graduates.

More recently, Shaffer (1998) has included multicultural competence in his array of human capital skills. This skill is not simply awareness of the existence of various cultures. Instead, Shaffer advocates an in-depth study of a specific geographic region of the world. This would include studying the history, cultures, languages, customs, politics, economics, and ideologies of the region, as well as recognizing one's own preconceptions, attitudes, and biases about the peoples of the region.

Obviously, academic advisors are in a position to assist students in maximizing their human capital through course and program selection and through nonacademic, lifestyle practices.

Conclusion

The use of assessment instruments in academic advising clearly enhances the productivity of the advising relationship. The reviews provided in this chapter might initially frustrate some advisors, advising administrators, and indeed academic administrators. The breadth of concepts and the array of available instruments along with the potential costs required to implement them can clearly seem ominous.

Rather than quickly dismiss such powerful potential, however, institutions should examine the opportunities made available through such assessment tools and seek to develop an assessment scheme that will facilitate a strong academic advising program and result in competent and satisfied students as graduates. Following are some observations and recommendations for developing such a scheme:

- A wealth of assessment instruments and data are available to advisors, including academic test scores, career aspirations, course placements, personality traits, and ongoing skill assessments. In fact, just about any type of information an academic advisor might need is likely to be made available through some assessment instrument.

- These instruments seem to be predominantly front-loaded. That is, a significant number and variety of them are geared to initial admission, initial course placement, and initial psychological, social, and personal adjustment to the campus. A number of specific instruments have been created to assess the culmination of the college experience. These are in fact new admission instruments for graduate and professional study, as well as indicators used in institutional outcomes assessment. By comparison, the middle part of the college experience is generally lacking in available instruments.

- Academic advisors cannot be expected to use any of the available instruments effectively without the benefit of specific training in their use. Score reports and raw data can be misinterpreted or misused without such a training effort. Further, to ensure training effectiveness, the selection, evaluation, and reward of academic advisors must also be considered. Part Four of this book addresses these aspects.

- Individual scores on many of the instruments described should always be used in a broad context. Even when specific cutoff scores determine a hard-and-fast decision (usually for course placement), the advisor must be alert and sensitive to other factors provided by the other data made available. For example, if a student is placed into a lower level course than expected, the advisor can compensate the student's discontent by explaining the relative skill levels of other students and the progression of skill development toward mastery. The advisor might acknowledge other strengths the student has shown (in or out of the classroom) and encourage the student to participate in and contribute to other campus programs, activities, and events.

- Advisors can, and indeed institutions should, determine what combination of assessments, skills, characteristics, and programs is most appropriate for their students. These might include specific assessment scores for academic skill performance, as well as a variety of measures of noncognitive variables that affect student performance and success. Whatever the combination, it should reflect an effort to meet student needs and goals, the advising program's objectives, and the institution's mission and goals.

Alverno College provides an excellent example of such an institutional effort. Faculty and staff at Alverno developed the Student as Learner Inventory to facilitate an integrative approach to teaching, learning, advising, and research that is specific to that campus, its curriculum, and its expected student outcomes (Deutsch and others, 1995).

This chapter has provided academic advisors with an awareness of the multiple types of assessment instruments available to them and of their potential use. Use of these instruments will enhance advisors' roles and the development of their students. This array of instruments and concepts provides many of the tools for assisting students in all aspects of their collegiate experience.

The instruments themselves simply provide data. Each institution's academic administration must ensure that these data are accessible and made available in the most timely, efficient, and effective ways. Each advising program administrator must ensure that adequate training efforts are provided for advisors. Each academic advisor must accept the responsibility to learn how to use, and must in fact use, the data made available to them. Students must ultimately assume responsibility for reviewing the data, for seeking advice, and for enacting behaviors that will contribute to their overall growth, development, and well-being. Only with such an integrated approach will the use of assessment instruments truly support academic advising.

References

Ancis, J. R., and Sedlacek, W. E. "Predicting the Academic Achievement of Female Students Using the SAT and Noncognitive Variables." *College and University*, 1997, *72*(3), 1–8.

Boyer, S. P., and Sedlacek, W. E. "Noncognitive Predictors of Academic Success for International Students: A Longitudinal Study." *Journal of College Student Development*, 1988, *29*(3), 218–223.

Brown, R. D., and Citrin, R. S. "A Student Development Transcript: Assumptions, Uses, and Formats." *Journal of College Student Personnel*, 1977, *18*(3), 163–168.

Chickering, A. W. *Education and Identity.* San Francisco: Jossey-Bass, 1969.

Deutsch, B., and others. "Integrating Teaching, Advising, and Research Tools: The Student as Learner Inventory as Retention and Learning Intervention." Paper presented at the Association for Institutional Research annual meeting, Boston, May 1995.

Dickson, G. L., and McMahon, T. R. *Advisor's Guide to the Developmental Advising Inventory.* Pullman: Washington State University, 1988.

Dickson, G. L., and McMahon, T. R. "The Developmental Advising Inventory: A New Approach to Academic Advising." *NACADA Journal*, 1991, *11*(1), 34–50.

Dickson, G. L., Sorochty, R. W., and Thayer, J. D. "Theory to Practice: Creating a Student Development Curriculum Using the Developmental Advising Inventory." *NASPA Journal*, 1998, *35*(2), 119–136.

Dickson, G. L., and Thayer, J. D. *Advisor's Guide to the Developmental Advising Inventory.* (Rev. ed.) Kettering, Ohio: Developmental Advising Inventories, 1993.

Fuertes, J. N., and Sedlacek, W. E. "Using Noncognitive Variables to Predict the Grades and Retention of Hispanic Students." *College Student Affairs Journal*, 1995, *14*(2), 30–36.

Gordon, V. N., and Carberry, J. D. "The Myers-Briggs Type Indicator: A Resource for Developmental Advising." *NACADA Journal,* 1984, *4*(2), 75–81.

Grites, T. J. "A Skills Approach to Career Development." *NACADA Journal,* 1983, *3*(1), 13–16.

Grites, T. J., and Colijn, G. J. "Coherent Curricular Choices: A Strategy to Enrich a College Education." *NACADA Journal,* 1989, *9*(2), 11–15.

Murray, G. L. "Improving Advising Through the Use of Cognitive Style." *NACADA Journal,* 1984, *4*(1), 17–22.

Sedlacek, W. E. "Black Students on White Campuses: Twenty Years of Research." *Journal of College Student Personnel,* 1987, *28*(6), 484–495.

Sedlacek, W. E. "Using Noncognitive Variables in Advising Nontraditional Students." *NACADA Journal,* 1991, *11*(1), 75–82.

Sedlacek, W. E., and Adams-Gaston, J. "Predicting the Academic Success of Student-Athletes Using SAT and Noncognitive Variables." *Journal of Counseling & Development,* 1992, *70*(6), 724–727.

Shaffer, L. S. "A Human Capital Approach to Academic Advising." *NACADA Journal,* 1997, *17*(1), 5–12.

Shaffer, L. S. "Maximizing Human Capital by Developing Multicultural Competence." *NACADA Journal,* 1998, *18*(2), 21–27.

Tracey, T. J., and Sedlacek, W. E. "Prediction of College Graduation Using Noncognitive Variables by Race." *Measurement and Evaluation in Counseling and Development,* 1987, *19,* 177–184.

Weinstein, C. E. *LASSI User's Manual.* Clearwater, Fla.: H & H, 1987.

Part Four

Training, Evaluation, and Recognition

At the core of every successful academic advising program are three fundamental components: training, evaluation, and recognition and reward. If academic advisors are to be successful in their work, they must be given the tools and provided with the experiences that will enhance their understanding, knowledge, and skills. In addition, there must be a mechanism through which the effectiveness of the advising program and the strengths and weaknesses of the advisors who deliver the program are evaluated. Finally, there must be a systematic effort to recognize and reward exemplary performance. It is so clear that the absence or weakness of only one of these three components compromises the effectiveness and reduces the quality of advising services on the campus. Yet the advising literature is consistent in its assertion that these three elements are the weakest links in the development of quality advising services. Because these three functions are so critical, they are the focus of Part Four of this book.

Margaret C. King, in Chapter Twenty, reviews the current status of academic advising training programs and provides a five-component framework for organizing the advisor training program. King continues by suggesting that good advisor training programs must attend to concepts, information, and relationship skills. She concludes with several practical suggestions for planning advisor training programs.

In Chapter Twenty-One, Linda C. Higginson expands the ideas presented by King. She proposes a framework for training advisors that consists of three critical components: supporting principles, delivery considerations, and assessment issues. Within this framework, Higginson weaves together the concepts, knowledge, and relationship skills discussed by King. Readers will find her extensive inventory of topics extremely useful.

In the final chapter on training issues, Phillip J. Farren and Faye Vowell provide a set of solid concepts that support best practices in advisor training. Focusing on diversity among institutions, and therefore among advisor training needs, Farren and Vowell present components of a model training program, key processes for improving advising, and several examples of best training practices in action.

Michael L. Lynch, in Chapter Twenty-Three, provides an overview of the important elements in the assessment of an advising program. Focusing on the standards delineated by the Council for the Advancement of Standards, Lynch brings clarity to the levels of program evaluation and the types of evaluation that should be undertaken. Finally, he effectively delineates the challenges associated with the assessment of campus advising.

Elizabeth G. Creamer and Delores W. Scott, the authors of Chapter Twenty-Four, concentrate on the evaluation of individual advisors. They review students' expectations that advisors be available, knowledgeable, and helpful, and they discuss the utility of several methods for collecting data on advisor effectiveness. The final section of this chapter defines four key elements in the development of an evaluation program for individual advisors.

Chapter Twenty-Five, the final chapter in Part Four, focuses on the area that is perhaps the weakest link in the development of quality advising programs: providing recognition and reward for exemplary performance as an advisor. Although most campus administrators agree on the importance of academic advising, there is little evidence that advising is valued on most college campuses. Thomas J. Kerr provides ample testimony on the lack of effective reward programs for academic advisors, but he also makes several suggestions for providing extrinsic rewards for advisors. Finally, Kerr proposes a model for categorizing advisor recognition programs and provides examples of programs that are currently in place on several college campuses.

Chapter Twenty

Designing Effective Training
for Academic Advisors

Margaret C. King

cademic advising has evolved from a simplistic, routine, perfunctory course-scheduling activity to a complex process of student development requiring comprehensive knowledge, skills, attitudes, and behaviors that can be learned and enhanced. As defined by David Crockett (1984, p. 3):

> Academic advising is a developmental process which assists students in the clarification of their life/career goals and in the development of educational plans for the realization of these goals. It is a decision-making process by which students realize their maximum educational potential through communication and information exchanges with an advisor; it is ongoing, multifaceted, and the responsibility of both students and advisor. The advisor serves as a facilitator of communication, a coordinator of learning experiences through course and career planning and academic progress review, and an agent of referral to other campus agencies as necessary.

The evolution in the complexity of advising has been caused by a variety of factors, including an increasingly diverse student population, curricular complexity, concern about student retention, and consumer awareness. To ensure that academic advisors are prepared to address these factors and to work with students effectively, a comprehensive and ongoing advisor training program is essential.

Another reason that advisor training is so important is noted by Thomas Brown (1998, p. 41): "There can be no accountability of equitable evaluation of the work that advisors do without an educational component that describes advising needs and expectations, defines roles and responsibilities, and provides opportunities to promote the skills fundamental to developmental advising.

Clearly, faculty and professional advisors have differing needs and responsibilities in academic advising; however, there are many advising skills, functions, and information that apply to all advisors." It should be noted that counselors, paraprofessionals, and peer advisors have different needs and responsibilities as well.

The primary goal of an advisor training program is to increase the effectiveness of advising services provided to students, thus increasing student satisfaction and persistence. There are, however, other benefits as well. Portia Weston (1993) has identified the following additional goals, or outcomes, of advisor training: enhanced communication among faculty and staff; better integration of the academic advisors into the culture of the college; reduced barriers between the academic, student affairs, and administrative divisions of the institution; creation of a better understanding of the contribution the individual advisor makes to the process of educating students; and creation of a more student-centered institution.

The Current Status of Advisor Training

Questions about the status of advisor training on college campuses have been asked in all five of the ACT national surveys of academic advising and are summarized by Wesley Habley and Ricardo Morales in the monograph *Current Practices in Academic Advising: Final Report on ACT's Fifth National Survey of Academic Advising* (1998). In 1983 the second survey noted that "many institutions are providing only a minimum of training to those involved in advising. This most often takes the form of an annual orientation meeting at the beginning of the fall term. Only about a quarter of the institutions conduct regularly scheduled in-service workshops during the year" (p. 4). In 1987 the survey was modified "to separate the advising done in academic units (departments) from that done in academic advising offices (centers)" (p. 4). In survey results from that year, a reference to training stated "the most significant methods by which advising can be improved are seen as both the least effective and the least improved areas in the organization and administration of campus advising programs" (p. 5). The fourth national survey noted that "training, accountability, evaluation and reward still rate below the midpoint on the effectiveness scale" (p. 5).

The results of the fifth survey showed the following:

- Training was provided for advisors by 34.8 percent of the academic departments; 23 percent of those departments required formal training.
- The most common format for training in the academic department continues to be a single workshop of one day or less per year (35 percent). Six percent of the institutions surveyed had a single workshop of more than one day per year, 20 percent had a series of short workshops throughout the year, and 33 percent provided individualized training based on advisor needs.

• The most common focus for training in the academic department continues to be on information and facts, with some attention paid to concepts such as definition and importance of advising. Skills received less emphasis than in previous surveys. Unfortunately, as Habley notes, data "support the traditional definition of advising as information giving that leads to the selection and scheduling of courses" (p. 27).

• Within advising offices, individualized training is the dominant training format (44 percent of institutions surveyed). Thirty-one percent offered a series of short workshops throughout the year, 16 percent offered a single workshop of one day or less per year, and 5 percent offered a single workshop of more than one day per year.

• Factual information continues to be the dominant focus of the training within advising offices, with a limited focus on advising concepts and relationship skills.

When asked to rate the effectiveness of their institutional advising program in terms of implementing training programs for advisors, the ranking was 2.89, up slightly from a 2.70 ranking in 1992 but still below the midpoint of the five-point effectiveness scale. As Habley and Morales note, "although we have made positive strides, there are many campuses that do not and will not see the importance of academic advising and, as a result, will never address important issues in academic advising" (p. 65). Training is one key issue.

An Organizing Framework for Planning an Academic Advisor Training Program

As an institution begins to design an academic advisor training program, consideration should be given to the following questions:

1. How is academic advising defined on your campus and how do you want it to be defined?
2. What knowledge, skills, and behaviors do advisors need to advise students successfully?
3. What knowledge, skills, and behaviors do advisors currently possess?
4. What needs to happen to close the gap between the skills needed and the skills currently possessed?

An organized approach to designing an advisor training program begins with one person in charge but with a team approach to the planning, which allows for different perspectives and promotes ownership. Ideally the team would include representatives of the group to be trained as well as representatives from academic affairs and student affairs, and students. The steps in designing and implementing an academic advising training program would include the following:

1. Reviewing the mission of the institution and the mission of advising
2. Identifying needs
3. Establishing goals and objectives
4. Selecting appropriate content, strategies, and methods
5. Implementing the program
6. Evaluating the program.

Reviewing the Institutional Mission

An advisor training program should evolve from the fundamental structure and function of the institution—in other words, from the institutional mission statement. It is important to articulate the relationship between advisor training and institutional mission, which is often done in an advising mission statement. If such a statement does not exist, it would be important to create one.

The *NACADA Faculty Advising Training Facilitator's Manual* (Kerr, 1996) discusses the relationship between institutional mission and advisor training, noting that "common phrases like 'development of the whole student,' 'lifelong learning,' 'preparing an informed citizenry' and 'develop broad intellectual skills' can become the focus of goals, objectives, and expected outcomes in an advisor development program" (p. 9).

Identifying Needs

It is important to determine the needs to be addressed by the training program. Data collected from both individual advisor and program evaluations can be an excellent source of ideas for training topics. Gathering input from experienced advisors as well as from those to be trained can be valuable. If evaluative data does not exist, a campuswide (macro) or program (micro) needs analysis could be done to identify the issues related to academic advising that the training program needs to address. It is critical that there be input from faculty, staff, and students in this process.

Establishing Goals and Objectives

Goals and objectives for the program need to be *s*pecific, *m*easurable, *a*chievable, *r*ealistic, and *t*angible—in other words, SMART. An example of a SMART objective could be to increase faculty understanding of the role and function of the career planning office. This objective is specific, it can be measured by determining if there is an increase in advisor referrals to the office, it is achievable by having staff from the office participate in the training program, it is realistic, and it is tangible. In establishing goals and objectives, it is important to consider the institutional attitude toward academic advising; for example, if there is not a strong institutional commitment to advising, there may be little or no support for training that goes beyond the information content. It is also important to look at any prior training and build on it.

Determining whether training will be preservice or in-service will be an issue as well. Preservice training topics might include a description of the advising system, the definition of advising, responsibilities of the advisor and advisee, tools for advising, how to access student records, review of procedures for drop-add and other advising activities, and so on—in other words, what an advisor needs to get started. In-service training topics might include a review of the preservice topics but with a greater focus on communication skills, referral skills, campus resources, and the like.

It is important that the goals and objectives for the training program be based on basic knowledge about the field of advising—the literature is full of information about advising philosophy, best practices, ethics, and so on—as well as an understanding of student development. As Virginia Gordon (1984) notes, viewing academic advising within a student development framework can provide direction and continuity. Understanding how students develop—intellectually, personally and socially—is important, as is viewing each student as a unique individual with different needs, rates of growth, and maturity.

Selecting Appropriate Content, Strategies, and Methods

There are three specific factors to be considered in planning advisor training. The first factor is content—What should the program include? Discussed in more depth in Chapter Twenty-One, content can be broken down into three major areas:

1. *Conceptual:* What do advisors need to understand—for example, definition of advising, the role of advising in student development, the relationship between advising and retention, and so on?

2. *Informational:* What do advisors need to know—for example, programs, policies, referral services, and so on?

3. *Relational:* What skills do advisors need to possess—such as listening skills, communication skills, interviewing skills, and so on?

The second factor is the audience—Who is going to receive this training? Are they faculty, full-time advisors, counselors, paraprofessionals, or peers? What is their skill level? How capable are they of understanding and applying the basic principles necessary to perform as an advisor? What is their level of experience? How long have they served as advisors? A training program for advisors new to the campus would be quite different from a program for experienced advisors. Finally, What is their willingness to participate in advising and in the training program?

Faculty advisors generally have knowledge of advising issues related to their specific disciplines. They can provide detailed information about courses and programs in their departments, and the rationale for course and program requirements. They are generally knowledgeable about educational and career opportunities related to their fields. However, faculty advisors may not have knowledge about student development theory, about the relationship between academic and career advising, and about the importance of communication skills in building a relationship with their advisees. Faculty also may not be as knowledgeable as full-time advisors about campus resources, policies, and procedures.

Faculty willingness to participate in training as well as in advising may be an issue as well. Among teaching, committee work, research, and the like, advising may have a low priority, particularly if the administrative priority is low. Some faculty simply are not interested. For many there is no reward. In some cases a collective bargaining agreement can limit what faculty can and will do. Also, some may subscribe to the "bootstraps philosophy," that students should be able to do things for themselves.

All of these things need to be considered in designing an advisor training program for faculty. Consequently, a comprehensive training program for faculty advisors will need to focus on all three content areas—conceptual, informational, and relational—and there will need to be real incentives to get faculty to participate.

Designing a training program for full-time advisors or counselors could be quite different. Here are staff who may not possess in-depth knowledge of courses, programs, and education and career opportunities in a given discipline, yet they are generally knowledgeable about the broad range of institutional programs, policies, and procedures. Other strengths may include knowledge of student development theory, knowledge of other services available to students, and knowledge of communication and referral skills. Consequently, depending on the background and skills they bring to their position, initial training for full-time advisors is critical, and the most important focus would be on information.

Training programs for paraprofessionals and peers would be different as well and would be based on the responsibilities they are expected to assume and the depth of knowledge they are expected to possess. Such training would include components that help the peer and paraprofessional deal with the importance of objectivity in communicating information, as well as components dealing with time and stress management for the advisor.

The third factor to be considered in planning an advisor training program is the strategies and methods to be used in conducting the training, such as external presenters, panel sessions, case studies, brainstorming activities, videos, discussion groups, and so on. These need to be selected on the basis of viewing advisors as adult learners. Adult learners are diverse, and they bring a variety of life experiences, interests, values, and commitments to the learning experience. Consequently, it is important that they be engaged in the learning process and that a variety of strategies and methods be used in training rather than delivering the training only in a lecture-presentation format. Examples of such methods can be found in Chapter Twenty-Five. Overall, it is important to remember that the goal is to help advisors clarify roles and responsibilities that will enhance the quality of their interaction with students.

In summary, "successful advisor development programs are derived from the integration of content areas with the skill, experience and willingness to participate of the advisors that the program is intended to serve" (Habley, 1992).

Implementing the Program

In preparing for implementation, the team coordinating the training should work to gain administrative support. This is critical to the success of the advisor training program because it reinforces the importance of the program. That support can be demonstrated early by letters from the president, provost, or dean who appoints individuals to the planning team, by having that individual address the planning team at its initial meeting, or by having him or her address the faculty and staff at the initial training session.

It is important to publicize the training program widely and, if possible, to offer incentives to attend, such as food, free materials, access to pin numbers, and inclusion in the reward structure. A letter from the president, provost, or dean inviting faculty and staff to the training would be ideal, as would inclusion of information about the training in campus publications and fliers and in public announcements at faculty senate meetings and other public forums. Clear support should also be expressed at dean and department head meetings.

The training program should be scheduled at times when faculty and staff are free. If that is not possible, multiple sessions should be offered. The bottom line is, make it as easy as possible for advisors to attend. The location of the training program should be appealing and could be either on or off campus. On campus may be more convenient, but interruptions are less likely off campus.

Upon completion of the training program or session, thank-you letters can be sent to participants, with copies sent to their supervisors.

Evaluating the Program

The evaluation process needs to be considered at the beginning of the planning process and should be directly related to the goals of the advisor training program. Evaluation can be designed for a single session or activity or for the entire training experience. Evaluation can focus on participant satisfaction with the training program or session or on what the participants have learned as a result of the training. For example, if a primary objective was to improve advisor knowledge of the correct procedure for dropping and adding classes, the measure of effectiveness might be a decrease in the number of drop-add forms filed improperly; or as mentioned earlier, if the objective was to increase advisor knowledge of the role and function of the career planning office, the measure of effectiveness might be an increase in advisor referrals to that office. Another way to evaluate is to review the program evaluation data that called attention to the need for specific training and see if there is improvement in that aspect of the program. The bottom line is, it is important to know whether people gained something from the program and whether there has been improvement in the needs or issues identified at the beginning of the process.

Conclusion

As this chapter has noted, academic advising has evolved into a complex process of student development requiring comprehensive knowledge, skills, attitudes, and behaviors. As a result, a comprehensive advisor training program is essential. The steps in designing and implementing such a program should include reviewing the mission of the institution and the mission of advising; identifying needs; establishing goals and objectives; selecting appropriate content, strategies, and methods; implementing the program; and evaluating the program.

A number of external resources are available to assist in the development and implementation of an advisor training program, including the following:

- *The NACADA Consultant's Bureau* provides assistance to colleges and universities in the review, establishment, development, and reorganization of advising services. Individuals and teams are available to assist institutions in any aspect of advising or to provide speakers and workshop facilitators.

- *The National Clearinghouse for Academic Advising* is a joint effort by NACADA and University College of the Ohio State University to promote the advancement of academic advising through the dissemination of resources and research pertinent to this educational endeavor.

- *The NACADA Faculty Advising Training Video and Manual* is a training package designed to increase understanding of the importance and complexity of advising, to describe a model of developmental advising and how it is best applied to advising situations, and to illustrate an unfolding advising relationship that demonstrates how informational, conceptual, and relational aspects can be applied when advising students. The video contains three types of material: eight advising scenarios (six of which show a developing relationship between a freshman student and her advisor and two of which are self-contained interviews), expert commentary on each scenario, and leading questions relating to each scenario. It is accompanied by a detailed facilitator's manual.

- *Academic Advising for Student Success and Retention* is a video-based training program that uses four videotapes ("Introduction and Foundation," "Communication and Relational Skills," "Advising Special Populations," and "Key Issues in Advising") as triggers to provide important content, introduce exercises and activities, and engage participant interest. A typical video segment lasts four to six minutes. The program also includes the "Leader's Guide" and the "Participant Book/Resource Guide."

- *The NACADA Summer Institute on Academic Advising* is a weeklong action-oriented institute that provides in-depth exploration of the issues and concerns of those involved with academic advising. The institute effectively integrates expert group presentations with small group discussions, workshops, and topical sessions led by skilled practitioners and organized by institutional type. Participants are asked to prepare and present an action plan for solving an advising challenge on their campus. Through these activities, participants develop a network of supportive colleagues across the nation.

References

Brown, T. "Designing Advisor Training/Development Programs." In *NACADA/ACT Academic Advising Summer Institute Session Guide.* Manhattan, Kans.: National Academic Advising Association, 1998.

Crockett, D. S. *Advising Skills, Techniques and Resources.* Iowa City, Iowa: American College Testing Program, 1984.

Gordon, V. N. "Training Professional and Paraprofessional Advisors." In R. B. Winston, T. K. Miller, S. C. Ender, and T. J. Grites (eds.), *Developmental Academic Advising: Addressing Students' Educational, Career, and Personal Needs.* San Francisco: Jossey Bass, 1984.

Habley, W. R. "Developing an Advisor Training Program." Unpublished outline of presentation at ACT Summer Institute on Academic Advising, 1992.

Habley, W. R., and Morales, R. H. *Current Practices in Academic Advising: Final Report on ACT's Fifth National Survey of Academic Advising.* National Academic Advising Association Monograph Series, no. 6. Manhattan, Kans.: National Academic Advising Association, 1998.

Kerr, T. J. (ed.). *NACADA Faculty Advising Training Facilitator's Manual.* Manhattan, Kans.: National Academic Advising Association, 1996.

Weston, P. "Adviser Training in the Community College." In M. C. King (ed.), *Academic Advising: Organizing and Delivering Services for Student Success.* New Directions for Community Colleges, no. 82. San Francisco: Jossey Bass, 1993.

Chapter Twenty-One

A Framework for
Training Program Content

Linda C. Higginson

The standards to guide professional practice in academic advising published by the Council for the Advancement of Standards (CAS) in Higher Education (Miller, 1997) include thirteen aspects of "best practice" for advising programs. Although the scope of these components (for example, mission, leadership, and financial resources) supercedes the role, function, and behavior of the individual academic advisor, expectations about the quality of advising services provided to students are embedded within all of the components. With best practice as a goal for all who provide academic advising, it seems reasonable to expect that individual advisors should possess the information, resources, and behavioral skills needed to enable high-quality experiences for students.

How do the full array of individuals performing academic advising—faculty, student affairs professionals, graduate and undergraduate students, and full-time and part-time advising personnel—become knowledgeable about the necessary information and resources, sharpen their interpersonal skills for relating effectively with students, and learn to use the appropriate information and strategies in the advising setting? Many writers (for example, Grites, 1978; Keller, 1988; Glennen and Vowell, 1995) have advocated during the past two decades that institutions must provide quality training experiences to address such advisor needs.

In discussing advisor training programs, a number of individuals have provided training program models and suggested lists of topics to be addressed in advisor orientation activities. Sensitive to the various types of individuals providing advising, Virginia Gordon (1984) points out that a number of basic functions are performed by all advising personnel (for example, orientation to the rationale for beginning and upper-division requirements, use of decision-making approaches, and provision of academic and cocurricular resources), regardless of their other institutional responsibilities. Donald and Elizabeth Creamer (1994) offer a conceptual model for developmental advising with specific student growth goals. This model requires that, to enable student learning and growth, the advisor's response to students must be grounded in understanding students' motivation for the questions they have posed in the advising interaction. Clearly this type of theoretical perspective has significant training implications in that advising personnel need to understand that students' questions go beyond mere information seeking. In her chapter on training faculty serving as academic advisors, Susan Frost (1995, p. 31) asserts that "the most effective training blends discussion about advising philosophy and campus practice." She also lists a half-dozen topics for inclusion in training programs, including findings about student outcomes, needs of special populations, registration procedures, and strategies for helping students examine their career and educational goals.

Current Status of Advisor Training Program Content

The results of American College Testing's (ACT's) fifth national survey of academic advising are provided in a monograph published by the National Academic Advising Association (Habley and Morales, 1998). Chapter Three in the present volume summarizes the findings from this latest comprehensive study of advising practice.

The monograph by Habley and Morales briefly summarizes the results of each of the first four ACT national academic advising surveys, conducted in 1979, 1983, 1987, and 1993. This careful summary enables analysis of progress made in various aspects of advising program delivery over the past two decades. In particular, several important insights are offered about the evolution and current offerings of advisor training programs. First, Habley and Morales note that advisor training efforts have remained focused primarily on students' and advisors' need for information, thus underscoring a narrow view of advising as "information giving that leads to the selection and scheduling of courses" (p. 27). Commenting on ACT's first national survey, conducted in 1979, and reporting on the recently completed fifth edition of the survey, they point out that a focus on information characterizes advisor training in both surveys and spans an eighteen-year period. According to the latest survey, "the most common topics included in faculty advisor training focus on information and facts while some attention is paid to concepts such as the definition of advising, and the importance of advising. Skills that focus on building strong relationships with advisees are receiving even less emphasis than in previous surveys" (Habley and Morales, 1998, p. 27).

Another finding in the latest national survey is concerned with support for and approaches to advisor training. Habley and Morales note that training for advisors, along with evaluation and recognition and reward, is not mentioned regularly in institutional policy statements. This current observation is discouraging, especially given that similar observations were made in the 1987 and 1993 surveys—that training experiences were offered at a minimum level, and that "training, accountability, evaluation, and reward still rate below the midpoint on the effectiveness scale" (Habley and Morales, 1998, p. 5).

Whatever the multiple, complex reasons for slow progress in regularizing the offerings and broadening the focus of advisor training programs, the increasing necessity of providing advising personnel with the information and skills to function successfully cannot be overstated. "Unlike teaching, which takes place in the company of departmental colleagues, advising is too often a service performed in virtual isolation" (Frost, 1995, p. 31). The relatively solitary advising experience described by Frost, the multiple professional expectations for those performing the advising role, and the increasing complexity of curricular information and of students' educational and personal needs all combine to necessitate the provision of high-quality training experiences.

Organizing Framework for Advisor Training

Over the years, a number of publications have provided excellent how-to suggestions for advisor-training programs (Grites, 1978; Ender and Winston, 1982; Kramer and Gardner, 1984; Vowell, 1995). In his paper "Advisor Training in the Context of a Teaching Enhancement Center," Habley (1995) asserts that three essential components are necessary to increase the likelihood that advisor training will be successful: presenting a balance of content topics; attending to training participants' skills, expertise, and willingness to participate (as well as to advise); and using suitable training approaches. However, few experts have offered a coordinated approach for connecting training methods, training program content, and assessment of training outcomes to one another. I believe that approaches to training programs (discussed in Chapter Twenty), assessment of training effectiveness (see Chapters Twenty and Twenty-Five), and training program content should be based on a unifying framework. The framework presented in this chapter has been developed jointly with Margaret King and Faye Vowell and is addressed in both Chapters Twenty and Twenty-Five.

We propose an organizing framework for training programs composed of three key elements—supporting principles, delivery considerations, and assessment issues. Earlier works by Gordon (1984) and Vowell (1995) have helped shape this framework as a unifying backdrop for coordinating the development of training program content, delivery strategies, and assessment. Gordon's reminder that training must include all types of individuals who provide advising (for example, recruitment and orientation personnel as well as faculty) is further supported by Vowell's perspective. She suggests that training program effectiveness is dependent in part on carefully framing program goals, relying on adult development theory, and using a needs assessment to determine the content focus.

The first element of the organizing framework presented here—supporting principles—includes four fundamental components that provide the foundation for developing appropriate and coordinated training program approaches, assessment strategies, and content topics for a specific group of advisors in training. These four foundation principles are (1) conducting a preparatory campus or program needs analysis, (2) reviewing the advising mission within the institution, (3) becoming informed about the broad field of advising, and (4) understanding student development. Delivery considerations constitute the second element of the organizing framework. This aspect focuses on the advisor as student and challenges program planners to be especially sensitive to effective learning strategies for advisors as adult learners. The third element, assessment issues, reminds training program developers that evaluation of program effectiveness must focus on both advisor and student outcomes.

Content Components for Advisor Training

With the organizing framework just presented as a foundation, the balance of this chapter focuses on desirable content components for advisor training programs. Strategies for training and program delivery methods are discussed in Chapter Twenty, and Chapter Twenty-Five addresses assessment of training program effectiveness.

Habley (1995) has envisioned a useful three-category approach to considering the components of training program content:

Concept components: These topics encompass what the advisor needs to understand about the student and about the institution's advising environment. They include such subjects as the definition of advising, students' expectations of advising, and the rights and responsibilities of advisors and advisees.

Information components: These are topics about which the advisor needs to be knowledgeable, including familiar items such as institutional rules and regulations, program and course offerings, and referral sources and services.

Relationship components: These are behaviors that the advisor needs to demonstrate in order to be effective in advising students, including demonstrating an attitude of warmth and welcome, asking questions that invite students' involvement in discussion, and helping students use effective decision-making strategies.

Commenting on this three-part classification of training program content topics, Habley (1995, p. 76) notes that "without understanding (conceptual elements), there is no context for the delivery of services. Without information, there is no substance to advising. And, without interpersonal skills (relational), the quality of the advisee/advisor interaction is left to chance." Many scholars recognize that the academic advising function, an activity that is common to virtually all colleges and universities, can be a key positive factor in student retention, especially as it occurs in the context of a personal relationship involving a student and a significant member of the institution's professional academic community.

The content categories identified by Habley—concept, information, and relationship—are discussed in the following sections. They are offered here to help institutions fulfill their educational responsibilities to students by nurturing in the advising setting high-quality interactions about substantive issues related to students' academic and personal growth. Results from the fifth national survey on academic advising (Habley and Morales, 1998) are used to frame the discussion of each category. That is, the lists of advising responsibilities, training topics, and reference materials cited by survey respondents serve as the beginning point for consideration of training program content topics. In addition, content that Glennen and Vowell (1995) found to be common in advisor training, as well as Kramer's (1995) view of attributes associated with successful advising, help expand the array of topics gleaned from the national survey results.

A broad list of suggested content topics is offered for each of the categories. However, as indicated in the organizing framework discussed earlier, selection of topics for inclusion in training experiences for particular groups of advisors should be informed collectively by the specific institutional mission, a current assessment of advisor and student needs, and attention to the learning preferences of the adult (advisor) learner.

The Concept Component

The advisor's conceptual understanding of the student and of the institution's advising environment serves as a crucial foundation for effective advising relationships. Topics that merit attention at this level are framed from two perspectives within the institution—the student and the role of advising.

The Student Within the Institution. Topics in this area enable advisors to understand college students in general as well as their own institution's student body. Subjects appropriate for emphasis include descriptive data about the characteristics of the students enrolled in the advisor's institution (for example, gender and racial composition, performance on standardized tests, and proportion of students receiving various types of financial aid) as well as data illustrating student attrition and retention patterns. Also, advisors need to understand students' educational and personal needs. Comprehending and appreciating both generic and specific student needs requires a focus on student development theory, on personal development issues for students (for example, alcohol use, conflict and stress, decision making, financing educational expenses, gender identification, learning styles, roommate relationships, and values clarification), and on the unique characteristics of special populations such as adult learners, student athletes, honors students, international students, racial and ethnic minorities, part-time students, preprofessional students, undecided students, underprepared and at-risk students, students with disabilities, and women.

Role of Advising Within the Institution. Awareness of the institution's mission and goals in the context of its local community and of higher education in general provides an important foundation for the advising function. Understanding the relationship of the advising function to those overarching institutional directions will position advisors to provide sensitive, relevant guidance to support student success. Topical areas suggested for emphasis include consideration of the importance of academic advising for students and the institution, and a definition of academic advising, including clarification of advisor and advisee responsibilities and privileges.

The Information Component

The fifth national survey on academic advising (Habley and Morales, 1998) shows that more than 55 percent of institutions now have formal policy statements relating to academic advising. Of these institutions, however, only a small proportion (28 to 38 percent, depending on the type of institution) address training for academic advising personnel in their policy statements. Findings from the fifth national survey also show that the typical approach to advisor training is a once-a-year workshop of one day or less. Further, as discussed previously, institutions report that their advisor training programs usually place considerable emphasis on providing relevant information to advisors. The almost exclusive emphasis on information and ACT's long experience in providing training in this area conveys that there seems to be no doubt that information does provide much of the substance of advising. The substantive information that academic advisors need to know falls into four groups—the internal environment, the external environment, student needs, and advisor self-knowledge.

Internal Institutional Structures and Functions. The context for academic advising is largely a reflection of the institution's internal environment. This environment is composed of the philosophical and historical underpinnings of the institution along with the current structures and functions that are in place to carry through the educational mission. To help students negotiate the institutional bureaucracy successfully, it is important for academic advisors to be knowledgeable about contemporary structures and functions. Training topics in this area include academic integrity; relevant advising technology (for example, on-line academic information programs and computerized degree audits); accommodations for students with disabilities; cocurricular opportunities to support academic success, such as honors programming and research involvement; course availability; degree program curricular requirements; honors program options; appropriate policies and procedures; publications such as the advising handbook and the institution's catalogue; campus referral sources and services; registration procedures; standards for course transfer from other institutions; and use of information sources such as transcripts and the results of standardized tests.

External Environment. The higher education community, the local community surrounding the campus, and the broad world of work supply additional context for the advising function. Advising personnel link to each of these arenas through their established professional and disciplinary networks and other referral sources and services. Through knowledge of the various aspects of the external environment, advisors are able to help students link their academic pursuits with real-world applications and settings (for example, cooperative education programs and internship experiences). Topics for advisor training on the external environment include cocurricular opportunities to support academic success, such as service learning experiences; employment outlook projections; professional associations and disciplinary societies; opportunities for graduate and professional continuing education; referral and information sources and services; and how to establish a personal network in the external environment.

Student Needs. Because the successful advising experience depends on the active involvement of advisees, advisors must be knowledgeable about how to address students' individual needs. Although the composition of the student body will differ from institution to institution, there are a number of universal student characteristics that may anchor this portion of the advisor training program. Related training topics include career and personal decision making, evaluation of multiple options, learning styles, effective learning strategies such as learning teams, analysis of the relationship between academic and occupational choice, special population issues (for example, curricular and occupational considerations for international students, veterans, and adult students), test preparation strategies, and time management.

Advisor Self-Knowledge. We have all heard advising colleagues express exasperation about the somewhat overwhelming quantity of information to be digested as part of the advisor role. Perhaps we have experienced those feelings personally. Yet attention to advisors has not been a typical training topic. To be successful in the classroom, instructors must attend to their own energy levels, interest in students, and personal issues outside the classroom. Effective counselors are aware of their levels of concentration, their personal values related to their clients' concerns, and the reactions of the client to the advisor's interventions. Academic advisors must have similar information about what they as individuals bring to the advising setting. For example, they should ask themselves, What attitudes do I have about student behavior—about alcohol use, sexual involvement, and academic dishonesty? What knowledge and beliefs do I possess about indecision about choice of major? What do I know and believe and what are my attitudes about students? Honest self-knowledge will enable the advisor to enter the advising relationship with integrity of purpose to focus on facilitating the student's personal and educational growth.

The Relationship Component

Results from the fifth national advising survey show that institutions have little experience training advisors in the relationship area. In particular, Habley and Morales (1998, p. 27) point out that few four-year public institutions include "relational skill areas in advisor training programs in all departments."

In his classic article describing academic advising as a form of teaching, Burns Crookston (1972, p. 12) defines a developmental approach to advising as "facilitating the student's rational processes, environmental and interpersonal interactions, behavioral awareness, and problem-solving, decision-making, and evaluation skills." Although a number of training topics are unique to the relationship component, in many ways the primary goal for this component is for the advisor to be able to use effectively the understanding and knowledge identified through the concept and information components. In Chapters Fifteen and Sixteen of this volume, the skills related to effective one-to-one and group advising approaches are discussed in detail.

The focus of this training component is for the advisor to convey effectively the understandings and knowledge obtained from the other components by establishing a personal relationship with student advisees through demonstrating appropriate advising behaviors. Use of such expert behaviors will enable the advisor to fulfill Crookston's vision and address students' needs fully. For example, advisor behaviors that derive from a conceptual understanding of and sensitivity to the special challenges of adult learners who face multiple competing responsibilities on a daily basis will likely result in the student feeling personally supported by the advisor. Similarly, advisor facility in explaining to students and helping them practice the use of various decision-making strategies is likely to lead to enhanced student confidence.

Training topics for this component include the following: accessing institutional and external information, behaving to communicate welcome and warmth, verbal and nonverbal interpersonal communication skills, interview and inquiry strategies, methods for teaching decision making, multicultural communication skills, establishment and maintenance of advising records, and use of advising tools such as computerized degree audits, academic planning worksheets, and articulation worksheets and agreements.

One final behavior that is paramount for advisors to demonstrate is accessibility. The importance of this behavior is emphasized by the results of a survey of students enrolled in the College of Business Administration at the University of North Texas (Kern and Engels, 1996). More than 90 percent of survey respondents included on their lists of needs three aspects of advisor accessibility—availability during evenings, access to a faculty advisor, and more time with an advisor. A training program can likely inform advisors in training about students' accessibility needs and expectations. However, no training experience can shape this behavior; it depends on the advisor's commitment.

Conclusion

This chapter has focused on the appropriate content topics to be addressed in training experiences for academic advisors. A three-factor organizing framework has been offered as a means to couple the choice of content topics with the approach to delivering and assessing the training program. This framework is composed of supporting principles, program delivery considerations, and assessment issues.

An extensive inventory of topics has been presented for each of three content areas—concept, information, and relationship. Topics in the concept component embody the necessary advisor understandings of both the student and the advising role within the institution. The information component includes topics in four areas: environment (both within the institution and external to it), student needs, and advisor knowledge of self. The last component centers on the personal relationship between the advisor and the student. Training topics for this component relate to the skills that the advisor must display during advising interactions. These behavioral attributes include various interpersonal communication skills, along with abilities to access informational resources and use available advising tools, and other facilitating behaviors.

The five national studies of academic advising conducted by ACT since 1979 (see Habley and Morales, 1998) show clearly that information has continued to make up the major portion of advisor training program content. In spite of this reliance on information for training, there have been no careful analyses of the effectiveness of these topics in achieving desirable advisor and advisee outcomes. Yet about half of institutions participating in the fifth national survey report that they regularly evaluate the overall effectiveness of their advising programs. To achieve necessary improvement in academic advising, stronger institutional commitments to quality training experiences for advisors are needed. These commitments must also require assessment of the effectiveness of training programs' content topics.

Using careful assessment of training program outcomes to inform future selection of content topics is an important step. In addition, the vision for advisor training programs must be determined by standards for best practice. This vision obligates advising experts to assess and share training program experiences, and to ensure that the CAS Academic Advising Standards and Guidelines (Miller, 1997) are enhanced to address training program requirements completely.

References

Creamer, D. G., and Creamer, E. G. "Practicing Developmental Advising: Theoretical Contexts and Functional Applications." *NACADA Journal*, 1994, *14*(2), 17–24.

Crookston, B. B. "A Developmental View of Academic Advising as Teaching." *Journal of College Student Personnel*, 1972, *13*, 12–17.

Ender, S. C., and Winston, R. B. "Training Allied Professional Academic Advisors." In R. B. Winston, S. C. Ender, and T. K. Miller (eds.), *Developmental Approaches to*

Academic Advising. New Directions for Student Services, no. 17. San Francisco: Jossey-Bass, 1982.

Frost, S. H. "Designing and Implementing a Faculty-Based Advising Program." In G. L. Kramer (ed.), *Reaffirming the Role of Faculty in Academic Advising.* NACADA Monograph Series, no. 1. Manhattan, Kans.: National Academic Advising Association, 1995.

Glennen, R. E., and Vowell, F. N. "Selecting, Training, Rewarding, and Recognizing Faculty Advisors." In M. L. Upcraft and G. L. Kramer (eds.), *First-Year Academic Advising: Patterns in the Present, Pathways to the Future.* Monograph Series, no. 18. Columbia: National Resource Center for the Freshman Year Experience and Students in Transition, University of South Carolina, 1995.

Gordon, V. N. "Training Professional and Paraprofessional Advisors." In R. B. Winston Jr., T. K. Miller, S. C. Ender, T. J. Grites (eds.), *Developmental Academic Advising: Addressing Students' Educational, Career, and Personal Needs.* San Francisco: Jossey-Bass, 1984.

Grites, T. J. "Training the Academic Advisor." In D. S. Crockett (ed.), *Academic Advising: A Resource Document.* Iowa City, Iowa: American College Testing Program, 1978.

Habley, W. "Advisor Training in the Context of a Teaching Enhancement Center." In R. E. Glennen and F. N. Vowell (eds.), *Academic Advising as a Comprehensive Campus Process.* National Academic Advising Association Monograph Series, no. 2. Manhattan, Kans.: National Academic Advising Association, 1995.

Habley, W. R., and Morales, R. H. (eds.). *Current Practices in Academic Advising: Final Report on ACT's Fifth National Survey of Academic Advising.* National Academic Advising Association Monograph Series, no. 6. Manhattan, Kans.: National Academic Advising Association, 1998.

Keller, M. C. "Advisor Training." In W. R. Habley (ed.), *The Status and Future of Academic Advising: Problems and Promise.* Iowa City, Iowa: American College Testing Program, 1988.

Kern, C. W., and Engels, D. W. "Developmental Academic Advising: A Paradigm Shift in a College of Business Administration." *Journal of College Student Development,* 1996, *37,* 95–96.

Kramer, G. L. "Redefining Faculty Roles for Academic Advising." In G. L. Kramer (ed.), *Reaffirming the Role of Faculty in Academic Advising.* National Academic Advising Association Monograph Series, no. 1, 1995. Manhattan, Kans.: National Academic Advising Association, 1995.

Kramer, H. C., and Gardner, R. E. "Improving Advising Knowledge and Skills Through Faculty Development." In R. B. Winston Jr., T. K. Miller, S. C. Ender, and T. J. Grites (eds.), *Developmental Academic Advising: Addressing Students' Educational, Career, and Personal Needs.* San Francisco: Jossey-Bass, 1984.

Miller, T. K. (ed.). *The Book of Professional Standards for Higher Education.* Washington, D.C.: Council for the Advancement of Standards in Higher Education, 1997.

Vowell, F. "Developing Faculty Potential as Excellent Advisors." In G. L. Kramer (ed.), *Reaffirming the Role of Faculty in Academic Advising.* National Academic Advising Association Monograph Series, no. 1. Manhattan, Kans.: National Academic Advising Association, 1995.

Chapter Twenty-Two

Model Training Programs

Phillip J. Farren, Faye Vowell

This chapter focuses on how to recognize best practices in advisor training and development programs. It builds on the information presented in Chapters Twenty and Twenty-One and presents specific examples of exemplary advisor training practices.

Considering Diversity

Advisor training programs should grow out of the mission of the institution and the role of advisors in that institution with regard to who advises and how the advising services are organized. Consider the diversity of institutions, each with a different mission: two-year, four-year, public, private, proprietary, comprehensive, liberal arts, church-related, research, and others. Then consider the variety of advisor types: peer or paraprofessional, faculty, professional, as well as others who may act as informal advisors such as admissions and orientation personnel.

Advisor training programs should be sensitive to these differences. For example, advisor training in two-year schools should enable advisors to be aware of the goals of individual students who may not want to pursue a degree but may instead prefer to focus on acquiring specific job skills. Four-year schools' advisor training goals may include giving advisors skills needed to enhance retention and graduation rates. Private schools are often smaller than their public counterparts, and they expect that the relationship between students and faculty will be closer because of more informal contact among faculty, staff, and students. If the institution is church related, there will often be emphasis on moral and ethical behavior outside the classroom as well as inside the classroom.

Proprietary schools have a more specific mission than other types of school, they are usually more career oriented, and they often have a shorter time to completion if they offer primarily certificate programs. Advisors at these schools are more likely to be professional advisors.

Research institutions also have different missions and concerns for advisor training. They are more likely to use a mixture of kinds of advisors and to use peer or paraprofessional advisors. Because of a variety of expectations, faculty members are less likely to advise undergraduates. This is in contrast to liberal arts institutions, which pride themselves on the involvement of faculty in advising.

Programs that use professional advisors often hire people with counseling skills or people skills and then need to help them understand the nature of advising as well as the particular requirements of the programs offered by that institution. Peer advisors or paraprofessionals may need to be made aware of the culture of higher education and the structure of their institution as well as of the particular skills, abilities, and knowledge needed to fulfill their role as advisors. Some faculty advisors may be uncomfortable in dealing with the affective issues that students bring to the advising relation, so they may need to receive training to become more comfortable with these issues.

So, a variety of issues are important when considering how to structure an advisor training program. Those who design and implement advisor training programs should be mindful of the mission of the institution and of the advising unit within the institution. They should also develop a purpose statement for the advisor training program that clearly delineates how it fits within institutional and unit missions. In addition, advisors need to know about the preparation, diversity, and socioeconomic needs of the students served. Are they first-generation college students? Do they need to work in addition to receiving financial aid? Are they well prepared or underprepared for the classes they will be taking? Finally, the purpose statement must take into account the characteristics expected of advisors. What skills and experiences should they have? What motivates them and what rewards are available to them?

Considering Best Practices

No matter whether one is trying to create a comprehensive and unified advisor training program for the first time or trying to revise an existing program, one way to increase the quality of the training program is to consider what best practices are being used by other training programs. In an article entitled "Benchmarking in Higher Education," C. Jackson Grayson Jr. (1998, p. 107) describes best practices as those judged to be "exemplary," "better," "good," or "successfully demonstrated." This chapter proposes to help creators of advisor training programs to accomplish some of the first steps by "benchmarking," or defining criteria for best practices and then giving examples for consideration.

Grayson outlines six basic steps in benchmarking. The first step is to identify the key processes critical to achieving the mission and goals of the training program; the second step is to analyze how those processes are being carried out. This chapter proposes a list of the processes and defines indicators of quality in them. Examples given of best practices in these areas will lead to the accomplishment of step three: to identify others who are doing the process better. Focusing on best practices will enable the process to be revised by adapting the ideas presented to a particular situation or by contacting the targeted institution to find out more about the process. Once the new process has been implemented, an evaluation can be made of the extent to which it is accomplishing the desired goal. Then one either goes through the benchmarking steps again with this process or works on another process. If readers wish to learn more about the quality process or benchmarking, we suggest that they look at *Benchmarking: A Tool for Continuous Improvement,* by C. J. McNair and Kathleen H. J. Leibfried (1992).

Components of a Model Program

A model advisor training program is based on the following foundational elements. First, the mission of the advising program must be clearly articulated and its connection to the institution's mission statement must be easily seen. A continuous process of needs analysis in regard to training should be in place. The person designing the advisor training program should be aware of national guidelines and expectations in the field of advising, such as those articulated by the Council for the Advancement of Standards (CAS) and the National Academic Advising Association (NACADA), and those found in the literature on advising. Designers of advisor training programs should also have a broad understanding of student development theory, especially as it relates to the students served at their institutions. With this background knowledge and preparation, designers have a firm foundation on which to construct their programs and to evaluate the best practices of other programs.

A model program of advisor training should also be mindful of its audience, and the format of the training should reflect the different learning styles of different types of learners. Most important in delivering a training program to faculty and staff is to treat them as adult learners and to structure programs for them in different ways than for peer or paraprofessional advisors.

Finally, a model advisor training program should focus on continuous evaluation of outcomes for both advisors, who are the audience for the training, and advisees, who are the recipients of improved knowledge and skills on the part of advisors.

Key Processes for Improving Advising

A number of key processes in advisor training can be isolated. They include needs assessment, marketing or advertising, selecting appropriate content and format, using appropriate resources, choosing the best presenters, and evaluation.

A needs assessment process should focus on the following as indicators of quality:

- The process reveals an understanding of advisor training needs by addressing informational, relational, and conceptual aspects.

- The process elicits perceived needs that are specific to the campus and to the advising unit.

- The needs assessment process is based on the mission and purpose of the institution.

- The needs assessment process is based on an understanding of the kinds of advisors used in the specific model of advising delivery, with particular attention to their skill level, their experience, and their willingness to participate.

Needs assessment can be done by using surveys and focus groups as well as by using information from advisor self-evaluations and evaluations by advisees. Aggregated data from other sources such as the American College Testing (ACT) assessment can provide a broader understanding of the support issues that students face, and this data can be used as a basis for training.

Marketing or advertising the training program is a key process that often is not considered, especially if training is considered mandatory or part of job responsibility. Indicators of quality in the marketing of advisor training should include the following:

- Marketing efforts should tell potential attendees what will be covered in each session so that they can determine a match between the content and their needs.

- Marketing efforts should create a sense of the value of training and build pride in the program.

- Marketing efforts should share results and show that the training program made a difference.

- Marketing programs should use different vehicles to reach different audiences.

- Marketing should be timely.

- Marketing efforts should fit the institutional mission and culture.

- More people should attend as marketing efforts improve.

- More inquiries about the training program should be received.

- More awareness about the training program should be seen campuswide.

Selecting appropriate content and formats for training sessions is a primary process for the creation of a successful advisor training program. Indicators of quality include the following:

- The purpose of training is clearly articulated and based on needs assessment.
- The content and format of the training sessions demonstrate sensitivity to the specific role of the advisors in the audience.
- Training sessions take into account experience and skill levels as well as readiness to learn.
- Training sessions show awareness of the different audiences: new advisors, returning advisors, part-time and full-time advisors, peer and paraprofessional advisors, faculty advisors, and professional advisors.
- Training sessions fit the institutional culture and mission.
- The content is balanced among the conceptual, relational, and informational areas of advising.
- The content is delivered in a variety of formats informed by the different developmental needs of the audience, such as role-playing, discussion, experiential learning, discussion of videos, panels of advisors, and panels of students.

Using appropriate resources and choosing appropriate presenters are processes that designers of advisor training programs frequently focus on. Best practices in these processes should consider the following:

- Presenters should have credibility with the targeted audience.
- Presenters represent a number of constituencies: experienced advisors, administrators, staff from areas that work closely with advisors, students, employers, and outside speakers.
- Presenters possess the necessary skills and experience to vary their presentation content and format to meet the needs of individual audiences.
- Presenters understand the mission and goals of the advising program and the specific training session in which they are participating.
- Presenters are experts in specific areas, such as advising students with disabilities, athletes, undecided or undeclared students, ethnically diverse students, and nontraditional students; or teaching student development theory and communication skills.
- The resources used support the goals of the training session.
- Resources are up-to-date, comprehensive, and user-friendly.

Evaluation of the training program is truly a process. Evaluation should be thought of as both short-term and long-term. The individual sessions of the training program need to be evaluated, as do the individual processes of the program. The whole training program also needs to be evaluated or assessed. Key indicators of successful evaluation plans include the following:

- Multiple forms of assessment are used.
- An increasing number of people participate in assessment activities.
- Individual evaluation instruments elicit specific data to improve the process.
- The evaluation instrument is keyed to different experience levels and different training activities
- Advisor performance improves.
- Outcomes are clearly identified.
- Outcomes match the desired goals. If not, the process is changed in order to better meet the goals.

Outcomes for successful advisor training programs should include an increase in the number of repeat attendees and an increase in the level of advisor satisfaction with training. Advisors should exhibit increased appreciation of the value of training over time. In addition, the training program should demonstrate that it has achieved stated goals. Finally, there should be a higher level of advisee satisfaction with advising if advisors are successful in transferring knowledge and skills gained in training to actual advising situations. Other quantifiable measures include a higher retention rate, a higher reported rate of students attaining their goals, a higher graduation rate, and a shorter time to graduation, as well as program goals specific to the institution.

Survey of Best Practices

In an effort to gather examples of best practices, we contacted ACT and NACADA award–winning programs that included training and asked that they complete a survey. In addition, we asked advisors to respond to a survey posted on NACADA's ACADV listserv and on a number of other NACADA listservs. Responses to the survey were measured against the criteria stated earlier, and best practices were identified.

Monroe Community College

A number of best practices can be seen at Monroe Community College, a public, two-year institution in Rochester, New York, with around fourteen thousand students. The three-hundred full-time faculty members are required by contract to advise fifteen hours a semester. Training hours can be used by faculty to fulfill this obligation. Approximately thirty student services personnel also advise. The advisor training program is offered through the counseling center. The training sessions are marketed through a monthly four-page flyer that includes a flowchart recommending a sequence for the fourteen workshops, a description of the content of each workshop, and a calendar giving date, time, place, and the presenter for each session. The times and workshops vary each month to meet the needs of different audiences. In addition, the workshop series is marketed in meetings with deans and departments, at new-faculty orientation, and in faculty recruitment materials.

The content of the training sessions, which target both faculty and professional advisors, constitutes a best practice worthy of note. Topics include "Introduction to Advisement," "On Course Training" (degree audit system training), "I Don't Know How to Begin," "Transfer Advising," "Placement Issues and Careers for the Twenty-First Century," "Student Development Theory and Its Relationship with Advisement," "Cross-Cultural Advising Strategies," and "Developmental Advising Theory in Practice." The handouts and materials are comprehensive and attractive.

Workshop sessions are created to respond to three levels of experience: beginning, having some experience with advising, and very experienced.

Beginning advisors are exposed to general education requirements; institutional policies and procedures; use of the student database, degree audit, and transcript analysis; campus resources; roles and responsibilities of advisor and advisees; typical advisee problem areas; basic communication and referral skills; basic concepts of developmental advising; campus demographics and traditions; test interpretation; and how to work with parents and significant others.

Advisors with some experience can take workshops on student development theory, career advising, crisis intervention, decision-making strategies, basic counseling techniques, how the campus culture interacts with advising, job market information about a major or program area, learning styles, and ethical issues in advising.

Very experienced advisors have access to the following workshops: how to advise special populations, such as honors students or students with disabilities; how to advise culturally different students, such as black and Hispanic students; human growth and development; retention strategies; decision-making theory; and learning theory.

Three levels of evaluation data are collected: workshop evaluations, pretesting and posttesting of participants, and evaluation of overall effectiveness. In addition, the following attendance data are collected: number of faculty and staff at each workshop, total attendance by division, and total attendance by semester.

The advising program at Monroe Community College has won two awards: a NACADA Outstanding Institutional Advising Certificate of Merit in 1996 and an Innovation of the Year Award in 1999 from the League for Innovation. (Material for this discussion was submitted by Denise Klein.)

Ball State University

The Office of Academic Systems at Ball State University offers an example of best practice in needs assessment. The Electronic Advising and Technology Committee, which is responsible for exploring possible uses of technology in support of academic advising, distributed a survey to all advisors. The purpose of the survey was to determine the level of expertise each advisor possessed in a number of advising and technology activities. The survey asked questions about Internet experience; experience with the degree-audit program and with the course transfer program; and experience with e-mail, the mainframe, the Windows operating system, and the Ball State Web site. The results of the survey were compiled and then training sessions were created to focus on the topics that revealed the greatest need. The Office of Academic Systems also has quick reference guides to facilitate the training of both professional staff and faculty advisors. (This information was submitted by Mike McCauley, director of the Office of Academic Systems.)

California State Polytechnic University, Pomona

Best practice in the area of marketing can be seen in the advisor training program offered through the Division of Student Affairs at California State Polytechnic University, Pomona. This four-year public polytechnic university has a campus community of 16,500. Staffed by full- and part-time professional advisors and peer advisors, the Division of Student Affairs provides in-house training for department advisors and peer advisors as well as faculty and professional advisor training for the larger campus community during fall convocation and once a month as part of an Advising Challenge Series that discusses special topics. The training is marketed in a weekly newsletter and in a flyer sent to all members of the campus community. Following is a sample of this marketing material:

> ### Motivating Underprepared Students—What Can We Do?
> Underprepared students are at risk of performing poorly in class, giving up, and leaving school. Finding ways to motivate and encourage students is critical to their success and retention. Join us for a discussion of how we can positively impact students through the advising process utilizing the Noel-Levitz *Academic Advising for Student Retention and Success* video series. This brown-bag session is open to everyone and will be held in the Faculty Center for Professional Development (Building 1, Room 227) from 12–1 P.M. on Tuesday, March 9th. Future programs in the Advising Challenge Series include "Avoiding Bias in Advising" and "Evaluating Your Strengths and Accomplishments as an Advisor." For more information, please contact Cathy Schmitt, University Advising Center, at extension 5257 or e-mail clschmitt@csupomona.edu.

Additional examples are provided in Exhibits 22.1 and 22.2. (These materials were submitted by Catherine Schmitt of the University Advising Center.)

Kennesaw State University

An example of best practices in marketing and delivery format is found at Kennesaw State University, Kennesaw, Georgia. This four-year public, 100 percent commuter school offers the Wise Owl Advising Information Certificate Program as part of a professional development program for faculty and staff. The certificate program is described in a brochure distributed to all faculty and staff each semester. It consists of three 1.5-hour workshops that have continuing education credit attached.

Meeting the Advising Challenge Series

Sessions to be held in the Faculty Center for Professional Development. For more information please call Cathy Schmitt at extension 5257.

October 15, 1999	3–5 pm	Advising Advisory Council meeting
November 19, 1999	12–1 pm	Motivating Underprepared Students
December 16, 1999	12–1 pm	Showing We Care: Communicating with Students
January 14, 1999	12–1 pm	Factors to Consider with Course Selection
February 11, 1999	3–5 pm	Advising Advisory Council meeting
March 10, 1999	12–1 pm	Assisting Students to Clarify Attitudes and Actions
April 8, 1999	12–1 pm	Avoiding Bias in Advising
May 17, 1999	3–5 pm	Advising Advisory Council meeting
June 9, 1999	12–1 pm	Evaluating Your Strengths and Accomplishments as an Advisor

Sponsored by the University Advising Center, Division of Student Affairs, Cal Poly Pomona

---

Exhibit 22.1.   Marketing Flyer Distributed to Campus Community, California State Polytechnic University, Pomona.

Meeting the Advising Challenge Series

These sessions will discuss the strengths-based approach to advising and the role this approach can have in promoting student success and retention utilizing the Noel-Levitz *Academic Advising for Student Retention and Success* video series. Each session will focus on a particular topic and on ways that academic advisors can promote the development of talent within students. These brown-bag lunch sessions will be held in the Faculty Center for Professional Development from 12–1 pm. For more information, please call Cathy Schmitt, University Advising Center, at extension 5257.

Topics include:

January 19, 1999	Factors to Consider During Course Selection
February 16, 1999	Showing We Care: Communicating with Students
March 9, 1999	Motivating Underprepared Students
April 20, 1999	Avoiding Bias in Advising
May 18, 1999	Evaluating Your Strengths and Accomplishments as an Advisor

---

Exhibit 22.2. Marketing Piece in Weekly Newsletter at Beginning of Advisor Training Series.

Note: Submitted by Catherine Schmitt, University Advising Center, California State Polytechnic University, Pomona.

In addition to marketing the training through the brochure, the program gives participants a certificate of completion and sends a letter to the head of each student's unit. Names of people who complete certificates are also showcased in the next version of the brochure. (This information was submitted by Brian Glankler, assistant director for Advising Services, and Donna Spetalnick, administrative coordinator for the Undeclared Advising Program.)

San Diego State University

Best practices in peer advisor training are demonstrated by San Diego State University. A peer advisor was directly involved in the design of the program. The program is based on Albert Bandura's, social learning theory, which encourages modeling good behavior for enhancing learning. The learning experience is integrated rather than being a series of discrete presentations. The peer advisor created a manual for peer advisor trainers to help them understand what is expected of them. It includes examples and case studies.

The training program itself lasts six to seven weeks and participants meet two hours each day on Monday, Wednesday, and Friday of those weeks. The Monday and Wednesday sessions are informational and are delivered by six senior advisors. For example, the general education requirement was presented by a faculty advisor who is also a history professor. The ethical issues session was presented by a faculty advisor who is a psychology professor with a particular interest in the topic. The Friday sessions focus on the use of technology, the availability of resources, and the application of information learned earlier in the week. (Information on this program was submitted by Sandra Cook, director of advising at San Diego State University. The peer advisor who was instrumental in the creation of the training program is Richard Moyer III.)

Indiana University-Purdue University at Indianapolis

The Department of Psychology in the School of Science at Indiana University-Purdue University at Indianapolis (IUPUI) offers another example of best practice in a peer advisor training program. IUPUI is a public, research, urban, commuter institution. The role of peer advisors is to serve as resources to their peers. They are not responsible for academic or career advising. They help students understand tools important to them in the advising process, help students learn what kinds of questions they should be asking, and do all scheduling of advising appointments with faculty advisors.

Students interested in peer advising experiences submit an application, are interviewed, and are accepted or denied on the basis of a set of academic and personal characteristics. Accepted students register for a one- to three-credit seminar course, "Professional Practice Program." For each credit hour of enrollment, they work three hours in the psychology advising office. Initially they go through an extensive daylong training to teach them about their roles as peer advisors as well as important logistics. They also attend a class every other week to explore such issues as developmental advising models, interpersonal communication, listening skills, and problem solving.

All peer advisors must complete a practical project designed to give them experience in research, reading, and reporting as well as furthering the development of the peer advising office. For example, one student chose the topic of stress management. He researched the topic, collected resources, developed an office file for future reference, and presented a workshop for students on the topic. (Information on this program was presented by Mikki Poynter Jeschke, director of student development.)

Linfield College

A number of schools offer examples of best practices in varying content and delivery format for different kinds of advisors. Linfield College in McMinville, Oregon, a four-year, private liberal arts school, trains both faculty and peer advisors. Linfield College won an Outstanding Program Award from NACADA in 1996. Peer advisors are trained in a six-hour spring retreat and a five-hour fall workshop. Faculty advisors receive training with peer advisors in the fall workshop and in a series of fifty-minute training sessions in the spring. These spring sessions have included the following presentations on important issues in advising: a faculty-peer advisor panel on e-mail advising, a presentation on discussion techniques delivered by a communications faculty member, a presentation on the interactive classroom delivered by an English faculty member, a summary of Cooperative Institutional Research Program (CIRP) results with implications for developmental advising delivered by a faculty member from the psychology department, a panel of successful faculty-peer advisor teams on what works, a slideshow on Generation X with a panel of freshman respondents, and training in using on-line access to student records. These optional workshop sessions are repeated at different hours to accommodate faculty with different schedules. Examples of agendas from a fall workshop and a peer advisor retreat can be found in Exhibits 22.3 and 22.4. (This information was provided by Deborah Olsen, director of academic advising.)

California State University, Hayward

California State University, Hayward (CSU Hayward), offers an example of best practices in tailoring the training of advisors to the different roles they play. CSU Hayward is a four-year public liberal arts school with 12,500 students. Full-time professional advisors receive two to three weeks of training when they are hired. Peer advisors are trained for six to eight weeks in the spring quarter. Student assistants who act as receptionists are trained for one to two weeks in the fall quarter. Graduate interns receive eight to ten weeks of training in the spring quarter. (This information was provided by Evette Castillo, interim coordinator, University Advisement Center.)

Western State College

Western State College in Gunnison, Colorado, is a four-year, public, undergraduate, liberal arts institution. It trains both faculty and peer advisors using a different format and content delivery method for each group. Faculty who advise

Morning Session (Approximately 9:30–11:30 A.M.)

1. Expectations
2. Get-to-know-you exercise
3. Purpose of colloquium
4. The first week at Linfield
5. Role of peer advisor and confidentiality

Short Break

6. Academic advising handbook scavenger hunt
7. Interactive exercise—Problems you anticipate/advice from the pros

Lunch Break

Be at Santa Fe Taqueria, 831 N.W. 23rd at 11:45 A.M.

After lunch, explore N.W. Portland

Workshop resumes at 1 P.M. promptly

Afternoon Sessions (1 P.M.–4:30 P.M.)

8. Letter to your advisees
9. Group-building activity
10. Videos and other resources available for colloquium

Short Break

11. One-on-one meetings with new students
12. Evaluation of the workshop

Exhibit 22.3. Peer Advisor Retreat, Linfield College, Portland Campus, Saturday, April 25, 1998.

as part of the Freshman Advisory Corp are trained each spring prior to the beginning of their summer duties in sessions that are repeated. Topics covered include developmental advising components (major information, skill development, communication, troubleshooting, and using advising tools such as the general education requirement worksheet), the role of advisors (responsibilities of advisors and students, rapport skills, respect, teaching and learning environment, policies and procedures, office hours, and records), advising in the nineties (population-specific issues including freshman, undecided, and transfer students; diverse populations; academically unprepared students; and students with disabilities), tools for advising (such as using the e-mail system to answer advising questions from students, prospective students, and other advisors), and support services.

Peer advisor training consists of a retreat with the resident assistant staff involving role-playing, and a two-day training and practical application session during the final summer orientation. Peer advisors also attend meetings that offer additional training and guidance throughout the semester. Issues included in the training are those that deal with first-year student adjustment issues, cooperating with resident advisors, team development, and advisors' role as peers. Peer advisors are required to attend training and are paid a $1,000

11:00–11:30	The day before college begins: Our new class and the faculty advisors' best resource.
11:30–11:40	Chocolate numeral awards.
11:40–12:15	An introduction to your notebooks. What's new?
12:15–12:30	Short break to pick up your lunches. Please return to Riley 201 to eat while workshop resumes.
12:30–1:00	Registration information: Barbara Seidman, associate dean of faculty, and Eileen Bourassa, associate registrar.
1:00–2:00	Completing the tour of your notebook.
2:00–2:15	Break
2:15–2:30	Changes in the tutoring services at Linfield: Dr. Judith Haynes.
2:30–2:45	New opportunities for student internships: Michael Hampton.
2:45–3:00	Expectations of good advisors; questions and wrap-up.
3:00–4:00	Studying the files and planning the first session—peer advisor/faculty advisor teams.
4:00–4:30	Brief meeting of peer advisors with Debbie.

Table of contents of this notebook:

Orientation schedule (small notebook)

Colloquium syllabus (white)

Placement exam schedule (yellow)

Math placement/advising form (white)

B. Seidman's memo re: spaces in LCs (blue)

Registration checklist (white)

Registration materials

IQs booklet (aqua)

Handbook of suggested activities (tan)

98–99 academic advising handbook (red covers)

Peer advisors only:

Peer advising meeting schedule (orange)

Computer proficiency checklist (purple)

The role of the peer advisor

Advice to the peer advisors from the veterans of 1997

Contents of colloquium box:

Academic files and list of your advisees

Camera and T-shirts

For distribution to students:

Linfield bulletins (catalogues)

Colloquium syllabi (white)

Registration materials

IQs booklet (aqua)

Practice schedules/LC worksheet (blue)

Registration checklist (white)

Placement exam schedule (yellow)

Math placement/advising form (white)

Faculty frowns/translating Linfield (green)

Study abroad flyer (yellow)

Web proficiency worksheet (purple)

Weekly schedule (white)

Exhibit 22.4. Colloquium Workshop, Friday, August 28, 1998.

stipend. (This information was provided by Julie Luekenga, academic advisor and career counselor.)

Western Illinois University

The University Advising and Academic Support Center at Western Illinois University offers a best practice in special training sessions that address topics as the need arises. For example, special sessions have been held to discuss a new graduation guarantee program, state general education mandates, and new technology to support advising. Western Illinois is a four-year public, comprehensive institution with full- and part-time professional advisors as well as faculty, peer, and paraprofessional advisors. (This information was supplied by Candace McLaughlin, director of the University Advising and Academic Support Center.)

William Rainey Harper College

William Rainey Harper College, a two-year public institution, illustrates a best practice in its intense training of faculty advisors in the Academic Advising and Counseling Center. The student development unit has eight full-time and four part-time counselors and ten faculty advisors who serve about fifteen thousand students. Initially advisors receive one to two weeks of intensive training, followed by a semester of observation. Observation entails advisors first observing advising sessions and then being observed by a veteran advisor. Then other training sessions are provided as needed two or three times a semester. (This material was provided by Janet Friend Westney, coordinator of academic advising and counseling.)

The Ohio State University

The Ohio State University's best practice is use of a Web site (http://www.uvc.ohio-state.edu/intra/gbcaltc.html) for advisor training and to offer materials for student use. The Web site contains the General Baccalaureate Curriculum and the Alternatives Advising Program Advising and Training Manual. It was created by the University College. Ohio State is a public research university. University College serves entering students with full-time professional advisors and half-time graduate associates. All new advisors receive three weeks of training and an additional two hours per week of extended training during the first quarter of their employment. All staff members participate in a 1- to 1.5-hour staff meeting each week. The Web site offers a wide variety of materials, including overviews of student development theories. It includes a section that focuses on the exploring student and is based on Gordon's work on career advising (Gordon, 1992). It is attractively designed and easy to navigate. Especially interesting are needs assessment inventories used by both the advisor and the advisee as well as on-line case studies that provide background on hypothetical students, including sample advising notes, and then pose questions for advisors in training.

Texas A&M University

Karl Mooney from Texas A&M University offers an example of a best practice in training advisors of student athletes. At the end of each term, an eligibility-review day is conducted. It is attended by advisors, graduate academic assistants, a clerk from the registrar's office who deals with eligibility, and at least one compliance office staff person. Live data from the university's Student Athlete Management Information System is projected onto a screen using a laptop and a data projector. The group first talks through a few cases of student athletes who are clearly eligible. Then they review all who are close or who need to have the averaging method applied. As the review progresses, the advising trainer references the National Collegiate Athletic Association bylaws for each case as needed. This practice reduces the likelihood of advising errors and serves as an excellent training procedure for graduate assistants and new full-time advisors as well as improving communication among the various offices that student athletes may visit for academic advising.

University of Texas at Arlington

The University Advising Center at the University of Texas at Arlington offers an example of a best practice in its emphasis on self-discovery as a part of advisor training. All advisors take the Myers-Briggs Type Indicator, the Strong Interest Inventory, and the Learning and Study Strategies Inventory to discover their own personality types, interests, and learning styles. Both faculty and professional advisors can participate in fifteen hours of training each semester. Certificates are offered to people completing the year-long thirty-hour training. The University of Texas at Arlington is a four-year public research institution. (This information was provided by Cubie Ward, director of the University Advising Center.)

Numerous other examples of best practices exist in higher education and outside of it. We urge you to seek out those best practices that would improve your advisor training and share them with other individuals and institutions.

Conclusion

Various institutions with different missions, different expectations for advisors, and different kinds of students need to be mindful of these differences when designing an advisor training program. The components of a model advisor training program include a clearly articulated mission, a continuous process of needs analysis, an awareness of national guidelines and of the advising literature, an understanding of student development theory, a knowledge of the format and delivery needs of the audience, and a process for continuous evaluation. Key processes can be identified in each of these areas. These processes form the basis for selection of examples of best practices that can be found in a variety of institutional settings.

References

Gordon, V. N. *Handbook of Academic Advising.* Westport, Conn.: Greenwood Press, 1992.

Grayson, C. J. Jr. "Benchmarking in Higher Education." In J. W. Myerson (ed.), *New Thinking on Higher Education: Creating a Context for Change.* Forum for the Future of Higher Education Series, Vol. 1. Bolton, Mass.: Anker, 1998.

McNair, C. J., and Leibfried, K.H.J. *Benchmarking: A Tool for Continuous Improvement.* New York: Wiley, 1992.

Chapter Twenty-Three

Assessing the Effectiveness of the Advising Program

Michael L. Lynch

Except for teaching, no other college activity seems to enjoy more legitimacy than academic advising. Regardless of the institution, somewhere within mission statements, strategic plans, goals, objectives, and so on will appear recognition of the importance of and commitment to quality academic advising. Given such recognition, one might expect that academic advising would be evaluated with somewhat the same regularity and thoroughness as classroom instruction. Such is not the case. In its fifth national survey of academic advising (Habley and Morales, 1998), American College Testing (ACT) found that the evaluation of advising programs and academic advisors received the ninth and tenth lowest effectiveness ratings out of the eleven criteria rated. Only the rewarding of good advising performance was rated lower. These low ratings were consistent across public and private and two-year and four-year institutions, and they were consistent across the last three national surveys, dating back to 1987. Rated slightly higher but still ranking among the five lowest criteria were advisor accountability and advisor training, two criteria that depend heavily on the evaluation of both advising programs and individual advisors.

Upcraft and Schuh (1996) suggest numerous reasons why assessment and evaluation should be a component of any student services program. These reasons can be summarized into two general reasons. First, program administrators and practitioners should want to know whether or not their efforts and resources are producing the desired effects. Do students feel they have access to and receive assistance from caring and knowledgeable advisors? Do they make timely progress toward their educational objectives with the fewest possible missteps? Are students who encounter academic or personal difficulties referred to the appropriate support services for assistance? The list could go on, but the basic question is whether or not the academic advising services are accomplishing what they are charged to do; and if not, why not?

Second, advising needs to be evaluated for political and economic reasons. In an age of increasing public skepticism on matters related to higher education, the general public and the politicians and governing boards who represent them are increasing their demands for accountability. Increasing competition for resources, both from within and outside higher education, is making it difficult for programs and services to maintain current budgets, and even more difficult to acquire additional resources. Failure to document accountability leads to both political and fiscal risk.

Combining today's political and economic realities with the findings of ACT's national advising survey places advising programs and advisors in a vulnerable position. With demands for demonstrated accountability increasing, limited time and resources are being devoted to determining whether or not programs and advisors are effective, providing the training and support needed to ensure effectiveness, and rewarding those programs and advisors who are effective.

Components of an Effective Advising Program

This chapter focuses on how to evaluate an institution's academic advising program—specifically, how to evaluate the advising process and the outcomes produced. While most scholars view the advising process and its outcomes as the primary indicators of a program's success or failure, this success or failure is influenced by other, often ignored components of the advising program. What are these other components and how might an institution assess or evaluate them? The Council for the Advancement of Standards in Higher Education (CAS) identifies thirteen standards (components) that should be included in an institution's academic advising program (Council for the Advancement of Standards in Higher Education, 1998). For each of the thirteen components, CAS provides a performance standard and guidelines that suggest actions that may be taken to meet the standard. The thirteen standards or components of an academic advising program are as follows:

1. *Mission (statement):* A clear delineation of the program's philosophy, goals, and objectives, with statements of expectations for advisors and advisees

2. *Program:* A delineation of program components along with a description of how they operate individually and collectively, and the expected outcomes

3. *Leadership:* An identifiable individual or individuals with designated responsibility, authority, and accountability for leading and managing the advising program

4. *Organization and management:* An organizational structure and management system that positions the advising program and its leadership in a manner that allows for the effective delivery of advising services

5. *Human resources:* Staffing sufficient to deliver advising services and accomplish program goals

6. *Financial resources:* A funding level sufficient to allow goal accomplishment

7. *Facilities, technology, and equipment:* The location of program components in facilities conducive to service delivery, and the provision of the technology and equipment necessary for service delivery

8. *Legal responsibilities:* Advising leadership and academic advisors who are knowledgeable of relevant laws, policies, and procedures and who provide advising services in accordance with these.

9. *Equal opportunity, access, and affirmative action:* Procedures, policies, and practices that ensure that program staffing and academic advising are conducted without discrimination on the basis of age, color, disability, gender, national origin, race, religion, sexual orientation, or veteran status

10. *Campus and community relations:* Creation and maintenance of effective working relationships with relevant campus and community offices and services

11. *Diversity:* Recognition of the value of diversity and the promotion of opportunities that foster awareness of and appreciation and respect for the cultures of other people

12. *Ethics:* Policies, procedures, and practices that ensure that advisors and the advising program adhere to high standards of personal and professional ethics

13. *Assessment and evaluation:* Routine quantitative and qualitative assessment and evaluation of the academic advising program for purposes of program and personnel accountability and improvement

Some of the CAS standards (program, organization and management, human resources, fiscal resources, and facilities, technology, and equipment) are more directly related than others to the delivery of advising services and the outcomes achieved. However, serious deficiencies in any one of the thirteen standards can impair the advising process and the program's ability to achieve its desired outcomes.

Before an institution develops an assessment and evaluation plan for academic advising, it may wish first to undertake a comprehensive self-assessment such as that outlined by CAS. Doing so will facilitate the planning and implementation of assessment and evaluation of the actual advising process and outcomes. The self-assessment process underscores the complexity of the advising program and helps delineate those areas that should be included in any program assessment. Further, the self-assessment will help identify problem areas and suggest improvement strategies in the event that the program evaluation discovers problems or deficiencies. For example, if the self-assessment reveals that the institution has failed to conceptualize a clear mission statement and definition of academic advising, this failure is likely to have an impact on the results of a process or outcomes evaluation. For institutions wishing to undertake such a self-assessment of their advising program, CAS provides a detailed self-assessment guide (CAS, 1998). (*Note:* Although phrased differently, many of the program components and practices included in the CAS standards are assessed in ACT's fifth national survey. Viewed together, the ACT results provide a national benchmark for some of the CAS standards.)

Levels of Evaluation

The assessment and evaluation of academic advising may appear to be an overwhelming task. Such perceptions are likely to exist in proportion to the size and complexity of the institution. While such perceptions are understandable, and even valid, evaluation of academic advising can occur on any one of four levels of increasing complexity: the individual advisor, the advising program, the advising unit, or institution-wide.

Individual advisor. Here the focus is on the quality of advising provided by a specific advisor. The results are most often utilized by the advisor or by the supervisor to guide the professional growth and improvement of the advisor or in decisions regarding reappointment, promotion, and tenure. The aggregation of individual advisor evaluations is an essential component of any program, unit, or institution-wide evaluation. The reader is referred to Chapter Twenty-Four for a more comprehensive discussion of the assessment and evaluation of individual advisors.

Advising program. An academic advising program is an intervention targeted to address the advising needs of a specific population of students (for example, a weekly advising seminar for at-risk freshmen; a special advising component for women in mathematics, science, or engineering; a peer advising program for entering students of color). The advising program may involve one or more advisors and functions as only one of multiple programmatic efforts within an advising unit.

Advising unit. An advising unit, as defined here, is an identifiable administrative or organizational entity that is allocated resources and charged with a mission or purpose that includes but may not be limited to providing academic advising. Such units include academic departments, advising centers, and so on. The advising unit usually has multiple academic advisors and is characterized by a program context from which advising services are delivered. Advising units frequently have responsibility for providing academic advising to specific populations or subpopulations of students (departmental majors, at-risk students, undecided students, disabled students, and so on). Whereas in the case of the individual advisor the focus is on the performance of that individ-ual, for the advising program and advising unit attention is also given to the interworking of the component members.

Institution-wide. In an institutional assessment, the focus encompasses indi-vidual advisors, advising programs, and advising units, but it goes beyond these separate components to include their interfacing with each other and with other program units that support academic advising (counseling services, learning centers, career services, admissions, the registrar, and so on). In an institutional assessment, the programs and services provided by these nonadvising services in support of academic advising are also included in the evaluation.

Types of Evaluation

For purposes of assessment and evaluation, academic advising is most appro-priately viewed as a complex process or system designed to produce outcomes. As such, any comprehensive evaluation of an institution's advising services should include two types of evaluation: process evaluation and outcomes eval-uation.

Process evaluation is the assessment of how effectively and efficiently advis-ing services are being delivered and to whom. Stated differently, Is the system working, and working on behalf of those for whom it is intended? Scheirer (1994) notes that process evaluation allows for examination of variations in pro-gram delivery. In academic advising, multiple delivery systems are common within a single institution. One may encounter faculty advisors, professional advisors, peer advisors, advising centers, and satellite programs responsible for advising subpopulations of students who cross all other academic and pro-grammatic boundaries (for example, learning disabled students, at-risk students, and so on). Process evaluation also provides information about the quality of service delivery and about which program components are contributing to pro-gram outcomes and which are not.

The second component of any complete program or service evaluation is an *outcomes assessment* or evaluation. Any well-defined program or service will have stated outcomes that it is supposed to accomplish. For academic advising this may be student retention, graduation within a given time frame, comple-tion of specified degree requirements, advisee enrollment in appropriate sup-port services, student and alumni satisfaction with the advising they have received, and so on. A comprehensive assessment and evaluation plan will include both process and outcomes components. The two approaches operate in a complimentary manner. Where outcomes fall short of desired levels, results from the process evaluation may offer suggested causes. In those cases where outcomes are achieved, results from the process evaluation may suggest avenues for even greater success or possible efficiencies through the identification of nonessential processes, policies, or procedures.

Challenges in the Assessment and Evaluation of Academic Advising

Developing an assessment plan for academic advising poses a number of challenges. First, the complexity of the advising process must be addressed. Academic advising should be viewed as a system much more complex than the advisor-advisee dyad. For this dyad to function well, information must flow back and forth, not only between advisor and advisee but also to and from the advising dyad and various campus offices and services, including admissions, the registrar, financial aid, learning assistance centers, career services, counseling services, student activities, and others. In some cases, the information flow is primarily inward to the advising dyad. In other cases, the flow results in information and referrals to the services. For still others, the relationship is one of reciprocity, in which information flows in both directions. Regardless of direction, any serious disruption of information or the failure of any one component can compromise the quality of academic advising. A comprehensive assessment or evaluation of academic advising must delineate these relationships and include them in the evaluation process—both as an entity to be evaluated and as a source of evaluative data.

A second challenge that must be addressed is the lack of a common definition and purpose for academic advising. Advisors and advisees differ in their opinions as to what should be included in academic advising. Definitions and expectations differ between underclass and upperclass students, among academic majors, between traditional and nontraditional students, and so on. These differences in definition and expectations lead to variations in program mission, goals, and objectives. The mission, goals, and objectives and in turn the definition of success must be used to determine the evaluative criteria to be assessed. When the evaluation moves beyond the individual advisor to encompass multiple advisors or multiple advising programs or units, a single set of evaluative criteria will no longer suffice. To meet this challenge, the evaluator must recognize these differences by tailoring the evaluative criteria to the specific situation.

A third challenge stems from the ethical consideration that all students are entitled to the institution's best advising efforts. This precludes experimentation with or manipulation of advising programs and services in a manner that might place advisees at risk. This in turn prevents use of several of the stronger evaluation designs that can determine cause and effect relationships. Instead, the evaluator must often rely on less powerful designs that reduce the certainty of the findings.

Considerations in Planning Assessment and Evaluation

The value of any program evaluation will be determined more by how the results are used than by the results themselves. This applies whether the focus of the evaluation is on the advising process or on advising outcomes, and it applies whether the focus is on the individual advisor, on an advising program or advising unit, or on an institution-wide advising system. Program evaluation is often viewed as a threat by those responsible for or involved in the program. Whether or not the results of an evaluation of academic advising are utilized as intended will be determined in part by whether or not they are viewed as valid and fair by those affected. If those to be affected by the evaluation results are involved in the planning and design of the evaluation, the threat is lessened and the evaluation is more likely to accomplish its intended purpose. Therefore the evaluation should be planned by a committee or team rather than by a single individual. The planning committee or team must include representatives from among the individuals likely to be affected by the results, such as academic advisors, advising administrators, faculty, student support services personnel, and students.

Prior to the actual planning of the evaluation, the planning team should focus on three issues. First, academic advising must be defined. Is there a general consensus as to the advising program's mission, goals, objectives, and priorities? If the institution or program does not have an official statement of mission, goals, and expectations for academic advising, reaching such consensus may be problematic. If such consensus does not exist or cannot be reached, the issue must be addressed by incorporating variations into the criteria to be assessed. Second, once advising is defined, the delivery system or systems must be identified and delineated. The planning team must understand how the delivery systems are supposed to operate, and they must identify the personnel and their responsibilities. Third, there should be general understanding and agreement as to the purpose of the evaluation and how the results will be used. Will they be used for evaluation of personnel, program improvement, or for other purposes?

Assuming a consensus can be reached on these issues, the planning committee can then move to planning the evaluation. First, the planning committee must identify the questions that the evaluation is supposed to answer. These questions will demonstrate whether the evaluation will concentrate on advising outcomes or on both the advising process and the outcomes. After the questions have been identified, the committee must define the focus of the evaluation. As explained previously, the focus may be on the individual advisor, on advising programs or units, or on the institution-wide advising system.

Once the questions have been identified and the focus of the evaluation determined, the committee must identify and operationally define valid indicators (data) that will indicate whether the advising process is working, whether desired outcomes are being achieved, or both. Finally, once the data to be collected have been determined, the committee must then identify the sources that can provide the needed information and the data collection methods.

When making these decisions, the planning committee may wish to refer to CAS standard 13 (assessment and evaluation) for guidance. If the assessment and evaluation process is to meet the CAS standard, six criteria are suggested:

1. Systematic qualitative evaluations
2. Systematic quantitative evaluations
3. Employment of a sufficient range of evaluation measures to ensure objectivity and comprehensiveness
4. Data collected directly from students and other affected constituencies
5. Utilization of results to revise and improve academic advising
6. Utilization of results to recognize advisor performance

Obviously the first four criteria speak to the evaluation process and the final two address the intended use of the results.

I recommend that the evaluation address both process and outcomes. The temptation may be to focus on outcomes only, in part because including the process greatly increases the complexity of the evaluation. However, when one moves beyond the course selection component of advising and into a more developmental model, advising becomes much less routine and much more complex. This complexity increases the need for effective communication and information flow among campus programs and services, thereby extending the scope of advising well beyond the advisor-advisee dyad. Process evaluation is necessary to assess the degree to which this wider range of programs, services, and players are interfacing effectively. If a desired outcome is not being achieved, it is the process analysis that may suggest avenues to improvement.

It has been noted that an evaluation may focus on any of four evaluation units: the individual advisor, an advising program, an advising unit, or the institution-wide advising system. As evaluation moves from the individual advisor to the institutional system, the task becomes increasingly complex. Depending on the institution, the evaluation units may exist in a variety of organizational structures (Habley and Morales, 1998). In those institutions with totally centralized advising systems, the institutional system and the aggregate of individual advisors may be one and the same.

Once the type (process, outcomes, or both) of evaluation and the focus (advisor, program, advising unit, or institution) have been determined, attention may be directed to the identification of indicators (variables) to be measured. Figure 23.1 lists possible process and outcome indicators. This listing is not all-inclusive and the appropriateness of a specific indicator will depend on the institution and how it defines advising. Note the complementary relationships that exist between the process indicators and the outcomes. The former are indicative of whether or not the desired or prescribed activities are occurring while the latter seek to assess whether or not the desired results have occurred.

After the planning committee has determined what data will be collected as process and outcome indicators, attention turns to the identification of data sources. Exhibit 23.2 suggests potential sources of both qualitative and quantitative information. These sources can be divided into people and documents.

Process Indicators	Outcome Indicators
Advisee follow-through on referrals	Academic performance (GPA)
Advisor accessibility	Advisee satisfaction ratings
Advisor assignments/loads	Alumni satisfaction ratings
Advisor utilization of referral services	Appropriate course selections
Advisor knowledge of	Appropriate referrals
career options	Cocurricular involvements
policies, procedures, and requirements	Courses failed
Advisor understanding/use of profile data	Drop-add transactions
Appropriate remedial assignments	Graduate/professional school admission rates
Availability of student profile information	Graduation rates
Course selections consistent with	Persistence rates
advisee degree objectives	Postgraduation career placements
advisee profiles	Time to graduation
prerequisite requirements and advisee's performance	
Number of advisor-initiated contacts	
Number of student-initiated contacts	
Number of students not receiving advising	
Referral follow-up with advisor and advisee	
Referrals to cocurricular activities	
Referrals to experiential education	
Requests for change of advisor and reasons	

Exhibit 23.1. Advising Process and Outcome Indicators.

The listing of potential data and data sources can be extensive. As a general rule, a given data element should be collected only if it will be used in the evaluation to answer an evaluation question. Also, those data elements that are available from university records, databases, and so on should not be collected again. If these criteria are applied and reapplied to each proposed data element, both the data elements collected and the sources involved can be limited to manageable numbers.

Data Collection

Finally, after the committee has identified who and what is to be evaluated, what evaluation questions are to be answered, what data are needed to answer these questions, and the sources from which the data can be collected, the com-

People	**Documents**
Academic deans/department heads	Academic transcripts
Admissions staff	Admission profiles
Advisees	Advisee course/class schedules
Advising administrators	Advisor notes/records
Advisors	Degree-audit reports (DARS)
Alumni	Developmental transcripts
Career planning staff	Grade reports
Counseling staff	Placement scores/profiles
Faculty	Registrar's student data file
Financial assistance staff	Student information files
Housing staff	Student tracking system
Graduating seniors	Transcripts/videos of advising
Learning assistance staff	
Registrar	
Students not advised	
Withdrawing students	

Exhibit 23.2. Potential Data Sources.

mittee must decide by what methods the data will be collected. A variety of collection methods are available for both qualitative and quantitative data. Several are discussed here. More detailed discussion of each methodology can be found in the relevant sources provided in the resources list.

Surveys

Surveys are usually conducted by one of three methods—mail, telephone, or in person—and are an efficient means of collecting information from large numbers of people at relatively low cost. Survey questions usually include multiple-choice options, rating scales, fill-in-the-blank questions, or short-answer questions. These response formats permit relatively simple analysis and interpretation. Open-ended questions are sometimes used but can be cumbersome to interpret and analyze.

If survey techniques are utilized, efforts should be made to keep the survey as short as possible. The longer the survey instrument is, the less likely it is that the respondent will be able to complete it. Avoid using the survey to collect data that are readily accessible from other sources (that is, age, class, gender, major, and so on). Also, the evaluator must decide who will be asked to complete the survey. Will all members of the group of interest be surveyed or will a subset or sample be surveyed? Various sampling techniques are available and are discussed in the sources listed in the resources list at the end of this chapter. Whatever methods are utilized, the evaluator must use a large-enough sample to ensure the desired level of confidence in the results. If the purpose of the evaluation is to focus on and compare various subgroups of the population (that is, freshmen compared to seniors, minority students, undecided students, students in preprofessional curricula, and so on), care must be taken to ensure that adequate numbers are sampled from each of the desired subpopulations.

Interviews

Interviews, either in person or by phone, are less efficient than surveys but can allow for more in-depth responses on the part of the interviewee. Again, as in the use of surveys, the interviews must be with a representative sample of the population or subpopulations under study.

Interviewers should be trained in interviewing techniques such as how to avoid asking leading questions, when to probe for elaboration on a response, how to record responses, and so on. The preferred means for establishing a degree of consistency across interviewers is to have each interviewer operate from a standard interview protocol. Whenever possible, audio or video recordings of the interviews should be made. These recordings ensure a complete record of the interviewee response and aid in the analysis.

Survey and interview methods are often utilized in conjunction with each other. Following the collection of the survey data, individuals are identified based on their responses to selected survey items, and follow-up interviews are conducted.

Focus Groups

Focus groups are small, informal groups whose discussion focuses on one or more issues of interest to the evaluator. The group's discussion is guided by a trained leader whose role is not to participate in the discussion but to keep the discussion focused on the questions or topics of concern. This may include the interjection of questions designed to elicit elaboration or more in-depth examination of the topic by the group membership. Stated differently, the leader should function not as a member of the group but as a facilitator of the discussion. An advantage of focus groups is that the interactions among the group members may provide information and insights not ordinarily obtained by survey or individual interview. For purposes of analysis, an audio or video recording of the group is recommended.

Field Observation

Field observation involves one or more nonparticipants observing an advising event, such as an advising conference, and systematically recording what takes place. Using field observation as a data collection method requires that the observers be trained in observation methods as well as in what events to record and how they are to be recorded. Interaction analysis protocols are frequently utilized to guide the observers and facilitate their recording of data, such as which party initiates an exchange, the topic of the exchange, the nature of the exchange (question, statement, request for information, and so on), and how the second party responds. As with interviews and focus groups, an audio or video recording of the event allows for postvalidation of the observer's observations. Reliability of observation data can be increased through the use of multiple observers. Care should be taken to make the observation process as unobtrusive as possible.

Document Analysis

For purposes of this discussion, document analysis means the collection of data from agency records (that is, registrar grade reports, student transcripts, student admission profiles, test score reports, enrollment transaction summaries, and so on) and advisor records such as those files normally maintained on each advisee. Document analyses can be very efficient, as in the downloading of data elements from the registrar's student data bank, or very laborious, as in the review of advisors' case notes. For those instances in which the information is to be gleaned from nonstructured databases (for example, advisors' notes, appointment schedules, and so on), the data recorders must be trained on what data is to be collected, how to identify this data, how to record ambiguous data, and so forth. The accuracy of such recorded audits can be greatly improved through the use of standard data recording forms that indicate what data elements are to be collected.

Field Experiments

Evaluators of academic advising will frequently wish to assess the impact of a particular advising program by assessing whether or not it had an impact or whether it is more or less effective than an alternative program. In either instance, the evaluator wishes to conclude that any change from the status quo or differences among the programs being compared are caused by the advising intervention or interventions. If circumstances allow, the evaluator will be best served by one of the true experimental designs discussed by Campbell and Stanley (1963). However, traditional experimental designs assume that the researcher can randomly select subjects and randomly assign them to the various treatments being compared (for example, advising programs). Because of ethical or logistical considerations or both, in academic advising research such randomization may not be possible. In these instances, the evaluator may be able to utilize a quasi-experimental design to achieve a similar level of design validity.

Data Analysis

The assessment and evaluation process discussed in this chapter provides the evaluation committee with a variety of both quantitative and qualitative information. Different analysis techniques are appropriate for each type of information. In analyzing the data and reporting the findings, the evaluator should utilize methodologies that can be understood by individuals with varying levels of statistical expertise and understanding. In general, strive for simplicity and brevity. Whenever possible, use basic descriptive statistics such as means, medians, frequencies, percentages, and so on. Employ graphs whenever possible. Basic descriptive statistics alone will suffice when the entire population of students or advisees is included in the database.

In those instances where data has been collected from samples, inferential methodologies should be employed. Inferential methodologies will allow the evaluator to accomplish three things. First, inferential methods should be utilized to place confidence limits around any descriptive statistics that are based on samples. Second, inferential methodologies will allow for the statistical comparison of various subgroupings of advisees, the comparison of multiple advising approaches or programs, the determination of relationships among various measurements, and the development of prediction models. Third, inferential statistics will allow for the determination of practical significance (as opposed to merely statistical significance), which should be the basis on which programmatic decisions are made. Commonly used statistical analysis software packages will provide the evaluator with the programs needed to conduct most descriptive and inferential procedures.

The analysis of qualitative data may appear to be much less structured than the analysis of quantitative date, and at times somewhat intimidating. The process will involve data reduction procedures in which the focus is on identifying recurring themes, issues, problems, and so on. Direct quotations from interviewees, focus group members, advisors' case notes, and such are frequently cited to illustrate the qualitative results. Triangulation is a procedure frequently utilized by qualitative researchers to establish the validity of what some critics see as being subjective data and findings. It is the process whereby qualitative researchers draw on data from multiple procedures (interviews, focus groups, observations, and so on) to cross-validate the existence of common themes, issues, problems, and so on.

Reporting Results and Recommendations

Depending on the complexity and scope of the evaluation, the final report of the assessment and evaluation committee may be a lengthy document. A full report of the study should be written to explain what was evaluated, who was evaluated, what data were collected, how they were collected, and from whom. Summaries of the descriptive statistics and any statistical analyses should be included. The purpose of the full report is to document what was done and to provide a reference document for administrators, policymakers, program managers, advisors, and other interested parties.

Although a lengthy evaluation report may be necessary, it is frequently a problem. The report's length and complexity will discourage all but the most dedicated from reading it. The evaluator's solution to this problem is the executive summary and recommendations. The executive summary should be no longer than three pages and provide a brief discussion of what was done, but it should focus mainly on the findings. Based on the evaluation committee's findings, a list of recommendations should be offered. Sonnichsen (1994) suggests that well-written recommendations possess five qualities. First, the recommendations must be made in a timely fashion. Obviously, the quality of academic advising was a priority when the evaluation team was given its charge. Recommendations that arrive after decisions have been made or after other priorities have replaced academic advising are less likely to be implemented. Second, to receive serious consideration, recommendations must have a realistic chance for implementation. The organizational structure of the institution, its formal and informal political power structure, and its budget realities should all be considered. Third, recommendations should be directed to those who will have final responsibility for implementation. This will include directors and coordinators of advising, academic advisors, and the directors and staff of relevant support services. Fourth, recommendations should be simple, specific, and understood by all affected. Finally, the connection between the recommendation and the findings should be obvious.

Conclusion

For purposes of evaluation, academic advising should be viewed as a complex process or system that is designed to produce outcomes. As such, any comprehensive evaluation of academic advising should focus on both the process and the outcomes. Process evaluation examines how effectively and efficiently advising services are being delivered and to whom. Outcomes evaluation seeks to answer whether or not the advising process is producing the desired results. The value of an assessment of academic advising will be determined by how the results are used. Because program assessment or evaluation is often viewed as a threat by those responsible for the program, steps should be taken to ensure that the evaluation process is viewed as valid and fair. Given the complexity of the advising process and the need to instill a sense of validity and fairness, an evaluation of academic advising is best undertaken by a project team that includes academic advisors, advising administrators, faculty, student support services personnel, and students.

An evaluation of academic advising may focus on any of four levels: the individual advisor, a specific advising program, an advising unit or the overall institutional advising system. Depending on the focus, the goals and objectives and even the definition of academic advising may vary. Because goals and objectives define success, each must be explicitly understood before evaluative criteria can be established. Once the evaluative criteria are established, the assessment should recognize the complexity of the advising process by utilizing both qualitative and quantitative methodologies.

Once the evaluation or assessment is completed, the project team or committee is usually expected to produce an evaluation report. Because the report is often lengthy, it should be accompanied by a much shorter executive summary. Depending on the results of the evaluation, recommendations for change or improvements may be warranted. Any such recommendations should be timely, follow logically from the findings, be simple and specific, have a reasonable chance for implementation, and be directed to those who will have responsibility for implementation.

Resources

Merriam, S. B. *Qualitative Research and Case Study Application in Education.* San Francisco: Jossey-Bass, 1998.

Rea, L. M., and Parker, R. A. *Designing and Conducting Survey Research.* San Francisco: Jossey-Bass, 1997.

Silverman, D. *Interpreting Qualitative Data: Methods for Analyzing Talk, Text and Interaction.* Thousand Oaks, Calif.: Sage, 1993.

Upcraft, M. L., and Schuh, J. H. *Assessment in Student Affairs: A Guide for Practitioners.* San Francisco: Jossey-Bass, 1996.

Wholey, J. S., Hatry, H. P., and Newcomer, K. E. (eds.). *Handbook of Practical Program Evaluation.* San Francisco: Jossey-Bass, 1994.

References

Campbell, D. T., and Stanley, J. C. *Experimental and Quasi-Experimental Designs for Research.* Boston: Houghton Mifflin, 1963.

Council for the Advancement of Standards in Higher Education. *Academic Advising Program Standards and Guidelines: Self-Assessment Guide.* Washington D.C.: Council for the Advancement of Standards in Higher Education, 1998.

Habley, W. R., and Morales, R. H. (eds.). *Current Practices in Academic Advising: Final Report on ACT's Fifth National Survey of Academic Advising.* National Academic Advising Association Monograph Series, no. 6. Manhattan, Kans.: National Academic Advising Association, 1998.

Miller, T. K. (ed.). *The Book of Professional Standards for Higher Education.* Washington, D.C.: Council for the Advancement of Standards in Higher Education, 1997.

Scheirer, M. A. "Designing and Using Process Evaluation." In J. S. Wholey, H. P. Hatry, and K. E. Newcomer (eds.), *Handbook of Practical Program Evaluation.* San Francisco: Jossey-Bass, 1994.

Sonnichsen, R. C. "Evaluators as Change Agents." In J. S. Wholey, H. P. Hatry, and K. E. Newcomer (eds.), *Handbook of Practical Program Evaluation.* San Francisco: Jossey-Bass, 1994.

Upcraft, M. L., and Schuh, J. H. *Assessment in Student Affairs: A Guide for Practitioners.* San Francisco: Jossey-Bass, 1996.

Chapter Twenty-Four

Assessing Individual Advisor Effectiveness

Elizabeth G. Creamer, Delores W. Scott

Evaluation is a judgment of value or worth. What is evaluated reflects what decision makers think is important (Brown and Sanstead, 1982). The main purpose of a systematic plan to evaluate advisors on a regular basis is to collect information that can contribute to improving advisor effectiveness in working with the student populations that are found in a particular setting. Like any judgment, it is subjective, based on the values and mission of a specific institutional context. Evaluating individual advisors is an important part of an overall strategy of program evaluation.

Slightly less than one-third of the institutions responding to American College Testing's fifth national survey of academic advising indicated that they evaluated the performance of advisors (Habley and Morales, 1998). Possibly reflecting the priority awarded to teaching, private institutions are more likely than public institutions to have systems in place to evaluate advisors. The failure of most institutions to conduct systematic evaluations of advisors is explained by a number of factors. These include a lack of resources, time, and expertise, and diverse delivery systems for advising within a single institution. It also includes the unspoken assumption that faculty should consider advising as part of their teaching or service assignment. The most potent reason, however, is probably that the traditional academic reward structure often blocks the ability to reward faculty who are genuinely committed to advising.

Characteristics of Effective Advising

The core elements of advisor behavior—availability, knowledge, and helpfulness— are central to the evaluation of advisors. Availability refers to the accessibility of an advisor to students and to whether the advisor honors posted office hours and meets scheduled appointments. Knowledge refers to both the accuracy and the timeliness of the information the advisor provides for students. Helpfulness refers to the extent that an advisor is perceived to express interest and concern for individual students and to provide information that is useful to the needs they articulate. These dimensions of an advisor's performance are most frequently assessed using feedback from students.

Administrative skills are an additional dimension of advisor effectiveness that is likely to require evaluative data from sources other than students. Administrative skills include handling of routine procedures, such as student records, as well as managing other responsibilities that accompany an advisor's role in addition to advising. This might include assignments on committees or projects related to advising. This is likely to be a larger component of the assignment of a professional advisor than of a faculty advisor.

While the core set of three advising skills applies to working with all students, effective advisors are likely to manifest or express these skills in somewhat different ways with students from different populations. Student expectations of advisors vary among older and traditional-age students, men and women, and between members of different racial or ethnic groups. Some of these differences are discussed in the next section.

Accessibility

White women and African Americans are the student groups most likely to demonstrate help-seeking behavior by taking the initiative to meet with an advisor. According to findings from the questions dealing with faculty on the 1991 and 1994 College Student Experiences Questionnaire (CSEQ), African American students were more likely than any other racial groups to have discussed personal problems or concerns with a faculty member. Findings from CSEQ also indicate that women were significantly more likely than men to have made an appointment to meet with a faculty member in his or her office and to have discussed career plans with a faculty member (Muffo, 1997).

These findings, among others, suggest that to be effective, advisors have to use different strategies to gain comparable access to members of different student groups. For some student populations, accessibility is accomplished by an open door and posted office hours. An informal, personal invitation or leaving the office to meet students informally in different locations across campus may be a more effective way to reach students who are unlikely to demonstrate help-seeking behavior.

Knowledge

Although both men and women prefer developmental to prescriptive advising, women have a significantly higher preference for developmental advising than men students (Herndon, Kaiser, and Creamer, 1996). Compared to prescriptive advising, developmental advising requires advisors to be knowledgeable on a broader range of topics. This is because the developmental approach is intentional about inviting the student to discuss the setting of personal, career, and life goals rather than just the requirements of a particular course or degree. This is an area in which the advisor's, the student's, and the supervisor's expectations may clash because not all advisors consider it in their domain of responsibility to discuss such an in-depth range of issues with students.

Helpfulness

Helpfulness is the dimension in which there is likely to be the widest differences in perception among members of different student groups. One way this dimension varies, for example, is in a preference for informal, out-of-class interaction with faculty. Informal interaction with faculty and advisors is more strongly associated with women's overall satisfaction than with men's (Light, 1990). African American and Asian American students are significantly more likely than other students to be dissatisfied with out-of-class availability of faculty (Muffo, 1997). This finding can be interpreted to reflect that these groups have high expectations for out-of-class interactions with faculty that are left largely unsatisfied.

Another way that some students may judge an advisor's helpfulness is by the advisor's willingness to raise or discuss issues related to race or gender. This is probably another example of an issue in which there are significant differences between the expectations of minority and majority students and between men and women students. African American and Asian American students are significantly more likely than other students to be dissatisfied with faculty attitudes toward students and racial harmony at their college or university. Women and members of minority groups are significantly more likely than men and members of the majority group to report needing help from faculty to cope with discrimination (Muffo, 1997). Black students see a culturally sensitive counselor or one who acknowledges their race or ethnicity as more competent than a culturally blind counselor (Pomales, Claiborn, and La Framboise, 1986).

While they have many of the same core needs and expectations of advisors, members of different student groups bring some different expectations that are likely to be reflected in how they evaluate the effectiveness of an academic advisor. Discussion of how expectations vary among members of different student populations, including among students at different stages of completing their degree, should be incorporated into the agenda of advisor training programs.

Methods of Evaluation

Four primary methods are utilized to evaluate advisors: student evaluation, self-evaluation, supervisory performance review, and peer review (Habley, 1988). In many cases, the process for conducting the evaluation must be negotiated with the campus human resources or personnel department.

Student Evaluations

Srebnik (1988) describes twelve pen-and-paper instruments that are available to collect student's perceptions about their advisors. These instruments generally assess student satisfaction with advisor behaviors and characteristics. They include standardized and nonstandardized instruments. Although pen-and-paper questionnaires have been the most common strategy for collecting information from students about advising, these kinds of data can also be collected through telephone interviews and through on-line or e-mail surveys. They are particularly valuable when they include open-ended questions that enable students to bring forward issues of concern to them that have not been addressed.

Focus Groups

A focus group occurs when a homogeneous group is convened to participate in a focused discussion about a particular topic. This method of data collection is effective in the evaluation of academic advising because it allows participants to express their thoughts, feelings, and perceptions in their own words. Many students find this format less intimidating than a one-to-one interview conducted by an official or authority figure associated with the university. When evaluating and assessing qualitative constructs such as advisor effectiveness and student satisfaction, this method facilitates the researcher's probing participants' opinions and perceptions and therefore provides for a more thorough understanding of the student's viewpoint.

Focus groups can be used to identify outstanding advisors as well as the traits students associate with effective advising. They lend themselves to discovery and exploration of aspects of the core skills of advisor effectiveness that may not have been anticipated. Assessing these variables through focus groups expands the evaluation beyond the dichotomous question of whether advising is effective or not. Because of the tool of probing, the information collected becomes more meaningful both to the advising process and to identifying areas in which improvement should occur. Whether advisors facilitate such discussion, are observers during the discussion, or gain the information by reading about it, the information derived from a focus group helps advisors to understand better how what they do is perceived by students.

Self-Assessment

Self-assessment is an important aspect of evaluation that has the goal of improving advisor effectiveness. A number of evaluation instruments are available for advisors to use to assess their attitudes about advising, the behaviors they use, and their perception of their level of support (Srebnik, 1988).

Research suggests that there is relatively high consistency between an advisor's stated philosophy of advising and the behaviors he or she actually utilizes (Daller, Creamer, and Creamer, 1997). The implication of this finding is that one way to assess advisors' behavior, if not necessarily their effectiveness, is to ask them to describe their philosophy of or approach to advising. Discussing philosophy with other advisors, as well as how they vary their approach among students, could be a valuable component of an advisor development program.

Peer or Collegial Assessment

Although it is a model used to evaluate college teaching, peer evaluation is the least frequently used method for evaluating advisors (Habley, 1988). Such a strategy is likely to include observation of performance in a number of settings, including with individuals and groups. Some advisors may find this type of evaluation less threatening than supervisor performance review. Another advantage of this approach is that many advisors are likely to find feedback from peers to be more credible than information from other sources, such as students.

Supervisor Assessment

Supervisor review is the most common form of advisor evaluation in advising offices (Habley and Morales, 1998). Supervisors are in a position to judge some aspects of advisor performance that students are not in a position to judge, such as the administrative dimensions of an advisor's role. These might include issues such as maintaining confidentiality and completing special projects, such as an advising newsletter or handbook. Supervisors, however, may no more be accurate judges than the advisor of students' perceptions and how they vary among different student populations.

Formative and Summative Evaluation

Evaluations differ in how the information or data collected are used.

Formative evaluation focuses most clearly on how to improve advisor effectiveness. Data collection tends to be iterative and ongoing. Information from formative evaluations can be used to guide individual goal setting and professional development plans. Summative evaluations for advisors are often in the form of annual performance reviews. This type of evaluation can be used to assist decision making, such as to guide personnel decisions or to identify advising award recipients. Summative evaluation can also be used to judge performance against a set of goals or criteria. The contribution of both forms of evaluation to improving advisor effectiveness is totally dependent on feeding the information back to the individual advisor in a constructive way. A summary of how information from formative and summative evaluations can be used appears in Exhibit 24.1.

Key Elements of Effective Evaluation Strategies

The quality of an evaluative strategy ultimately depends on the usefulness of the information collected to the particular institutional context and whether it contributes to improving advisor effectiveness. Effective evaluative strategies

Formative Evaluation

> Identify areas for staff development.
>
> Guide training activities.
>
> Guide individual goal setting.
>
> Define areas for professional development.

Summative Evaluation

> Judge performance relative to established goals or standards.
>
> Identify advising award recipients.
>
> Measure change in behaviors.
>
> Compare advisor's performance.
>
> Assist personnel decisions, such as to determine merit increases.

Exhibit 24.1. Uses of Formative and Summative Evaluations to Assess Advisor Effectiveness.

for advisors include the use of multiple sources and kinds of data, that procedures be in place so that evaluation is an ongoing or iterative process, that evaluation be linked to opportunities for professional development, and that it be linked to rewards.

Multiple Sources and Kinds of Data

No one type or source of data can provide a multidimensional assessment of advisor effectiveness. Feedback from more than one constituency and using more than one method is a way to get the full picture of an advisor's performance in a number of different settings.

While measures of student satisfaction with an advisor are a central element of most evaluations, they should be only one of many sources of data, because student evaluations of advising, like teaching, are influenced by extraneous factors, such as the race, sex, and perceived status of the advisor. In addition, student satisfaction measures cannot capture long-term outcomes and may be influenced by unrealistic or uninformed expectations about the role of an advisor. Finally, student learning is frequently the outcome of an uncomfortable situation in which a student's attitudes and preconceptions are challenged. This might be the case, for example, when a student who is unable to dissect a fetal pig in a first-year biology class is questioned by an advisor about how that reaction fits with the student's ambition to be a physician. This is exactly the kind of situation that may have long-term, positive consequences for a student, but that a student might evaluate negatively in the short-term.

An Ongoing or Iterative Process

Feedback from data collected in the process of conducting an evaluation is most likely to affect an advisor's behavior when it is part of an ongoing, regularly scheduled process of data collection in which advisors have full access to data collected from a variety of sources and using a variety of methods. Anecdotal comments or an occasional letter from a student, whether positive or negative, hardly suffices as an adequate measure of an advisor's effectiveness over time and among different student populations.

Linked to Opportunities for Professional Development and Goal Setting

Findings from evaluations are most likely to affect attitudes and behaviors when the advisors to be evaluated participate in developing a systematic plan for evaluation and in determining the types of data that will be collected. This approach can be effective only when it takes into account other aspects of an advisor's work assignment.

Linked to Rewards

Just as about two-thirds if institutions do not evaluate the performance of advisors, more than two-thirds of institutions do not recognize, reward, or compensate faculty for academic advising (Habley and Morales, 1998). The two strategies are obviously linked. The linking of rewards to effective academic advising is a clear indication of an institution's commitment to advising weighed against other, competing demands on faculty time.

Recognition of faculty's advising roles can come in many different forms. These include release time from instruction or committee work, financial incentives, considering advising as part of the tenure and promotion process as either teaching or service, travel funds, the opportunity to attend conferences related to advising, reference materials about advising, and awards for excellence in advising. While there is often a core group of faculty whose commitment to students is reflected in high-quality teaching and advising, it is unrealistic to expect most faculty members to allocate more than the minimum required attention to advising when doing so means sacrificing other areas of faculty performance that are evaluated for tenure and promotion. Advising should be clearly identified as part of the expectations for the teaching component of faculty responsibilities. Institutions that have no system of rewards in place for academic advising are not fully committed to it as an element of either teaching or service.

Following is a list of resources for developing and implementing a plan to evaluate advisors:

Resources Provided by Related Professional Associations

Miller, T. K. (ed.). "Standards and Guidelines for Academic Advising." CAS Blue Book. Washington, D.C.: Council for the Advancement of Standards for Student Services/Development Programs, 1999.

National Clearinghouse for Academic Advising, Ohio State University, and National Academic Advising Association. "Annotated Bibliography on Evaluation and Assessment." www.uvc-ohio-state.edu/chouse.html

National Academic Advising Association. *Statement of Core Values.* Manhattan, Kans.: National Academic Advising Association, 1994.

Standardized Instruments Completed by Students

ACT Survey of Academic Advising

The Academic Advising Inventory (Winston and Sandor, 1984).

The Developmental Advising Inventory (Dickson and Thayer, 1993)

Conclusion

A common theme throughout higher education is the critical role of strong leadership and vision in supporting the advising function. Because of the positive impact of effective advising on student retention and graduation, college and university administrators must be willing to view the function of advisors as integral to the institution's commitment to student success. Fundamental to this is the existence of an institutional mission statement that clearly recognizes the advising role to be at the core of teaching and learning.

Top-level leadership is important to operationalize the institutional mission and make a commitment to advising as a component of student success. Operationalizing a mission statement that includes an emphasis on advising means having organizational processes and structures in place that reward and recognize effective advising and that provide opportunities for advisors across campus to engage in dialogue about their advising roles. Effective advising is not an outcome that occurs from just routinely meeting with students and giving them advice; rather, it is one that requires creative and systematic strategies to promote student development. Institutions that communicate through their mission statement and goals that advising is important are likely to have positive outcomes both in the quality of student learning experiences and in retention and graduation rates. Positive outcomes in these areas ultimately result in satisfied alumni and increased enrollments, and might suggest a stable institutional economy. If the value of effective advising is entrenched in the institutional mission, the potential resulting fiscal stability can provide an opportunity for allocation of additional resources to advisor training, evaluation and assessment, and effectiveness.

How resources are allocated within an institution is directly related to the institution's goals and mission. Because of the importance of advisor training and evaluation and assessment, resource allocation is key to articulating the importance of appointing people who are committed to advising and to cultivating exceptional skills among advisors. These resources can and should be reflected by rewarding advisors through increased salaries, recognition, rewards, facilities, training, technology, and assessment through other strategies.

Valuing advising as a major part of teaching and learning, providing rewards for effective advising, and allocating resources to support advising programs can be outcomes of an institutional mission that values advising and the role of advisors in student satisfaction and retention. When combined with championship or advocacy for the advising function by top-level leaders, these variables demonstrate a commitment to advising that will make the difference between the successful or unsuccessful advisor in American colleges and universities.

If individual advisors are to be effective, then it is essential that they receive feedback from a number of sources about their performance. The value of both formative and summative evaluations is in how effectively the information generated is used. This chapter has reviewed the characteristics of effective advising and ways to collect information about advisor effectiveness, and it has described a variety of resources that assist the practitioner in the development of formative and summative evaluations.

References

Brown, R. D., and Sanstead, M. J. "Using Evaluation to Make Decisions About Academic Advising Programs." In R. B. Winston Jr., S. C. Ender, & T. K. Miller (eds.), *Developmental Approaches to Academic Advising* . San Francisco: Jossey-Bass, 1982.

Daller, M. L., Creamer, E. G., and Creamer, D. G. "Advising Styles Observable in Practice: Counselor, Scheduler, and Teacher." *NACADA Journal*, 1997, *17*(20), 31–38.

Dickson, G. L., and Thayer, J. D. *The Developmental Advising Inventory.* Kettering, Ohio: Developmental Advising Inventories, 1993.

Habley, W. R, (ed.). *The Status and Future of Academic Advising: Problems and Promises.* Iowa City, Iowa: American College Testing Program, 1988.

Habley, W. R., and Morales, R. H. *Current Practices in Academic Advising: Final Report on ACT's Fifth National Survey of Academic Advising.* National Academic Advising Association Monograph Series, no. 6. Manhattan, Kans.: National Academic Advising Association, 1998.

Herndon, J. B., Kaiser, J., and Creamer, D. G. "Student Preferences for Advising Style in Community College Environments." *Journal of College Student Development,* 1996, *37*(6), 637–648.

Light, R. J. "Explorations with Students and Faculty About Teaching, Learning, and Student Life." *Harvard Assessment Seminars.* Cambridge, Mass.: Harvard University, 1990.

Miller, T. K. (ed.). "Standards and Guidelines for Academic Advising." CAS Blue Book. Washington, D.C.: Council for the Advancement of Standards for Student Services/Development Programs, 1999.

Muffo, J. "In Dealing with Students, Race and Gender Do Matter." *Quality Improvement in Action: Reports from the Academic Assessment Program.* Blacksburg, Va.: Virginia Polytechnic Institute and State University, Mar. 1997.

National Clearinghouse for Academic Advising, Ohio State University, and National Academic Advising Association. "Annotated Bibliography on Evaluation and Assessment." www.uvc-ohio-state.edu/chouse.html

Pomales, J., Claiborn, C. D., and La Framboise, T. D. "Effects of Black Students' Racial Identity on Perceptions of White Counselors in Varying Cultural Settings." *Journal of Counseling Psychology,* 1986, *33*(1), 57–61.

Srebnik, D. S. "Academic Advising Evaluation: A Review of Assessment Instruments." *NACADA Journal,* 1988, *8*(1), 52–62.

Winston, R. B., and Sandor, J. A. *The Academic Advising Inventory.* Athens, Ga.: Student Development Associates, 1984.

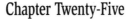

Chapter Twenty-Five

Recognition and Reward for Excellence in Advising

Thomas J. Kerr

Is it a simple idea or a complicated issue? On the surface, who could argue that advisors should not be recognized or rewarded for their efforts in providing advising to students at our institutions of higher learning? If a survey of college and university presidents was commissioned and they were asked, Should advisors at your institution be recognized or rewarded for providing academic advising? it would not surprise anyone that the response would be an overwhelming if not unanimous affirmative. In a similar manner if faculty and professional advisors were surveyed on the same issue, a similar response would be expected. Then what is the problem? There has been no agreement on the level of recognition or reward that is appropriate. The issue gets more complicated when the recognition or reward requires a commitment of scarce resources. A scarce resource does not always mean money; it could include other things, such as space, professional time, limited tenured faculty positions, and so on. Multiple levels of recognition and rewards can be used to honor advisors for exemplary performance.

This chapter focuses on what is involved in implementing a program at various levels of commitment, examines some current practices, and makes some suggestions on how to implement a program at each level.

Characteristics of a Profession

To implement a recognition and reward program that has an institutional impact is a difficult task because it requires that all stakeholders of the institution buy into the program. A typical program would include academic advising in the promotion and tenure review process for faculty advisors. There is an inherent problem, however, in that academic advising is not viewed as a profession by many of the individuals who are seeking to be recognized and rewarded for their efforts. The status of academic advising must be elevated and it must be recognized as a profession before recognition and reward programs at the institutional level will be commonplace.

Christensen (1980) outlines five major, interrelated components of a profession that could apply to advising: (1) history and philosophy, (2) relevant theories, (3) models and practice, (4) professional competencies, and (5) management and organizational competencies. Although the professional identity of advisors is fairly new, these five components can be identified as part of the awareness of individuals currently practicing in the profession. Perhaps the best view is presented by Young (1988), who suggests that student affairs (and advising) should be thought of as dynamic and professionalizing rather than as static and fully professionalized.

While at present advising does not qualify as a full profession under many of the criteria set forth by Christensen (1980), it can be viewed as an "emerging" profession with many of the earmarks of a profession in place. A professional identity has been established, national standards have been set, a broad range of autonomy exists for individual practitioners, national organizations have been formed, and a code of ethics has been developed (Gordon, 1992).

Although academic advising may be viewed as an emerging profession, how far has it really progressed? The existence of a well-articulated policy statement, the establishment of a means to measure effectiveness, the existence of training and evaluation, and finally, recognition and reward are cornerstones of performance in every established, recognized profession. These very factors, however, have been the Achilles heel for the field of advising as confirmed by the data generated by the five national surveys of academic advising produced by American College Testing (ACT).

Factors in Academic Advising Becoming a Profession

Four major factors need to be considered for academic advising to become a profession: a policy statement, a means to measure the effectiveness of advising, implementation of training and evaluation, and finally, a means to provide recognition and reward.

Policy Statement

Perhaps the key component to establishing a field as a profession is not simply the existence of a policy statement but what is included and, even more importantly, not included in the statement. Between the 1987 and 1992 surveys there was a significant increase in the number of institutions reporting existence of a written policy statement, but this appears to have leveled off at 61 percent, as reported by the 1997 survey. Of those reporting that they have a policy statement, most (more than half) included statements on philosophy, goals of advising, delivery strategies, responsibilities of advisors, and responsibilities of advisees. Not emphasized in policy were the other cornerstones of advising: training (30 percent), accountability and evaluation (18 percent), and recognition and reward of advisors (7 percent). Recognition and reward has in fact taken a step backward. In 1997, only 10 percent of the institutions reported having a policy statement about recognition and reward—not a positive sign for the future of advising as it strives to become a profession.

Measuring the Effectiveness of Advising

The effectiveness of advising was measured by asking respondents to indicate how effective they felt their institution's advising program was in terms of eleven variables and according to the following scale: (1) very ineffective, (2) ineffective, (3) neutral, (4) effective, and (5) very effective. The good news is that the mean of all the variables remained slightly above the midpoint, at 3.1. The achievement of effectiveness across all institutional types saw a gain on nine of the eleven variables. The bad news was that even though there were positive and incremental gains in the mean for effectiveness across all institutional types, advisor accountability (2.96), training (2.89), program evaluation (2.68), advisor evaluation (2.63), and recognition and reward (2.16) fell, as in all of the previous surveys, below the midpoint on the effectiveness scale (Habley and Morales, 1998). The worst news was that recognition and reward trailed the cornerstone components that were considered important in moving toward advising being considered a profession.

Training and Evaluation

Thirty-five percent of academic departments across all institutional types provide some type of formal training, but only 23 percent require training for academic advisors. Of those institutions that provide training, the most common methods of delivery are a single workshop of one day or less per year, or individualized training based on advisors' needs. The dominant topics covered continue to be informational topics such as academic regulations, policies, registration procedures, and campus referral sources. Relational as well as conceptual topics have decreased significantly as training topics since the 1992 survey. This supports the traditional definition of advising as information giving that leads to selection and scheduling of courses, and if this view is not changed, it will prohibit academic advising from achieving the status of a profession.

The evaluation of advisors is not much better than the training of advisors. Only 29 percent of faculty advisors are evaluated. Of this group, the predominant method of evaluation is either self-evaluation or student evaluation. Only 2 percent of these evaluations are done by peer review, and 12 percent are done by a supervisor. The evaluation done in advising offices or centers is better than that done in other settings in that 66 percent of institutions that use this form of advising report that advisors are evaluated. However, only 9 percent are reviewed by a peer.

For advising to be elevated to the status of profession, a higher percentage of advisors must be evaluated. It must become commonplace to have peer evaluations as the norm rather than as the exception, as is the case in faculty evaluation of teaching.

Recognition and Reward

The news only gets worse. Fewer than one in three, or 31 percent, of campuses recognize, reward, or compensate faculty for academic advising. There has been a consistent decline in all types of faculty advisor recognition strategies from 1987 until the present. In 1992, on 23 percent of campuses, academic advising was a major consideration in tenure or promotion decisions in some or all departments, and this fell to only 7 percent in 1997. Worse still, in 1992, on 54 percent of campuses academic advising was a minor consideration in tenure and promotion decisions in some or all departments. In 1997 this percentage dropped dramatically to 14 percent. Is all lost? Probably not yet, but academic advising is definitely at the crossroads of not being recognized as a profession in the near future unless we make a dramatic about-face.

These are the problems that currently face the field of academic advising as it strives to achieve status as a profession, and the resulting barriers that impede institutions in implementing a recognition and reward program that has an institutional impact. What follows are examples of how we can recognize and reward advising.

Recognizing and Rewarding Advising

The intrinsic rewards that advisors receive by helping students navigate the educational pathways of our institutions, and the satisfaction and personal fulfillment they receive in watching students grow and develop as individuals, are enough for many advisors. However, as Wesley Habley (1995) states, "The function of advising is too critical to be left solely to those who intrinsically cherish it." Extrinsic rewards for both the individual advisor and the institution are important because they make visible the importance of academic advising as an integral component of the infrastructure of the institution. Following are some ways to provide extrinsic rewards.

Consideration in tenure, promotion, and merit decisions. This is the ultimate in extrinsic rewards. As discussed previously, this consideration must be more than a statement in a contract or position description. An institutional policy or mission statement must include advising. There must be a method to evaluate the effectiveness of advising, and training and evaluation procedures must be in place.

Release time. This is a very effective method for rewarding advisors. The release time does not always have to be from teaching. It could also be from committee work or other service responsibilities.

Credit for instruction. If advising is considered a component of teaching, then credit for advising can be considered a component of the teaching load for a faculty member.

Stipends. Monetary compensation is most always an incentive.

Other compensation rewards. Support for travel to conferences, secretarial support, a private parking space, priority for summer teaching, a teaching or graduate assistant, and support for a professional development activity such as attending the National Academic Advising Association's (NACADA) Summer Institute on Academic Advising are just some of the ways to reward and recognize advising.

Annual awards. The committee that selects recipients of annual awards should be as comprehensive as possible, including colleagues from across the campus—senior administrators as well as students. If there is an award for outstanding teaching, the outstanding advisor award should have equal status and be presented at the same event.

External recognition. Consider, when possible, having outstanding advisers receive recognition from external organizations. NACADA's National Awards Program for Academic Advising honors individuals and institutions who are making significant contributions to the field of advising. NACADA Outstanding Advisor Awards recognize effective advising qualities and practices that distinguish the recipient as an outstanding academic advisor, including but not necessarily limited to the following:

- Demonstrates a caring attitude toward advisees
- Is available to advisees
- Meets advisees in information settings
- Provides evidence of students' success
- Is perceived by colleagues as having strong advising skills
- Is recognized by the institution for outstanding advising
- Exhibits intrusive behavior designed to build a strong relationship with advisees
- Monitors student progress toward academic and career goals
- Attends and supports advisor development programs
- Demonstrates effective interpersonal skills
- Has frequent contact with advisees
- Uses appropriate information sources
- Undertakes advisee evaluations
- Exhibits appropriate referral activity
- Is able to engage in developmental advising
- Shows mastery of institutional regulations, policies, and procedures

NACADA's Outstanding Institutional Advising Program Awards. These awards recognize programs that can document innovative or exemplary practices that have resulted in the improvement of the institution's academic advising services. These outstanding programs demonstrate innovative quality, creativity, current relevancy, institutional commitment to advising, positive impact on student and institutional outcomes, and transferability of the program to a wide variety of institutions.

Acknowledgement. A simple thank-you letter or a free lunch can generate a lot of goodwill. Tickets to campus events, award certificates, or T-shirts are just a few ways that advisors can be shown they are appreciated. Providing publicity by submitting articles to campus newspapers, creating specially designed nameplates, or posting a list of outstanding advisors in strategic campus locations are other ways to acknowledge and recognize the importance of advisors.

As these examples show, a recognition and reward program does not always require a significant use of resources. It does require, however, that advising be considered an important and integral component of the educational mission of the institution. The next section provides some examples of institutions that are currently bucking the odds and providing what are referred to as *best practices* of recognition and reward programs for academic advising.

Best Practices in Advising

As described previously, there are many ways in which academic advising can be recognized and rewarded. These can be categorized according to the impact they have on the institution as well as the impact they have on the individual advisor:

> *Level One.* A program of recognition and reward that has an impact not only on the individual but also on the institution.
>
> *Level Two.* A program of recognition and reward that has an impact on the individual and provides recognition at the institutional level.
>
> *Level Three.* A program of recognition and reward that has an impact on individuals as well as on their colleagues at the departmental level.

Examples of Programs at Level One

These are programs of recognition and reward that have an impact not only on the individual but also on the institution.

Iowa State University. The policy and procedures manual at Iowa State University describes promotion and tenure as including teaching, research and scholarship or artistic activities, and extension or professional practice and service. To be promoted or tenured, a faculty member must demonstrate excellence in at least one of the three areas and competence in the other areas relevant to their appointment. Following is an excerpt from the July 1995 Faculty Handbook that describes how advising is considered a component of teaching:

Excellence in Teaching
Teaching refers to academic activities that promote learning among those individuals or groups with whom a faculty member interacts. Faculty members who excel in teaching exhibit their command over the subject matter in classroom discussions or lectures, and they present material to students in an objective, organized way that promotes the learning process. They present the subject matter with logic and conviction, and are able to awaken in students an awareness of the relationship of their subject to other classes, fields of knowledge, and cultures. They display concern and respect for their students. They are recognized by their students and university colleagues as persons who guide and inspire their students. They strive continuously to broaden and deepen their knowledge and understanding of their discipline, seek to improve the methods of teaching their subject, keep informed about new developments in their field, use appropriate instructional technologies, and prepare educational materials that are up-to-date and well-written. Their influence and reputation as teachers may be demonstrated further by student and peer evaluation as well as by authoring textbooks and by lectures and publications on pedagogy, by the publication of such instructional materials as laboratory manuals and videotapes, or by significant contributions to professional associations that seek to improve teaching.

Excellence in academic advising may serve to augment evidence of excellence in teaching. Faculty members whose teaching responsibilities include academic advising should interact constructively with their advisees. They are expected to be knowledgeable about scheduling and about curricular and extracurricular matters, to keep informed of current policies and procedures, and to aid students in making use of university resources to enhance their educational and personal development. They assist students in learning to make intelligent decisions for themselves. Evidence of excellence in advising may be demonstrated by student and peer evaluation, by advising awards, by active participation in local and national advising conferences and seminars, by writing and presenting advising papers, and by preparing in-house advising documents.

Pennsylvania State University: Altoona College. Altoona College, which is part of the Pennsylvania State University system, is governed by the promotion and tenure document of Penn State. However, each unit within the system can further refine the document for itself. Following is the refinement developed by Altoona College with regard to teaching ability and effectiveness.

Elaboration of the Three Basic Criteria for Tenure and Promotion
Teaching ability and effectiveness. In accordance with our mission, the Altoona College highly values the teaching and advising roles of its faculty. Faculty members must possess an ongoing commitment to teaching and in particular must demonstrate success in communicating their specialized knowledge to students. This commitment and communication are essential to the educational process. Effectiveness in this area will be measured primarily by input from students and

faculty colleagues in the form of course and advising evaluations, peer evaluations, student interviews, letters from former students, evaluation of course syllabi and other course materials, and any other means that will attest to the candidate's teaching and advising effectiveness.

University of Wisconsin: College of Letters and Sciences. All departments in the College of Letters and Sciences include advising in their documents for promotion and tenure. In general, advising is considered a component of teaching, with each department determining how advising will be reported and the extent to which it will factor into the assessment. Following are excerpts from three departments:

> Advising is more than helping students select courses—it also includes a mentoring function. As such, it is related to teaching. It also serves the purpose of helping students complete their course of studies in a timely and efficient manner which best utilizes the resources of the department. As such, it is a service to the well-being and effectiveness of the program. It is expected that advising will be well done with a minimum average level of 3.5 on the grand mean of the Department's Advisor Perception Inventory. Barring other evidence to the contrary, it may be assumed that advising is minimally satisfactory. If evidence to the contrary is considered in making personnel decisions, the faculty members shall be notified of this matter in a timely manner so that change can be effected and will also be discussed as part of the post-review counseling.

> Academic advising and other out-of-class activities is evaluated by the number of students advised, quality of advising, tutorial instruction provided to students during office hours, etc.

> Documented evidence of successful student advising. This should be demonstrated by participation in college or university-sponsored advising workshops, preview activities, participating in other university or college advising opportunities, advising student clubs, and maintenance of a regular advising schedule.

These are considered drafts and are currently under review by the university as it examines its promotion and tenure standards.

Examples of Programs at Level Two

These are programs of recognition and reward that have an impact on the individual and provide recognition at the institutional level.

Western Illinois University: Outstanding Academic Adviser Award. Recipients of this award are selected by the Outstanding Academic Adviser Award Committee, which is composed of the assistant academic vice president (the chair), the previous year's recipient, a representative of the faculty senate, a representative of the Council of Academic Advisers, and a representative of the Student Government Association. Eligibility is open to full- or part-time faculty members or academic support personnel responsible for the academic advising of undergraduate students. Documentation of excellence in two or more of the following categories is expected: (1) service to students as an adviser; (2) student perceptions of adviser's abilities based on evaluations; (3) size, composition, and effective management of caseload, with emphasis on qualitative management; (4) knowledge of advising principles and university rules and regulations; and (5) meeting student needs beyond the expectations of the position.

The award is presented in conjunction with the annual Outstanding Teaching Award. The recipient receives a $250 cash award from the Alumni Association, $2,500 in line-item expenditures from Faculty Development, and a plaque.

University of North Florida: Outstanding Academic Advising Award. Recipients of this award are selected by the Outstanding Academic Advising Award Selection Committee, which consists of seven members: two students selected by the student government, one faculty member, one student affairs representative, two academic advisors, and one enrollment services representative. Eligibility is restricted to individuals with primary responsibility for undergraduate advising. Selection is made on the basis of the following criteria: (1) the individual has made outstanding contributions to the field of academic advising; (2) has demonstrated innovation and made contributions that have had positive impacts on the advising process; (3) has thorough knowledge of college programs and university policies and procedures; (4) has made an effort to remain current on important advising issues as well as university programs and support services; (5) has genuine concern for students' academic and personal welfare, including career and life planning; (6) has excellent interpersonal communication skills with a high degree of patience, willingness, and sensitivity in assisting students; (7) is able to interact and work with colleagues, faculty, administrators, and support personnel for the benefit of students (is a strong student advocate); (8) has philosophical beliefs that are consistent and reflect a positive attitude toward the advising process and the mission of the university; (9) is a consummate professional and good representative of the university; and (10) overall contributions to academic advising have been superb.

A plaque is given at an end-of-year awards convocation and the advisor's name appears in the catalogue. A cash stipend is currently provided in the amount of $2,000.

Pennsylvania State University: Excellence in Advising Award. This award was established by the Undergraduate Student Government's Academic Assembly to encourage advising excellence at Penn State. The selection committee evaluates the impact of the nominee in the following categories: advising philosophy, assistance in academic and career decision making, enthusiasm, and other services for students. An award consisting of an appropriately inscribed memento and a cash gift is presented at the President's Award Convocation. Recipients of the award are expected to share their successful advising techniques and expertise with other Penn State faculty and graduate assistants by participating in lectures, workshops, and symposia throughout the year.

Examples of Programs at Level Three

These are programs of recognition and reward that have an impact on individuals as well as on their colleagues at the departmental level.

Southwest Missouri State University: Master Advisors. The Master Advisor Program was created to increase the quality of academic advising for Southwest Missouri State University (SMSU) students by systematically providing faculty and professional staff advisors with appropriate training, evaluation, and recognition. The Advisement Center staff designed the program, which focuses on three main competencies in advisors: an ability to relate with students, an understanding of basic concepts of advising, and a strong working knowledge of academic information and campus resources. Both the *Master Advisor Handbook* and the Master Advisor Workshop were organized around these competencies.

In the first year of the program, 112 advisors from across the campus voluntarily participated in one of six intensive sixteen-hour advising workshops. Participants earned the designation "Master Advisor," received a framed certificate, were commended to their deans and department heads, and became eligible for Excellence in Advising awards. Since that time, Master Advisors have received annual updates to the *Master Advisor Handbook* and attended refresher workshops at least every three years.

Pretests and posttests of advising information were administered to all participants. Participants showed an average gain in advising knowledge of 17 percent from pretest to posttest. Because the 112 current Master Advisors advise 6,673 students, the program is affecting the quality of advising offered to a large proportion of SMSU's 14,309 undergraduate students.

University of Memphis: Plaque. In University College, where nontraditional students work closely with faculty advisors to create interdisciplinary programs, all graduates are invited to nominate their faculty advisors for an award provided by the college. Students respond to a Likert-scale questionnaire and are urged to provide anecdotal comments. Professional advisors and previous winning advisors are invited, along with their department chairs and deans, to an elegant spring awards ceremony and are given a plaque.

Cloud County Community College: Release Time. Initially, a program was in place to compensate faculty advisors with stipends. Although the advisors appreciated the money, they indicated that time was a more important compensation. To provide this time, a program was established to assign some of the advisors' committee work to nonadvising faculty. While this saved money, it did not work effectively because those who advise tend to be the best committee members. The program now in place provides release time for faculty advisors from part of their teaching load. A full-time teaching load is fifteen credit hours per semester. Advisors receive three credit hours of release time for every fifty advisees.

Ohio University: Stipends to Support Advising. Since the early 1980s, the University College of Ohio University has operated under a dual-advising model, utilizing more than one hundred volunteer faculty members from across campus as well as full-time advisors to advise first-year undecided students. First-year students have the advantage of working with both a faculty advisor and a University College advisor. Experienced faculty who enjoy working with first-year students are selected from all areas of the university to advise University College students. They meet with assigned students each quarter to provide registration materials and discuss such matters as course selection, academic policies, and major program options.

Advisors are given the opportunity to meet their new advisees at a welcoming reception and advising information session at the beginning of each fall quarter. Faculty, professional, and peer advisors and first-year students gather informally for an introduction to the academic advising and registration system and for refreshments.

Faculty contact with students outside the formal advising realm is encouraged through the Advisor's Fund, which provides an allocation for faculty and students to attend theater productions, lectures, or sporting events or to meet over coffee, lunch, or pizza.

Walla Walla College: Gift Certificates. During winter quarter, Walla Walla College gives each student an advisor evaluation form to complete. The survey contains fifteen statements about advisors. The students are asked to respond to each statement on a scale of 1 to 5. The last statement on the survey explains the Excellence in Advising Award. Students are asked to write a paragraph nominating their advisor if they feel he or she is an excellent advisor. The faculty advisor who receives the award is presented with a $200 check and a plaque. The award is presented during graduation when the teacher awards are presented. The award has been given out for the last six years and it is funded by the president's office.

Five additional faculty advisors are presented with gift certificates during the Advisers in Service meeting before the beginning of the autumn quarter. The gift certificates are funded by the Advisement Office budget.

Temple University: Release Time. Temple University has an arrangement with its Academic Advising Center that provides one course reduction per semester for eight hours of advising or one course reduction a year for four hours per semester of advising. Several additional recommendations for release time are being considered:

- A cumulative banking system that would encourage departmental advising, one credit per semester with one course reduction accrued after three credits have been banked

- Package release time for advising that would include teaching a freshman seminar and developing and teaching a College of Liberal Arts Discovery Series course

- A course reduction for faculty members who want to develop a technology-based on-line Discovery Series course for their departments as well as to plan for its maintenance

- Setting aside one merit unit per department per year from the teaching category in order to reward advising, because advising is teaching in the best sense of both words

Conclusion

What has not been discussed in detail are the intrinsic rewards of advising. Good advisors receive many intrinsic rewards from the knowledge that they have helped a student in their quest for knowledge and from watching students grow and develop through the advising experience. Of course this cannot be enough if we want to elevate the importance of advising on our campuses. The function of advising is too critical to be left solely to those who intrinsically cherish it.

It is clear from the data produced in ACT's fifth national survey that there is no consistent campuswide practice that recognizes and rewards academic advisors (Habley and Morales, 1998). In fact, as noted earlier, there has been a consistent decline in all types of advisor recognition strategies from the 1987 survey to the present. Thirty-one percent of the institutions surveyed recognized or rewarded advisors for academic advising. Of those institutions, in 1987 release time from instruction, committee work, or research expectations in all or some departments was 43 percent. This fell to 18 percent in 1997. Academic advising as a major consideration in tenure and promotion decisions in all or some departments was at 21 percent in 1987 and fell to 7 percent in 1997. Likewise, the consideration of academic advising as a minor component in tenure and promotion decisions was at 46 percent in 1987 and at 14 percent in 1997.

How do institutions initiate a turnaround to recognize and reward advisors for their efforts? As a profession, academic advising has to do a better job of selling its importance. It is not enough to continue to preach to the converted. It is important to move beyond telling advising colleagues how important advising is and to begin to convince the decision makers and resource allocators on our campuses how important a role academic advising plays in the fabric of the institution. Grites and Kelley (1994, pp. 1, 10) developed a formula for quantifying the importance of advising:

> One of the ways in which an advising program might be able to demonstrate clearly that it has an economic value to the institution is to conduct a functional analysis of its operation. This analysis is intended to demonstrate an actual dollar value for each of the functions performed by the advising office or program. An outline of the process is described below:
>
> First, the advising unit must identify all of the functions it performs, that is, assign students to advisors, develop advising materials, conduct workshops, etc.

Second, all possible alternatives to each function must be identified and analyzed for possible effects. For example, will another office assume the function? Will other personnel perform the function? Will the function be eliminated?

Each alternative, for every function, must then be plotted to determine the anticipated results of such action. This is probably best done in a flow-chart format.

The third part of this analysis is to determine a dollar value for each result. For example, if the purchase of new computer software is an alternative, then the cost of that software would likely be the dollar value of that alternative; or if more academic appeals would likely be generated, then the personnel cost of handling these additional appeals would likely be the dollar value of that alternative.

One very likely result from many of the alternatives to the functions normally performed by academic advising offices programs is higher attrition of students. In these cases it is important to know the dollar value of a retained student so that those advising functions that are shown to contribute to retention are represented in real dollar figures.

A most conservative (and simple) method for calculating the dollar value of a retained student is to divide the total annual budget for recruitment and admissions by the annual "yield" of students, that is, the number of new students who actually enroll. This figure can be considered a replacement cost that does not have to be incurred for each student that has been retained.

Therefore, each function that is shown to result in student retention represents a dollar value equal to the number of students retained (by the function) times the dollar value of replacement as calculated above. [Grites and Kelley, 1994, pp. 1, 10]

This excerpt is provided as an example of how as a profession we must be assertive and provide indisputable convincing arguments to the decision makers and resource allocators that advising makes a difference. If advisors want to have their institutions commit resources (more positions and more fiscal support) to advising that are being competed for by all constituents, they must provide them with compelling, persuasive, and indisputable arguments that advising not only improves the quality of students' experience but also improves and affects the reputation, fiscal well-being, effectiveness, and prestige of the institution.

Accept the challenge and start the movement to have academic advising considered a profession. This will have a direct impact on the level and importance that academic advising will receive in the arena of recognition and reward. As the data from the 1997 ACT survey confirms, the time to start is now.

References

Christensen, V. R. "Bringing About Change." In U. Delworth and G. R. Hanson (eds.), *Student Services.* San Francisco: Jossey-Bass, 1980.

Gordon, V. N. *Handbook of Academic Advising.* Westport, Conn.: Greenwood Press, 1992.

Grites, T. J., and Kelley, J. "Meeting the Assault in Advising: The Economics of Advising." *Newsletter of the National Academic Advising Association,* 1994, *16*(1), pp. 1, 10.

Habley, W. R. "Advisor Training in the Context of a Teaching Enhancement Center." In R. E. Glennen and F. N. Vowell (eds.), *Academic Advising as a Comprehensive Campus Process.* National Academic Advising Association Monograph Series, no. 2. Manhattan, Kans.: National Academic Advising Association, 1995.

Habley, W. R., and Morales, R. H. *Current Practices in Academic Advising: Final Report on ACT's Fifth National Survey of Academic Advising.* National Academic Advising Association Monograph Series, no. 6. Manhattan, Kans.: National Academic Advising Association, 1998.

Young, D. P. "Legal Issues Regarding Academic Advising: An Update." *NACADA Journal,* 1988, *4,* 89–95.

Part Five

Dealing with Change in the Future of Academic Advising

S o far this book has outlined the historical foundations and other issues critical to the practice of academic advising. Looking to the future is just as important if advising is to advance and effect positive change. Victoria A. McGillin, in Chapter Twenty-Six, describes the critical issues that will face the field of academic advising in the future and suggests areas for research based on what current research identifies.

In Chapter Twenty-Seven, Virginia N. Gordon looks into the needs of tomorrow's students and at the competencies that students must acquire while in college if they are to be successful in the workplace. Because tomorrow's workplace will be very different from the workplaces of the past and the present, this chapter speculates on how advising, as part of higher education, can adapt to this inevitable change in order to help students prepare for their future careers and lifestyles.

The final chapter in this volume, Chapter Twenty-Eight, by Herta Teitelbaum, discusses how higher education might change and how our degree of preparedness for this change will influence advising as a moving force in preparing students for the next few decades. The chapter provides some possible scenarios and offers suggestions for how specific actions can be implemented to ensure that advising in the future is relevant to the new age.

Taking into account current issues in academic advising, Part Five projects those issues into the future and attempts to offer suggestions and solutions. As we enter the next millennium, it is important for academic advisors to anticipate and adapt to changes that will affect them, the environment in which they work, and the students they advise. If advising is to become a moving force in preparing students for the next few decades, it must not only anticipate change, but must also determine its role in adapting to these changes.

Chapter Twenty-Six

Current Issues in Advising Research

Victoria A. McGillin

When the National Academic Advising Association (NACADA) polled members in 1980 and 1985, asking them to identify critical issues in advising, the low quality and availability of advising and the poor training of faculty advisors were consistently reported as the highest priorities (Polson and Cashin, 1981; Polson and Gordon, 1988). Divorced from the disciplinary base through which an increasingly specialized faculty found their primary roles and rewards, faculty advisors were hard-pressed to shift their focus away from the research and teaching activities tied to tenure and toward an activity of uncertain status and recognition.

Despite growing concerns about the quality of advising and student retention, and the developing insistence of reaccreditation boards that colleges and universities provide demonstrable evidence of effectiveness (Kramer and Peterson, 1983), at the time of the NACADA polls there was very little research on which to build a case for the importance of academic advising. Research was necessary to document the impact of advising on higher education outcomes, to gain support from campus leadership, to defend the field, and to elevate the status of advising in higher education (Habley, 1988). Although the dearth of research on advising was attributed to barriers within higher education (Polson and Cashin, 1981), many within the higher education community joined the call for further study of academic planning and innovative advising programs (for example, McGlaughlin and Starr, 1982; Matthews, 1982).

The Status of Current Research in Advising

Academic advising research owes much to the social sciences for the methods it has selected, the instruments it has designed, the paradigms it has tested, and the theories it has explored. Much of advising's theoretical base comes from the fields of psychology, cognition, sociology, and counseling and psychotherapy. Heavy reliance on clinical or counseling models, however, has resulted in problematization of normal concerns, such as the tendency to label undecidedness as symptomatic of emotional distress.

Although willing to borrow a wide range of social science theories, research in advising has rarely borrowed more than one or two methodologies. With almost exclusive reliance on survey data (McGlaughlin and Starr, 1982), single-source survey data has dominated the field. Reliance on surveys also delayed the introduction of qualitative and contextualized analysis, the missing link in theory-building both for advising and for higher education (Pascarella and Terenzini, 1982). There have been few efforts to validate the constructs assessed, and minimal attention has been paid to rudimentary reliability studies. Few studies of advising have investigated the advisor's contribution to the advising relationship. Finally, advising research has failed to evaluate advising processes, which is common to research in higher education (Stage, 1989).

Design flaws have characterized much advising research. Other than a few cross-sectional comparisons (for example, lower- versus upper-division students), few scholars have actually employed developmental designs (such as longitudinal or cross-sequential data collection) even when purporting to measure developmental phenomena. There was no employment of experimental design in advising research at the time. Quasi-experimental designs have been most common but have frequently lacked control groups, randomization of subjects, or matched samples. Also lacking have been replications, applications to other populations, and reliability or validity studies. This has stymied theory development, impaired instrument development, and retarded the development of the field (Tinsley and Irelan, 1989). Most published research has also been hampered by reliance on small, single-institution, majority population samples. Similar to most higher education research, advising research could be criticized for the limited relevance of measures to assess student change; for failure to attend to individual differences, such as age, gender, ethnicity, and life course; for inattention to the indirect effect of the college experience; for blindness to long-term outcomes; and for failure to validate instruments (Pascarella, 1991).

Critical Issues Facing the Field of Advising

In the spring of 1997, a stratified sample of the NACADA membership was again questioned about the critical issues in advising. They identified retention, faculty role, technology, organizational structures, management of institutional change, career and major advising, institutional support for advising, advising workloads, advisor development and training, developmental and holistic advising, advising special populations, advisor recognition and reward, and assessment of advising. These can be loosely collected into the domains of student issues, advisor issues, and organizational issues. The following three sections review and critique the published advising research within the broader framework of higher education research.

Student Advising Issues

Critical student issues in advising were identified by the NACADA membership as including documentation of developmental or holistic advising as a primary model of advising delivery, the link between retention and advising, and the myriad issues posed by advising special populations of students.

Developmental or Holistic Advising. Developmental or holistic models of advising are most often loosely assembled from the cognitive, epistemological, and social developmental literature. Research supporting or challenging these models is rare, and the diverse results are as much a function of the poorly operationalized constructs as the concomitant weaknesses of instruments designed to assess them.

A number of studies have employed the Academic Advising Inventory (AAI) (Winston and Sandor, 1984), which was designed to measure the developmental and prescriptive ends of an advising continuum. Although this was one of the first advising instruments to assess more than satisfaction, the lack of validation studies and questions about the bipolar, unidimensional continuum and item construction have rendered suspect the repeated endorsement of the developmental end of the continuum (Herndon, Kaiser, and Creamer, 1996). High developmental advising scores have been correlated with high levels of faculty-student contact (Alexitch, 1997) and with higher levels of intellectual performance in some groups (for example, Novels and Ender, 1988). One recent attempt to observe behavioral indices of the two ends of the AAI continuum, however, demonstrated that no advisor could be so simply classified (Daller, Creamer, and Creamer, 1997).

In contrast, other instruments challenged the model of advising as a bipolar, unidimensional continuum and described two independent dimensions of advising: person-centered activities (defining interests and goals, relating academic options to careers) and information-centered activities (clerical, information-giving, and monitoring activities) (Andrews, Andrews, Long, and Henton, 1988; Fielstein, Scoles and Webb, 1992). Students in one study rated informational activities as more important than person-centered activities (Fielstein, Scoles, and Webb, 1992). However, several studies have documented that some groups of students (such as African Americans and women) consistently received lower levels of person-centered advising than desired and that the differences between groups of students were nonrandom (Fielstein, Scoles, and Webb, 1992; Herndon, Kaiser, and Creamer, 1996).

This gap between preferred advising and received advising may be a function of faculty perceptions of their own behavior. Although advisors were observed to behave consistently across students (Daller, Creamer, and Creamer, 1997), Grites (1981) found that students rated advisors differently than advisors rated themselves. Student preferences for advisor styles also differed by gender, race, personality characteristics, age, and experience (Andrews, Andrews, Long, and Henton, 1988; Alexitch, 1997). Despite these results, belief in the primacy of a single model of developmental advising remain unchallenged.

Similar conceptual, psychometric, and design flaws have weakened efforts to assess the developmental impact of college on students overall (Hanson, 1988). Although theorists have debated the degree to which development is seen as cumulative, directional, and predictable, most have advocated research on the student's total experience rather than piecemeal investigations of academic and cocurricular life (Pascarella and others, 1996).

Retention and Advising. Advising's place in the national debate in retention began with Beal and Noel's 1979 publication *What Works in Student Retention,* which reported that poor advising was a significant reason for leaving college, and a significant relationship with someone at school was found to be most important in retention. While institutional integration has since been more broadly defined to address both social and academic connections with the college (Tinto, 1990), the presumptive link between advising and retention remains. Greater faculty-student contact and sound academic advising have been seen as the core of campus retention efforts (for example, Beasley-Fielstein, 1986; Clark, 1989). However, the vast majority of subsequent studies have used either single-institution samples, small samples, or both, critically masking institutional differences in the impact of faculty on retention (Terenzini and others, 1981). Since 1979, only one study has contradicted the conclusion that correlations between improved advising services and retention are causative (Mark and Romano, 1982).

In the broader higher education research, retention was consistently found to be dependent on a combination of academic and personal needs, calling for collaborative efforts (Tinto, 1998) to enhance students' integration into the learning community (Dougherty, 1987; Bedford and Durkee, 1989). However, this research was similarly limited by sample size, single effects, and statistical and theoretical flaws (Dey and Astin, 1993).

Advising Special Populations. Academic advising involves encounters with a wide range of student populations, such as undecided, underprepared and at-risk, transfer, part-time, adult, disabled, and multicultural students (Habley and Morales, 1998a). Each group is capable of generating a literature all its own (Strommer, 1995). Research on advising with special populations, however, has been constrained to a very few groups and most often merely documents needs (for example, Stoynoff, 1997).

Many of the problems in advising research on special populations can be characterized by the difficulties paramount in the study of two such groups: undecided and multicultural students. Research on undecided students, while prolific, has been severely hampered by the classification of all students without majors as undecided (Lewallen, 1995). The majority of studies have employed samples from single institutions with differing policies on major declaration, which has confounded comparison. Studies employing schemas for categorizing forms of undecidedness, such as Gordon's (1995) model, found a modest relationship between decided status and advising outcomes (Hagstrom, Skovholt, and Rivers, 1997; Peterson and Barrett, 1987).

Multicultural students have also been treated as a single research population, despite presenting ethnicity-specific issues to academic advisors. For example, some of the limited research in this area has documented, among other results, that Asian American students prefer academic counseling over personal counseling (Atkinson, Lowe, and Matthews, 1995), that higher-performing African American males are dissatisfied with academic advising (Oliver, Smith, and Wilson, 1989), and that cocurricular activities have a negative impact on multicultural students' participation in faculty advising (Giles-Gee; 1989). As problematic as the advising research on special populations has proved to be, higher education research with special populations has suffered the same limitations, imposed when all members of special populations were treated as a single, coherent group (for example, Greenland, 1989).

Career and Major Advising. The tension between major and career advising reflects the tensions between traditional academics, who are married to their disciplines (Hogan, 1991), and the forces for change that have demanded greater accountability to the life goals of students, investments in the institution, and responsibilities to the state. The psychological and sociological literature has addressed the need for greater career advising embedded within advising in the major (Wilder, 1982; Matthews, 1982; Hogan, 1991). While there has been considerable documentation of this need, advisors have not recognized major and career advising to be as significant as their advisees have (Eddy and Essarum, 1989), and they have questioned their own ability to serve as sources of career decision-making skills (Russel and Sullivan, 1979).

In contrast to the advising literature, two trends have emerged in the limited higher education research comparing majors and careers: the power of disciplines to uniquely acculturate their students' values (for example, Latucca and Stark, 1995) and the consistent reports that liberal arts graduates have felt underprepared and lacking in the skills necessary for entry-level positions (for example, Sherohman and Havir, 1989).

Advisor Issues

The issues best gathered under the heading of advisor concerns include questions about the faculty role in advising, and about advisor workloads, advisor training and assessment, and advisor recognition and reward. These have been most timely in the era of downsizing and quality assurance.

Faculty Role in Advising. The faculty role in advising has been at the heart of the debate between advising as teaching and advising as service. This has situated advising in the recognition and reward structure of higher education. While a 1980 study of collective bargaining agreements and institutional documents found little reference to advising (Teague and Grites, 1980), there is recent evidence that most disciplines have placed advising squarely under teaching (Diamond and Adam, 1995).

Survey research has characterized the limited scholarship on faculty roles in advising, focusing primarily on discrepancies between student and advisor perceptions of these roles (for example, Fielstein and Lammers, 1992). Faculty advisors have agreed that their roles include the tasks of helper, educator, and mentor (Kelly, 1995) and they have been found generally to meet the informational goals and basic job expectations of their students while falling short of the students' priorities around personal well-being. This has proved critical as student satisfaction has been related to fewer discrepancies between what students have valued in advisors and their advisors' behaviors (Fielstein, 1987; Ray, Moore, and Oliver, 1991).

The higher education debate over faculty roles has taken on national significance with renewed calls for attention to teaching and students, but little research to back the calls. Some of the limited research has documented discrepancies between actual faculty roles and desired roles, which have resulted in role stress (Endres and Wearden, 1996), or role conflict, particularly for women faculty (Zhang and Farley, 1995).

Advising Workloads. Research-based discussions of advisor workloads have been rare, perhaps resulting from a reluctance to document the labor-intensive nature of this activity. The most comprehensive examinations, completed by Habley and colleagues (Carstensen and Silberhorn, 1979; Crockett and Levitz, 1983; Habley, 1988, 1983; Habley and Morales, 1998a), has documented a growth in faculty responsibility for advising, with instructional faculty serving as advisors within academic departments in more than 80 percent of the institutions assessed. Advising loads have been relatively consistent (between thirty and thirty-eight advisees per advisor) as have been the numbers of contacts reported by faculty (between two to three per semester), accounting for 12 percent of faculty time (Habley and Morales, 1998a). Faculty self-reports have proved suspect, however, as students have reported fewer advising contacts with faculty (one per year) than did their faculty advisors (Creedon, 1990).

Over the past ten years, staffing in centralized advising offices shifted from partial use of faculty to reliance on full-time professional advisors, who managed, on average, loads of more than 250 advisees. Extrapolating from the Habley and Morales (1998a) data, direct contact with advisees accounted for more than 78 percent of professional advisors' time. Not surprisingly, advisor satisfaction was found to vary directly with workload (Fielstein and Lammers, 1992).

Driven by demands for accountability, higher education research has focused almost exclusively on faculty work (that is, teaching, research, and service). Given that service has rarely figured into assessments while teaching and research have been treated as zero-sum situations (more focus on one must result in less focus on the other), efforts by higher education to investigate workloads has resulted in inconsistent findings,

Advisor Recognition and Reward. Research on the recognition and reward of advisors has been limited to surveys of practices, while evidence of effectiveness has been lacking (Sherbo, 1983). While surveys of faculty (Kelly, 1995) and staff (Krupka and Vener, 1980) have identified reward and recognition systems as the top campus need, advising, in contrast, has consistently been rated very low in status and in the traditional reward structure (Larsen and Brown, 1983).

When advising has been considered part of teaching, it has been seen as less connected to the disciplines and therefore less central to faculty professional identity (Wade and Yoder, 1995). However, in a recent report from the disciplinary organizations, advising was included in the discipline-specific language of teaching for eleven of the scholarly societies surveyed (Diamond and Adam, 1995), providing an opening for the revision of advising rewards.

In their nationally stratified survey of advising, Habley and Morales (1998a) reported that between 24 and 37 percent of the schools surveyed offered some form of advising recognition or reward to departmental advisors, but these programs peaked in the late eighties, and there have been recent declines in every category of faculty reward and recognition. Minor consideration in tenure, while the most frequently employed form of reward, also showed the most precipitous decline since 1992.

Research on faculty recognition and reward has proved richer in the higher education literature, where both use and effectiveness have been explored. However, surveys, which are critical for advising's role in teaching, have repeatedly documented the discrepancy between stated valuation of teaching and the primacy of research in the reward structure (Fairweather, 1994; Krik, 1996).

Assessment of Advising. The research on assessment of advising has included studies of the advising process and explorations of advising outcomes. Process research from the field of communications and narrative studies have found advisor language to reflect institutional identities, to problematize otherwise nonproblematic concerns, to mark status, and to collaborate on stories begun by students, primarily to display the advisor's knowledge (for example, He, 1994, 1996; Adams and others, 1990). The effect may differ, given the social identity (race, gender, or ethnicity) of the student and advisor (Bardovi-Harlig and Hartford, 1993; Nadler and Nadler, 1993).

National surveys have reported that less than one-third of all academic departments evaluate their advisors annually (Habley and Morales, 1998a). In contrast, the majority of centralized advising offices evaluate their mostly professional staffs annually, using supervisor, student, or self-assessments (Habley and Morales, 1998a). These advisor assessment instruments vary in their reliability and validity, and there have been conflicting reports about which factors best correlate with effectiveness ratings (Iaccino, 1991; Kelley and Lynch, 1990). Studies that compared student assessments of faculty and professional advisors produced conflicting results (Jaffe and Huba, 1990; Kelley and Lynch, 1990). Given variations in students' assessments, it is not surprising to note that advisors have attributed positive advising outcomes to personal efforts and have rejected responsibility for negative outcomes (Kramer, 1982).

Some methodological concerns have included reliance on global quantitative measures of satisfaction (Hanson and Raney, 1993) and instrument reliability. Assessments have also failed to evaluate advising as it was actually experienced, that is, as episodic, short bursts of intensive activity followed by long gaps in contact,

In contrast, assessment of higher education outcomes has moved to the center of reaccredidation activities, and by 1989 most institutions surveyed evaluated the curriculum and institutional effectiveness. While colleges and universities have made commitments to assessing their outcomes, formal studies of high quality have been rare. Serious methodological concerns have limited most higher education assessment efforts.

Advisor Development and Training. Little formal research has documented advisor training (Kramer, 1986) or the informational, conceptual, and skills components needed. While one-third of all institutions questioned provided advisor training, less than one-quarter of the institutions required training for advisors within academic departments (Habley and Morales, 1998a). Some critics have even questioned the legitimacy of training academics as advisors (Waggenspack and Hensley, 1992).

Single-day workshops have predominated as have reliance on informational and, to a lesser extent, conceptual topics. Relational skills have consistently been neglected in faculty training, and have been found in less than one-third of professional advisor training programs (Habley and Morales, 1998a).

In contrast to the very limited research on advisor training, faculty development has been the focus of considerable scholarship in higher education (for example, Sorcinelli, 1994). However, research on higher education staff training has been as modest as that on academic advising.

Organizational Issues

When advisors have raised questions about institutional support, they have addressed two separate but related topics: resource allocation and the status of advising. Institutions have been unwilling to support academic advising unless they have seen it as a high-status role for faculty or professionals, but advising's status will not change until its importance can be documented. The issues of institutional support for advisors fall into the categories of structure, institutional change, and technology.

Organizational Structures. Organizational research on advising has either documented reporting lines and organizational models or assessed the effectiveness of those different models. Over the past ten years there has been a decrease in the proportion of advising coordinators who report directly to college presidents, and growth (to 46 percent) in the proportion who report to academic affairs (Habley and Morales, 1998a), reflecting the early reliance on the Faculty-

Only Model (Carstensen and Silberhorn, 1979). Using a model of advising delivery based on the relative authority of faculty or centralized administrative advisors, Habley and Morales (1998a) documented a decline in the Faculty-Only Model and an increase in the Supplementary and Split Models, representing significant movement toward a model of shared responsibility.

Research on the relative effectiveness of different models of advising has been scarce and contradictory (for example, Jaffe and Huba, 1990; Kelley and Lynch 1990). The search for the best organizational model has proved as specious as the search for the best model of advising. Different advising organizational models are needed to fit different institutional cultures (Habley and Morales, 1998b).

The higher education organizational literature, which looks at the institution as a whole, has repeatedly called for collaborations across academic and student divisions. This collaboration, however, may have been hampered by documented differences in management styles in academic and administrative culture (for example, Terpstra and Olson, 1984).

Managing Institutional Change. Advising-related studies of institutional change have been limited. One survey reported that 61 percent of the colleges and universities responding planned some sort of change in their advising programs, particularly in public institutions (Creamer and Creamer, 1994). The process of change in advising units has also been found to be circular and recursive, and responsive to ongoing needs assessments (Frank, 1993).

To understand the sources of this change, it is instructive to review the forces shaping change in higher education overall. These forces have included changing student expectations, changing forms of the disciplines, and increased demands for accountability of faculty as a resource (Plater, 1995). Faculty, however, while favoring change, have not actively sought it (Downie and Maden, 1981), potentially limiting the effect of any force for change.

Technology and Advising. Although a number of authors have written on the potential impact of technology on advising (for example, Lowry and Grites, 1982), financial constraints have resulted in a significant delay in the implementation of technological innovations. Initial aversion to flawed, early degree audits and the subsequent job-security anxiety resulting from the newer, more effective audits may have also contributed to hesitation by advisors (Kramer, 1996). In fact, use of computerized degree audits has declined over the last ten years (Habley and Morales, 1998a).

Formal research on the impact of technology on advising has been very limited, documenting usage patterns (Lyon and Carpinelli, 1996), satisfaction and convenience (Sotto, 1996), and impact on retention, advancement, and advisor contacts (Severy and Singer, 1996). While advice about electronic resources and electronic learners is widely available (for example, Lieberman, 1996), solid research is missing.

Higher education has similarly struggled to produce a research-based literature addressing the pedagogic issues associated with the introduction of information technology. This was hampered early on by the lack of computer literacy among faculty (Hofmann, 1991), by faculty skepticism concerning gains in critical thinking (DeSieno, 1995), and by the early demonstration that electronic fixes do not work for all academic problems. The impact of technology on student learning has been variable, affecting attitude but not achievement (Grimes and others, 1989).

Conclusion: The Future of Advising Research

It is evident that the research agenda for academic advising must become a national priority. The very status of advising as a field and of roles, institutional support, training, and recognition will all depend on the generation of qualitative and quantitative research documenting what advisors do. The field can no longer afford to stand outside the national demand for documented outcomes in higher education.

We must first clarify what advising is and is not by generating a theory of academic advising. We must better conceptualize the multidimensional nature of advising encounters and ensure advising's place as a critical component of faculty teaching activities and as the professional responsibility of full-time advisors. Advising must also be reconceptualized within the larger issues facing higher education, such as general education reform, roles, and rewards.

Second, we must study what advisors do. Observational and reflective studies of advising encounters may provide understanding of effective practices and of the meanings generated by both advisor and advisee. We must better understand the effects of institutional and disciplinary culture as well as the impact of rater knowledge on assessment results. The process of advising over time must be explored through longitudinal approaches. Methodologically, the field must free itself from reliance on unidimensional student surveys of advisor behaviors or preferences. Advising scholars must establish instrument reliability and validity. Research must also move beyond single-campus, single-program investigations.

Third, the link between advising and retention must be documented anew. Specifically, we need to understand better the role of bad advising as separate from the role of a positive relationship in retaining students. The multiple natures of advisors as well as the multiplicity of advisees complicate and enrich the research questions. How do these differences affect both the content and the process of an advising encounter? How do these individual differences affect not only preferences but also actual behaviors?

Fourth, research on advisors, not just on advisees, is critical. How do professional advisors differ from faculty advisors in what they do? Given the need to evaluate faculty as whole persons, not just as individuals who spend 12 percent of their time advising, how can advising best be integrated into the academic role? What is the impact of differential reward structures on advising's status? Is the effect different for men and women, professionals and faculty advisors? How effective are different advisor training methods?

Fifth, advising researchers must take the lead in establishing critical collaborations. Given the importance of recent national initiatives in higher education, advising as a discipline must join the national debate on faculty roles and rewards, innovations in teaching, faculty-student encounters, and the creation of learning communities. Through scholarship on the relation between advising and these topics, we can create entrees into the national discourse.

Finally, and potentially most critically, advising scholars must explore collaborations within the disciplines. Rather than viewing disciplinarity as a barrier, advisors should join with discipline-based scholars to make sense of how advising fits within their field. Tying advising practices into the disciplines may create the most effective link between advising professionals and their discipline-based colleagues. The search for a single model of good advising must give way to the documentation and celebration of the multiplicity of advising encounters across advisors, students, disciplines, and institutions.

References

Adams, R. J., and others. "Effects of Form of Address on Advisees' Perceptions of Advisors." *NACADA Journal,* 1990, *10*(2), 12–19.

Alexitch, L. R. "Student Educational Orientation and Preferences for Advising from University Professors." *Journal of College Student Development,* 1997, *38*(4), 333–343.

Andrews, M., Andrews, D., Long, E., and Henton, J. "Student Characteristics as Predictors of Perceived Academic Advising Needs." *Journal of College Student Personnel,* 1988, *28*(1), 60–65.

Atkinson, D. R., Lowe, S., and Matthews, L. "Asian-American Acculturation, Gender, and Willingness to Seek Counseling." *Journal of Multicultural Counseling and Development,* 1995, *23*(3), 130–138.

Bardovi-Harlig, K., and Hartford, B. S. "The Language of Comembership." *Research on Language and Social Interaction,* 1993, *26*(3), 227–257.

Beal, P. E., and Noel, L. *What Works in Student Retention: A Preliminary Summary of a National Survey.* Iowa City, Iowa: American College Testing Program; and Boulder City, Colo.: National Center for Higher Education Management Systems, 1979.

Beasley-Fielstein, L. "Student Perceptions of Developmental Advisor-Advisee Relationship." *NACADA Journal,* 1986, *6*(2), 107–117.

Bedford, M. H., and Durkee, P. E. "Retention: Some More Ideas." *NASPA Journal,* 1989, *27*(2), 168–171.

Carstensen, D. C., and Silberhorn, C. *Final Report: A National Survey of Academic Advising.* Iowa City, Iowa: American College Testing Program, 1979.

Clark, E. E. "The Importance of a Comprehensive Advising System in Improving Student Retention and Graduation Rates." *Australian Universities' Review,* 1989, *32*(1), 27–29.

Creamer, E. G., and Creamer, D. G. "Planned Change Projects in Academic Advising: A NACADA Research Grant Report." *NACADA Journal*, 1994, *14*(1), 43–45.

Creedon, J. E. "Components of Good Advising: Differences in Faculty and Student Perceptions." *NACADA Journal*, 1990, *10*(2), 30–36.

Crockett, D. S., and Levitz, R. S. *Final Report on ACT's Second National Survey of Academic Advising.* Iowa City, Iowa: American College Testing Program, 1983.

Daller, M. L., Creamer, E. G., and Creamer, D. G. "Advising Styles Observable in Practice: Counselor, Scheduler and Teacher." *NACADA Journal*, 1997, *17*(2), 31–38.

DeSieno, R. "The Faculty and Digital Technology." *EDUCOM Review*, 1995, *30*(4), 46–48.

Dey, E. L., and Astin, A. W. "Statistical Alternatives for Studying College Student Retention: A Comparative Analysis of Logit, Probit, and Linear Regression." *Research in Higher Education*, 1993, *34*(5), 569–581.

Diamond, R. M., and Adam, B. E. (eds.). *The Disciplines Speak: Rewarding the Scholarly, Professional and Creative Work of Faculty.* Washington, D.C.: American Association for Higher Education, 1995.

Dougherty, D. "Developing a Residential Retention Program." *Journal of College & University Student Housing*, 1987, *17*(1), 11–16.

Downie, R., and Maden, R. "Teaching Methods in Biology: How Can We Get Information to Flow." *Journal of Biological Education*, 1981, *15*(1), 47–50.

Eddy, J. P., and Essarum, C. C. "Student and Faculty Perception of an Undergraduate Academic Advising Process." *College Student Affairs Journal*, 1989, *9*(2), 6–13.

Endres, F. F., and Wearden, S. T. "Job-Related Stress Among Mass Communication Faculty." *Journalism and Mass Communication Educator*, 1996, *51*(3), 32.

Fairweather, J. S. "Faculty Rewards: The Comprehensive College and University Study." *Metropolitan Universities: An International Forum*, 1994, *5*(1), 54–61.

Fielstein, L. L. "Student Preferences for Personal Contact in Student-Faculty Advising Relationships." *NACADA Journal*, 1987, *7*(2), 34–42.

Fielstein, L. L., and Lammers, W. J. "The Relationship of Student Satisfaction with Advising to Administrative Support for Advising Services." *NACADA Journal*, 1992, *12*(1), 15–21.

Fielstein, L. L., Scoles, M., and Webb, K. "Differences in Traditional and Nontraditional Students' Preferences for Advising Services and Perceptions of Services Received." *NACADA Journal*, 1992, *12*(2), 5–12.

Frank, C. P. "An Integrated Model of Academic Advising Program Development." *NACADA Journal*, 1993, *13*(1), 62–73.

Giles-Gee, H. F. "Increasing the Retention of Black Students: A Multimethod Approach." *Journal of College Student Development*, 1989, *30*(3), 196–200.

Gordon, V. N. *The Undecided College Student: An Academic and Career Advising Challenge* (2nd ed.). Springfield, Ill.: Thomas, 1995.

Greenland, A. E. "Responsiveness to Adult Undergraduates in a Traditional Land-Grant University: An Institution-Wide Self-Assessment." *Equity and Excellence*, 1989, *24*(3), 13–19.

Grimes, P. W., and others. "The Effectiveness of 'Economics U$A' on Learning and Attitudes." *Journal of Economic Education*, 1989, *20*(2), 139–152.

Grites, T. J. "Student and Self-Rating of Teacher-Advisors." *NACADA Journal,* 1981, *1*(1), 29–33.

Habley, W. R. *Fulfilling the Promise?* Iowa City, Iowa: American College Testing Program, 1983.

Habley, W. R. *The Status and Future of Academic Advising: Problems and Promise.* Iowa City, Iowa: American College Testing Program, 1988.

Habley, W. R., and Morales, R. H. *Current Practices in Academic Advising: Final Report on ACT's Fifth National Survey of Academic Advising.* National Academic Advising Association Monograph Series, no. 6. Manhattan, Kans.: National Academic Advising Association, 1998a.

Habley, W. R., and Morales, R. H. "Advising Models: Goal Achievement and Program Effectiveness." *NACADA Journal,* 1998b, *18*(1) 35–41.

Hagstrom, S. J., Skovholt, T. M., and Rivers, D. A. "The Advanced Undecided College Student: A Qualitative Study." *NACADA Journal,* 1997, *17*(2), 23–30.

Hanson, G. R. "These Truths Are Self-Evident, but . . ." *Journal of College Student Development*, 1988, *29*(6), 501–503.

Hanson, G. R., and Raney, M. W. "Evaluating Academic Advising in a Multiversity Setting." *NACADA Journal,* 1993, *13*(1), 34–42.

He, A. "Withholding Academic Advice: Institutional Context and Discourse Practice." *Discourse Processes,* 1994, *18*(3), 297–316.

He, A. "Stories as Academic Counseling Resources." *Journal of Narrative and Life History,* 1996, *6*(2), 107–121.

Herndon, J. B., Kaiser, D., and Creamer, D. G. "Student Preferences for Advising Style in Community College Environments." *Journal of College Student Development,* 1996, *37*(6), 637–648.

Hofmann, L. A. "Computers in Education: A Triumph of Process Over Purpose." *Collegiate Microcomputer,* 1991, *9*(4), 215–218.

Hogan, P. M. "Vocational Preparation with a Liberal Arts Framework: Suggested Directions for Undergraduate Psychology Programs." *Teaching of Psychology*, 1991, *18*(3), 148–153.

Iaccino, J. F. "Assessment and Comparison of Advising for Freshmen and Upperclassmen." *Journal of the Freshman Year Experience,* 1991, *3*(2), 75–90.

Jaffe, W. F., and Huba, M. E. "Engineering Students Use of and Satisfaction with Faculty and Professional Academic Advising Systems." *NACADA Journal,* 1990, *10*(2), 37–43,

Kelley, K. N., and Lynch, M. J. "Factors Students Use When Evaluating Advisors." *NACADA Journal,* 1990, *11*(1), 26–33.

Kelly, J. "Faculty Speak to Advising." A. G. Reinarz and E. R. White (eds.), *Teaching Through Academic Advising: A Faculty Perspective.* New Directions for Teaching and Learning, no. 62. San Francisco: Jossey-Bass, 1995.

Kramer, G. L. "The Human-Technology Nexus." In Kramer, G. L., and Childs, M. W. (eds.). *Transforming Academic Advising Through the Use of Information Technology.* NACADA Monograph Series, no. 4, Manhattan, Kans.: National Academic Advising Association, 1996.

Kramer, G. L., and Peterson, E. D. "Utilizing an Accreditation Model to Evaluate Academic Advisement." *NASPA Journal,* 1983, *20*(3), 42–50.

Kramer, H. C. "Advising and Causal Attribution Theory." *NACADA Journal,* 1982, *2*(1), 1–7.

Kramer, H. C. "Faculty Development: The Advising Coordinator's Changing Scene." *NACADA Journal,* 1986, *6*(2), 31–42.

Krik, J. J. "Predictors of Salary Level for HRD Academes." *Human Resource Development Quarterly,* 1996, *7*(4), 359–367.

Krupka, L. R., and Vener, A. M. "Academic Advising/Career Counseling and the 'New' College Student." *Journal of College Student Personnel,* 1980, *21*(3), 270–274.

Larsen, M. D., and Brown, B. M. "Rewards for Academic Advising: An Evaluation." *NACADA Journal,* 1983, *3*(2), 53–60.

Latucca, L. R., and Stark, J. S. "Modifying the Major: Discretionary Thoughts from Ten Disciplines." *Journal of Higher Education,* 1995, *18*(3), 315–344.

Lewallen, W. C. "Students Decided and Undecided About Career Choice: A Comparison of College Achievement and Student Involvement." *NACADA Journal,* 1995, *15*(1), 22–30.

Lieberman, S. J. "Cyber Adviser: High-Tech, High-Touch Advising." *T.H.E. Journal,* 1996, *24*(4), 111–114.

Lowry, G. R., and Grites, T. J. "The Classroom as an Institutional Resource: An Example in Computer-Assisted Advising." *NACADA Journal,* 1982, *2*(2), 76–89.

Lyon, J. L., and Carpinelli, M. S. "The Use of the Kiosk Systems Technology in Academic Support Services." In Kramer, G. L., and Childs, M. W. (eds.), *Transforming Academic Advising Through the Use of Information Technology.* National Academic Advising Association Monograph Series, no. 4. Manhattan, Kans.: National Academic Advising Association, 1996.

Mark, M. M., and Romano, J. J. "The Freshman Seminar Program: Experimental Evaluation of an Introduction to the Liberal Arts." *Evaluation Review,* 1982, *6*(6), 901–810.

Matthews, J. R. "Evaluation: A Major Challenge for the 1980s." *Teaching of Psychology,* 1982, *9*(1), 49–52.

McGlaughlin, B. M., and Starr, E. A. "Academic Advising Literature Since 1965: A College Student Personnel Abstracts Review." *NACADA Journal,* 1982, *2*(2), 14–23.

Nadler, M. K., and Nadler, L. B. "The Influence of Student Sex and Instructor Sex on Academic Advising Communication." *Journal on Excellence in College Teaching,* 1993, *4*, 119–130.

Novels, A. N., and Ender, S. C. "The Impact of Developmental Advising for High-Achieving Minority Students." *NACADA Journal,* 1988, *8*(2), 23–26.

Oliver, M. L., Smith, A. W., and Wilson, K. R. "Supporting Successful Black Students: Personal, Organizational and Institutional Factors." *National Journal of Sociology,* 1989, *3*(2), 2–21.

Pascarella, E. T. "The Impact of College on Students: The Nature of the Evidence." *Review of Higher Education,* 1991, *14*(4), 453–466.

Pascarella, E. T., and Terenzini, P. T. "Contextual Analysis as a Method for Assessing Residence Group Effects." *Journal of College Student Personnel,* 1982, *23*(2), 108–114.

Pascarella, E. T., and others. "What Have We Learned from the First Year of the National Study of Student Learning?" *Journal of College Student Development,"* 1996, *37*(2), 182–192.

Peterson, C., and Barrett, L. C. "Explanatory Style and Academic Performance Among University Freshmen.*" Journal of Personality and Social Psychology,* 1987, *53*(3), 603–607.

Plater, W. M. "Future Work: Faculty Time in the Twenty-First Century." *Change,* 1995, *27*(3), 22–34.

Polson, C. J., and Cashin, W. E. "Research Priorities for Academic Advising: Results of Survey of NACADA Membership." *NACADA Journal,* 1981, *1*(1), 34–43.

Polson, C. J., and Gordon, V. N. "Issues in Academic Advising Revisited." *NACADA Journal,* 1988, *8*(2), 49–58.

Ray, H. N., Moore, W. K., and Oliver, J. E. "Evaluation of a Computer-Assisted Advising System." *NACADA Journal,* 1991, *11*(2), 21–27.

Russel, J. H., and Sullivan, T. "Student Acquisition of Career Decision-Making Skills as a Result of Faculty Advisor Intervention." *Journal of College Student Personnel,* 1979, *20*(4), 291–296.

Severy, L. J., and Singer, P. J. "The University of Florida's Monitoring Academic Progress Policy (MAPP)." In G. L. Kramer and M. W. Childs (eds.), *Transforming Academic Advising Through the Use of Information Technology.* NACADA Monograph Series, no. 4, Manhattan, Kans.: National Academic Advising Association, 1996.

Sherbo, I. "Academic Advising in England and in the United States: A Comparison." *NACADA Journal,* 1983, *3*(2), 39–46.

Sherohman, J., and Havir, L. "Preparing Undergraduates for Practice: Implications from a Survey of Graduates." *Clinical Sociology Review,* 1989, *7*, 212–224.

Sorcinelli, M. D. "Effective Approaches to New Faculty Development." *Journal of Counseling and Development,* 1994, *72*(5), 474–479.

Sotto, R. R. "Interactive Video Advising." In G. L. Kramer and M. W. Childs (eds.), *Transforming Academic Advising Through the Use of Information Technology.* NACADA Monograph Series, no. 4, Manhattan, Kans.: National Academic Advising Association, 1996.

Stage, F. K. "College Outcomes and Student Development: Filling in the Gaps." *Review of Higher Education,* 1989, *12*(3), 293–304.

Stoynoff, S. "Factors Associated with International Students' Academic Achievement." *Journal of Instructional Psychology,* 1997, *24*(1), 56–68.

Strommer, D. W. "Advising Special Populations of Students." A. G. Reinarz and E. R. White (eds.), *Teaching Through Academic Advising: A Faculty Perspective.* New Directions for Teaching and Learning, no. 62. San Francisco: Jossey-Bass, 1995.

Teague, G. V., and Grites, T. J. "Faculty Contracts and Academic Advising." *Journal of College Student Personnel,* 1980, *21*(1), 40–44.

Terenzini, P. T., and others. "Predicting Freshman Persistence and Voluntary Dropout Decisions: A Replication." *Research in Higher Education,* 1981, *15*(2), 109–127.

Terpstra, D. E., and Olson, P. D. "Sources of Resistance to Management-by-Objectives Among University Faculty." *Education,* 1984, *104*(4), 435–443.

Tinsley, D. J., and Irelan, T. M. "Instruments Used in College Student Affairs Research: An Analysis of the Measurement Base of a Young Profession." *Journal of College Student Development,* 1989, *30*(4), 440–447.

Tinto, V. S. "Principles of Effective Retention." *Journal of the Freshman Experience,* 1990, *2,* 35–48.

Tinto, V. S. "Colleges as Communities: Taking Research on Student Persistence Seriously." *Review of Higher Education,* 1998, *21*(2), 167–177.

Wade, B. K., and Yoder, E. P. "The Professional Status of Teachers and Academic Advisers: It Matters." A. G. Reinarz and E. R. White (eds.), *Teaching Through Academic Advising: A Faculty Perspective.* New Directions for Teaching and Learning, no. 62. San Francisco: Jossey-Bass, 1995.

Waggenspack, B. M., and Hensley, W. E. "The State of Communication Undergraduate Academic Advising." *ACA Bulletin,* 1992, *82,* 18–27.

Wilder, J. R. "Academic and Career Advising: Institutional Commitment and Program Recommendations." *Peabody Journal of Education,* 1982, *59*(2), 107–111.

Winston, R. B., and Sandor, J. A. *The Academic Advising Inventory.* Athens, Ga.: Student Development Associates, 1984.

Zhang, C., and Farley, J. E. "Gender and the Distribution of Household Work: A Comparison of Self-Reports by Female Faculty in the United States and China." *Journal of Comparative Family Studies,* 1995, *26*(2), 195–206.

Chapter Twenty-Seven

Meeting the Needs of Tomorrow's Learners and Tomorrow's Workplace

Virginia N. Gordon

As we contemplate the future of higher education and academic advising, we need to think creatively about how advising can serve the students who will inhabit our campuses and prepare them for a world that is changing dramatically. Currently we are bombarded with visions of a new technological century in which our personal and professional lives will be affected by change that is hard to imagine. Although we and our students face an unknown future, we must plan for these changes with a proactive stance that anticipates and controls change in a positive, beneficial way.

Costanza (1998) outlines four visions of the century ahead from a perspective that looks back from the year 2100. Two of the scenarios are based on a *technological optimist* worldview and reflect the continuation of current trends. Costanza calls the positive version "Star Trek" and the negative version "Mad Max." The positive version is based on an optimistic view of free competition, unlimited resources, and most importantly, technology's ability to meet any challenge. If these assumptions are wrong, the negative or "Mad Max" version could take place. In this scenario, the oil supply is depleted and alternative energy sources fail to materialize or be cost-effective. In this scenario, financial markets collapse, governments weaken, and the world is run by transnational corporations.

The other two possible scenarios that Costanza envisions for the century ahead are based on *technological skepticism*. In these two views, "Big Government" triumphs over private enterprise and "Ecotopia" sees the environment as the primary concern as "consumerism" is replaced with a "sustainable lifestyle." In these two versions of the future, resources are limited, and progress depends less on technology and more on social and community development.

Many of us would probably select one of the three sustainable scenarios (excluding Mad Max) because they are closer to the present version of society. Our personal view of the progress of technology (whether it will have a positive or negative impact) will influence which worldview we desire. Regardless of choice, our goal must be to create advising services rationally, to reflect our values in the way we manage human activities. As Costanza points out, we each have our own private vision of the world in which we really want to live. And although we have little control over technology as individuals, we do have some influence on the world immediately around us.

If any of these four visions (or any other scenario, for that matter) turns out to be real, advising's small niche in the world of higher education will reflect our and society's reaction to these technological and societal changes. We must strive to maintain the type of environment that constantly focuses on the needs of individual students and uses technology as a positive force.

Tomorrow's Work World

Much has been written about the impact of technology on the workplace of tomorrow. Our present culture has been in "future shock" for many years. The rapid development of new technologies has literally transformed our lives in a few short decades. We are finding ourselves moving at "warp speed" and trying to adjust to the increasing velocity of our lives in many arenas. Bertman (1998) describes this new mode of operating as the "power of now," which he defines as "the intense energy of an unconditional present, a present uncompromised by any other dimension of time. . . . The 'power of now' replaces the long term with the short term, duration with immediacy, permanence with transience, memory with sensation, insight with impulse" (pp. 20–21). In a recent survey nearly 40 percent of Americans reported that they feel rushed all the time. To resist this condition, Bertman suggests, we should restrain our technology by defining the kind of life we want, both personally and communally, and we should "select the technologies that truly serve those ends . . . and have the courage to reject technologies that take more than they give" (p. 22).

Information technology, or infotech, consists of "computing combined with telecommunications and networking" (Hines, 1996, p. 7). Hines predicts that in the future there will be no jobs that will not be influenced by infotech—at least 90 percent of the workforce will be affected by 2010. According to the Commerce Department, the demand for information technology workers alone will reach a million by 2005 (Challenger, 1998, p. 18).

Hines indicates that infotech will affect future workers on two levels: their jobs will be done through computers or expert systems and their jobs will be redesigned because of the use of these intermediary capabilities. For example, the teachers of 2010 will be more facilitators or coaches than lecturers. Teachers will help students customize their education depending on the individual student's needs. We like to think that truly committed academic advisors are already helping students customize their education. With the help of creatively designed personalized computer systems, this task should become even more effective and exciting. Advisors, however, must be involved in the teams designing these systems. Too often we have been handed systems that are not responsive to our or our advisees' needs. In the future, as these systems become a reality, advisors will need to be more proactive.

Peter Drucker (1998, p. 16) discusses the changing workplace as "the future that has already happened." Economic growth will no longer come from putting more people to work; it will come from the productivity of knowledge work and of knowledge workers. Unlike past workers in manufacturing, knowledge workers "own the means of production: They carry that knowledge in their heads and can therefore take it with them" (p. 18). Drucker insists that the most important area in which new methods and practices for the workplace need to be developed is managing society's knowledge resources, specifically education and health care, "both of which are today overadministered and undermanaged" (p. 18).

Although educating knowledge workers and managing knowledge resources are two critical roles currently challenging higher education, they will become even more important in the future. Because of infotech, Hines (1996, p. 11) indicates, future workers will be engaged in activities that involve "gathering, creating, manipulating, storing, and distributing information related to products, services, and customer needs." It is interesting to speculate how future advisors might gather, create, manipulate, store, and distribute information, because disseminating information is such an integral advising task. As proposed earlier, advisors must be involved in these activities in the way they will be expected and want to be involved.

Tomorrow's Workers

By the year 2030, middle-aged Generation Xers (born from 1965–1976) will make up most of the workforce and their baby boomer parents (born from 1946–1964) will have retired. The U.S. population over age seventy at that time will have doubled from what it is now. The demographics of the workforce will change, particularly as the number of teens and those over fifty increases. Challenger (1998) suggests that population changes will be just as important as technology in influencing the future workplace. Employers will need to be constantly aware of the potential for polarity among such a diverse workforce, which could influence the climate of the workplace (Thau and Heflin, 1997).

According to a recent Shell Oil Company (1998) poll, there are six types of worker-personality types in the workforce. Each type has a distinctive approach to work. Understanding these differences is especially important to employers, who will find it increasingly difficult to hire and retain effective workers. The six types are as follows:

- *Fulfillment seekers.* These workers seek jobs that will help them make the world a better place. They describe themselves as team players rather than as leaders. They express high satisfaction with their work. Typical occupations, according to the poll, are teachers, nurses, and public defenders.
- *Risk takers.* Members of this group want to get rich quickly and are constantly trying to find financial opportunities. They frequently move from one employer to another, always looking for the better job. Forty percent have incomes of $50,000 or more. Typical occupations are software entrepreneurs and car salespersons.
- *High achievers.* These are the leaders of the workplace. They take initiative and are noted for their careful planning skills. They are the highest income group, with one-fourth earning $75,000 a year or more. They are lawyers, surgeons, architects, and so on.
- *Clock punchers.* Many workers in this group say they are in their jobs by chance. They had the lowest satisfaction level of the six groups. They would have made a different career choice if they had had the chance. Many had a high school diploma or less. Typical jobs were cashiering, waitressing, and being a hospital orderly.
- *Ladder climbers.* These workers prefer to stay with one company because of the stability. They are loyal and would rather have a stable income than a high one. They have a modest education but good income. Forty-eight percent earn more than $50,000 a year. Corporate middle managers and skilled blue-collar supervisors are examples of workers in this group.
- *Paycheck cashers.* These workers would rather have a good income and benefits than the opportunity to use their capabilities or change the world. Most do not have a college degree. Typical jobs are factory work and entry-level word processing.

These types illustrate the importance of understanding the values and goals of individuals, because future workers will increasingly choose their employers on the basis of how the workers perceive the organization's aims and values (Herman and Gioia, 1998). Meaningful work will be important to many workers, and organizations will need to consider this if they want to maintain a high-performance workforce. Quality-of-life issues and the opportunity for personal and professional growth are becoming more important to many job seekers.

As advisors, do we see students whose attitudes, values, and goals are similar to any of these six worker-personality types? For example, students who are destined to become fulfillment seekers might want to discuss career options involving the importance of satisfying work through helping others. High achievers, who seem to have carefully planned their career path from an early age and who aspire to a profession, might express concern about the leadership and income values they seek in relation to major and career choices. Learning about the values and goals of advisees is important, especially as they make decisions affecting who they want to be as future workers.

Mitchell (1998) discusses the generation shift in values among the Generation Xers who are beginning their family-forming years. One important factor is the high educational levels of the baby boomers and Xers. Mitchell writes, "Education greatly influences people's attitudes and values, wants and needs" (p. 16). She also says that the terms *conservative* and *liberal* are misleading because they are becoming less useful in predicting public opinion on issues. Mitchell argues that it is important to understand the values and beliefs of the younger, or "replacement," generation because they are the ones who will be shaping the future of society.

Goleman (1998) suggests that a worker's emotional skills may be more important to an employer in the future than technical skills (which many workers will have). Emotional intelligence, according to Goleman, includes both self-awareness and awareness of others. His Emotional Competence Framework incorporates both personal and social competencies. Personal competence includes self-awareness, self-regulation, and motivation. Social competence includes empathy and social skills. As the work of the future becomes more complex and collaborative, the emotionally intelligent worker will be in demand. Top performers must master a mix of these competencies, not just a few.

The successful workers of the twenty-first century will need to be creative, flexible, and motivated to become lifelong learners. In the early 1990s the U.S. Secretary of Labor appointed a special commission to define the types of work skills that would be needed for the next century. The Secretary's Commission on Achieving Necessary Skills (SCANS, 1991) defined five competencies and a three-part foundation of skills and personal qualities that were deemed important for the workplace of the future. The commission suggested that effective workers can productively use resources, interpersonal skills, information, systems, and technology. The commission also emphasized more basic skills, such as the fundamental skills of reading, writing, and mathematics as well as speaking and listening skills. The personal qualities that the commission deemed important included responsibility, self-esteem, self-management, sociability, and integrity. High standards of attendance, enthusiasm, vitality, and optimism in approaching and completing work were also identified.

Some advisors have found it helpful to have the SCANS list of competencies, skills, and personal qualities available during an advising session to encourage students to schedule classes where these skills are taught. In addition to coursework, advisors can emphasize the importance of obtaining these essential competencies through other avenues (such as volunteer work, internships, campus activities, and work experiences).

Herman and Gioia (1998) also describe certain skills that future workers must acquire if they are to be successful. In addition to technical and technological skills, they will need visionary skills, the ability to organize, persuasive skills, communication skills, and the ability to learn. The most successful workers in the twenty-first century will seek balance, growth, and fulfillment in both their work and home environments. While opportunities exist on today's campuses for students to acquire many of these skills, more emphasis will need to be placed on how and when these and other skills can be learned during the college experience.

Higher Education: The Knowledge Factory

Our institutions of higher learning were built on a foundation deep in tradition. Joseph Pelton (1996) points out that since the age of Socrates, almost 2,500 years ago, we have created a world of rocketships, genetic engineering, chaos theory, and supercomputers. But education in colleges and universities, says Pelton, is still "putting students in a classroom with an authority figure who lectures for a prescribed period of time" (p. 17). In other words, little has changed from the way students were taught in Socrates' time. Pelton admits that the challenge of reforming global education is "a more awesome undertaking than the Apollo Moon Project, the Great Wall of China, and the Great Pyramids of Egypt combined" (p. 17).

In the past century the main forces shaping universities in particular have been science and democracy. These two forces greatly influenced the stability of the university in the twentieth century. A global survey of universities (or "knowledge factories") carried out by *The Economist* ("A Survey of Universities," 1997) determined that "the university is not just a creator of knowledge, a trainer of young minds, and a transmitter of culture, but also a major agent of economic growth" (p. 4). The survey indicated that the university is "not so much a moral or cultural force, [but] more of an incubator of new industries in a technologically dominated economy" (p. 5). The university is already struggling to reconcile its ancient mission of "creator of knowledge" with the demands of mass higher education, and economics and politics will continue to influence its future role in society.

As the survey of universities in *The Economist* asks, Can the university meet the new demands being placed on it and remain true to its tradition of being a community of scholars and to offering a quality undergraduate education? Rather than altering higher education to an unrecognizable form, cyberspace can offer innovative ways of helping students learn in many new and different settings. New connections between disciplines and between institutions can also offer new and exciting ways of communicating and cooperating in teaching and research. Through technology the university will truly become a community of scholars, not so much being encumbered with *how* education is delivered but caring about *what* is delivered in terms of content and learning services. Advising must take on a more definitive role in the learning process as this transformation takes place.

Levine and Cureton (1998) poignantly write about our current transitional generation of students who, as all before them, are affected by the cycles of history. These authors remind us of past cycles of the "wakeful, strenuous, and even frenetic activity" of society, followed by "periods of rest" (p. 146). A cycle of wakefulness is a *period of community ascendancy,* which is future oriented. The 1960s, through the Vietnam War, is an example of this period. During periods of rest, *individual ascendancy* is the hallmark. These periods are oriented to the present and are more concerned with individual rights. After World War II, for example, people were weary and wanted a period of rest.

What we are caught in now, according to Levine and Cureton, is a rare time in our history when profound change is occurring. Not since the industrial revolution have we witnessed such upheaval in our society. This world of massive social and economic change is the one that college students are facing today. Levine and Cureton suggest that the "education we offered previous generations, whether successful or not, will not work for these students" (1998, p. 157). They suggest a formal college curriculum that is grounded in the life needs of students rather than the current one, which is rooted in traditional academic disciplines. The elements in this new curriculum include helping students acquire the *communication and critical thinking skills* needed for a new age; an understanding of our *human heritage* (and how societies have responded to change in the past); a respect for our *global environment* (including scientific literacy and citizens who can make effective environmental policies); an understanding of the many *roles* students will play in the future (that is, individual, family member, worker, citizen, leader, and follower); an opportunity to acquire in college the knowledge and experiences that will help them function effectively in these roles; and an understanding of how *values,* which underlie each of the other attributes, function in their lives and in society. As advisors we can have a great impact on how students respond to the challenges set forth in this "curriculum for living" and how each of these attributes will be absorbed by the future transitional generations we will advise.

Advising for the Future

How will academic advising change or be influenced by the future demands of the workplace and the need to educate people for a new age? Who will our future students be? How will technology continue to change how we interact with students? How can a liberal education serve students in a technological society? How can students acquire the skills needed for the future workplace? Or from a broader perspective, How will advising systems continue to respond to the needs of students, departments, and institutions? How will future organizational functions change advising systems? How can we more effectively evaluate what we do and how we do it? These and other issues must be confronted if academic advising is to meet the challenges ahead.

Learning Technologies

Technology has already had a tremendous impact on the nitty-gritty aspects of advising, such as registration and monitoring students' progress toward a degree. Other technological innovations will have great impact on advisors and students alike. Through *telelearning,* students of the future will select when they wish to learn according to their personal schedules (Halal and Liebowitz, 1996). While not new, intelligent tutoring systems will become common. Through intelligent multimedia computer programs, students will be guided individually to their own personal levels of understanding.

Distance learning is an example of how technology is changing our approaches to education. Many older students wish to pursue new career directions and need to enhance their educational preparation. Others are not geographically near the source of the education they need or desire. Technology has given higher education (along with all other educational levels) the capability of reaching thousands of students who would not have participated before.

Halal and Liebowitz (1996) describe some changes in the way students will be exposed to different approaches to learning. Students will attend televised lectures in their residence halls and use their computers to access library materials. Although electronic instruction will be provided, part of instruction will be in small informal classes with faculty. Local area networks will help integrate different aspects of college life. Nonresidential students will access lectures and library resources from their homes or workplaces. Libraries will increasingly reduce reference space and increase computer space.

There is concern that electronic education will lack the caring element that dialogue in the classroom offers. The caring teacher will still be needed, but as an advisor or consultant rather than as a lecturer. Teachers will focus on the more complex issues in learning for which machines cannot provide. Advisors will assume a much broader role as teacher and communicator of information and ideas, and as an important part of students' support networks.

Career Advising

Advising that offers career information and actively supports career planning can and should play a more important role in the future. The traditional career planning model that is recognized today assumes a stable, fixed career path. Students are encouraged (and sometimes even forced) early in their college years to set goals that are generally perceived as long-term. Barner (1996), however, insists that future workers will need to become career strategists rather than career planners. He predicts that career paths will be "fragmented and subject to change" (p. 16). Future employees will be more interested in personal satisfaction and short-term objectives. They will need to be more flexible, constantly reassessing their goals and tracking their progress based on fulfilling their personal needs. Future workers can no longer rely on organizations for a career track but must assume responsibility for their own career path.

Academic advisors can play a critical role in helping students understand the importance of educational and vocational planning fashioned in this new light. Students will need to become career strategists when they enter college, if not before. They will need to acquire the skills of lifelong learning, recognizing the importance of adapting to change and constantly reevaluating their personal needs and desires.

These shifts in career strategies will also affect educators. More pressure will be exerted to make our teaching and advising practices more user-friendly. Actually, many of our recognized developmental advising practices will be carried over into the classroom. Barner (1996) indicates that university teachers will need to "demonstrate solid presentation and training skills and provide supplemental coaching and guidance to needy students" (p. 17).

Barner also lists four key survival skills that everyone should learn. The first is *environmental scanning,* which includes the ability to access computer and other networks to gage one's skills in order to prevent technological obsolescence and identify fast-breaking employment opportunities. The second is to *acquire portable skills,* which are easily transferable, such as knowledge of financial software or project management. The third key skill is *self-management* when either working alone or with a team. The last skill is in the area of *communication* and includes both verbal and written skills. This last ability will be especially important in working with diverse coworkers and in high-stress or time-limited situations.

In Chapter Eleven of this volume, Betsy McCalla-Wriggins outlines the elements of effective career planning and emphasizes the need to integrate academic and career information when advising students. With such vast amounts of information about the work world available through technology, students can be overwhelmed quickly and become frustrated. Academic advisors will be increasingly involved in helping students access, gather, analyze, and synthesize career information, and will help them apply it to their own personal values and goals.

Advisors as Communicators

Communication skills will become even more important in future advising because of the great diversity expected in the student population. Advisors will need to be more sensitive to the cultural influences affecting their advisees who are from backgrounds different from their own. They will need to expand and refine their knowledge about the cultures represented by the students they advise while honestly checking their own attitudes and biases. They should be trained to understand the developmental issues of diverse groups of students so they can communicate with sensitivity and skill.

The ability to prioritize, condense, and convey information will be one of the most important advisor skills in the future. We are already feeling the pressures of an information glut, and the amount of information that bombards us constantly will only increase. Advisors will assume a critical role in acting as intermediaries between students and information resources and will need to help their advisees acquire, process, and evaluate diverse and sometimes complex types of information.

Advisors not only must continue to improve and refine their own communication skills, but also will need to impress on their advisees the importance of communication and thinking skills. Levine and Cureton (1998) emphasize how critical these skills will be in the future and how important it is for today's learners to acquire them for tomorrow's workplace. They outline three transitional skills that must be mastered. First, *critical thinking* is important in a world where so much information is available so readily. This skill includes the ability to cut through vast amounts of constantly changing information, to determine what is relevant and true for a particular problem, and to apply it in both familiar and changing situations. Second, as stated earlier, we must impress on students the inevitability of *continuous learning*, because they will need to assimilate new knowledge and acquire fresh skills throughout the rest of their lives. *Creativity* is the third skill that Levine and Cureton list as essential for the worker of the future. Old ways of thinking and acting will often be useless, and creatively developed new ones will be required.

Advisors as Collaborators

Schroeder, Minor, and Tarkow (1999) observe that "as institutions have become complex, we have attempted to address complexities through specialization, and in the process our organizations have become increasingly fragmented" (p. 61). The need for coordination and collaboration among the organizational components of our campuses has never been greater. Collaborative efforts are being encouraged across many campuses today and will continue because of pressures for higher education reform.

Collaborative initiatives such as learning communities, multicultural studies, and retention efforts have required many areas of the campus community to work together. Academic advisors have been involved in many of these collaborative efforts, including living-learning centers, first-year student experience programs, capstone programs, and service learning. These cooperative practices will become even more important in the future as different types of units are asked to work together to solve problems or create new programs. As Tuckey (1996) states, "the vitality of the advising system depends on how it is linked to the lifeblood of the institution" (p. 11). Tuckey suggests that there needs to be a systems coordinator of academic advising to monitor how the total campus advising system functions and evolves.

Advisors as Futurists

Academic advisors can no longer rely on advising habits that reflect the status quo. They will need to seek out new sources of information, educate themselves about the broader trends in higher education, and most importantly, monitor the changing needs of their diverse advisees. They should be able to answer students' questions about the kinds of skills and knowledge they will need in certain fields. Knowledge of the avenues for helping students understand and acquire the skills needed to be successful in the future workplace will be part of advisors' repertoire. Helping students in this way will require a new type of advisor role whose responsibilities will include researching and disseminating information for student use through many types of technological media. Technology now makes it possible to do this individually or in groups through advisors' listservs or Web pages (Vowell, 1996).

The implications for training future advisors, who will need to acquire broad and complex knowledge as well as opportunities to refine technical and communication skills, are obvious. Advisor development can no longer be a once-a-year event; urgency dictates frequently offered sessions in which new skills are taught and new information is disseminated and processed.

Many experienced advisors may agree that our work is constantly evolving to accommodate the changes taking place in our institutions and in our student bodies. We can either be frustrated by increased workloads, confusing organizational systems, and waning resources, or we can meet these challenges with dedication and renewed faith in the value of our work. We must resist getting caught up in the power of now at the expense of building meaningful relationships and creating responsible advising environments. Increasingly students will need a haven where they can feel secure in expressing their concerns and making decisions that require careful thought. As Bertman (1998) observes, we must prevent our "hyperculture" from obscuring history and memory. A balance of the past, present, and future must be preserved if we are to provide our students with a stable, humane environment in which to live, learn, and work.

Conclusion

As we contemplate the future of higher education and our roles as advisors, we must always be cognizant of society's accelerated rate of change and how it will affect our personal and professional lives. Advisors must never lose sight of their noble purpose of providing students with an accepting and challenging environment in which they can learn and grow to their full potential.

In the future, advisors will need continually to develop new technological skills, expand their expertise in career advising, learn new skills as communicators and interpreters of complex information, and become more involved as collaborators with both institutional and community resources. A new role—that of advisor as futurist—will be essential if we are to help ourselves and our students succeed in a rapidly changing world.

References

"A Survey of Universities: The Knowledge Factory." *The Economist,* Oct. 4, 1997, pp. 3–22.

Barner, R. "The New Career Strategist." In E. Cornish (ed.), *Exploring Your Future: Living, Learning, and Working in the Information Age.* Bethesda, Md.: World Future Society, 1996.

Bertman, S. *Hyperculture: The Human Cost of Speed.* New York: Praeger, 1998.

Challenger, J. A. "There Is No Future for the Workplace" *The Futurist,* 1998, *32*(7), 16–20.

Costanza, R. "Four Visions of the Century Ahead." *The Futurist,* 1998, *32*(7), 16–20.

Drucker, P. *Peter Drucker on the Profession of Management.* Boston: Harvard Business School Press, 1998.

Goleman, D. *Working with Emotional Intelligence.* New York: Bantam Books, 1998.

Halal, W. E., and Liebowitz, J. "Telelearning: The Multimedia Revolution in Education." In E. Cornish (ed.), *Exploring Your Future: Living, Learning, and Working in the Information Age.* Bethesda, Md.: World Future Society, 1996.

Herman, R. E., and Gioia, J. L. "Making Work Meaningful." *The Futurist,* 1998, *32*(9), 24–38.

Hines, A. "Jobs and Infotech," In E. Cornish (ed.), *Exploring Your Future: Living, Learning, and Working in the Information Age.* Bethesda, Md.: World Future Society, 1996.

Levine, A., and Cureton, J. S. *When Hope and Fear Collide.* San Francisco: Jossey-Bass, 1998.

Mitchell, S. *American Generations: Who They Are, How They Live, What They Think.* New York: New Strategist, 1998.

Pelton, J. N. "Cyberlearning vs. the University." *The Futurist,* 1996, *30*(2), 17–20.

Schroeder, C. C., Minor, F. D., and Tarkow, T. A. "Learning Communities: Partnerships Between Academic and Student Affairs." In J. H. Levine (ed.), *Learning Communities: New Structures, New Partnerships for Learning.* Columbia, S.C.: National Resource Center for the First-Year Experience and Students in Transition, 1999.

Secretary's Commission on Achieving Necessary Skills. *Learning A Living: A Blueprint for High Performance.* Washington, D.C.: U.S. Department of Labor, 1991.

Shell Oil Company. "The Shell Poll." Houston, Tex.: Shell Oil Company, Sept. 1998.

Thau, R. D., and Heflin, J. S. (ed.), *Generations Apart: Xers vs. Boomers vs. the Elderly.* Amherst, N.Y.: Prometheus Books, 1997.

Tuckey, D. D. "Academic Advising as a Multisystem, Collaborative Enterprise." *NACADA Journal,* 1996, *16*(1), 6–13.

Vowell, F. "Using the Internet in Advising: The World Wide Web, E-Mail, and Listservs." In G. L. Kramer and W. Childs (eds.), *Transforming Academic Advising Through the Use of Information Technology.* National Academic Advising Association Monograph Series, no. 4. Manhattan, Kans.: National Academic Advising Association, 1996.

Chapter Twenty-Eight

Anticipating, Implementing, and Adapting to Changes in Academic Advising

Herta Teitelbaum

In his article "Another Century's End, Another Revolution for Higher Education," Kennedy (1995) presages a transformation of higher education for the new millennium, not unlike the profound changes that marked the end of the nineteenth century and the first half of the twentieth century and ultimately produced a system of higher education in the United States that was the envy of the world. The United States is currently in the midst of transforming itself from an industrial and agricultural environment to an information and service society. The forces driving these changes have already begun to alter the face of higher education. Academic advisors must identify changes already under way and those that are yet to come in order to respond effectively to the evolving educational environment.

The first part of this chapter outlines the major pressures affecting higher education and forcing institutions to reconsider their roles and activities. The second part examines the likely effects of these changes on current advising practices and the ways in which advisors can evaluate the environment on their own campus to understand the local effects of these trends. The last two sections suggest strategies for meeting new challenges, not only to survive but also to bring new vitality to academic advising.

The Changing Face of Higher Education

American colleges and universities are social institutions embedded in the general economy. Consequently, changes that are now reshaping American businesses and organizations inevitably influence higher education as well. Resource scarcity, increased competitiveness, downsizing and outsourcing, and a generally more turbulent, less predictable environment are the characteristics of the postindustrial environment in which business enterprises now find themselves. Modern technology has altered the expectations of consumers and the behavior of service providers. Businesses that successfully take advantage of technological innovations are able to create efficiencies that allow them to recapture and sustain a high level of productivity and competitiveness.

Ortmann (1997) notes a number of parallel developments in higher education and the broad industrial setting, and universities have begun to explore the implications of these developments. Through the Pew Higher Education Roundtable program, faculty, administrators, trustees, and staff from hundreds of institutions of higher education have, since 1993, begun conversations about impending changes and ways to restructure the academy. The American Council on Education has also developed a Kellogg-funded network of colleges and universities to deal with the restructuring entailed by those changes (Guskin, 1996).

The Increasing Cost of Higher Education and the Impact of Expected Enrollment Growth

Just as the higher costs of technology and human resources have affected business organizations, the steadily increasing cost of delivering higher education programs, coupled with enrollment increases predicted for the next decade, will create serious challenges for all, and particularly for public educational institutions. Many economists and higher education administrators believe that the economic and financial future of higher education is in jeopardy (Brinkman and Morgan, 1994; Institute for Research on Higher Education at the University of Pennsylvania, 1996). During the past two decades, per-student expenditures have increased while government student support and legislative funding for public higher education have declined. Tuition at both private and public college has soared to levels that are alarming to the public and likely cannot be continued. Without changes in the delivery of higher education, aggregate budget shortfalls at U.S. colleges and universities are expected to rise dramatically as we move into the next century (Hammonds and others, 1997).

Undergraduate enrollment in institutions of higher education will likely rise by 12 percent overall between 1996 and 2008. The traditional college-age population of eighteen- to twenty-four-year-olds is projected to increase at a greater rate, by 18 percent, and is expected to make up 60 percent of the enrollment by 2008. Students twenty-five and older are estimated to account for 40 percent of enrollments by that date (U.S. Department of Education, 1997a). Enrollment growth is a cause for concern rather than a solution to educational finance problems because tuition revenues cover only about one-third of the actual cost of public higher education. Declining federal and state government support will not make up the difference (Winston, 1997; Macunovich, 1997). Cost containment and finding new funding sources are clearly the primary challenges for higher education administrators.

The Demand for Constituent-Based Education and Rapid Changes in the Labor Market

Plater (1995) observes that learning cannot be separated from the needs of society and the expectations of students. In this respect, he believes, institutions of higher education are no different from every other industrial and service sector of American economic life. Survival and success are now clearly a function of the delivery of valued outcomes. Late-twentieth-century students are highly goal oriented and consider a college degree an investment in a better life—a down payment on a career that will give them the skills and credentials they need in the current and future labor market and provide them with greater economic security. Students are surely correct in seeing the economic value of higher education. The gap in earnings between those with a high school degree and those with various levels of higher education has steadily widened (U.S. Department of Commerce, 1995; Cosca, 1998). Moreover, industrial employment, which relies less on a college-educated labor force, has declined while the demand for better-educated workers in the information and service industry has risen (McPherson and Schapiro, 1995).

Not only have the required credentials for employment changed but so has the work environment. The turbulent nature of the economy, the speed of technological innovations, and the continuing restructuring and reengineering of business all imply that jobs in the twenty-first century will look very different from the jobs of today. The fastest growing occupations are expected to be in the managerial, professional, and technical fields, requiring a high level of education and skill. Contemporary students need to be prepared to adjust to changes in the job market, to make career changes more frequently than was necessary in the past, and to retrain and acquire new skills to adapt to the increasingly unpredictable work environment (Krannich and Krannich, 1998).

Students, parents, and businesses will bring pressure on higher education to provide a curriculum more obviously relevant to employment and career requirements. Career planning will become a major focus in education programs and new emphasis will be placed on specialization and flexibility in career preparation (Krannich and Krannich, 1998). Although some in the academy resist acknowledging this vocational aspect of higher education, it has been the reality for quite some time. Increased emphasis on career-oriented learning is readily apparent in the changing demand for majors. The number of students majoring in occupational fields such as business, health-related programs, and engineering has grown substantially since 1970. At the same time, the proportion of bachelor degrees in traditional disciplines such as English, philosophy, and mathematics has declined precipitously since then (U.S. Department of Education, 1997b).

Although it may seem otherwise, the increasing interest in and demand for occupationally orientated majors should not be thought inconsistent with continued emphasis on liberal learning. The unpredictable nature of the employment market will result in dramatically different working patterns in the future.

Current and future graduates will not remain in the job for which they prepared in college but will undertake a number of different careers in their lives. What they learn in college must therefore provide knowledge and competencies that are useful across occupational categories. Continuing education will become an ever more important vehicle for skill development within and across occupations. Ultimately, however, college graduates will have to bring to the workplace the ability to adapt, to be flexible, and to learn new things, which are precisely the skills a liberal or general education seeks to foster (McPherson and Schapiro, 1995).

Focus on Student Learning and Outcome Measures

In recent years, the academy has begun to shift its emphasis from teaching to learning. It has also started to examine seriously the meaning of a bachelor's degree, seeing it not in the traditional terms measured by the accumulation of courses and credits but through assessment of acquired knowledge and competencies. Nonetheless, many employers still express dissatisfaction with the overall quality of education of graduates. A 1993 report from the Wingspread Group on Higher Education paints a disappointing picture of degree recipients—30 percent of degree holders took no mathematics courses, 40 percent had no credits in English or American literature, and 25 percent did not take a single history class. Moreover, only about one-half of the graduates demonstrated intermediate levels of competence in reading, writing, and quantitative skills (Plater, 1998).

For their part, legislators seek increasingly to influence the management of public colleges and to hold these institutions accountable for student outcomes. In addition, the private sector is beginning to present a serious challenge to the traditional higher educational market. The number of corporate "universities" offering in-house, job-related training has increased from about 1,000 to 1,400, some 40 percent, in five years (Hammonds and others, 1997). Moreover, for-profit institutions offering accredited degree programs have been successful in attracting large numbers of adult students who are not well served by traditional colleges. These are specialized institutions with a clearly defined mission and a focus on specific program goals that are client-based and responsive to the educational and personal needs of the surge of adults seeking convenient ways to begin or continue their education. With an enrollment of sixty thousand students, the University of Phoenix is one example of a successful education enterprise that provides for working adults a limited number of degree and certification programs in high-demand areas such as business, health care, and information technology. Taking advantage of the Internet and interactive TV, organizations such as the Knowledge Universe, the College Connection, the Jones International University, and more recently the Western Governors University have entered the higher education market promising affordable degree programs to vast numbers of students in many locations. These businesses know they will succeed only if they can produce results and if they are able to certify the outcomes of student learning (Hammonds and others, 1997; Winston, 1999).

The message to traditional colleges and universities should be clear. A serious review and restructuring of the academy is essential to continued prominence in an increasingly competitive higher education environment.

The Role of Technology in Higher Education

Technology clearly has been the primary transforming factor as we move into a postindustrial society. In industry, technology accounts for much of the impetus to downsize firms, for the popularity of outsourcing, for the surge in value-adding partnerships, and for the flattening of hierarchies (Ortmann, 1997). Modern information technology has changed dramatically the way scholars and students access information in higher education and is beginning to alter the forms of teaching and learning in the future. Traditionally, faculty and students were bound to the physical space of colleges and universities because these were the central depositories of information in their libraries. Information technology now allows universities to shift from investing in the physical storage of information to creating electronic databases. Ready access to discipline-based information through electronic means increasingly frees scholars and students from the limitations of physical space and time. Faculty can now easily interact with their colleagues at distant places and pursue their research in a global environment. Technology will also dramatically change the delivery of instruction and the way students learn. Instead of coming to a campus, students will have access to a wide variety of electronic curricula. They will be able to communicate electronically with their instructors and learn by utilizing interactive reading materials and study exercises (Noam, 1995; Massy and Zemsky, 1995). Distance learners will be credentialed through competency-based certification of degrees. For-profit organizations are expected to take the lead in providing electronic educational programs, and this will increase the latitude available to students as they choose their educational paths. Electronic curricula will be especially appealing to the growing number of students who, because of work-related factors or family commitments, cannot pursue a traditional, campus-based education (Noam, 1995).

Cost reduction is of course one of the primary reasons that traditional institutions of higher education as well as for-profit organizations are particularly interested in moving into the electronic education market. After the initial investment in hardware and software and the creation of electronic curricula, courses and programs are accessible to thousands of students around the world for relatively small further investments.

The Impact of Change on Academic Advising

The changes that are reshaping higher education will necessarily affect advising practices. This section examines how the changes outlined in the previous section may alter the ways in which colleges advise students in the future, and proposes some ideas for both rethinking traditional advising processes and restructuring advising offices.

Strategies for Addressing Resource Constraints

Over the next decade, higher education institutions will continue to experience declining resources, making staff additions in advising offices unlikely. At the same time, undergraduate enrollments are expected to increase. As a result, advisors will be called on to serve larger numbers of students with existing or, in some cases, even reduced resources. The obvious challenge is to advise more students with no additional staff while maintaining high-quality services. Reconciling these seemingly contradictory goals will require advisors to examine seriously their traditional ways of doing business—current advising structure and practices—and identify strategies for increasing efficiencies. These demands closely resemble the experience in recent years of American businesses that have had to reinvent themselves through rethinking and restructuring their business practices in order to function effectively in changed circumstances.

Restructuring the Advising Office

A hypothetical strategic planning exercise may illustrate one approach to reassessing the delivery of advising services. This exercise requires evaluation of staffing requirements and identification of alternative and perhaps more cost-effective ways for satisfying student demand. To begin, let us differentiate among the different kinds of advising assistance offered to students and match those with the level of advisor expertise necessary to satisfy those needs. The matrix in Exhibit 28.1 displays this information in a simplified fashion. Column one looks at student needs as a continuum ranging from basic information to more complex student problems. The second column matches the level of advisor expertise with the student needs. Finally, the last column lists potential alternative ways for meeting advising demands.

This matrix suggests different ways of staffing an advising office as well as relatively low-cost alternatives to the traditional way of providing services to students. A proportion of student needs can adequately be fulfilled through avenues that are less costly than paying for the time of experienced faculty or professional advisors. For instance, the information needs of students could be met by referring students to existing literature or to well-designed and easily accessible Web sites with answers to frequently asked questions. These Web sites could also link students to the e-mail address of an advisor who can clarify Web site information and answer specific questions. Students increasingly use computers for all aspects of college life—to register for courses, to change their course schedule, to obtain their course grades at the end of the academic term, to access catalogue information, and to investigate databases for research projects. Academic advising offices can take advantage of these skills to provide students with the information they need, without an office visit.

Group advising sessions can also be a successful tool for providing introductory information to students. Orientation programs have for years relied on

Student Advising Need	Level of Advisor Experience Required	Alternatives for Satisfying Need
Information	Low	Printed information
		Web-based information with FAQs and linked to e-mail
		Group advising
Straightforward advising situations (such as degree progress check, class scheduling)	Medium	Undergraduate advisors (paraprofessionals)
		Graduate student advisors
More complex advising situations (such as probation students, undecided students)	High	Faculty or professional advisors
		Graduate student advisors

Exhibit 28.1. Types of Student Advising Needs with Corresponding Advisor Experience Levels and Alternative Advising Modalities.

this approach to provide large numbers of students with common, basic information. Other opportunities for group advising include general information sessions for students interested in a particular major, or workshops for undecided students on strategies for identifying a major and a career. A question-and-answer period at the end of the session can address additional questions students might have. Students who need customized help can then arrange individual advisor appointments. Group sessions reduce advising loads and relieve advisors from the tedium of having to repeat the same information in one-to-one advising sessions. They are also more cost-effective because they require fewer staff resources.

At the other end of the spectrum of student advising needs are more complex situations best handled by individual conferences with experienced advisors. Advising probation students or students who are undecided about a major or career illustrate these situations.

As the matrix suggests, advising offices might consider employing a mix of advising staff consisting of experienced faculty or professional advisors to deal with students' most difficult advising issues, and well-trained part-time undergraduates (paraprofessionals) to assist students with more straightforward advising situations. This scheme would allow advising offices to realize cost savings without reducing the quality of service. Student advisors relate well to younger students and have the advantage of sharing direct knowledge of college life and courses with their advisees. In addition, student advisors gain valuable communication, teaching, and leadership skills from their advising experience. Advising offices might also consider hiring graduate students, who could be trained to assist in all areas. While their hourly rate will be higher than that of undergraduates, it will be considerably less than the cost of faculty or professional advisors. Moreover, graduate advisors provide a potential pool from which to draw future advising professionals if vacancies occur. (For references on student advising, the reader should consult the National Clearinghouse for Academic Advising < http://www.uvc.ohio-state.edu/chouse.html >).

Responding to the Changing Needs of Students

The ultimate goal of advising offices is to meet the needs of students effectively and efficiently. Accordingly, advisors must be knowledgeable about current and predictable characteristics, needs, and expectations of the student population they serve.

Diversity. It has been apparent for some time that the college population is becoming more diverse in its composition, level of academic preparation, and educational and career goals. Participation in higher education by students of color will continue to increase because most minority groups have higher growth rates than the majority population. Far fewer matriculants will fit the traditional full-time student profile. In the near future, fully 40 percent of undergraduates will be attending school on a part-time basis either at the outset of or sometime during their academic careers, or they will return to school after a period for additional education and training (U.S. Department of Education, 1997a). This part-time student group will include college students in the traditional age range who work to help pay for the increasing cost of tuition, and older working adults who seek a degree or additional education to advance within or change their employment.

Yet a further change concerns the preparation of students prior to enrollment at a university. Rather than coming directly from high school and completing their degrees at the college in which they initially matriculate, students often enroll in two or more institutions before completing a degree. Because the cost of attending a community or junior college is generally significantly lower than the tuition at four-year institutions, the number of students who begin their college career at a two-year institution has risen and will probably continue to increase. As a result, the number of transfer students at four-year colleges and universities is growing, particularly in large urban areas. This latter trend requires advising programs to address issues such as the articulation of two- and four-year college courses, access to major fields for students who have not been premajors in those fields, and the choice of majors for those who have not previously considered that question with care.

Nontraditional Access to Advising Services. As noted, diversity with respect to race, ethnicity, age, and purpose makes it essential for advisors to design programs and services directed to the differing needs of their clientele. They must also consider their availability to provide that advice. Many students with full-time jobs can take classes only in the evening and often find advising offices closed at that time. In addition, with the expansion of coursework and degree programs that are delivered electronically, an increasing proportion of students will rarely set foot on a campus. Those students will come to expect that their advising needs will also be met in nontraditional ways.

Practices in business and health care provide some ideas of how these new advising needs might be met. Interactive electronic conference sessions are already employed in industry because they are convenient and cost-effective. For example, nursing services to elderly outpatients are delivered in some locations through electronic interactivity, allowing both parties to see each other on a monitor. This technology can increase the contact between nurses and patients and also increase the number of patients served because of substantial savings in travel time. In turn, the elderly are able to continue living independently, which many want to do as long as possible (Horiuchi, 1999).

The same technology will allow universities to provide advising services electronically. Even now, students on many campuses have ready access to their academic records, automated degree-audit reports, and Web pages that provide important academic information. These media provide the high-tech but not the "high-touch" aspect that comes with individual guidance by an academic advisor. However, it is also true that advisors increasingly use e-mail to assist students who cannot come to campus. Beyond e-mail, interactive electronic advising sessions in which advisors sit in their offices and can see their distant students on a video screen are well within our current technical capacity and will be conducive to an educational environment where a substantial number of students find it inconvenient or impossible to come to a campus. The marriage of high-tech and high-touch may provide the setting for enhanced efficiency without loss of the human relationships and expert guidance that are important for students who present complex educational issues. For example, Rio Hondo Community College in Whittier, California (http://www.rh.cc.ca.us/online/counseling) has already pioneered a video-advising program for high school students in the Southern Los Angeles area. College counselors use interactive video technology to advise high school students in real time, answering their questions about admission, registration, academic programs, and careers.

Identifying Environmental Changes. The many changes discussed earlier will occur to greater and lesser extents at various universities and colleges depending on size, urban or rural location, regional or national identity, and perhaps local demographics. To engage in strategic planning for their own institutions, advisors must understand the characteristics, needs, and expectations of their own clientele. In evaluating a local situation, two primary sources of information should be consulted—institutional data and information from students themselves. Most universities and colleges maintain an institutional research office that can provide a comprehensive profile of prospective and enrolled students, including demographic as well as academic background information. Researchers in these offices are also frequently familiar with national and local trends that might lead to future changes in student characteristics. Student surveys can produce generalized information on student experiences, needs, and expectations, and focus groups of students can provide important qualitative information on these questions. All of these sources of data are useful in guiding advisors as they shape programs and services to respond to environmental changes.

Academic advisors are often the first on campus to be aware of changes in the campus environment and to recognize that current programs, services, and policies no longer meet students' needs. This knowledge provides an opportunity for advisors to propose and initiate change in the delivery of student services on campus. It is also clear that changes frequently affect not only advising offices but all parts of an institution. The challenges of staging an institutional response to changes in the campus environment are discussed in greater detail in the following sections.

Campuswide Coordination Through the Development of Cooperative and Collaborative Relationships

Although university administrators and faculty often think of advising as a single activity, the responsibility for advising is often distributed among a variety of offices and carried out by a variety of personnel. At most large institutions and many smaller ones, personnel in academic departments and other campus offices meet with students and are involved in some form of advising activity. Advising assignments may be made to faculty, to professional advisors, to staff, to students, or to some combination of personnel. A centralized office employing faculty or professional and sometimes student advisors may carry out some range of advising functions, usually those thought common to all university students. In addition, advising services are often also provided by offices concerned with special student populations such as student athletes, disabled students, and international students, to name a few. The functions of a number of other campus offices, which may or may not include academic advising as part of their mandate, substantially affect students in ways relevant to advising. Decisions made by admissions offices—perhaps to admit students with marginal qualifications—will affect academic advisors; a registrar's office may be responsible for degree audits that are directly relevant to advising students as they plan for graduation. Faculty and program committees determine and sometimes change the requirements for entrance into and completion of a major or program. Such decisions are often made without information about their effects on students and sometimes without communication to advisors on campus.

The variety of agencies engaged in advising and the number of offices whose activities crucially affect advising make clear the importance of campuswide coordination to create an advising system in which all parts of the community participate in addressing critical campuswide advising issues and arrive at institutionally coherent solutions that benefit students. Whatever the advising structure and the identity of advising personnel, everyone involved in some form of student advising activities shares common interests, needs, and concerns that can be more effectively addressed at the institutional level through campuswide coordination rather than through separate efforts by individual offices.

Achieving this goal requires serious institutional attention whatever the size of the institution. The National Academic Advising Association's Monograph *Current Practices in Academic Advising* (Habley and Morales, 1998) presents the results of the fifth national survey of academic advising sponsored by American College Testing and provides an assessment of the current status of academic advising based on a broad spectrum of institutions across the nation. The authors found that while four out of five campuses have identified an individual to coordinate advising, the majority of individuals with coordinating responsibilities spend insufficient time in this role. Moreover, only limited progress has been made over the years in developing institutional mission and goal statements for advising and program evaluation. In addition, academic advising remains an undervalued activity on most campuses, and institutional support for faculty and staff advisors in the areas of training, evaluation, and rewards remains problematic. A comparison of advising practices among different types of institutions reveals that the quality of advising services at many four-year public colleges that enroll large numbers of students is considerably lower than the quality of services found at two-year public and private as well as four-year private institutions.

Coordination Strategies

Regardless of how daunting may seem the task of coordinating academic advising across a broad spectrum of campus units under these conditions, continued lack of coordination is even more troublesome. To begin with, an individual with coordinating responsibilities must be appointed by a high-level administrator. This both ensures that the campus perceives coordination to be an important institutional responsibility, and gives the designated person the authority to carry out the coordinating functions. The coordinator must develop a set of broad goals to be accomplished, which might include the following:

- Developing mission and goal statements for advising that are consistent with the mission of the institution and linked to demonstrable outcomes such as student satisfaction and retention
- Facilitating the information flow of important academic and advising-related information to all offices involved with advising students
- Identifying and addressing campuswide advising concerns and improving the quality of advising services
- Developing and implementing a campuswide advisor training and professional development program
- Increasing the visibility of academic advising on campus
- Enhancing opportunities for advisor recognition and awards

- Implementing an assessment component to evaluate the effectiveness of academic advising programs and services.

It is also important that the coordinator report to and have the support of a high-level administrator and submit an annual report outlining accomplishments as well as identifying future goals and needs. The coordinator may want to establish a committee to assist with coordinating tasks. Committee members should include representatives from advising offices, from other campus offices involved in advising-related activities (such as the orientation office or student support programs), and representatives from departments such as admissions and registration whose activities and decisions affect students and advisors. A committee of this kind facilitates discussion and resolution of critical advising issues in a cooperative and collaborative fashion. Subcommittees can be established to work on specific problems and report back to the full committee with their recommendations.

Other Strategies for Campus Involvement and for Creating Partnerships Through Collaboration

There are of course many other ways of developing connections among campus offices and becoming involved in campuswide activities. Advisors frequently serve on faculty committees or ad hoc task forces that deal with aspects of undergraduate education. In these settings, advisors can articulate their understandings of the student perspective and perhaps influence the outcome of proposed changes in policies and program requirements in a way that reconciles felt student needs and the academic mission of the institution. At many institutions, faculty and professional advisors teach in academic departments. All of these activities provide opportunities to demonstrate the importance of academic advising to the educational enterprise.

With the increased career orientation of students, faculty and professional advisors recognize the relationship between academic and career advising. Creating that relationship is more difficult than recognizing it. On most campuses, career advising and academic advising take place in separate offices, often with reporting lines to different vice presidents. While students do not see questions regarding a major and a career as separate inquiries, organizational structures often require referral to an administrative office to investigate careers and to an academic department in a different building and with a different schedule for help in identifying a major. Assuming that far-reaching changes in university structure are unlikely, advisors should explore the creation of collaborative programs between academic departments and student services offices to ease the burden on students. Courses or workshops might be established for undecided students in which staff from career services and from the advising office responsible for undecided students jointly present information on strategies for making career and major decisions. Similarly, department advisors and staff from career services offices can sponsor joint workshops for majors in particular disciplines that will provide students with information on careers related to their major.

Such cooperative programming enables students to approach the decision-making process as they now see it—as a single search for a major and a career.

With the increase of students transferring from one institution to another, collaborative programs between institutions are also appearing with greater frequency. To take only one example, in some locations where a two-year institution is a major feeder institution for a four-year college, cooperative arrangements now allow advisors from four-year colleges to advise students at the community college on a regular basis. These arrangements help students with respect to the decision to transfer, prepare students for transition to the four-year institution, and make the transition to the receiving institution as seamless as possible.

Planning Change

This last section discusses ways we can anticipate change and prepare for it. A proactive approach will help avoid situations in which advisors merely react to change or, worse yet, in which crisis management rather than thoughtful planning and programming prevails.

Anticipating Change

Factors driving change in organizations are often apparent long before they are reflected in institutional actions, programs, and policies. For instance, declining budgets in higher education and changing demographics in the college population have been known for some time. It is essential that advisors become informed about national, local, and institution-specific trends that might affect academic advising. At the national level, useful information is available from the *NACADA Journal,* the *Chronicle of Higher Education, Change* magazine, the *Journal of College Student Development,* or the *Journal of Higher Education,* among other publications. Local sources of information include strategic planning reports from governing boards for the state's higher education institutions as well as legislative reports dealing with education issues. At the institutional level, strategic planning documents, reports from the institutional research office, or campus committee reports can reveal institutional concerns and the direction in which the campus is moving.

Organizing Change

An organized plan for change will facilitate movement of an organization or a department in a new direction. Typically the change process includes three major phases—developing a proposal, securing support, and implementing and evaluating the change (Teitelbaum, 1994).

The proposal should include clear identification of the problem to be addressed, its causes, and any potential negative consequences for both students and the institution. Supporting research and data should be set out, as well as information about other institutions that have experienced a similar problem. The proposal should also examine the range of potential solutions and suggest an approach that seems most promising in light of existing institutional considerations. A persuasive proposal will attend to the steps needed to bring about the suggested change, a probable time frame, and the resources realistically required for its accomplishment. Finally, the proposal should include a specific method for evaluation.

In addition to these administrative concerns, the proposal should include a component that examines various conceptual, political, and practical aspects associated with its adoption and implementation (Schlossberg, Lynch, and Chickering, 1989). Conceptual issues include the relationship of the proposed change to the institutional mission, educational theory, and human development. Political issues include anticipation of the ways in which a proposed change may be perceived as a threat to the interests of various campus constituents, and identification of ways of presenting the proposal so that it will be understood to comport with those interests. Issues of feasibility require candid examination of the sources from which needed resources, whether financial or human, will be drawn; the availability of plans to secure those resources; and exploration of the possibility of deriving long-range financial benefits from the change.

The proposal should accordingly reveal the support that must be developed from three critical sources—affected constituents, those who will be called on to implement the initiative, and (in the case of major institutional change) campus policymakers. The nature and extent of the proposed change ultimately determines the complexity and extent of this aspect of planned change. Some proposals—for example, for internal modification of an advising program—will require support only from personnel in a single unit—in this case, the advising staff. In contrast, a proposal to change institutional policy typically entails campuswide approval. Not only acquiescence but also active sponsorship will be necessary from those policymakers who hold the organizational power and influence necessary to legitimate change (Gorman, 1989). The task of the proposal's author or initiator is to enable high-level administrators to understand the problem, the need for the proposed change, and its benefits.

After support and commitment for change have been secured, the final phase of planned change is implementation and evaluation. The nature and scope of change will determine the duration and steps required for implementation. Any successful implementation depends on structure and discipline. "Change management is not haphazard or unplanned. It is a systematic understanding of how people react to change and how to motivate them" (Hughes, 1989, p. 87).

To effect a proposed change, the reasons for modifying patterns of behavior and the ways in which this will be done must be understood by all involved. Administrators must be sensitive to potential resistance at this point and allow enough time to inform and prepare those whose activities will be affected (Farmer, 1990). Students or faculty must be informed of what they must do and why; it may be necessary to train staff to carry out their revised jobs effectively. It is also important to be aware of the stress levels experienced by staff as they implement the initiative and to provide support for those who find adjustment difficult. Finally, it is helpful to allow staff an opportunity to discuss problems as they emerge. Continuing analysis by all involved will not only improve the process but also build commitment to the change.

The Role of Advisors in Changing the Campus Climate

As intermediaries between the institution and students, academic advisors are in a unique position to initiate change. Because of their daily interaction with students, they are often the first on campus to be aware of problems such as outdated policies, obsolete programs, or student needs that are not being met. They also know how those systemic inadequacies can adversely affect student satisfaction and retention, as well as institutional effectiveness. Those situations represent opportunities for advisors to effect change on campus through identifying problems, developing options for solving them, and persuading campus policymakers of the need for change for the benefit of students and the institution itself (Teitelbaum, 1994).

Conclusion

This chapter has outlined—in broad strokes—the major external and internal factors that are expected to alter the face of higher education in the future and in turn affect academic advising practices. Clearly local and institutional circumstances have much to do with the ways in which those changes will manifest themselves on individual campuses. Nevertheless, a common concern for all advisors, regardless of geographic location, type of institution, or advising structure, is to anticipate and prepare for change. The advising profession must foresee and respond to new circumstances to meet these challenges and continue its centrally important contributions to students and the institution it serves.

References

Brinkman, P. T., and Morgan, A. W. "The Future of Higher Education Finance." In T. R. Sanford (ed.), *Preparing for the Information Needs of the Twenty-First Century.* San Francisco: Jossey-Bass, 1994.

Cosca, T. "Earnings of College Graduates in 1996." *Occupational Outlook Quarterly,* 1998, *3,* 21–29.

Farmer, D. W. "Strategies for Change." In D. W. Steeples (ed.), *Managing Change in Higher Education.* San Francisco: Jossey-Bass, 1990.

Gorman, B. "The Role and Responsibility of the Sponsor." In K. S. Hughes and D. Conner (eds.), *Managing Change in Higher Education: Preparing for the Twenty-First Century.* Washington, D.C.: College and University Personnel Association, 1989.

Guskin, A. E. "Facing the Future: The Change Process in Restructuring Universities." *Change,* 1996, *4,* 27–37.

Habley, W. R., and Morales, R. H. *Current Practices in Academic Advising: Final Report on ACT's Fifth National Survey of Academic Advising.* National Academic Advising Association Monograph Series, no. 6. Manhattan, Kans.: National Academic Advising Association, 1998.

Hammonds, K. H., and others. "The New 'U': A Tough Market Is Reshaping Colleges." *Business Week,* Dec. 22, 1997, pp. 96–102.

Horiuchi, V. "Unit Harks Back to Days of the House Call." *Salt Lake Tribune,* Mar. 27, 1999, p. D8.

Hughes, K. S. "Taking a Structured and Disciplined Approach to Managing Change." In K. S. Hughes and D. Conner (eds.), *Managing Change in Higher Education: Preparing for the Twenty-First Century.* Washington D.C.: College and University Personnel Association, 1989.

Institute for Research on Higher Education at the University of Pennsylvania. "Footing the Bill: The Shifting Burden of Higher Education Finance." *Change,* 1996, *5,* 49–52.

Kennedy, D. "Another Century's End, Another Revolution for Higher Education." *Change,* 1995, *3,* 8–15.

Krannich, R., and Krannich, C. R. *The Best Jobs for the Twenty-First Century.* Manassas Park, Va.: Impact, 1998.

Macunovich, D. J. "Will There Be a Boom in the Demand for U.S. Higher Education Among Eighteen- to Twenty-Four-Year-Olds?" *Change,* 1997, *3,* 34–44.

Massy, W. F., and Zemsky, R. *Using Information Technology to Enhance Academic Productivity.* Washington, D.C.: Educom, Interuniversity Communications Council, 1995.

McPherson, M. S., and Schapiro, M. O. "Skills, Innovations, and Values—Future Needs for Postsecondary Education." *Change,* 1995, *4,* 26–32.

Noam, E. M. "Electronics and the Dim Future of the University." *Science,* 1995, *270,* 247–249.

Ortmann, A. "How to Survive in Postindustrial Environments." *Journal of Higher Education,* 1997, *68*(5), 483–501.

Plater, W. M. "Future Work: Faculty Time in the Twenty-First Century." *Change,* 1995, *27*(3), 22–33.

Plater, W. M. "So, Why Aren't We Taking Learning Seriously?" *About Campus,* 1998, *6,* 9–14.

Schlossberg, N. K., Lynch, A. Q., and Chickering, A. W. *Improving Higher Education Environments for Adults.* San Francisco: Jossey-Bass, 1989.

Teitelbaum, H. "Changing the Campus Environment." *NACADA Journal,* 1994, *14*(1), 32–37.

U.S. Department of Commerce, Bureau of the Census. *How Much We Earn—Factors That Make a Difference.* Washington, D.C.: U.S. Department of Commerce, 1995.

U.S. Department of Education, National Center for Education Statistics. *Projections of Education Statistics to 2008.* NCES 98–016. Washington, D.C.: U.S. Department of Education, 1997a.

U.S. Department of Education, National Center for Education Statistics. *Chartbook of Degrees Conferred, 1969–70 to 1993–94.* NCES 98–071. Washington, D.C.: U.S. Department of Education, 1997b.

Winston, G. C. "Why Can't a College Be More Like a Firm?" *Change,* 1997, *5,* 33–38.

Winston, G. "For-Profit Higher Education." *Change,* 1999, *1,* 13–19.

Appendix A

NACADA's Core Values

The National Academic Advising Association (NACADA) is an organization of professional advisors, faculty, administrators, students, and others from a variety of settings who do academic advising or otherwise work to promote quality academic advising on college and university campuses. As members of this organization or of the profession of academic advising, or as others who advise or provide related programs and services to students, we must recognize our responsibility not only to students and the institutions in which the advising is done, but also to society, to colleagues, and to ourselves.

While not all those who do academic advising are professional advisors, anyone carrying out advising functions should be expected to perform in a professional manner. The Core Values identified and discussed here provide a framework against which those who advise can measure their own performance.

In no way does this Core Values statement try to dictate that all academic advising needs to be done in precisely the same way by everyone or that there is one particular advising philosophy or model. Instead, these are reference points for professionals to use. Furthermore, the Core Values do not carry equal weight. Advisors will find some Core Values more important than others, depending on their own philosophies and those of their colleges or universities.

The Power of Academic Advising

Few events in students' postsecondary experiences have as much potential for influencing their development as does academic advising.

Through regular contact with students—whether face-to-face, through the mail, on the telephone, or through computer-mediated systems—advisors gain meaningful insights into students' academic, social, and personal experiences and needs. Advisors use these insights to help students feel a part of the academic community, develop sound academic and career goals, and ultimately be successful learners.

Because of the nature of academic advising, advisors often develop a broad vision of the institution. Advisors can therefore play an important interpretive role with administrators, faculty, and staff, helping them further understand students' academic and personal development needs. Advisors can teach others to identify students who, with additional attention from academic support staff, may achieve their goals to succeed academically and personally.

Students place a great deal of trust in their advisors. That trust warrants quality programs and services. It is through our Core Values that students' expectations of academic advising are honored.

Beliefs About Students

Like other educators, academic advisors work to strengthen the importance, dignity, potential, and unique nature of each individual served within the academic setting. Our work as advisors is guided by our beliefs that

- *Students can be responsible for their own behavior*
- *Students can be successful as a result of their individual goals and efforts*
- *Students have a desire to learn*
- *Learning needs vary according to individual skills, goals, and experiences*
- *Students hold their own beliefs and opinions*

Why Our Core Values Are Important

Out of these beliefs grow our Core Values. Regardless of our professional preparation and experience, each of us in the field of academic advising is ultimately guided in our work by what we perceive as important, what we value, and what we believe about those we serve—primarily students, but also others in the institutions within which we work, and even the institutions themselves.

We recognize the complex nature of academic advising, the wide variety of settings and tasks for which academic advisors are responsible, and the diverse backgrounds and experiences of academic advisors. Yet while values and beliefs are by their very nature individual, there are many that are subscribed to by those who advise students. Through this statement of Core Values we communicate to others what they can expect from us. These Core Values may be used to validate our conduct in our diverse roles and our relationships within the academic community.

The Core Values

Students deserve dependable, accurate, respectful, honest, friendly, and professional service. Academic advisors understand that in order to serve students well they are responsible to many constituents who compose our academic communities. This is the foundation on which the following Core Values rest.

Advisors are responsible to the students and individuals they serve. The cooperative efforts of all who advise help to deliver quality programs and services to students. These include, but are not limited to, giving accurate and timely information, maintaining regular office hours, and keeping appointments.

Advisors help students develop a perception of themselves and their relationship to the future. Advisors introduce students in a nurturing way to the world they are entering—teaching them to value the learning process, put the college experience into perspective, become more responsible, set priorities and evaluate sequences of events, and be honest with themselves.

Advisors encourage self-reliance by helping students make informed and responsible decisions, set realistic goals, and develop thinking, learning, and life management skills to meet present and future needs. Advisors work with students to help them accomplish the goals and objectives they have established for themselves. Advisors encourage students to be responsible for their own success and progress. They respect students' rights to their individual beliefs and opinions but are not dictated to by students.

Advisors work to modify barriers to student progress; to identify burdensome, ineffective, and inefficient policies and procedures; and to effect change. When the needs of students and the institution are in conflict, advisors seek a resolution that is in the best interests of both parties. Advisors inform students about appropriate grievance procedures in cases where students find the resolution unsatisfactory.

Advisors recognize the changing nature of the college and university environment and student body. They support students in appropriate ways (for instance, as advocates at the administrative level for recognition of these changes, by offering varied office hours, and by acknowledging the special needs of all students and the pressures on them to juggle study with work, family, and other interpersonal demands).

Advisors are knowledgeable about and sensitive to federal, state, and their own institution's policies and procedures, especially those governing such matters as sexual harassment, personal relationships with students, privacy of student information, equal treatment, equal access, and equal opportunity.

Advisors respect the rights of students to have information about themselves kept confidential. Advisors share information with others about students and their programs only when both advisor and student believe that information is relevant and will result in increased information or assistance, assessment, and provision of appropriate services to the student.

Advisors gain access to and use computerized information about students only when that information is relevant to the advising they are doing with that particular student. Advisors enter or change information on students' records only when legitimately authorized to do so.

Advisors need to document advising contacts adequately to aid subsequent advising interactions.

Advisors are responsible for involving others, when appropriate, in the advising process. Effective advising requires a broad-based, or holistic, approach to working with students. Academic advisors develop crucial ties with others who assist students in diverse areas such as admissions, orientation, financial aid, housing, health services, athletics, course selection and satisfaction of academic requirements, special physical and educational needs (such as disabilities, study skills, and psychological counseling), foreign study, career development, cocurricular programs, and graduation clearance.

Advisors are facilitators and mediators. Responsible academic advisors recognize their limitations and use their specialized knowledge effectively.

To make connections between academic advising and other aspects of students' lives, advisors seek out resources provided by others. Referrals to these resources provide students with further assessment of their needs and access to appropriate programs and services. Along with others, advisors are responsible for helping students integrate the information they are confronted with and for helping them make well-informed academic decisions.

If peer advisors are used, the supervising advisor will closely monitor the peer adviser regarding adherence to appropriate policies and practices.

Advisors are responsible to the college or university in which they work. Advisors respect the opinions of their colleagues; remain neutral when students present them with comments, questions, or opinions about other faculty or staff; and are nonjudgmental about academic programs.

Advisors increase their collective professional strength by sharing their philosophies and techniques with colleagues.

Advisors keep administrators who are not involved directly in the advising process informed and aware of the importance of academic advising in students' lives and of the need for administrative support of advising and related activities.

Advisors abide by the specific policies, procedures, and values of the department and institution for which they work. Where injustices occur and might interfere with students' learning, advisors advocate with the institution's administration, faculty, and staff for change on behalf of students.

Advisors are responsible to higher education generally. Academic advisors honor (and are protected by) the concept of academic freedom as practiced on our campuses. In this spirit, advisors hold a variety of points of view. Academic advisors are free to base their work with students on the most appropriate and optimum theories of college student development and models of delivery for academic advising programs and services.

Advisors accept that one of the goals of education is to introduce students to the world of ideas. One goal of academic advising is to establish a partnership between student and advisor to guide students through their academic programs so they may attain the knowledge gained and offered by faculty.

Academic advisors believe that it is ultimately the responsibility of students to apply what they learn to everyday situations. Advisors help students in understanding this process.

Advisors advocate for students' educational achievement at the highest attainable standard and they support student goals as well as the educational mission of the institution.

Advisors advocate for the creation or strengthening of programs and services that are compatible with students' academic needs.

Advisors are responsible to the community (including the local community, state, and region in which the institution is located). Academic advisors interpret the institution's mission, standards, goals, and values to its community, including public and private schools from which the college or university draws its student body. Likewise, advisors understand their student body and regularly inform the schools from which their students come about appropriate preparation so that students may perform successfully in higher education.

Advisors are sensitive to the values and mores of the surrounding community, sharing these with and interpreting them to students. Advisors are aware of community programs and services and may become models for students by participating in community activities themselves.

Advisors are responsible to their professional role as advisors and to themselves personally. To keep advising skills honed and interest high, advisors are encouraged to seek opportunities for professional development through classes, workshops, conferences, reading, consultation with others, and interaction in formal groups with other advisors (such as professional organizations like NACADA).

Advisors understand the demands on themselves that emerge from the service nature of the work they do. Advisors develop skills for taking care of themselves physically, emotionally, and spiritually. They learn how to detach themselves from students' problems while maintaining a keen listening ear and providing sensitive responses. They establish and maintain appropriate boundaries. They need to be nurtured by others within the profession and they need to nurture their colleagues. They seek support for themselves within and outside the institution.

Academic advising lends itself well to research. Advisors may engage in research related to advising and are encouraged to engage in research related to their own particular training and disciplinary backgrounds. Each research agenda must honor the institution's safeguards for privacy and humane treatment of subjects.

The intention of the Statement of Core Values is to provide the guidance that many academic advisors have sought. The statement should be reviewed periodically, adding relevant material and rewording existing language to bring the statement in line with current professional practices and thinking. The National Academic Advising Association encourages institutions to adopt this Statement of Core Values, to embrace its principles, and to support the work of those who do academic advising.

Council for the Advancement of Standards (CAS)

Academic advising is an essential element of a student's collegiate experience. It evolves from the institution's culture, values, and practices and is delivered in accordance with these factors. Academic advising is one of the few endeavors universal to all college and university students and plays a significant role in their education. Advising practice draws from various educational and human development strategies and theories (for example, teaching and counseling, the psychology of learning, communication studies, theories of decision making and information transfer, and storytelling as a mechanism for understanding human experience).

Academic advising was long the purview solely of faculty who accepted the responsibility in earnest. However, with the advent of electives into the curriculum, academic advising has been delivered by professional, full-time staff members outside the faculty tenure track structure as well as by graduate and undergraduate students. Today's academic advising is well supported by contemporary computing technologies, particularly in activities such as registration, information dissemination, and auditing of student progress in meeting degree requirements.

Academic advising is one of the few institutional functions that connect all students to the institution. As higher education curricula become increasingly complex and as educational options expand, pressure to make the educational experience as meaningful as possible for students has increased as well. Higher education, in turn, has responded with renewed attention to the need for quality academic advising.

The establishment of the National Academic Advising Association (NACADA) following the first national conference on advising in 1977 was a significant turning point in according recognition to those in higher education who consider their work in academic advising as purposeful and unique. Today, NACADA is flourishing, with membership numbering more than 5,200 and national and regional meetings attracting more than 4,000 participants annually during the 1990s. Responding to the growing need for ethical principles to guide advising practice and to enable all academic advisors to examine their behavior within a professional framework, NACADA developed a Statement of Core Values that was last revised in 1994.

Academic advising became a significant category in the professional literature during the 1980s, and this trend has continued during the past decade; for example, see Gordon's chapter in *Teaching Through Academic Advising: A Faculty Perspective* (Reinarz & White, 1995) and *Current Practices in Academic Advising: Final Report on ACT's Fifth National Survey of Academic Advisors* (Habley & Morales, 1998). NACADA publishes a monograph series that examines various aspects of advising. Additional resources, including annotated bibliographies, are available from the Clearinghouse on Academic Advising. Information about NACADA's publications, as well as a link to the clearinghouse, can be located electronically via the NACADA Web site on the World Wide Web. The NACADA Executive Office is an excellent source of general information as well.

Academic advising has been described as a crucial component of all students' experiences in higher education. Within this context, students can find meaning in their lives, make significant decisions about the future, be supported to achieve to their maximum potential, and access all that higher education has to offer. When practiced with competence and dedication, academic advising can enhance retention rates. In an age often characterized by impersonality and detachment, academic advising provides a vital personal connection that students need and frequently seek.

References, Readings, and Resources

Cramer, G. L., & Childs, M. W. (eds.) (1996). *Transforming academic advising through the use of information technology.* Monograph No. 4. Manhattan, KS: National Academic Advising Association.

Frost, S. H. (1991). *Academic advising for student success: A system of shared responsibility.* ASHE-ERIC Higher Education Report No. 3. Washington, DC: The George Washington University.

Glennen, R. E., & Vowell, F. N. (eds.) (1995). *Academic advising as a comprehensive campus process.* Monograph No. 2. Manhattan, KS: National Academic Advising Association.

Gordon, V. N. (1994). *Academic advising: An annotated bibliography.* Westport, CT: Greenwood Press.

Habley, W. R., & Morales, R. H. (eds.) (1998). *Current practices in academic advising: Final report on ACT's fifth national survey of academic advising.* Monograph No. 6. Manhattan, KS: National Academic Advising Association.

Reinarz, A. G., & White, E. R. (eds.) (1995). *Teaching through academic advising: A faculty perspective.* San Francisco: Jossey-Bass.

Upcraft, M. L., & Cramer, G. L. (eds.) (1995). *First-year academic advising: Patterns in the present, pathways to the future.* Monograph No. 18. Columbia, SC: National Resource Center for the Freshman Year Experience and Students in Transition.

Winston, R. B., Jr., Ender, S. C., & Miller, T. K. (eds.) (1982). *Developmental approaches to academic advising.* New Directions for Student Services, No. 17. San Francisco: Jossey-Bass.

Winston, R. B., Jr., Miller, T. K., & Ender, S. C., Grites, T. J. (eds.) (1984). *Developmental academic advising: Addressing students' educational, career, and personal needs.* San Francisco: Jossey-Bass.

Clearinghouse on Academic Advising, 110 Enarson Hall, The Ohio State University, Columbus, OH 43210.

National Academic Advising Association, 2323 Anderson Avenue, Manhattan, KS 66502–2912; (785) 532–5717; Fax (785) 532–7732; Web page: www.ksu.edu/nacada.

Academic Advising
CAS Standards and Guidelines

Part 1. Mission

The academic advising program must develop, record. disseminate, implement, and regularly review its mission and goals. Mission statements must be consistent with the mission and goals of the institution and with the standards in this document.

The primary purpose of the academic advising program is to assist students in the development of meaningful educational plans that are compatible with their life goals.

The institution must have a clearly written statement of philosophy pertaining to academic advising, which must include program goals and expectations of advisors and advisees.

> The ultimate responsibility for making decisions about educational plans and life goals rests with the individual student. The academic advisor should assist by helping to identify and assess alternatives and the consequences of decisions. Institutional goals for academic advising should include:

- development of suitable educational plans;
- clarification of career and life goals;
- selection of appropriate courses and other educational experiences;

- interpretation of institutional requirements;
- enhancement of student awareness about educational resources available (e.g., internship, study abroad, honors, and learning assistance programs);
- evaluation of student progress toward established goals;
- development of decision-making skills;
- reinforcement of student self-direction;
- referral to and use of institutional and community support services; and
- collection and distribution of data regarding student needs, preferences, and performance for use in making institutional decisions and policies.

Part 2. Program

The formal education of students is purposeful and holistic and consists of the curriculum and the cocurriculum.

The academic advising program must be (a) intentional; (b) coherent; (c) based on theories and knowledge of teaching, learning, and human development; (d) reflective of developmental and demographic profiles of the student population; and (e) responsive to the special needs of individuals.

The academic advising program must promote learning and development in students by encouraging experiences which lead to intellectual growth, ability to communicate effectively, realistic self-appraisal, enhanced self-esteem, clarification of values, appropriate career choices, leadership development, physical fitness, meaningful interpersonal relations, ability to work independently and collaboratively, social responsibility, satisfying and productive lifestyles, appreciation of aesthetic and cultural diversity, and achievement of personal goals.

The academic advising program must assist students in overcoming educational and personal problems and skill deficiencies.

The academic advising program must identify environmental conditions that may negatively influence student academic achievement and propose interventions that may neutralize such conditions.

The academic advisor must review and use available data about students' academic and educational needs, performance, aspirations, and problems.

The academic advising program must ensure that academic advisors collaborate in the collection of relevant data about students for use in individual academic advising conferences.

Individual academic advising conferences must be available to students each academic term.

Through private, individual conferences with students, the academic advisors should provide assistance in refining goals and objectives, understanding available choices, and assessing the consequences of alternative courses of action. Course selection, understanding and meeting institutional requirements, and providing clear and accurate information regarding institutional policies, procedures, resources, and programs may be carried out individually or in groups.

The academic status of the student being advised should be taken into consideration when determining caseloads. For example, first-year, undecided, underprepared, and honors students may require more advising time than upper-division students who have declared their majors.

Academic advising caseloads must be consistent with the time required for the effective performance of this activity.

> When determining the workloads it should be recognized that advisors may work with students not officially assigned to them and that contacts regarding advising may extend beyond direct contact with the student.

The academic advising program must provide current and accurate advising information to academic advisors.

> Supplemental systems for the delivery of advising information, such as on-line computer programs, may be employed.
> Referrals to appropriate institutional or community support services should be made as needed.
> The academic advising program should make available to academic advisors all pertinent research (e.g., about students, the academic advising program, and perceptions of the institution).

Part 3. Leadership

The institution must appoint, position, and empower the leader of the academic advising program to accomplish stated missions. Leaders at various levels must be selected on the basis of formal education and training, relevant work experience, personal attributes, and other professional credentials. Expectations of accountability must be defined for academic advising program leaders, and their performance must be fairly assessed.

Leaders of academic advising programs must exercise authority over those resources for which they are responsible to achieve their respective missions. Leaders must articulate a vision for their organization; set goals and objectives; prescribe and practice ethical behavior; recruit, select, supervise, and develop others in the organization; manage, plan, budget, and evaluate; communicate effectively; and marshal cooperative action from colleagues, employees, other institutional constituencies, and persons outside the organization. Leaders must address individual, organizational, or environmental conditions that inhibit the achievement of goals. Leaders must improve programs and services continuously in response to changing student needs and institutional priorities.

Part 4. Organization and Management

The academic advising program must be structured purposefully and managed effectively to achieve its stated goals. Evidence of appropriate structure must include current and accessible policies and procedures, written expectations for performance of all employees, and organizational charts. Effective management practices must be evident, including clear sources and channels of authority, effective communication, procedures to make decisions and resolve conflicts, responsiveness to changing conditions, accountability systems, and recognition and reward processes.

The academic advising program must provide channels within its organization for regular review of administrative policies and procedures.

The design of the academic advising program must be compatible with the institution's organizational structure and its students' needs. Specific advisor responsibilities must be clearly delineated, published, and disseminated to both advisors and advisees.

In some institutions academic advising is a centralized function while in others it is decentralized, with a variety of people throughout the institution assuming responsibilities. Whatever system is used, students, faculty advisors, and professional staff should be informed of their respective advising responsibilities.

Part 5. Human Resources

The academic advising program must be staffed adequately by individuals qualified to accomplish its mission and goals. The academic advising program must establish procedures for selection, training, and evaluation of advisors; set expectations for supervision; and provide appropriate professional development opportunities.

An academic advisor must hold an earned graduate degree or must possess an appropriate combination of education and experience.

Graduate students, interns, others in training, student employees, peer advisors, and volunteers must be carefully selected and adequately trained, supervised, and evaluated. When their knowledge and skills are not adequate for particular situations, they must refer students or others in need of assistance to a qualified professional staff member.

The academic advising program must have sufficient support personnel to accomplish its mission. Such staff must be technologically proficient and qualified to perform activities including reception duties, office equipment operation, records maintenance, and mail handling.

Appropriate salary levels and fringe benefits for academic advising program personnel must be commensurate with those for comparable positions within the institution, in similar institutions, and in the relevant geographic area.

The academic advising program must intentionally employ advisors who reflect the diversity of the institution's student population, to ensure the existence of readily identifiable role models for students, and/or to enrich the campus community.

Affirmative action must occur in hiring and promotion practices to ensure diverse staffing profiles as required by institutional policy and local, state/provincial, and federal law.

The institution must designate a specific individual to direct the academic advising program.

The director of an academic advising program must possess either an earned graduate degree or an equivalent combination of academic and educational experience, previous experience as an academic advisor, and knowledge of the literature of academic advising. The director must be skilled in fiscal management, personnel selection and training, conceptualization, planning, and evaluation tasks.

Academic advisors should have an understanding of student development; a comprehensive knowledge of the institution's programs, academic requirements, majors, minors, and support services; a demonstrated interest in working with and assisting students; a willingness to participate in pre-service and in-service workshops and other professional activities; and demonstrated interpersonal skills.

Sufficient personnel should be available to meet students' advising needs without unreasonable delay. Advisors should allow an appropriate amount of time for students to discuss plans, programs, courses, academic progress, and other subjects related to their educational programs.

Academic advising personnel may be organized in various ways. They may be full-time or part-time professional who have advising as their primary function or they may be faculty whose responsibilities include academic advising. Paraprofessionals (e.g., graduate students in practice, interns, or assistants) or peer advisors may also assist advisors.

Support personnel should maintain student records, organize resource materials, receive students, make appointments, and handle correspondence and other operational needs. Technical staff may be used in research, data collection, systems development, and special projects.

Technical and support personnel should be carefully selected and adequately trained, supervised, and evaluated.

Part 6. Financial Resources

The academic advising program must have adequate funding to accomplish its mission and goals. Priorities, whether set periodically or as a result of extraordinary conditions, must be determined within the context of the stated mission, goals, and resources.

Special consideration should be given to providing funding for training and development of advisors, particularly those for whom the advisory function is a part-time and/or secondary assignment.

Financial resources should be sufficient to provide high-quality print and nonprint information for students and training materials for advisors. Also, there should be sufficient resources to promote the academic advising program.

Part 7. Facilities, Technology, and Equipment

The academic advising program must have adequate and suitably located facilities, technology, and equipment to support its mission and goals. Facilities, technology, and equipment must be in compliance with relevant federal, state/provincial, and local requirements to provide for access, health, and safety.

The academic advising program must ensure that technology-assisted advising includes appropriate approvals, consultations, and referrals.

Computing equipment and access to local networks, student databases, and the Internet should be available to academic advisors.

Privacy and freedom from visual and auditory distractions should be considerations in designing appropriate facilities.

Part 8. Legal Responsibilities

Academic advisors must be knowledgeable about and responsive to law and regulations that relate to the academic advising program. Sources for legal obligations and limitations include constitutional, statutory, regulatory, and case law; mandatory laws and orders emanating from federal, state/provincial, and local governments; and the institution through its policies.

Academic advisors must use reasonable and informed practices to limit the liability exposure of the institution and its officers, employees, and agents. Academic advisors must be informed about institutional policies regarding personal liability and related insurance coverage options.

The institution must provide access to legal advice for academic advisors as needed to carry out assigned responsibilities.

The institution must inform academic advisors and students, in a timely and systematic fashion, about extraordinary or changing legal obligations and potential liabilities.

Part 9. Equal Opportunity, Access, and Affirmative Action

The academic advising program must ensure that services are provided on a fair and equitable basis and are accessible to all students. Hours of operation must be responsive to the needs of all students. The academic advising program must adhere to the spirit and intent of equal opportunity laws.

The academic advising program must not be discriminatory on the basis of age, color, disability, gender, national origin, race, religious creed, sexual orientation, and/or veteran status. Exceptions are appropriate only where provided by relevant law and institutional policy.

Consistent with mission and goals, the academic advising program must take affirmative action to remedy significant imbalances in student participation and staffing patterns.

Part 10. Campus and Community Relations

The academic advising program must establish, maintain, and promote effective relations with relevant campus offices and external agencies.

Academic advising is integral to the educational process and depends on close working relationships with other institutional agencies and the administration. The academic advising program should be fully integrated into other processes of the institution.

For referral purposes, the academic advising program should provide academic advisors with a comprehensive list of relevant external agencies, campus offices, and opportunities.

Part 11. Diversity

Within the context of the institution's unique mission, multidimensional diversity enriches the community and enhances the collegiate experience for all; therefore, the academic advising program must nurture environments where similarities and differences among people are recognized and honored.

The academic advising program must promote cultural educational experiences that are characterized by open and continuous communication, that deepen understanding of one's own culture and heritage, and that respect and educate about similarities, differences, and histories of cultures.

The academic advising program must address the characteristics and needs of a diverse population when establishing and implementing policies and procedures.

Part 12. Ethics

All persons involved in the delivery of the academic advising program must adhere to the highest principles of ethical behavior. The academic advising program must implement statements of ethical practice. The academic advising program must publish these statements and ensure their periodic review by all concerned.

Ethical standards or other statements from relevant professional associations should be considered.

The academic advising program must ensure that confidentiality is maintained for all records and communications (i.e., paper and electronic), unless exempted by law.

Information disclosed in individual academic advising sessions must remain confidential, unless written permission to divulge the information is given by the student. However, all academic advising personnel must disclose to appropriate authorities information judged to be of an emergency nature, especially when the health and safety of the individual or others are involved. Information in students' educational records must not be disclosed to noninstitutional third parties without appropriate consent, unless classified as "Directory" information or when the information is subpoenaed by law. The academic advising program must apply a similar dedication to privacy and confidentiality to research data concerning individuals.

All academic advising personnel must be aware of and avoid personal conflict of interest or the appearance thereof in their transactions with students and others. All academic advising personnel must strive to ensure fair, objective, and impartial treatment of all persons with whom they interact.

When handling institutional funds, all academic advising personnel must ensure that such funds are managed in accordance with established and responsible accounting procedures.

All academic advising personnel must not participate in any form of harassment that demeans persons or creates an intimidating, hostile, or offensive campus environment.

All academic advising personnel must perform their duties within the limits of their training, expertise, and competence. When these limits are exceeded, individuals in need of further assistance must be referred to persons possessing appropriate qualifications.

All academic advising personnel must use suitable means to confront unethical behavior exhibited within the educational community.

Part 13. Assessment and Evaluation

The academic advising program must regularly conduct systematic qualitative and quantitative evaluations of program quality to determine the extent to which the stated mission and goals are being met. Although methods of assessment may vary, the academic advising program must employ a sufficient range of measures to ensure objectivity and comprehensiveness. Data collected must include responses from students and other affected constituencies. Results of these evaluations must be used in revising and improving the performance of personnel.

NACADA Resources

National Academic Advising Association
Kansas State University
2323 Anderson Avenue, Suite 225
Manhattan, KS 66502
www.ksu.edu/nacada or nacada@ksu.edu
Phone: 785–532–5717   Fax: 785–532–7732

Publications

Literature addressing current issues in advising

- Journal—semiannual refereed journal
- Newsletter—quarterly information about advising and NACADA resources
- Advisor Training Manual
- Monographs
  Reaffirming the Role of Faculty in Academic Advising
  Academic Advising as a Comprehensive Campus Process
  Advising First-Year Students
  Transforming Academic Advising Through Technology
  Advising Students with Disabilities
  Current Practices in Academic Advising: A National Survey

Training Video

A training aid for advising enhancement

- Basic premises of advising
- Complete facilitator's manual
- Vignettes to demonstrate effective advising

Videotape of 1999 Teleconference

Academic Advising: Fostering Retention

Overview of current advising issue to heighten awareness of advising on your campus

- Current advising research
- Advising organizational models
- Advising as teaching
- Advisor training
- Evaluation/recognition/reward

Clearinghouse on Academic Advising

Easy reference source for advising issues

- Comprehensive annotated bibliographies
- Advising publications samples
- Advising resources

Consultants Bureau

Outside expertise to assist you

- External reviews/evaluators
- Workshop leaders
- Speakers
- Consultants

CAS Standards

Assistance in assessing your advising programs

- Guidelines for programs
- Self-assessment materials

Awards

Recognizing and valuing advising

- Outstanding advisor recognition
- Outstanding institutional advising program recognition

- Advising publications recognition
- Research grants and scholarships

Membership/Networks

Enhancing professional development

- Commissions—to address specific advising areas/populations
- Regions—to share with nearby colleagues
- Listservs—immediate access to colleagues worldwide
- Leadership opportunities—to contribute to your profession
- Career services—a list of employment opportunities

Ordered by: *Ship to:*

Name: _____   Name: _____

Institution: _____   Institution: _____

Address: _____   Street Address & Room # (UPS will not ship to box #):

City: _____ State: ____ Zip: _____   _____

Phone: _____ Fax: _____   City: _____ State: ____ Zip: _____

E-Mail: _____   Phone: _____

Monographs

Prices: *NACADA Member: $25 each*   View full descriptions at
Nonmember: $30 each   **http://www.ksu.edu/nacada**

M01	Reaffirming the Role of Faculty in Academic Advising (1995)	____ @ $____ = $____
M02	Advising as a Comprehensive Campus Process(1995)	____ @ $____ = $____
M03	First-Year Student Academic Advising (1996)	____ @ $____ = $____
M04	Transforming Advising Through the Use of Technology (1996)	____ @ $____ = $____
M05	Advising Students with Disabilities (1997)	____ @ $____ = $____
M06	Current Practices in Academic Advising (1998)	____ @ $____ = $____

Special Resources

M00	Designing an Effective Advising Training Program (1993)	____ @ $ 15.00 = $____
P04	Status and Future of Academic Advising (1988)	____ @ $ 15.00 = $____
V01	NACADA Faculty Advising Training Video (1996)	____ @ $205.00 = $____
	(V01 price includes $195 for video + $10 shipping/handling)	
V02	Fostering Retention (1999 teleconference videotape)	____ @ $285.00 = $____

Task Force Reports

P01	Advising Students in Oversubscribed and Selective Majors (1985)	____ @ $ 5.00 = $____
P02	Advising Adult Learners (1986)	____ @ $ 5.00 = $____
P03	Advising as a Profession (1987)	____ @ $ 5.00 = $____

NACADA Journal

Latest issue: ____ @ $ 15.00 = $____

Back copies are available for all issues. Some issues may be photocopied.

Please list volume and no.

Vol./Yr. _____   No./Issue _____

Vol./Yr. _____   No./Issue _____   Total back copies ____ @ $ 10.00 = $____

(Index for Volumes 1–15 included with Vol. 15, No. 2, Fall 1995 or on NACADA Web site)

Total Amount Due and Enclosed $____

____ Check enclosed

____ Charge (indicate card)   Card No.:_____   Exp. Date:_____

   ____ Visa

   ____ Mastercard   Signature:_____

   ____ American Express   Print Cardholder Name:_____

PAYMENT MUST ACCOMPANY ORDERS (Our FEIN# is 48–1114759)

NACADA Publications Order, Kansas State University, 2323 Anderson Ave., Ste. 225, Manhattan, KS 66502

Questions? PH: 785–532–5717 or FAX: 785–532–7732   E-Mail: nacada@ksu.edu   Web: http://www.ksu.edu/nacada

Name Index

Subject Index